Human Development and Behavior

Bernard D. Starr, Ph.D.

Associate Professor, City University of New York, Brooklyn College
Clinical Psychologist, State University of New York, Downstate Medical Center

Harris S. Goldstein, M.D., D.Med.Sc.

Director, Outpatient Department, Division of Child and Adolescent Psychiatry,
Director, Family Studies, Department of Psychiatry,
State University of New York, Downstate Medical Center

With a Foreword by Anne J. Doyle, R.N., M.S.

Associate Professor, City College School of Nursing, New York

Human Development and Behavior: Psychology in Nursing
by Bernard D. Starr and Harris S. Goldstein

Copyright © 1975 by Springer Publishing Company, Inc.

Springer Publishing Company, Inc.
200 Park Avenue South
New York, N.Y. 10003

Designed by Patrick Vitacco

75 76 77 78 79 / 10 9 8 7 6 5 4 3 2 1

Library of Congress Cataloging in Publication Data
Starr, Bernard D
  Human development and behavior.
  Bibliography: p.
  Includes index.
  1. Nurses and nursing—Psychological aspects. 2. Developmental psychobiology. 3. Human behavior. 4. Medicine and psychology.
I. Goldstein, Harris S., 1934-   joint author. II. Title [DNLM:
1. Psychology—Nursing texts. WY87 S796h]
RT86.S68   610.73'01'9   73-92205   ISBN 0-8261-1550-0

Printed in the United States of America

HUMAN DEVELOPMENT AND BEHAVIOR

Psychology in Nursing

Springer Publishing Company/ New York

Foreword

Human Development and Behavior, with its special focus on nursing practice, will be a welcome addition to both students and practitioners of nursing. In it are delineated the major psychological concepts as they relate to the life cycle of individuals in periods of health as well as illness. What emerges is an overview of behavior that enables the nurse to intervene more effectively with her clients to promote better psychological adaptation.

What makes the book especially appealing is its timeliness for students in integrated programs of nursing. Despite nearly a decade of movement toward integration, that progress is seldom reflected in textbooks. Indeed, few developmental texts even span the entire life cycle or consider aging and dying as important components of the life process. But this book goes much further, presenting relevant findings from developmental research in a total context of sociocultural influences. It even includes a searching look at the issue of role behavior as a product of physiological difference and social conditioning.

The book steers clear of a specific conceptual framework or bias. Instead it presents views of the major theorists—Freud, Erikson, Piaget, and Sullivan, to mention only a few—in a clear, concise, and comprehensive overview. The authors' eclectic approach spans the principles of behavior therapy relevant to nursing practice. Finally, the book offers elements of research methodology that will help the nurse not only to pursue further studies in developmental literature but also to gather and organize data about human behavior—thus enabling her to improve the quality of her own practice and, perhaps, to contribute to an expanded nursing theory.

As nursing moves ahead toward increasing professionalism, much emphasis will surely be given to the role of the nurse in health maintenance and primary prevention. Certainly this text takes a long step toward the beginning preparation of the nurse for this role.

ANNE J. DOYLE

v

Contents

Acknowledgments

We are indebted to many people who very generously gave their time to read and comment on various parts of the manuscript. The book is stronger for their contributions. We would like to thank: Dr. Laura Barbanel, Ms. Helen Behnke, Dr. Robert Boorstyn, Professor Anne J. Doyle, Major Merlan O. Ellis, Ms. Suzanne Embree, Major Ann Frederico, Professor George Fried, Dr. Solomon Garb, Mr. David Gewirtzman, Dr. Lorraine Harner, Dr. Jacob Kagan, Dr. Milton Klein, Dr. Barry Lubetkin, and Professor Angela Barron McBride. Brigitte Goldstein and Jana Starr assisted in almost every phase of the manuscript production. Special thanks also go to Patrick Vitacco, the editor and designer, who extended himself so much for this project.

Chapter *I*

Introduction:
Understanding People

THIS BOOK is about people and how they function. More specifically, it explores the entire span of human development and behavior, from conception through old age and death. Human psychology is a subject that is close to all of us—we live it every day of our lives. In that sense, studying psychology is unlike studying any other science. There is hardly a topic in the field of human behavior that we can't relate to in a personal way. The fact that psychology is an integral part of our experience helps to explain why understanding people seems, at the same time, both simple and very complex: simple because almost everyone has a strong opinion about "what makes people tick," yet complex because as we get close to behavior and want to act on our assumptions we find ourselves frequently baffled. Our initial feeling of familiarity deceives us, and we soon realize that there are no simple explanations.

1

PSYCHOLOGY AND NURSING

For the nurse psychology is even more complex than for other students of behavior, because the nurse comes into contact with people at every stage of the life cycle. Furthermore, the nurse most often enters into professional relationships with people when they are in a state of crisis. Illness, hospitalization, disability, physical decline, and fear of death are some of the most painful and agonizing human experiences that nurses must live through with their patients. Others may talk about these topics, but in nursing they are concrete realities.

The nurse's concern for people extends, of course, beyond patients in crisis. The social context of health care brings the nurse outside of institutions and into involvement with family, community, and society. In these broader areas of concern an understanding of healthy development and behavior is essential.

How does knowledge of psychology contribute to health care? After all, as is well known, most people recover from illness even with little intervention. Psychology and psychologizing are popular, but in what ways can our concern for the emotional and distinctly human side of the person help our patients or clients?

Physical and Emotional Health

It is important to bear in mind that the physical and emotional aspects of the person are inseparably related. Apathy, anger, fear, love, hate, as well as other feelings and emotions, all have physical concomitants. Some of these *affective states* contribute to a person's well-being, while others are physically harmful. Anger, for example, is frequently accompanied by anxiety. In a state of anxiety, pulse rate is increased and the heart works harder (it may go from 72 beats per minute to 120 beats per minute), various glands increase their activity, and in general the body is in a tense state prepared for danger. These physiological reactions can be useful at times to get the person ready for stressful situations, but they can be dangerous for patients suffering from a host of illnesses. The negative effects of emotions have been demonstrated experimentally with animals. In one study monkeys who were otherwise healthy developed ulcers when placed under prolonged psychological stress (Brady, 1958). Other investigators have suggested that human susceptibility to serious illnesses, even to cancer, can result from emotions of despair and hopelessness (Schmale and Iker, 1966; Schmale and Engel, 1967). On the other hand, it has been found that positive emotional states can aid recovery from illness (McDaniel, 1969).

It would therefore appear that, while most patients do recover, attention to psychological needs can speed up recovery, make recovery complete, reduce the probability of relapse, and engender a positive attitude toward health care.

The nurse, having the greatest amount of person-to-person contact in patient care, can play a vital role in the emotional states of her patients. The sensitive, well-trained nurse can alter and direct the emotional reactions of her patients to facilitate treatment and recovery. The nurse can in some cases quickly promote a desired reaction. In other cases more prolonged work is necessary to establish a relationship with a patient that can mediate emotional impact in a desired direction. Take the case of a hospitalized child whose initial reaction is a violent one—he screams, cries, complains of severe pain, clings to his mother. Recognition of underlying infantilism and dependency can lead the nurse to respond in an appropriately supportive and nurturant manner. This reaction can establish a sense of trust in the child and in general make him feel better and respond more positively to the nurse. If the child, on the other hand, attempts to cover up his dependency through a facade of bravado and denial of pain and hurt, the nurse might choose to praise the child for his "bravery" and thereby gain his confidence by offering support in a form that he can accept. An overly nurturant reaction, in this instance, could make the child feel uncomfortable; he may associate affection with being treated like a baby—something he may desire but wishes to deny. Even in more serious medical cases, as well as with healthy clients of all ages, the nurse may similarly have to adjust her behavior to meet the psychological dynamics of the situation. In applying psychological knowledge in this manner, the nurse is not necessarily aiming to change the person. The goal is rather to provide the client with emotional gratification in terms of his particular needs in order to enhance the treatment process.

The Need To Relate

Human beings by virtue of their emotional makeup have a need for human contact and relationships. There is ample research evidence demonstrating the pathology resulting from a lack of human relationships. As we will see in Chapter 2, when infants and young children are denied constant, intensive, and personalized human relationships, severe problems arise in their overall functioning. Humans are raised in interpersonal and social environments, and this upbringing heightens the need throughout life for intimacy, contact, and understanding. Especially during times of illness and hospitalization, these emotional needs come to the fore. The need for relating and contact may take different forms depending on the patient's personality, but it is always there. Even in cases where closeness or sympathy seems to be shunned, closer examination will find a deep hurt that makes the person cover up emotional needs. In fact, such people often have overwhelming strivings for contact that they are unable to accept. The nurse must address herself to the emotional life of her patients because of her recognition of the basic social and emotional nature of humans.

UNDERSTANDING THE INDIVIDUAL
Differences and Personality Dynamics

When you walk into a patient area, whether it be a clinic or a hospital, what do you see? Where is your attention drawn? What should you be looking for? What should you focus on? What are your personal feelings and reactions?

A superficial look will tell you some important facts. Are the patients young or old? Male or female? A glance at the charts will give you physical findings, the diagnosis, the treatment plan, physiological signs, and so on. Chances are that the patient will receive excellent physical care and will recover.

But what about the patient as a person—a unique person? Clearly, people are different. Not only do they differ in physical appearances, illnesses, and rates of recovery, but they are different as people— that is, they have different personalities. They feel differently, they see situations differently, and they respond differently to the same situation. For example, consider an 8-year-old child who falls down and scrapes his knee. Can we predict his response to this incident? Not with any certainty, even if we know the extent of physical injury. Yet this situation is relatively simple compared with the ones faced by nurses in their everyday work. Why can't we predict the child's behavior? Generalizations about behavior are very difficult, because so many factors determine how a person will react in a given situation. Using your own personal reaction—"How would I feel if I sustained such an injury?"—or a generalization—"How should an 8-year-old react?"—as a guide can be helpful, but often it does not provide an accurate answer. An important guideline to keep in mind is that *there is no single right way to view a situation.* The following self-administered exercise demonstrates this point.

Examine the picture on the opposite page. Very quickly, without giving it much thought, describe what you see and make up a story about the picture with a beginning and an end.

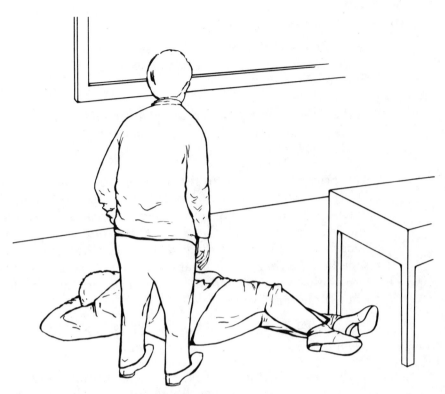

From I. L. Solomon and B. D. Starr, *The School Apperception Method* (New York: Springer, 1968).

Compare your story with those of the other students. Did you all interpret the picture in the same way? Usually the range of interpretations is great. Some see the child on the floor as ill and the other boy as a helper. Some see a fight scene which ranges from horsing around to violent aggression. Others call it a scene from a school play. The outcomes of the stories about the picture also differ.

This *projective stimulus* dramatizes the differences in people's perceptions and interactions with their environments. There is no "correct" interpretation of the picture. In fact, the picture really doesn't tell you much beyond some descriptive details: there are two boys, one on the floor and one standing, and their faces are not visible. If the picture tells so little, where do the various interpretations come from? They come from within the person making up the story. The descriptive factors interact with the individual's unique psychological needs and general personality characteristics to produce particular interpretations. It is these individual dynamics that provide each person with his interpretation of what is "correct" or "real."

Principles of Uniqueness

If people respond differently because their inner worlds, needs, and personalities differ, then we can arrive at an important principle of human relations.

> *We must know a great deal about an individual and his inner world in order to understand the meaning of his behavior.*

This principle directs us to the study of *developmental psychology*. Developmental psychology provides the basis of understanding how unique experiences and environments shape unique personalities and behaviors. To return to our 8-year-old, how do we explain a marked reaction to the scraped knee when the wound seems rather superficial? What is the meaning of this behavior? A number of hypotheses come to mind, all of which require further information. Thus our next principle:

> *Understanding behavior requires the refinement of hypotheses through information-gathering.*

In this instance, the child may be injured more seriously than is apparent—a possibility that should not be overlooked. On the other hand, the boy may be an infantile and dependent child who uses every situation to elicit support and sympathy from his parents and other adults. Or his behavior may be more situational and temporary. For example, there may be a new sibling in the home and consequently the 8-year-old is going through a temporary *regression,* i.e., a return to infantile behavior because of having lost his prized position in the family. Or the child may have suffered some disappointment that has made him hypersensitive for the moment. Another possibility is that his mother's overreaction and panic at the sight of the knee triggered his extreme reaction. The hypotheses could go on but the point is evident: *behavior is very complex.* A simplistic approach that assumes one "correct" interpretation overlooks the complexity of behavior and detracts from a professional approach to the understanding of the whole person.

Once we have determined the major precipitating cause of a behavior, we should recognize that there are other causes as well. Many factors converge to produce a slice of behavior. Usually there are a number of psychological components. Therefore, our next principle states:

Behavior is multidetermined.

Freud called this principle *overdetermination of behavior.* It strikes at the heart of a dynamic approach to human personality. The principle emphasizes the unique configuration of multiple causes for each behavioral act.

The example of our injured child can be applied to a person of any age group. A young adult or a middle-aged or aging person might react in a manner similar to the 8-year-old with his bruised knee. Think of the hospitalized patient, of whatever age or sex, who complains bitterly at the slightest discomfort, who places great demands on the nursing staff, who never seems to be satisfied in spite of receiving more attention than more seriously ill patients, and who never seems appreciative of services rendered, never says "thank you," and never offers any friendly exchange. The same infantile dynamics may be operating as in the case of the child, but they are being manifested in a different manner. The fact that a patient is chronologically adult or elderly should not keep us from recognizing the presence of infantile behaviors alongside more mature ones. The next principle therefore states:

Every person functions on many levels simultaneously.

While this principle is more obvious in the excessively demanding person, it can also apply to patients who appear just the opposite— the ones who never complain, never ask for anything, seem grateful for the least bit of attention, and never give sufficient feedback on their condition. These patients may have similar underlying dynamics as the dependent type, and they can pose equally serious problems for nursing care.

Our final principle of uniqueness calls attention to the environment in which the person grows and behaves.

Behavior must be evaluated in a social context.

Not only is the individual unique; so are the social forces of family and culture that surround him and leave their mark on him. Social influences are especially pronounced in the area of emotional expression. In some cultural settings 8-year-old boys (and adults as well) are expected to cry and show emotions even in response to minor stress. Other cultures indoctrinate the "stiff upper lip" reaction. We will have much more to say about cultural influences on behavior in Chapter 13.

We have offered some principles and illustrations at this point to emphasize the diversity of personalities, the uniqueness of the individual, and the distinction between overt behavior and underlying dynamics. The various types of personality and behavior likely to be associated with behavioral reactions and styles will be discussed in greater detail in Chapter 16 on psychopathology.

LEARNING ABOUT PEOPLE

Keeping in mind the principle of individual uniqueness, how do we go about gathering information about people? General principles or theories are useful for establishing a framework for our understanding of people, as we will see in Chapters 8 to 12, but we still need methods for learning about a particular person. Human relations specialists have developed a variety of techniques for probing the inner worlds and personalities of individuals. All of these techniques are valuable tools, but some are especially pertinent to nursing and health-care situations.

Self-Report

Asking direct questions is one way to learn about people. This approach is suitable for some data, but not for others. A person can report his date of birth, the size of his family, some aspects of his medical history, as well as some other objective facts. But when it comes to behavior and personality, people become less reliable. Even seemingly objective facts are frequently distorted. For example, pediatricians often report the inaccuracy of parents' recollections of landmarks in their children's development. Children are reported to walk earlier, talk earlier, and toilet-train sooner than they do in reality. Some parents state that their children have suffered diseases that they did not have while others neglect to report diseases that did occur. The dangers of self-report were dramatized in a study by Robbins (1963) in which parents of 3-year-olds showed inaccuracies in recalling the onset of bowel training, standing, walking, introduction of the cup, and type of feeding schedule. What was really striking about this study was that the parents had been part of a broader study on child development requiring a periodic review of the developmental data, and hence could be expected to be very much up on their children's landmarks. Also interesting was the tendency for the parents to be inaccurate in the the direction of recommendations made by experts on child-rearing. To generalize, people not only make errors in self-reporting but they will also distort in the direction of the greatest social approval. People will frequently tell you what they think you want to hear.

When someone is asked to make self-assessments and to report feelings and attitudes, distortions are even greater than in the case of "objective data." Why should this occur? Everyone has a need to preserve his self-esteem and will therefore present himself in a more positive light than accuracy would justify. This is usually an unconscious process. Depending on the person's emotional strength, his ability to view himself objectively will vary. The person who needs to see himself as super-independent will not readily report feelings of inadequacy. On the other hand, a dependent person may not want to show that he is really capable of functioning in a grown-up, independent fashion. Consequently, self-report must be used with caution if we are to gather accurate information about the deeper levels of personality and behavior.

Interview

The interview is a form of verbal interaction with the aim of obtaining information about a person. The range of interviewing techniques is very great. An interview can be highly structured, with well-defined questions that limit the possible responses: e.g., the interview can present the client with multiple-choice questions. Other structured interviews, while not multiple-choice, may still consist of predetermined questions in a fixed order. At the other extreme is the nondirective interview, in which the client is given great latitude in responding. Directions like "tell me about yourself" or "just say anything that comes into your mind" are examples of highly unstructured interviewing approaches. The unstructured method sets the stage for the client to reveal many facets of his functioning and unique personality. Choice of interviewing technique will depend on the kind of information desired. If you want to know the specifics of a person's work and health history, it is best to ask him directly in a structured manner. If, however, you want to "get a feel" for the person's emotional reactions, worries, and personality style, an unstructured approach might be best. In some instances, the verbal interaction of the interview is not as significant as the opportunity it presents to observe the patient informally. The unstructured method requires great skill and training in order to be able to handle the spontaneity, unpredictability, and open-ended nature of the interaction. The interview is an important information-gathering tool for the nurse, because some form of verbal interaction is always taking place with patients. The acquisition of interviewing skills can make these interactions much more fruitful. The interview is also part of other methods of information-gathering (e.g., self-report and observation).

Psychological Tests

Psychologists administer a variety of tests to learn about people. Tests are used for assessing intelligence, personality, interests, attitudes, adjustment, and many other psychological characteristics. They are useful in making such assessments because they are based on standards that establish a means of comparing the performance of different individuals. The concept of "normal" or "average" and "deviations" for the trait being measured can be determined when there is a common frame of reference. Some tests are objective, requiring specific delineated responses (e.g., multiple-choice) while others are more subjective and allow for open-ended unpredictable responses (e.g., projective tests). But whatever the test, it usually requires specialized skills and training for administration and scoring as well as a formal test setting. Many nurses use modified tests in the form of rating scales to measure traits such as cooperativeness, passivity, and general adjustment of patients. But for the most part psychological tests are too lengthy for regular use and would interfere with the spontaneous nurse-client interaction.

Informal Observation

Observation can be formal or informal. Formal observation is very much related to tests in that it requires a highly systematic and controlled approach and usually involves ratings and/or measures of behavior. Formal observation can be very useful when we want to pinpoint areas of behavior for examination or when we are conducting psychological research. Informal observation, on the other hand, is a technique that does not require an artificial or strained situation, only the usual nurse-client setting. This technique is probably the most feasible and valuable day-to-day tool for nurses. The term *informal* should not be interpreted as casual or simple. Informal observation requires that the nurse be a knowledgeable and keen observer.

It means, first of all, that the nurse must be open to all avenues of communication, nonverbal as well as verbal. Nonverbal communication can provide much information. A patient may say one thing while his body language signals convey a different message. Julius Fast in his book *Body Language* (1970) cites the case of an adolescent boy in therapy who made a suicide attempt shortly after a therapy session. The boy's suicidal intent was communicated in his listless posture, unresponsiveness, and empty face. The therapist had an uneasy feeling after the session and, knowing other things about the boy, went to the patient's home, arriving in time to save him from an overdose of pills.

We live in a very literate, verbal society and therefore tend to disregard or distrust nonverbal communication. An example of this is the finding by Baer and her associates (1970) that nurses, physicians, and social workers indicated greater recognition of verbal than of nonverbal expressions of pain. Baer et al. concluded, "we tend to denigrate the vocal patient calling him all sorts of unpleasant names, yet we find in this study that it is those who do vocalize who are assumed to be suffering greatest pain, and thus may receive the most attention." It is therefore important for the nurse to become sensitive to nonverbal communications and learn to interpret, trust, and respond to them.

For informal observation to be effective and fruitful, it is necessary to develop the following attitudes:

Respect for the Individual. Each person is valuable and deserves our concern and interest. Respect for the individual entails empathy for the felt experiences of the person and a willingness to explore and participate in the person's universe of feelings.

Nonjudgmental Attitude. As health practitioners, we must not allow our own values and attitudes to distort our observations. Everyone has personal likes and dislikes. Some people will appeal to you and others will not. Some personality styles, values, mores, mannerisms, political philosophies, as well as other characteristics may sharply contrast with your own preferences. In your personal life there may be people and situations that you avoid and others that you seek out, depending on your preferences. Certainly health professionals must constantly make judgments in the sense of decision-making. But it is necessary to set value judgments aside and to avoid placing "right" and "wrong" labels on people. A nonjudgmental attitude is not easy to develop. It is an aspect of the health-care professional's training that must begin early and develop over many years. Even trained psychotherapists are concerned with their personal reactions to patients as a factor that can impede helping the patient, and they use the term *countertransference* to describe these reactions.

Open-Ended Listening and Observing. The trained observer attends to every aspect of the person's behavior without arriving at premature conclusions. Observations are noted and stored, but closure is delayed until sufficient data are obtained. Conclusions based on limited observations can be faulty. It is necessary to permit the person to present himself as fully as possible before developing hypotheses, and even then conclusions should be regarded as tentative and always subject to revision.

Patient-Oriented Attitude. The aim of the nurse–client relationship is to help the client. A large degree of selflessness is demanded of the nurse, for she does not deal with an ordinary social relationship, in which give and take may be expected or demanded. The nurse–client relationship frequently feels one-sided. Patients may be hostile, demanding, and sometimes even abusive. In all such instances the nurse's first goal in her professional work is the establishment of an understanding relationship with the patient. This goal cannot be achieved if the usual social amenities are expected of patients. Nursing care situations often evoke very primitive and infantile mechanisms in people, which the nurse must strive to understand in the context of the stress on the coping resources of the person involved. Here again, training and experience are required.

Consider a situation in which a patient accuses the nurse of not attending to his needs and giving more attention to other patients. The patient might make all sorts of accusations against the nurse and say he will hold her responsible if he does not recover. The nurse may have actually given more attention to him than to other patients and perhaps even used some free time to serve this overdemanding and abusive person. If she becomes indignant and angry as a result of the patient's ungratefulness and threatens to withdraw all the extras she has given, she is reacting personally rather than professionally. That is not to say that firm handling should be avoided. Frequently it is necessary to point out infantile behavior to a patient and to set limits. But it must be done in an atmosphere of understanding and acceptance so that the patient can make constructive use of the communication. Strategy in such cases must be well thought out and presented to the patient in a controlled manner. To accomplish this it is necessary to separate personal needs, conflicts, and frustrations from the professional role. This of course is more easily said than done. Training in human relations and perhaps personal therapy or counseling may be required to achieve the level of self-understanding and security for mastery of the patient-oriented attitude.

Scientific Attitude. To sustain a high scientific level of our observations, it is necessary to be systematic and critical. Informal observational data are no less scientific than any other source of acquiring information. In fact, in vivo observation has a long history and tradition in medicine. The central factor in the scientific caliber of observations is the technique and attitude of the observer. In examining the data provided by a person it is important to note trends, consistencies, and inconsistencies of behavior. Each inconsistency must be accounted for. When explanations for inconsistencies are not present the questions must be left open, and the nurse should be constantly on the lookout for data that can shed light on the contradiction.

Flexibility is an important part of the scientific attitude. There should be no precommitment to a preferred point of view. Specific data should always determine hypotheses and conclusions. Hunches and feelings are important aspects of the scientific attitude, but they must be supported eventually by objective data. We must not be afraid to change our views. Accuracy is much more important than being proven right. Open-mindedness is also a vital part of the scientific attitude. Not only must the scientist listen to differing points of view but he also has the obligation of treating opposing views seriously.

Perhaps most crucial to the scientific attitude is respect for the work and knowledge of others. Nursing is essentially a helping profession, but in order to accomplish its humanistic goals, it must utilize the insights and information that psychology can offer regarding human development and behavior. Learning and understanding the concepts presented in this book will help you apply psychology in your professional work.

SUMMARY

Human development is a complex subject that covers the span from conception through old age and death. For nurses and other health professionals the study of psychology must extend beyond the traditional topics to include areas of special concern to those who work with people in crisis situations. Application of psychology to health care emphasizes the relation between physical and emotional health, and the interpersonal needs of people.

The uniqueness of each person is a basic postulate of our approach to human psychology. Understanding the unique composite of a person's attitudes, needs, and behavior requires a great deal of information about the individual and his inner world, refinement of hypotheses through information-gathering, recognition of the multi-determined nature of behavior, recognition that behavior occurs simultaneously on many levels, and recognition of the social context of behavior.

There are many ways to learn about people—self-report, interviews, psychological tests, and observation. Informal observation is the most convenient and appropriate method for health professionals. A number of attitudes must be mastered to make informal observation valid: respect for the individual, nonjudgmental attitude, open-ended listening and observing, patient-oriented attitude, and scientific attitude.

SUGGESTED READINGS

Dorroh, T. L. *Between patient and health worker.* New York: McGraw-Hill, 1974.

Lipkin, G. B., and Cohen, R. G. *Effective approaches to patients' behavior.* New York: Springer, 1973.

Travelbee, J. *Interpersonal aspects of nursing.* Philadelphia: F. H. Davis, 1971.

Ujhely, G. B. *Determinants of the nurse-patient relationship.* New York: Springer, 1968.

Part *I*

The Life Cycle

EACH PERSON'S LIFE is unique, and no psychology can hope to account for all our individual variations and differences. Yet we all share in certain experiences that mark our progress from birth to death, and we all pass through predictable stages or landmarks of development in the course of our lives. Human existence is a dynamic process. In order to understand it properly we must first consider the whole span of the life cycle, investigating those experiences that are common to us all. Part I, then, is a chapter-by-chapter presentation of the principal stages of the life cycle: childhood, adolescence, early and middle adulthood, aging, and death. A separate chapter is devoted to the family, the primary structure that shapes human development.

As you read through these chapters, bear in mind that they are intended as an overview. A synthesis of many viewpoints and of many different psychological theories, they are by no means complete in their account of human development and behavior. Nor are they intended to be. Human behavior is extremely complex, and, just as no single encounter with another person can reveal that person's full richness and complexity, no single account of human psychology can examine all its aspects in sufficient detail. Therefore we will return to many of the topics and themes treated in Part I in later chapters, considering them from the viewpoint of psychologists who have carried out intensive study and research in particular areas. Thus, for example, early childhood development is treated briefly in Chapter 2; later it is considered again in the light of the theories of Sigmund Freud, Jean Piaget, and the behaviorists, among others. We will also take account of the various external factors that can shape individual development in particular ways. (A glance at the Contents will give some idea of the range of the book, and you can, of course, skip ahead at any time to gain additional information on those topics of particular interest to you.)

Just as people are always growing and becoming, so too with our knowledge of them. As we look at people from different angles and from different points of view, we will expand our understanding and, along with it, our sense of the infinite complexity and mystery of human existence.

Chapter 2

Childhood

A MAJOR CHARACTERISTIC of our species is the great length of time an individual requires to reach maturity. The extended period of childhood and adolescence is needed for the acquisition of the complex social and cognitive skills that are uniquely human. Even in adulthood, the individual continues to change, although the rate of change is not as rapid and the type of change not as dramatic as during childhood and adolescence.

We will start this chapter with a brief look at the fascinating discoveries of modern genetics. Next, we will trace the developing organism from the one-cell stage through the embryonic and fetal stages. Finally we will survey the developmental periods of infancy (birth to 2 years), early childhood (2 to 6 years), and middle childhood (6 to 12 years).

HEREDITY

Personality development really begins before birth. We know relatively little about prenatal effects on the organism, but recent work has demonstrated that certain personality characteristics can be assessed even in the neonate. Stella Chess and her coworkers (Thomas et al., 1968) have shown that infants manifest markedly different temperaments from the time of birth. Such characteristics are probably inherited, although we are far from understanding the subtleties of inherited personality attributes. It is essential, however, to gain an understanding of mechanisms of inheritance, as these will become increasingly important as research progresses.

Much about the mechanisms of heredity has been unravelled, and we can now obtain at least some understanding of how development is controlled. Even with our present state of sophistication in scientific matters, however, it staggers the imagination to contemplate how the complete plans for the growth and development of a human being are packed into the microscopic and submicroscopic particles of the nucleus of a single cell, the *zygote*.

It is important from the outset to think of heredity as the transfer of information, rather than of specific traits, from generation to generation. Only then will the mechanisms involved in heredity make sense. The nucleus of the zygote contains complex codes that instruct the developing organism on how to develop. In order to gain an understanding of normal development as well as of hereditary diseases, it is necessary to know some of the basic elements of genetics: the genes (the bearers of the code), chromosomes, genotype and phenotype, and the principle of dominance.

Genes

Only in the last 30 years have technical capabilities progressed to the point where it is possible to probe the submicroscopic world of the gene, the bearer of the hereditary code. This has been made possible by a combination of advances in light and electron microscopy, in biochemistry, biophysics, and molecular biology. Of course, even before these technical advances had been made, many of the laws governing the outcome of the intergenerational transmission of hereditary information were already known. The observations of Gregor Mendel, an Austrian monk, in the middle of the nineteenth century established the scientific basis for the study of heredity long before the mechanisms began to be understood.

What is the gene? The gene is a biochemical template or form.

Through the arrangement of its chemical elements, the gene induces the synthesis of proteins of a type and in a sequence that results in the unfolding of the organism's characteristics. The biochemical name for the group of substances forming this template is desoxyribonucleic acid (DNA). Genes are made up of DNA. The specific arrangements of the elements of the DNA molecule constitute a genetic code. The DNA acts as a template to form a similar but slightly different molecule, ribonucleic acid (RNA), which acts as a messenger. The messenger RNA travels to a special cytoplasmic protein-building structure in the cell, the ribosome, where its code induces the formation of specific proteins at specific times. The proteins include enzymes needed for the development of the cell in certain directions as well as substances with other functions. The process by which the RNA-induced protein synthesis progresses to cellular specialization (that is, how it induces a liver cell to form at one time and a brain cell at another) is not yet known.

Chromosomes

Each chromosome is an aggregate of millions of genes. Chromosomes are visible with the aid of a microscope and usually appear as bar-like structures in the form of Xs. The fact that they stain a dark color in cell preparations has given them their name (*chromo* = color, *some* = body, i.e., colored body). There are 46 chromosomes in the human cell. Until 1956 it was believed that there were 48, but in that year Tjio and Levan were able to identify the number correctly as 46. The work of these two scientists is, in fact, taken by many as the starting point of human cytogenetics.

Since each chromosome consists of countless genes, it is evident that any abnormality in a chromosome is likely to have a catastrophic effect on development. It is thought, however, that most chromosomal aberrations are lethal and result in an unnoticed spontaneous abortion—that is, the developing organism is not able to maintain itself and is passed in the menstrual flow.

The 46 chromosomes represent 23 pairs. One chromosome of each pair comes from the female parent as part of the ovum and the other from the male parent as part of the sperm. There are two major types of chromosomes, the 22 pairs of autosomal chromosomes and the single pair of sex chromosomes. The sex chromosomes determine whether an organism is to develop as a male or female. Unlike the paired autosomal chromosomes, which are identical to each other in appearance, the sex chromosomes are of two different types: the X chromosome and the Y chromosome. The Y chromosome is much

Figure 2.1 **Photograph of a Man's Chromosomes, Arranged in Corresponding Pairs**
(Courtesy of Harold P. Klinger, M.D., Ph.D., Albert Einstein College of Medicine, N.Y.)

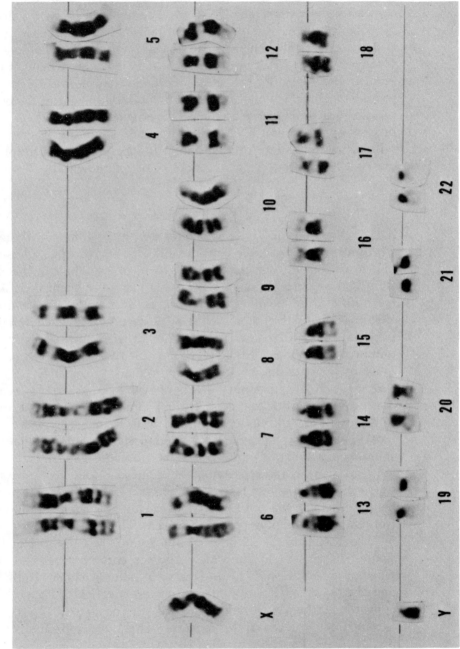

smaller than the X and has the appearance of a chromosome fragment. From the ovum the new organism always receives an X chromosome; from the sperm it may receive either an X or a Y. If the organism receives an XX pair it will be female; if it receives an XY pair it will be male.

Genotype and Phenotype

The genetic code represents the plan for the organism's development. This plan may or may not be carried out, depending on the nature of the messages and the environment in which the organism develops. For instance, a chemical may interfere with some aspect of development for which the genetic code is present. Thalidomide, a drug widely prescribed as a sedative in Europe, was found to interfere with limb formation of fetuses when given to pregnant women. The tragedy that resulted from the use of this medication caused widespread public indignation.

A further complication arises from the fact that in most instances at least two genes are operating to send messages about the same event. That is because there are two paired chromosomes with the same type of genes for all but the sex chromosomes. For example, the female parent contributes a gene whose code takes part in the formation of iris pigment, and the male parent does likewise. Now it is a characteristic of genes that their messages may be either strong or weak. A strong message will override a weak one and determine the organism's development. A weak message will determine development if it is the only one heard. An example will clarify this characteristic. The two most frequent eye colors in the United States are brown and blue. A gene coded for brown eyes carries a strong message, and a gene for blue eyes carries a weak message. If one parent provides a brown-eye gene and the other a blue-eye gene, the brown-eye gene will be responded to and the child will have brown eyes. For a child to have blue eyes, a blue-eye gene needs to come from both parents. Geneticists term the strong-message gene *dominant* and the weak-message gene *recessive.* A blue-eyed person *must* have a blue-blue pair of eye-color genes in his cells, but a brown-eyed person may have either of two combinations of eye-color gene pairs: brown-brown or brown-blue. Consequently, without knowing the eye color of the grandparents, one cannot tell whether a brown-eyed child has a recessive blue-eye gene or not.

The actual genetic makeup of an individual is not necessarily reflected in his physical makeup, since not all genes become expressed. That is why a distinction is made between genotype and phenotype. The *genotype* is the genetic makeup of the organism, including recessive genes that never become physically evident. The *phenotype* is the sum of physical characteristics of the individual. In our example, if a child received a brown-eye gene and a blue-eye gene from his parents, his genotype for eye color would be brown-blue. His phenotype, however, would be brown eye color.

Mixed Dominance. What happens if two dominant genes are present as a pair for a single trait? Then *both* genes gain expression. Let us take the example of blood groups A, B, and O. Genes for types A and B are both *dominant*, whereas genes for O are *recessive*. If an individual's genotype is AA or AO, he will have type A blood; if his genotype is BB or BO, he will have type B blood. But if his genotype is AB, he will have type AB blood.

Genetic Diseases

Diseases due to abnormal genes are probably much more frequent than we realize. If the abnormal gene affects early cellular growth in a critical way, the cells simply will not multiply beyond a certain point. On the other hand, the genetic abnormality may be subtle, appearing not as a gross organismic disturbance early in development but surfacing later as, say, a lessened capacity to withstand the process of aging, as evidenced by the early onset of arteriosclerosis. In other cases there appears a single enzyme deficiency as a consequence of a genetic abnormality. Such is the case in galactosemia, in which there is an absence of the enzyme necessary to the digestion of galactose, the sugar in milk.

There will always be genetic alterations occurring, because there is a spontaneous rate of molecular shift that results in a rearrangement of the genetic code. These rearrangements of genetic material are called *mutations*. The rate of mutation is increased by radiation, by the ingestion of certain toxins, and possibly by viral infections. Most mutations probably lead to nonviable forms. Some may lead to changes that increase adaptive capacity, and these are the basis for the evolution of specie differences. These evolutionary, genetically successful changes take place slowly, of course, as in the case of man's progressively more complex brain capacity, which has been evolving over millions of years.

Chromosomal Aberrations

During the time of cell cleavage or splitting of cells it sometimes happens that as the chromosomes separate into the two daughter cells a chromosome breaks or fails to split off at the right moment. This results in too few or too many chromosomes in the daughter cells. Again, as with genetic changes, most such occurrences affect vital cellular functions so grossly as to prevent further cellular growth. Some organisms survive, but usually with major organismic defects. Examples of such chromosomally based congenital syndromes are Down's syndrome and Klinefelter's syndrome. In Down's syndrome or mongolism there are three number 21 chromosomes (trisomy 21), and the individual has a characteristic physical appearance and is mentally retarded. In Klinefelter's syndrome there are two Xs and a Y chromosome (XXY configuration), resulting in chromosomal hermaphroditism (that is, being both male and female), with mental retardation commonly present. In humans the only factor known to increase the likelihood of chromosomal aberrations is aging in the mother. Down's syndrome is much commoner among births to women in their 40s.

PRENATAL DEVELOPMENT

Now that we have some understanding of the means by which the plans for development are transmitted from generation to generation, let us consider the development process from its inception to the birth of the child.

The Zygote

The zygote is the single cell that is formed from the fusion of the two germ cells, the ovum and the sperm. In all higher animals the embryo develops by such a fusion, which involves the coming together into one cell of the genetic material from male and female germ cells. The germ cells or *gametes* differ in some important respects from the other cells in the human body. Both gametes (ovum and sperm) have one-half the number of chromosomes that the other cells of the organism have. This one-half chromosomal complement is called the *haploid* (= single, i.e., not a pair) number; in humans, it is 23. The fusion of the two haploid gametes produces a cell with the species-specific number of 23 pairs of chromosomes. The zygote thus has the full complement or *diploid* number of chromosomes.

The process by which the gametes achieve their haploid number of chromosomes is called *meiosis*. Meiosis is a specialized form of cell division in which the cells divide twice but reproduce their chromosomes only once. The result is a reduction of the chromosome number to the haploid number.

This process leads to some interesting consequences in the similarity of family members. Since the two chromosomes that form each of the 23 pairs can and do have quite different hereditary attributes, which one of the pair a parent contributes is important to the determination of the constitutional makeup of the offspring. However, it is a matter of pure chance which member of the pair of a given chromosome will in fact be present in the gamete.

Thus, *siblings* may have from 0 to 46 chromosomes in common. Based on random distribution, the most common case will be that they have 50 percent of their chromosomes in common; that is, 50 percent of their genes are identical. Nonetheless, it becomes evident that two children in the same family can be, in a hereditary sense, totally different; although they have the same parents, they may have none of the same genetic material.

The gametes, apart from being different in chromosomal content from other cells, have additional special characteristics. The ovum has nutrients stored in the cell that will supply the growth needs of the embryo during the first weeks of growth. The ovum has no independent motile capacity, although it does travel from the ovary to the uterus via the Fallopian tubes. The sperm is much smaller than the ovary, and its minute mass is made up mainly of nucleus and tail. The tail provides locomotion for the sperm, which enters the uterus via the cervix. The sperm traverses the uterus and fuses with the ovum, usually in the oviducts (Fallopian tubes). The process of fusion is called *fertilization*, and the product of fertilization is the zygote.

The organism that develops from the single-celled zygote goes through numerous stages and in a sense recapitulates phylogeny; that is, the organism repeats in its development the stages in the evolution of the species. Until all the major organs are formed the developing organism is termed an *embryo*. After the organ formation is complete and until birth, the developing organism is called a *fetus*. The early stages of embryonic development are characterized by rapid growth and development and occupy the first 10 to 12 weeks of *gestation*. The period of fetal development is one of continuing elaboration and maturing of the organs laid down in the embryonic phase.

The Embryo

The study of embryology is a fascinating one, but we will review only briefly some major aspects of this early period of development. Within a few hours after fertilization, cleavage of the zygote takes place, with complete genetic material being passed on to each daughter cell by the process of nuclear splitting called *mitosis*.

By the time the embryo enters the uterine cavity from its course down the oviducts on the fourth day, it has become a solid sphere of cells called a *blastula*. This solid sphere develops a cavity, becoming a *blastocyst*, and then attaches itself to the wall of the uterus on the fifth day. The lining of the uterus proliferates, and by the thirteenth day the embryo is completely buried in the uterine wall. In this early phase of development necessary nutrients simply traverse the wall of the embryo from the highly vascularized uterine wall. However, the organism's complexity soon requires a more adequate system of intraembryonic transport. By the fourth week the arteries and veins are sufficiently connected by the developing capillary networks that circulation is possible, and the first heart movements occur. Electrocardiograms have been recorded from the embryo as early as 7 weeks.

By 27 days (4 weeks) the embryo is 5 millimeters (1/5 inch) long and the head is already clearly discernible. The heart has divided into four chambers and arm buds have appeared. The progress of organ formation (organogenesis) is completed by 12 weeks, and the end of the first trimester marks the beginning of the fetal phase. Although new organs as such are not laid down in the fetal period, it is not for another three calendar months, or at the end of the second trimester, that the fetus, if born, has a chance to live. The maturing process continues right up to the time of birth, and in the newborn nursery different levels of maturity of infants are readily evident. The infant born early will have a receding chin, and, since it will not yet have much subcutaneous fat, it will look old and wrinkled. The "immature" baby, however, quickly catches up with its full-faced neighbors whose buccal (cheek) fat pads give them the typical round baby face.

The child's personality, in some respects, has probably already been developing in utero. We suspect but do not know how much the rhythmic movements of the mother's body and her chemistry are influencing the fetal responses. Once the infant is born, however, we can see him develop. It is at this point, then, that psychological processes are first clearly discernible.

INFANCY

We will consider infancy the period in a child's life from birth to 2 years of age. As we must repeatedly remind ourselves, the life cycle is a continuum; but, because the human mind needs landmarks to assimilate data, we resort to periods, although periodization results in much futile controversy—such as whether infancy should extend from birth to 12 months, to 18 months, to 2 years, or whatever. In fact, there is no such truly demarcated period as infancy or early childhood, except as we use such practical divisions for purposes of speaking with one another.

During infancy there are many events that are primarily determined by the maturation of the nervous system. The human infant's brain at birth is similar in functional capacity to the reptilian brain. The more evolutionally advanced brain tissue is nonfunctional, maturing only gradually during the first months of life. In fact, the brain is not completely mature until the individual reaches puberty. In the healthy infant, as the neurological apparatus becomes functional the various abilities unfold: sitting, crawling, standing, walking. These skills are fairly automatic and, unless he is restrained, a child will spontaneously develop them. Other abilities that also cannot take place until the neurological apparatus is functional require in addition an adequate human environment with its stimulation and affection. Examples of these abilities are speech, bowel and bladder control, and social smiling.

The unfolding of abilities in infancy and early childhood varies greatly. Within wide margins, there is no known relation between the age at which a child develops skills and his level of functioning later in life. Beyond certain limits, however, we begin to suspect developmental abnormalities. Still the range is wide. For instance, an infant may speak in simple sentences as early as 1 year of age or as late as 3 years of age and be quite normal. Table 2.1 (pp. 36–37) gives a very approximate idea of the age at which children display skills.

The Neonate

The newborn child enters the world in a state of distress. Prior to birth, the infant resided in a warm (98.6° F.), stable, protective, liquid intrauterine environment in which oxygen and nourishment were provided by the mother's body. At birth, the child is thrust into a comparatively cold (75° F.) environment, in which he must survive with mechanisms that do not work perfectly at first. Oxygen intake may be irregular and sucking ineffective in getting adequate nourishment. It may take weeks before regularity and equilibrium of body functions are established. The distress of the infant can be seen in the periods of intense crying and generalized body reactions. How these very early experiences affect development and personality is still unclear, but some psychologists and psychiatrists have attributed great significance to the initial distress period of the infant. Otto Rank referred to the "birth trauma." More recently,

Arthur Janov has proposed that early experiences of pain even in the birth process can establish prototypic patterns that affect how the individual will handle stress throughout his life. Whether or not these speculations are accurate, we should be sensitive to the difficult adjustments that are required of the neonate.

Physical Growth and Development

Growth is the increase in size of the organism, while development refers to the increase in structural and functional complexity which usually accompanies growth. Infancy is a period of very rapid growth and development. At birth the average infant weighs 7.5 lbs. (3.3 kg.) and measures 20 inches (51 cm.) in length. With legs drawn up in the fetal position, the newborn looks even smaller and can be readily held by one hand and forearm. However, it does not remain such a small bundle for long. The birth weight doubles between the fourth and fifth months and triples by the end of the first year. By 2 years of age, the average child weighs 27 lbs. and is 34 inches tall.

There are some general principles of growth and development that are especially evident in infancy. One such principle is that growth and development proceed in a *cephalo-caudal* direction. This means that the head end of the body develops earlier, and maturation proceeds from the head toward the feet. Thus head movement is under the infant's voluntary control long before he can control the rest of his body. The head is also disproportionately large in relation to the remainder of the body, accounting for one fourth of total body length at birth, whereas in the adult, the head constitutes one-tenth of the individual's height. The body catches up in the course of later development.

Development also exhibits a gradient in a *proximo-distal* direction. That is, development proceeds from the central axis of the body outward, with the result that the arms come under voluntary control before the hands and the legs before the feet.

At birth the infant's bones are just beginning to harden or ossify. It is the softness of the skull bones that makes possible the molding of the head as it passes through the birth canal. The soft spots or fontanelles may not completely ossify until 2 years of age. The ossification of all the bones of the body follows a very regular course, so much so that the age of a child can be determined by the extent of ossification of the skeleton. The complete ossification of the long bones, such as the humerus and femur, is not complete until adolescence. The rate of skeletal development is genetically determined, although systemic illness may markedly influence growth rates.

Tooth erruption is quite variable. Some children are born with one or more teeth being present, while others may not have their first ones until after their first birthday. On the average, the first tooth (a lower incisor) appears at about 7 months. By the end of the first year infants average 6 primary or deciduous teeth, and by the end of the second year all 20 primary teeth of most infants will have erupted.

Muscle development takes the form of increases in size and in control. The infant is born with all the muscle fibers it will ever have, just as it is born with all its nerve cells. The muscles are small, however, relative to the infant's size, and all the "voluntary" muscles are not under its control. Muscle mass shows a steady increase throughout infancy, with males having slightly greater muscle development.

Motor Development

Owing to the immaturity of the higher nervous centers, the young infant is dominated by subcortical neurological mechanisms. When startled by any sudden, intense stimulation, the whole body tenses in the startle or *Moro reflex*. This disappears at about 4 months of age. When hungry, the infant displays a characteristic *rooting reflex*, with head turning and mouth opening. And when its head is turned, the arm on the side to which the head turns automatically stretches out while the opposite arm is drawn in. This reflex, called the *tonic-neck reflex*, occurs normally during the first 3 months of life. The infant at birth also automatically grasps if its palm is stimulated, but it cannot let go.

As the nervous system develops, the infant becomes less regulated by these automatic responses, and voluntary, purposive movements become predominant. At about 5 months the infant is capable of intentionally reaching for an object such as a rattle or spoon and grasping it. At 6-7 months, it can manipulate these simple objects. For instance, it can shake a rattle and bang a spoon on the table. By 10 months it is able to use a *pincer grasp* (thumb and forefinger) to pick up a small pellet or string.

Postural control and locomotion also progress as the nervous system matures. By 8 months the infant can sit without support and by 9 months it can crawl on hands and knees. At about a year, most infants are able to balance themselves sufficiently to be able to stand alone for at least a few moments. Walking without help usually begins at about 15 months. By 2 the infant runs and is able to walk up and down stairs alone.

Sensory Development

At birth all the senses are intact, although those that provide knowledge of the immediate environment, the near receptors—touch, movement, and temperature—are the most important ones in the early months. While the distant receptors—vision and hearing—are functional, they do not appear to be well differentiated at first. The newborn can distinguish light from dark but cannot make out faces. By 4 weeks the infant will stare at faces, although it is not until 4 months that he achieves binocular vision—both eyes focusing on the same object, yielding three-dimensional vision. By this time the infant also recognizes familiar objects, such as a baby bottle. Hearing is similarly present from birth, but specific responses to sound are only gradually developed. However, the mother's voice will elicit a turning of the infant's head relatively early—some report it even in the newborn period.

Language Development

For most of infancy the child is preverbal. The word "infancy" actually means the period without speech (*in* = "without" and *fari* = "to speak"), although the period is no longer defined this way. It is not until the last half of the second year that speech has reached a level where communication of needs is regularly made using words. Language is one of the most important developmental acquisitions of the infant, and it enhances the child's social and intellectual development.

The cry is the earliest sound that the infant makes. Crying is a spontaneous reaction to pain and discomfort that continues throughout infancy. The infant makes other spontaneous sounds, some of which are associated with physical states; they include yawns, sneezes, sighs, grunts, coughs, and whines. All of these sounds are universal, produced even by deaf children. At first these various sounds are not communicative, that is, they are not directed at anyone with the intent of eliciting a reaction. However, by about 3 months the infant learns that he can get a response to crying, and at that point vocalization begins to evolve into communication. The young infant's immature vocal apparatus makes his speech quite limited. The range of acquisition of speech is highly variable, yet there is a definite sequence that almost all infants pass through in developing language.

The first vocalizations other than crying occur at about 4 weeks and consist of small throaty noises. By 12 weeks the infant is cooing, which consists of fairly clear vowel sounds such as "oo," "ah," "ee." This is closely followed by babbling, the vocalizing of single and multiple syllables. Babbling appears to be a self-perpetuating activity that infants enjoy; they can keep it up for long periods of time. The experience gained in babbling helps the further development of the speech apparatus and leads to an increase in the number and variety of basic speech sounds (phonemes). By 12 months of age the infant can control his speech apparatus and knows that speech can communicate. He is therefore ready to talk. By this time infants will utter on the average two to three recognizable words (such as "mama," "dada," "bye"). This will expand to four to six words by 13 months; a rapid increase in vocabulary follows thereafter. During the early stage of talking the infant will also use many meaningless sounds that resemble speech, and it appears as if the infant is holding a conversation. This period is called the jargon phase.

The first words for all children are nouns that name familiar things—mama, bottle, bed, blanket, milk, and the like. Once the infant has acquired a number of nouns related to the people and objects in his immediate environment, he begins to use verbs—"want milk," "go television." At about 1½ years of age adjectives and adverbs are added. Prepositions and pronouns are the last parts of speech to develop. By age 2 the child has a vocabulary of 200 to 300 words, and although he is capable of speaking in single complete sentences, communications still consist mostly of one- and two-word phrases.

Receptive language (i.e., understanding) develops earlier than expressive language (speaking); thus the infant can understand simple commands such as "put the block in the cup" at 12 months of age but can only utter a few words at that time. While a gap between receptive and expressive language exists through most of childhood, the disparity diminishes as the child gets older. In infancy language is not very highly differentiated and is used egocentrically to express a variety of meanings. The infant will apply the same word to many different objects and situations. As the child's vocabulary expands and his perceptual discrimination becomes more refined, language takes on greater precision and specificity.

Social Development

Let us consider a 3-month-old infant girl. When she is hungry she will cry to be fed, and when she has had a bowel movement she will cry to be changed. She also knows that when she wants attention crying will eventually bring someone to her. When she is picked up, her crying will subside. And after she is comforted, if she is smiled at and the comforter's eyes catch hers, she may smile in return. When smiling first appears at two months, it is automatic, a reflex, but it soon develops into a response to something pleasurable. What is going on inside this infant girl as she acts, is reacted to, and reacts herself? She is learning the effect of communicating about basic needs—hunger, discomfort, wanting to be held. Most importantly, she is learning that her communications are affecting those around her; she is influencing them to provide for her. The gradually developed awareness that her basic needs—food, cleansing, holding—are responded to develops in her a sense of security, the feeling that she can affect her environment and that the environment can be counted on for fulfillment of needs. Here we can see the beginning of the interpersonal trust and security so important for social development.

What if this infant's physiological needs were met, but on a schedule that ignored her communications? Such a situation tended to exist in large orphanages, a situation that is generally but not entirely of the past. Under such conditions, the busy caretakers fed the infant on the caretakers' schedule. They had little opportunity to respond to the infant's cries for handling or changing, but rather changed the child by the clock instead of by announced need. The unfortunate consequence was that the infants could not develop a sense of the effectiveness of communication. They did not feel that they could influence the important people around them, and they had no basis for developing a sense of confidence in their ability to cope with the environment. The Self was completely passive in this infant-caretaker interaction. The result was disastrous. Retardation of growth and development was widespread (Provence and Lipton, 1962; Skeels, 1966), and children with a capacity for normal personality growth languished. Although they grew physically, their intellectual and emotional development was stunted; they had abnormally low I.Q.s and experienced difficulties in developing social skills and relating to other people. (In Chapter 15 we will discuss the effects of institutionalization in greater detail.)

Ethical considerations do not permit experimental deprivation of human infants. Animal studies of monkeys (Harlow, 1959), however, permit us to infer what the effect of total social deprivation might be on humans. Infant monkeys were reared in isolation, without contact with their mothers or with humans, and fed through bottles placed in holders. Later, when placed with other monkeys, they were unable to relate to them, and this inability persisted into adulthood, resisting change even over very prolonged contacts with normal monkeys. The devastating effect of such deprivation manifested itself in greatly limited social and emotional capacities. The monkeys raised in this way were very timid. When other monkeys approached them in a friendly manner, they became unduly aggressive. At maturity they were unable to engage in "instinctive" heterosexual behavior; the males could not mount females in heat, and females were unable to assume the position for copulation. When females who had been deprived of contact with other monkeys as infants did occasionally become pregnant, they were unable to provide even the most rudimentary nurturance for their babies. In fact, they cruelly rejected their infants, chasing them and pushing them away despite the intense efforts of the infant monkeys to nurse and be near their mothers.

We can only conclude from these studies that a consistent affectional bond with a responsive person is required for adequate infant development.

Let us return to the example of our baby girl. In early infancy, while she is not passive, she has things mainly done for her. Toward the end of the first year, however, the infant has acquired many abilities—she sits, crawls, carries objects, points to things she wants, generously rewards people she likes with affection—so that, in terms of social interaction, more is done by her than for her. She now seeks out, by crawling or haltingly walking, those she wants to be with. She explores with enthusiasm. She seems to understand a loud "No!" although she does not seem to retain the message very long.

The infant at this time communicates a real sense of Self, of a distinct personality. She shows this early sense of self in numerous ways. She is jealous of her siblings now and wants especially to be held if a parent is holding someone else. She has clearer preferences for foods, for toys, and for people. She has also, usually, learned ways of engaging others, so that she can prolong a social exchange by various "tricks."

To highlight the characteristics of this period, it is instructive to consider the earliest form of severe emotional disturbance, *infantile autism*. This earliest of the psychoses usually originates in the first year of life, and the autistic child is commonly described by his parents as being unresponsive even at the age of 1. The comings and goings of parents or others are not greeted with signs of either pleasure or distress. As long as the child is fed and permitted to be in a familiar physical environment, he appears satisfied. The people around him don't seem to count. Often the child appears not to care whether his parents or others attend to him.

Fortunately infantile autism is rare, although it is indeed tragic for the child and the family when it occurs. What this disturbance does make clear is the high level of social skills attained by and expected of the normal 1-year-old.

EARLY CHILDHOOD
Motor Development

During the preschool years of 2 to 6, bodily activity is a central aspect of behavior. Walking and running become smooth, and 2- and 3-year-olds obtain much pleasure from the sensation of movement. They enjoy using their new skills in coordination to climb, ride cars, and pull wagons. By 3 they are able to pedal a tricycle and this adds to their enjoyment of being in motion. Between 2 and 6 there is also a steady increase in the child's fine coordination skills. Activities requiring precision such as block building are challenging activities for the 3-year-old and become elaborate, imaginative constructions for the 4- and 5-year-old. Similarly, the visual-motor coordination involved in drawing shows a steady progression and becomes an outlet for creative and imaginative interests. Sometime during the 4-5-year-old period most children become capable of drawing a simple potato-man figure that is gradually elaborated on. These drawings express to some extent the developing body awareness and self-concept of the child.

Language Development

In the third and fourth year of life language mastery reaches a level where verbal communication becomes the major mode of expression. By the age of 3 vocabulary has increased to about 800 words, by 4 to 1,500 words, by 5 to 2,000 words, and by 6 to 2,500 words. In the early phase of language development the infant does not apply grammatical rules. But there is a rapid acquisition of grammar: by age 4 the basic rules of the native language are evident in the child's speech, and by age 6 the rules have been pretty well absorbed, and all parts of speech are used.

The acquisition of vocabulary and verbal skills is greatly influenced by environmental stimulation, and socioeconomic factors play a major role in determining the rate and nature of a child's language development. A socioecononomically disadvantaged home is usually associated with less verbal stimulation, and as a consequence children from such homes often lag in verbal skills. Preschool educational intervention and other enrichment experiences are very helpful in accelerating language development.

As the child passes through the preschool years, his manner of expressing himself also becomes more complex. Sentences are longer, reaching an average of more than five words by age 6, and use is made of compound sentence structure. There is also a progression in these years from what Jean Piaget calls egocentric speech to socialized speech, that is, from the self-directed monologue to speech clearly addressed to others for some purpose (e.g., exchanging ideas, obtaining something).

General intelligence is inextricably associated with language development. Words are symbols that serve and enrich thought processes. Concept formation, abstractions, and the acquisition of information about the world depend greatly upon word symbols. Many types of problem-solving require the presence of an adequate vocabulary, because analysis of a situation largely depends on defining and labeling component parts. Thus the child deprived of adequate verbal stimulation is handicapped both in the acquisition of information communicated in written or spoken form and in the development of complex mental functions.

Social Development

Not infrequently parents will say they long for the time when their child was an infant. What they usually mean is that they wish the child were not so difficult to manage. What is it that changes a seemingly easygoing good-natured infant into a difficult-to-manage boy or girl? Let us go back to our little girl. As an infant, she needs to have most things done for her. At the age of 1, she gets into many things—by crawling or walking —and empties out drawers and goes for electric sockets. But most of these incidents are handled quickly and relatively easily. Supervision is pretty constant, but with the help of gates or a playpen the area of supervision can be kept fairly limited. Not so when the child reaches 1½ or 2. Now she moves about quickly on her feet. She reaches to open doors. Sometimes she is successful when one does not expect it and gets into a dangerous situation—climbing on the toilet bowl or the stove. There is also a change in her attitude. A few months earlier, she seemed to have learned that certain things were "off limits," such as going out the front door. Now all that is disregarded, and she tries all over again to do the "no" behaviors. When limits are set, she has a tantrum, cries, kicks her feet, and throws herself on the floor; she gives every appearance of being terribly insulted. Somehow the new capacities that are unfolding—walking, beginning to use words to communicate, feeding herself—bring her into frequent opposition to what is safe for her and permissible in relation to the needs of others. Gates are not insurmountable. Chairs can be moved to get at high places. Other children who get in the way can be hit or bitten with harmful force.

In spite of all this, the child is in a most exciting phase of development, a phase in which her personality crystallizes itself and becomes more defined. Her capacities are a delight as well as a burden—but a heavy burden of supervision and giving. While the 1½- to 2½-year-old is rapidly developing skills that can take her into a more self-sustaining life style, at the same time she is continually making contact with her parents for comfort and assurance that her well of affectional security is safely there.

As the child's capacities, strength, coordination, and verbal and intellectual abilities increase, the environment's expectations increase also. Pressure begins to be applied to delay and to cooperate. Pressures to delay take the form of deferring need gratification—getting food, play materials, etc. Crying no longer simply elicits something to eat; there is a requirement that everyone wait his turn.

Developing Controls.   The process of learning to mesh one's needs with those of the "others" in the environment is one of the most important tasks of childhood. This process is called *socialization*, and it begins in earnest in late infancy and early childhood. Socialization is often defined as learning to follow society's rules. This definition makes the process sound heavy-handed and oppressive. Perhaps more appropriately, socialization should be defined as the process of teaching a child what will make survival successful in the culture into which he is born. The act of reprimanding a 2-year-old for attempting to break open the head of his enemy-for-the-moment with a board is part of socialization. It is obviously not adaptive to attempt to destroy whoever frustrates us—although that is our earliest and remains our most common initial feeling-response. By adaptive we mean that which makes for survival and/or success in a given environment.

It is at about age 2 that both child and parents begin to feel the pressures for rules to be learned and the child to be "civilized." Why age 2? Actually, 2 is just an approximate age; if families were carefully assessed we would probably find wide variation in the age at which the pressures to conform become a major point of focus. What mostly determines the age is the individual child's physical and personality development. Most parents intuitively respond when the child is both capable and needful of learning the rules. The child with

Table 2.1   **The First Six Years**

Age	Motor Development	Language	Social and Self Help
1 mo.	Lifts head briefly when prone	Small throaty sounds Mostly crying vocalizations	Looks at faces Less active when talked to
2 mo.	Lifts chest a short distance when prone	Single vowel sounds, *a-e-i*	Smiles socially
3 mo.	Turns from back to side	Babbling begins	Holds rattle when placed in hand
4 mo.	Holds head steady when carried	Laughs aloud	Reaches for familiar faces
5 mo.	No head lag when pulled to sitting position	Squeals	Occupies self
6 mo.	Rolls from back to stomach	Imitates simple sounds	Assisted, drinks from cup Grasps toy with one hand
7 mo.	Sits briefly when placed	Consonants used (dada)	Demands attention Transfers toy from hand to hand
8 mo.	Sits alone	Babbling at its peak	Separation anxiety intense
9 mo.	Crawls	Imitates some words	Grasps small toy between thumb and index finger
10 mo.	Pulls to standing position	Says 1-2 words: Dada, Mama	Waves bye-bye

normal motor development is by age 2 adept at getting into dangerous situations. By 2 the child has developed enough language ability so that the parents can use words to explain what they are doing, at least to some extent. The child can also indicate his needs by simple phrases or his own jargon. It is also at this time that voluntary control over the sphincters begins to be present. Some children have the neuromuscular maturity to establish bowel control before the age of 2, but it is more usual after 2, and many children do not establish complete control until 3. As in most neurologically deter-

Age	Motor Development	Language	Social and Self Help
12 mo.	Walks with hand held	Says 3-6 words	Cooperates in dressing
15 mo.	Walks alone	Uses jargon	Hugs a doll or teddy
18 mo.	Climbs stairs holding on	Uses 10 words Names pictures	Plays alongside other children Feeds self with spilling
2 yrs.	Walks up and down stairs alone Runs	Uses phrases and 3 word sentences Uses pronouns	Handles cup well Turns pages of book one at a time Initiates own play activities Asks to go to toilet
3 yrs.	Pedals tricycle Draws a circle from a copy	Talks in full sentences Answers simple questions	Plays with other children Feeds self with little spilling
4 yrs.	Copies a cross	Uses conjunctions and prepositions	Cares for self at toilet Engages in dramatic play
5 yrs.	Draws triangle from copy	Sentence structure more complex	Dresses self except for tying shoes
6 yrs.	Uses pencil for printing letters	Rapid progress in reading	Plays simple table games

mined abilities, girls on the average develop sphincter control considerably earlier than boys. In fact, the whole process of socialization proceeds with greater ease for girls than for boys. This sex difference, while known to most parents and teachers, is too often disregarded, leading to inappropriate expectations for one or the other sex. If a family has girls and then a boy comes along, they may expect the boy to achieve sphincter control as easily as his sisters did, and be as "mature." When he cannot fulfill these expectations he may be seen as stubborn, negativistic, or bad. The 3-year-old girl who leads the way for the 3-year-old boy may be seen as bossy, when in truth she is simply neurologically older and therefore in many important ways more capable.

Learning To Play with Others. In the brief but important pre-school years, the young child learns how to relate, how to get along with other children, and how to assert himself appropriately. Our 3-year-old girl has a great deal of trouble sharing her toys, although unlike six months earlier, she now wants to play with other children (associative play) not just be near them (parallel play). She is struggling to learn how to do it. Wanting to play with others but not wanting to share possessions leads to unending squabbles. Whining, crying, and being insulted are the rules of the day, and parents are constantly called upon to arbitrate disputes. But the disputes are never taken very seriously by the children—though adults sometimes become alienated because of such episodes—and almost immediately return to playing with one another.

As the child proceeds into the fourth and fifth years she becomes an adept responder to the subtle cues of interpersonal relations. Greater distinction is now made among people. Likes and dislikes are more clearly articulated, and definite preferences in playmates are established, based increasingly on personality characteristics.

It is at this age that many children will be attending a nursery school, day-care center, or community center for from a few hours a week to all day, five days a week. Nursery schools and day-care centers provide an opportunity for supervised play with many other children, an opportunity often not available to the child at home or in the neighborhood. There is also a wider variety of toys and activities available than at home. Most importantly, the well-trained early-childhood educator who supervises the children can help to stimulate and enhance social and cognitive development. The children can learn to use their senses more fully through special games, and they can come to realize that there are safe and pleasurable experiences to be had away from home. A shy child can be helped to become an active group participant. The experience will also help to prepare children for school. However, not every child is ready for even half a day's separation from home at the age of 4. Most children are, but those who are not need to be recognized and worked with; attendance at nursery school should be delayed or the separation made more gradually in such cases.

Readiness for School. By the time our little girl enters school, socialization has to a great extent been achieved. Controls are comfortably established over bowel and bladder functions.

Aggressive impulses are well in hand, and frustration does not call forth tantrums. She can dress herself, she has a sense of what is appropriate behavior with adults, and she can find pleasure in playing with friends with only an occasional dispute. She can also separate from her family and in a sense be on her own for a part of each day.

MIDDLE CHILDHOOD

Middle childhood spans the years from 6 to 12. It is a period in which the child learns to cope in earnest outside the family. The relationships in the family remain important, but two new sets of relationships—the school and the peer group—become increasingly influential in the child's social development.

School

From 6 to 12 the child progresses from the first through the sixth grade. Many children attend nursery school, and most attend kindergarten before entering first grade; nonetheless, the first grade represents something quite different to the youngster. The school experiences of nursery and kindergarten are focused on group play and developing readiness for learning in a group setting. The first-grader, however, is expected to be ready to learn, and the school requires it. Most children look forward to the new challenge that school presents, wanting to be considered grown-up and capable. They also approach the school experience with an insatiable curiosity and a strong desire to know how things function. The pleasure of exploring new areas leads to learning about the social and material environment. But the curiosity needs to be channeled to meet the demands of a group-learning situation. To learn in a class setting, a child must be able to maintain attention and concentration, follow rules and regulations, and share the teacher's time and attention with other children. Although early childhood education today tends to be relatively open and unstructured—making allowances for the young child's need for movement, variety, and self-directed activities—the pressures for control and concentration will increase with entrance into first grade.

This new world of learning is an exciting one for the child, especially if the teacher is able to capture the child's interest and make provisions for the students' individual differences. Not all children are developing at the same cognitive and emotional rate, and the early tasks of reading, writing, and arithmetic will be met with corresponding ease or difficulty. A child whose perceptual-motor development is somewhat immature will experience a more difficult time recognizing words and keeping his letters between the lines than will his more mature neighbor. This difference in maturity does not mean that the less mature child will not catch up and perhaps even surpass his more mature classmate, but for the time being he will have to struggle harder to master the tasks at hand.

By the third grade, children have usually "hit their stride." Those who have matured a little more slowly will usually have caught up. The classroom routine is now a familiar, and for most a comfortable, part of their day. The age differences among classmates, which can be as much as a year, are now less noticeable with respect to cognitive ability. The children's attitudes toward learning are more differentiated and tend to reflect the attitudes of their parents. The effects of a positive educational orientation in the family will increasingly be expressed in the children's approach to the school experience.

By 12 the child has amassed a great deal of information, can read a book with ease, and has fairly well established a pattern or style of learning, be it efficient or inefficient. He is still limited in his ability for abstract thinking and conceptualization, but in most areas of learning he demonstrates a remarkable capacity.

The Peer Group

Middle childhood is sometimes referred to as the age of the gang, because it is between the ages of 6 and 12 that the peer group takes on such immense importance. The middle-childhood gang is primarily a play group, but it also aids social development through the cooperation and interaction that are required. The transition from group play to the formation of an intimate peer group is a gradual process that begins in middle childhood and reaches its peak in adolescence. Of course the preschooler has already developed friendships, but these friendships do not possess the group dynamic characteristics of the neighborhood group.

An important aspect of these social groupings of children is that they are separate and autonomous from the adult world. The gang or clique of middle childhood has its secrets, rules, and rituals that belong to the children alone and are neither shared with nor, for the most part, observed by adults. The treehouse and clubhouse typify and concretize the separateness from the adult world and the special sense of belongingness that are so valued by children at this age. Not to be a member of one of these peer groups is to feel rejected, isolated, and vulnerable. It is not that each child must be a part of these groups (certainly many are not and become productive individuals); but to be an outsider is usually painful and raises within the child self-doubt and the fear that he is not "good enough" in some mysterious way.

Another characteristic of the peer groups of middle childhood is the separation of the sexes. Sex role typing is very clearly evident in the activities of middle childhood (we will discuss the topic of sex typing at the end of this chapter). The preferred activities of boys and girls differ in some respects, but these differences do not fully account for the degree of separation of their play. Boys play marbles, spin tops, play cops and robbers, wrestle, and engage in team sports—baseball, football, hockey. Girls generally spend little time in group games and are more apt than boys to enage in dramatic play. There are, of course, many girls who do not follow this pattern but prefer to join the boys in their games. The "tomboy" is usually an accepted variation in a girl's development, unlike the boy who is rejected if he is "feminine" in his interests. Girls also tend to spend more time at home or visiting in the homes of other girls. Many other activities, of course, are the same; both boys and girls bicycle, swim, roller-skate and ice-skate, play "hide and seek," checkers, cards, and the like. Yet they are not likely to participate in these activities together. This separation of the sexes, a long-established cultural pattern, probably developed as a means of fostering identification with one's own sex and teaching the sexual role skills important to the culture. Thus boys learn from other boys what is expected of boys and men. One can see this in the way younger boys—the 7- and 8-year-olds—are taught the rules of a game and the behavior expected of a good sport by the older boys in the group, the 10- or 11-year-olds.

Older boys and girls "socialize" the younger ones by demanding that they conform to the rules of the games as the group and culture define them. Such socialization by the peer group is an important and powerful source of learning. A major danger for the child in this period of development is that he will find it difficult not to conform to these peer group standards. If these demands are for behavior of a delinquent type, the child can adopt antisocial standards. Most parents, however, are able to supervise their children's activities closely enough during middle childhood to prevent the adoption of standards the parents do not approve of. During the next phase of development, adolescence, this supervision is often not as feasible or as desirable, making it all the more important that social values be firmly established by the end of middle childhood.

The child who must grow up in an urban ghetto faces special diffi-culties in this period as well as in adolescence. To survive, he must be able to protect himself in the schoolyard and the street. To be able to fight under such circumstances is important. He must, however, be able to discriminate between the times when aggressive responses are appropriate and when they are not. Such discrimination is not always easy, and a too explosive temper may create serious difficulties for the child—when, for instance, it surfaces in the classroom.

Ralph was 9 when first brought to the clinic. The school had sent him because he kept getting into fights in the classroom. His fighting was responsible for his having been kept back the year before. Ralph had an 11-year-old sister and 6-year-old sister. His mother couldn't understand "what got into the boy." He just wouldn't listen. He got into trouble in the neighborhood as well as in school. He broke windows, climbed into empty houses, got into fights. There was no father in the home and there had not been one for several years. Ralph possessed good intellectual ability but was always on guard that some boy was going to get the best of him. He was "hypermasculine." He displayed a tough bravado that sought to compensate for not having the security of a father. At home such behavior was a burden but in school it was simply not tolerated. He was suspended and referred for treatment.

The Chum

Toward 10 or 11 there usually develops a special friendship that takes precedence over all others. This special friend or chum becomes the confidant, the extra-loyal friend and sharer of secret dreams and thoughts. This chum relationship was considered especially important by Sullivan (see Chapter 12) as a phase in the development of the capacity for adult intimacy. The chum also serves importantly as a source of support and reality-testing in that self-doubts and fantasies can be safely discussed with this one comrade. The turbulent early period of adolescence is much easier to cope with when the fresh surge of sexual interest and the new push for independence from the family can be shared. The preadolescent or adolescent does not feel that he or she is strange or deviant; the chum is there to validate the new inner experiences and to provide the reassurance that they are not peculiar after all.

Children's Fears

Children show many different fears and distress reactions in the course of growing up. Many infants cry and show general distress reactions when left alone or when they are hungry or experiencing some other pain. Infants will also show a startle reaction to sudden, unexpected, or intense sensory experiences such as loud noises, flashing lights, and falling. In early childhood fears become more specific, reflecting the increased ability to make discriminations and to represent the world symbolically. Typically, children fear the dark, ghosts, robbers, monsters, and bad dreams. Early childhood fears may persist into middle childhood. But at about 5 to 6 years of age the child's separation fears become heightened by his entrance into nursery school or kindergarten. Separation anxiety is reflected in fears of harm, accidents, or injury from real or imaginary sources (e.g., animals, ghosts, etc.). The awareness of death as a concrete reality also emerges during middle childhood, generating many specific and symbolic fears with the theme of death.

Most childhood fears are normal and transient. Fears that are more deeply rooted in emotional problems can, however, interfere with the child's functioning and necessitate psychological help. For example, the child might develop sleep disturbances, school phobia, obsessions, compulsions, or painful somatic complaints and symptoms.

CHILDHOOD SEXUALITY

Adult sexuality is the result of a complex process of genetically and hormonally regulated bodily growth and development that takes place at the time of puberty. Before puberty, sexual development is quite limited. In boys the penis is relatively small, and the testes produce neither sperm nor appreciable amounts of androgen, the male sex hormone. In girls, the ovaries are dormant; no ova are released, nor is estrogen produced. In both boys and girls there are demonstrable, though small, amounts of androgens and estrogens—both hormones being present in the same amount in both sexes. They are probably produced by the adrenals. The genitals are responsive to hormones, but under normal circumstances the rise in hormone level that induces growth in the genitals waits for pubertal age.

There are exceptions. A normal exception is routinely seen at birth. The mother's circulating estrogen stimulates development of the vulva in the fetus in utero, and the nurse can see the enlarged genitals quite clearly in the newborn. Frequently there is also slight breast development in both girls and boys at birth. These effects recede in the first week.

Other exceptions to normal puberty are seen in precocious puberty, which may occur as early as 4 or 5 years of age. Occasionally hormones given to a pregnant woman cause stimulation of clitoral growth in the fetus. In such instances the clitoris may be large enough to be mistaken for a penis, and mislabeling of the child's sex is known to have occurred.

Before puberty sexual excitement is relatively limited. The child can and does become sexually stimulated (and may have orgasms), but childhood sexuality does not have the same quality as adult sexuality. During infancy children explore their bodies, and exploration includes the genitalia. The boy will pull on his penis, examine it, and play with it. The pleasure experienced is part of the child's general interest and sensual pleasure in his body. Similarly, a girl will examine her vulva and vaginal orifice.

Probably because of the anatomical differences, the amount of handling and genital play is usually greater among boys than among girls. The penis is more visible, more readily handled, and subject to erections. In fact, penile erections are frequent from birth through old age, and while they may be associated with sexual excitement, most often in childhood they are not. For instance erections occur regularly in sleep during the REM (rapid-eye-movement) periods of "physiologic storm," which coincide with the periods of dreaming. Of course, in the adult male sexual dreams are not infrequent, but penile erection occurs during these periods regardless of sexual content and from birth (and even in utero!). The erections are expressions of a general physiologic excitation. The nurses in the newborn nursery as well as on the pediatric service frequently observe this phenomenon. Children do experience sexual excitement, but nurses and other professionals should be aware that the various sources of genital excitation are not exclusively sexual.

Sexual Identity

The felt sex role or gender identity develops very early. A child of 18 months is probably already aware of his own sex and that of important others in his life. By 3 years this sense of sexual identity is firmly established if not verbalized by all children. This fact is evident in studies in which mislabeling of sex (pseudohermaphroditism) has occurred as a result of hormonal abnormalities or developmental anomalies. For instance, a male infant may have undescended testes with hypospadis, a congenital condition in which the urethra fails to close; when severe, this may produce the appearance of female genitalia. It has been found in such cases that, even with corrective treatment, if the sexual mislabeling was not corrected by the age of 3 the individual experienced himself in later life according to the mislabeling. This occurred even though hormonal and sexual characteristics were opposite to the felt sex. If change was instituted prior to 3, mislabeling could be corrected (Money, 1963). Thus the most powerful determinant of an individual's sexual identity would seem to be what his family labels him. A careful examination of the neonate is essential in order to avoid irreparable damage in the establishment of the appropriate sexual identity.

Sex Differences in Behavior

Boys and girls display different behavior patterns and characteristics that can be readily observed. As we have noted, the sexes usually play separately and pursue different interests. Boys tend toward more physical and manipulative activities and girls toward more passive activities. Also, boys show more aggression while girls are described as nurturant. In the area of ability and achievement, no differences in overall intelligence have been found between boys and girls (Matarazzo, 1972). But girls do better in reading, word fluency, grammar, and spelling, particularly in the early elementary school grades. Boys tend to do better in analytic and inductive reasoning and in spatial visualization. Boys of high school age do better than do girls in math—although there are no differences in elementary school—and this difference continues into adulthood. Boys also display greater mechanical ability than girls. (These trends, we must emphasize, apply to large groups and not to a particular boy or girl who may be poor or outstanding in any given skill or area.)

How can we account for these differences? Are they biologically determined or socially conditioned? While we cannot say conclusively that some differences between males and females do not have a biological basis, glaring differences in role training and social conditioning play a major role. It is also important to recognize that none of the proposed differences have any bearing on potential for outstanding achievement, competence, or creativity in any area of life, professional or otherwise.

Hormones and Sex Role Behavior

To separate hormonal effects from environmental influences is exceedingly difficult, since we know that from birth parents treat female and male infants differently. One avenue of exploration has been the investigation of subtle differences in infant behavior soon after birth, before environmental influences can have exerted their effect. These studies have led to some interesting though hard-to-interpret findings. Bell and Costello (1964) found that newborn females reacted more to having a covering blanket removed and were more sensitive to air-jet stimulation of the abdomen. Bell and Darling (1965) found that newborn males raise their heads higher than did newborn females. Wolff (1969) found female newborns more sensitive than male to skin contact. Korner (1973) found early male-female differences in hand-to-mouth activity, with females displaying mouth-dominated movements and males hand-dominated movements. Korner also reviewed the studies of behavioral sex differences in newborns, and she concluded that findings were generally consistent in pointing to greater tactile sensitivity in females and greater initial muscular strength in males. She raised the question whether some of the differences in the way parents handle infants (e.g., parents tend to provide male infants with more tactile stimulation) may be a response to subtle sex differences in the infants. That is, the infant may be eliciting from the parents certain behaviors at the same time that the parents foster specific behaviors in the infant.

How do these sex differences in the newborn originate? Hamburg and Lunde (1966) among others attribute the origin of these differences to the prenatal action of hormones. There is a critical period in the third fetal month in which the fetal testes produce androgens that induce the formation of the male reproductive organs. If androgens are not produced by the testes at this critical period, the fetus fails to develop male characteristics. The presence of circulating androgens prenatally could cause greater muscular strength at birth in males. Korner also postulates that the androgens may suppress the male skin sensitivity.

An interesting study of the effects of prenatal hormones on later personality development was carried out by Yalom et al. (1973). They made use of the fact that diabetic mothers are often given female hormones (estrogen and progesterone) during their pregnancy to help prevent abortions, which occur frequently with them. The investigators located twenty 6-year-old boys and twenty 16-year-old boys whose mothers had been so treated. They compared these boys with same-age children of diabetic mothers who had not been given hormones. The comparisons included many measures of psychosexual behavior and the raters of the children's behavior did not know which of the children had been exposed to hormones and which had not. It was found that the boys exposed to the estrogen-progesterone treatment were rated significantly less assertive and displayed less athletic ability than the boys not so exposed. However, the mechanism by which the hormones exerted their influence on the boys' psychosexual development was not clarified.

Thus there is evidence that male and female infants exhibit behavioral differences at birth and that prenatal hormonal influences may help to shape later personality development.

Role Training

Whatever biological propensities may be present become over-shadowed by the different social conditioning that begins at birth. Boys and girls are dressed differently, talked to differently, talked about differently, and bombarded with different expectations. There are countless behaviors that are encouraged or discouraged on the basis of the sex of the child.

In one study mothers talking about sons and daughters empha-sized different qualities for each. Terms such as poise, politeness, and charm were applied to daughters while self-confidence, competitiveness, achievement, and independence were stressed for sons (Hill, 1964). Parents will encourage and reinforce at a very early age the preferred behaviors while overtly and subtly dis-couraging the "unmasculine" or "unfeminine" behaviors. For instance, aggression is more tolerated in boys than in girls. Boys will be ridiculed for playing with dolls and girls for being too rough or too "tomboyish." On the other hand, nurturing attitudes and playing house are more expected in girls. It does not take the child long to sense the rules for approval or disapproval.

Social stereotyping reaches into almost every area of functioning. Whether it be school, play, social relations, or family life, there are usually clear-cut roles along sex lines. The relentless and repetitive concurrence of the role stereotypes gives them an overwhelmingly convincing impact, and eventually they become an "instinctive" part of the child's sense of right and wrong behaviors. Biological effects at this point become clouded. The powerful result of early role teaching is illustrated in a study by Looft (1971), in which 6- to 8-year-old children were asked the familiar question "What do you want to be when you grow up?" The two most popular categories for girls were the roles of nurse and teacher. These two choices were selected by 75% of the girls. The two most popular choices for boys, of football player and fireman, were selected by only 10% of the boys. Furthermore, the choices of the boys were spread out over 18 occu-pational categories, while the girls confined their choices to only 8 categories. It would appear from these data that the social rein-forcers that emphasize role distinctions between the sexes have far-reaching implications for the life choices and self-images of individuals.

The subtle manifestations of social conditioning can also be seen in books that children are exposed to at a young age. As early as 1946 researchers noted differences in characterizations and representations of males and females in children's textbooks. Not only were females represented less often in the third-grade texts examined, but the usual stereotypes prevailed. Boys were active, aggressive, and achievement-oriented, while girls were passive, uncreative, kind, and showing little ambition. Fathers were active problem-solvers and mothers mindless and passive homemakers (Child, Potter, and Levine, 1946). Saario et al. (1973) report the results of a more detailed study of recent children's textbooks. Many of the earlier stereotypes still persisted. In all, 270 stories in four popular reading series were examined (Bank Street, Ginn, Harper & Row, and Scott Foresman). There were still significantly fewer female than male characters. This cannot, of course, be justified as reflecting reality since in fact children are generally exposed to more women than men (e.g., mother and teacher). Other significant differences showed boys to be more aggressive, more physically assertive, and better problem-solvers. Girls were more frequently characterized by greater fantasy and more preoccupation with self. Adult females came across with greater conformity and greater verbal behavior. Male adults were portrayed more frequently as productive, assertive, and problem-solving. The stereotypes increased with the progression from kindergarten to third-grade-level readers.

Role stereotyping exists in many school curricula. There is commonly early separation into supposed male and female activities—boys to shop and mechanical activities and girls to home economics and sewing. Specialized high schools and vocational schools have also been cited for discriminatory entrance requirements. How often are youngsters told that boys are more scientifically and mathematically inclined and girls more expressively inclined? To what extent stereotyped role depictions become self-fulfilling prophesies is difficult to estimate, but the attitudes behind these practices undoubtedly contribute to the constricted aspirations of women. The United States government has recently taken note of the widespread discriminatory practices in schools and employment, and this has led to legislation prohibiting discrimination in federally supported programs.

How the sex role stereotyping affects male–female relationships and attitudes is indicated by research at Harvard University reported by Gornick (1973). Harvard undergraduates were asked to write stories based on the following cue: "After first-term finals, Anne finds herself at the top of her medical school class." Most of the responses were along these lines:

Anne is not a woman. She is really a computer. . . .

Anne rushes out of her smelly formaldehyde laboratory and runs to the university bar where she knows she will find Bruno! The perfect man! . . .

Anne is paralyzed from the waist down. She sits in a wheel chair and studies for medical school. . . .

Outstanding success for women becomes dissociated from normality and femininity in the eyes of these undergraduate males. Stories were quite different when it was a male who was presented as the student at the top of his class:

John is a conscientious young man who has worked hard. He is pleased with himself. John has always wanted to go into medicine and is very dedicated. . . . John continues working hard and eventually graduates at the top of his class.

Success is more compatible with the male image and therefore does not have to be presented as a compensation or peculiarity. On the other side are the pseudomasculine needs of many men, which drive them to avoid characteristics that do not fit the male image. In the final analysis sex typing along a broad spectrum of behaviors is counterproductive to the fullest expression and fulfillment of human potentialities.

SUMMARY

The plans for the development of an organism are contained in its genes, which are located on the chromosomes. In humans, there are 23 pairs of chromosomes. The genes are biochemical templates made up of DNA. They transmit their codes by forming another substance, RNA, which acts as a messenger to the protein-building structure of the cell.

The fusion of the male gamete (sperm) and female gamete (ovum) forms the zygote and marks the beginning of the new organism's development. The first phase of intrauterine development is called the embryonic stage. It is the period of organ formation. The second and longer phase is the fetal stage, when growth and maturation of the organs take place.

Physical growth and development are very rapid during infancy. Birth weight triples by the end of the first year. At birth, the infant is neurologically immature and displays a number of reflexes (Moro, rooting, tonic-neck reflex) that disappear as the organism matures.

Postural control and locomotion progress takes place in an orderly sequence, starting with head control and proceeding to walking. For most of infancy the child is preverbal. An invariant sequence of development of speech occurs, with a vocabulary of 200 to 300 words being attained by 2 years of age.

The infant requires a responding environment for adequate intellectual and emotional development. It needs to develop confidence in its ability to communicate its needs and to develop a basic trust in human relationships.

During the preschool years coordination becomes smooth and skilled. Language ability increases rapidly, both in extent of vocabulary and in complexity of sentence structures. Socialization begins in earnest, and the child learns to control its impulses. The preschool child learns to share toys and to play with peers.

In middle childhood relationships outside the home assume major importance. A large portion of each day is spent in school. Teachers and learning become dominant experiences. As middle childhood progresses, the peer group is increasingly influential in the child's life.

While interest in the genitals is normally present in childhood, sexual excitement remains limited. Gender identity develops very early, at least by 3 years of age. Sexual differences in behavior are mainly due to social conditioning, although hormonal factors may play a role. Sexual stereotypes often work to the disadvantage of the individual in modern society.

SUGGESTED READINGS

Prenatal

Moore, K. L. *Before we are born: basic embryology and birth deficits.* Philadelphia: W. B. Saunders, 1974.

Roberts, J. A. F. *An introduction to medical genetics.* 6th ed. London: Oxford University Press, 1973.

Watson, J. D. *The double helix: a personal account of the discovery of the structure of DNA.* New York: Atheneum, 1969.

Infancy

Church, J. *Understanding your child from birth to three.* New York: Random House, 1973.

Fraiberg, S. H. *The magic years.* New York: Scribner's, 1959.

Gesell, A. *The first five years of life.* New York: Harper, 1940.

Provence, S. A., and Lipton, R. C. *Infants in institutions.* New York: International Universities Press, 1962.

Spock, B. *Baby and child care.* New York: Hawthorns, 1968.

Childhood

Erikson, E. H. *Childhood and society.* 2nd ed. New York: Norton, 1963.

Gesell, A., and Ilg, F. S. *The child from five to ten.* New York: Harper & Row, 1946.

Hartley, R. *Understanding children's play.* New York: New York University Press, 1952.

Illingsworth, R. S. *The normal child.* 5th ed. Baltimore: Williams and Wilkins, 1972.

Lewis, M. *Clinical aspects of child development.* Philadelphia: Lea and Febiger, 1971.

Maccoby, E. E., ed. *The development of sex differences.* Stanford, Calif.: Stanford University Press, 1966.

Smart, M. S., and Smart R. C. *Preschool children.* New York: Macmillan, 1973.

Stone, L. J., and Church, J. *Childhood and adolescence.* 3rd ed. New York: Random House, 1973.

Chapter 3

Adolescence

ADOLESCENCE MEANS literally "growing into maturity." It refers to the variable period of time that forms the transition from childhood to adulthood. Although adolescence is considered by many as the last phase of childhood, it is in reality a time when the individual is no longer a child but not yet an adult. It is more difficult to set the boundaries for adolescence than for any other period in the life cycle. The onset of puberty is frequently taken as the beginning of adolescence, but in fact there are great individual differences in age of onset of puberty. Although the psychological development that takes place during adolescence is greatly influenced by the physiological changes of puberty, it is not fully determined by them. Other aspects of the inner self and the outer environment, such as cognitive development, peer group activities, and family attitudes, will determine when this transition phase is entered. For our purposes, we will take 13 as the age at which adolescence begins for both boys and girls.

When does adolescence end and adulthood begin? In the United States it is frequently said that adolescence has been prolonged into the 20s. If one considers economic independence as the hallmark of the adult, it is true that such independence is reached later and later. Of those graduating from high school today, more than half go on to college, which means that they do not enter full-time employment until their 20s. However, economic independence per se need not be the primary indicator of adulthood. Rather, adulthood may be defined as beginning when one is responsible for one's own actions. In the United States, 18 is increasingly being taken as the age at which one expects such responsibility, and this has been given legal sanction by the law conferring voting rights on 18-year-olds. Consequently we will call 18 the upper limit of adolescence, realizing nonetheless that there will be wide individual differences as well as other definitions of adulthood.

PUBERTY

Although the prepubertal child is capable of experiencing sexual excitation, it is at puberty that sexual curiosity changes to sexual need. Puberty comes not as a sudden change but as a gradual progression of physical and psychological changes that take place over the course of 3 to 5 years.

Puberty begins earlier in girls, on the average two years sooner than it does in boys, and it takes three to four years before complete sexual maturity is reached. The first sign of puberty in girls is breast development, which usually begins between 8 and 13 years of age; their growth is followed in about a year by the appearance of pubic hair, a height spurt, and changes in general physique (widening of the hips). The average age for the beginning of the menses (the menarche) is 13 years, with a normal range of occurrence at 10 to $16\frac{1}{2}$ years. (In this context "normal" is taken to mean that 90% of girls have their first menses between 10 and $16\frac{1}{2}$ years of age.)

In boys puberty begins with an increased rate of growth of the testes and scrotum; at first there is slight, then greater growth of pubic hair. At the same time the penis, proportionately small until puberty, grows. There is also a height spurt and enlargement of the larynx with a deepening of the voice.

Until puberty boys and girls are similar in height. With the earlier onset of puberty in girls, there is a two-year period during which they are on the average taller than boys. The height spurt of the boys, however, is greater, and by 16 the average boy is taller than the average girl. Approximately two years after the beginning of the growth of pubic hair in boys, axillary and facial hair appear. There are also changes in physique, with marked development of muscular strength. These changes require three to five years from the time the accelerated growth of the testes and penis begins. Further, even though the first ejaculation in boys occurs on the average at the age of 14, it is within the normal range for a boy to experience his first ejaculation at any time between 11 and 15 years of age.

For both boys and girls, the growth spurt and increased physical strength that accompany puberty foster a greater interest and participation in competitive sports. It is in such activities that differences in the rate of physical maturation are often keenly felt. One study of 15-year-old boys showed an average difference of 8 inches in height and 30 pounds in weight between early maturers and late maturers (Jones and Bayley, 1950). Such a difference in physical stature could readily determine whether a boy is able to compete successfully in team sports. Even in sports such as swimming, where height and weight are not as important, muscle mass is crucial, and the increase in androgens at puberty is responsible for a marked increase in muscular capacity. The late-maturing boy is likely as a consequence of this temporary disadvantage to be more shy and to have lower self-esteem. These traits also tend to persist even when the late maturer has caught up physically (Eichorn, 1963). Among girls the early maturers appear to be under more stress. Their sexual development may make them feel embarrassingly different from their physically more childlike peers. This suggests that a strictly chronological grouping of adolescents does not serve their diverse social and developmental needs.

Not only motor skills are rapidly developing in early adolescence. At 13 to 14 years of age, the adolescent becomes capable of the adult type of abstract reasoning (see formal operations of Piaget, Chapter 11). With this new cognitive ability comes the adolescent's passion for the higher "truths" and for ideological causes. Although cognitive ability alone has limited value unless coupled with knowledge, the new intellectual skills can lead to solid achievements. In areas such as mathematics and music, in which a large body of knowledge need not necessarily be acquired, a creative mind can make significant contributions at a relatively young age.

SOCIAL DEVELOPMENT

In early adolescence children are entering puberty at different ages, and so physiologically based heterosexual interest develops at quite varied times. Most youngsters, even those who have reached puberty earlier than have their peers, engage in social activities primarily with other adolescents of the same sex. While this is a time of awakening interest in the opposite sex, this interest is largely expressed in talk rather than in extended social contact. A close, dependent relationship with someone of the same sex is more typical of late childhood and early adolescence. Adolescent "chum" relationships, which are usually carried over from middle childhood, are invested with a new intensity and meaning. Interest is now focused on the boy or girl friend of the same sex as an individual. Friends want to know everything about each other—feelings, reactions, wishes, habits, and so on. Perceptions of the other person become much more discriminating. These intimate and intense chum relationships serve as a bridge to mature socialization. The adolescent, in effect, tries himself or herself out in these relatively "safe" friendships. Also, the empathy, self-awareness, and role-playing involved in chum relationships pave the way for the more anxiety-provoking heterosexual relationships.

While the chum relationship is a vital link in the chain of social development, some adolescents are unable to establish such a bond. The fragile, easily threatened self-esteem of the adolescent can scare him off from any form of real intimacy. Social isolation, with its profound sense of loneliness and depression, is one such escape from intimacy. "Hanging around" with a large group and not relating to any one individual is another solution. The emotional ups and downs of adolescence can be great as each success and failure is encountered. Mood swings as well as erratic patterns of behavior are not uncommon.

Adolescent cliques or gangs also serve the identity needs of the adolescent. Fearful of the demands of achieving independence, many adolescents submerge themselves into a group identity, which for the moment gives a feeling of importance and belonging. The clique insulates the adolescent from the adult world while establishing its own norms that he can achieve. The standards, values, and opinions of the peer group may exert much more influence on the adolescent than do parents or other adults. While the clique has the positive effect of testing out roles and styles of relating in preparation for adulthood, it can also have a negative influence. Pressures for conformity in the peer group can be even more intense than they were in middle childhood. The need for acceptance can reign supreme, leading the adolescent to experiment with drugs or sex at a time when he or she is not prepared to handle the emotional aspects of these experiences. Of course, individual maturity will determine how each adolescent navigates in the peer group. From this point of view, dealing with the peer group is not *just* preparation for adult life but another developmental task in the ongoing process of establishing individual identity.

For the adolescent from a poverty environment the clique or gang may take on even greater importance. The higher incidence of school failure, lack of skills, few opportunities, constricted aspirations, and social instability all conspire to convey a feeling of low self-esteem to the adolescent from a poverty culture. The clique becomes the oasis where self-esteem is possible. But in relating to the humiliation inflicted by society the poverty clique must take drastic action. Antisocial acts having high status in the peer group are a quick avenue to a feeling of worth; apathy, withdrawal, dropping out, and passive acceptance of clique norms are other responses.

A Separate Culture

Adolescents are separated both from younger children and from adults by the organization of the school system. In order to provide rich educational experiences, including youth-oriented social life and special-interest clubs, high schools have expanded their facilities for adolescents. This expansion of programs has its definite advantages, offering all adolescents resources for activities that few families could afford, such as costly sports equipment, chemistry laboratories, and swimming pools. In line with this trend, many families have come to provide "rec-rooms" for their youngsters, where they can engage in their own activities. In short, our society has, with all good intentions, created the setting and the means for a "youth culture" the likes of which has never existed in any other society. In addition, school attendance up to age 18 for a majority of adolescents works to extend the period of childlike dependence.

Unfortunately, this "separate culture" often results in a sense of alienation from the rest of society. For some this alienation stimulates a desire to find a deeper meaning in life, leading to study and involvement in mystical experiences, Zen Buddhism, astrology, and similar attemps at cosmic understanding. For others the alienation produces escapism of various forms, one of the most harmful of these being the use of drugs. Perhaps in rebellion against their parents' society, and as a symbol of belonging to their own subculture, adolescents today make widespread use of marijuana. While marijuana is probably no more harmful than alcohol, intoxicants do result in lessened judgment, and hence they are especially dangerous when used by those of high school age.

One characteristic of this separate culture is its strong reliance on age-mates as models. The heroes of today's adolescents are usually very close to their own age—rock singers, for instance. Anyone over 30 is considered alien and not likely to share youth's values. Another characteristic of adolescents is their identification with the underdog. There is a strong feeling of empathy for those who, like themselves, are alienated from society. They are therefore quick to rally to antiestablishment political causes; they tend to regard existing institutions as oppressive and seek to change them. Although these characteristics increase the tension between the generations, they may also help society to grow rather than stagnate. However, the separateness and alienation can be costly, especially when young people fail to make use of existing institutions for their own growth and development. When their alienation leads them to use narcotics or to drop out of school at a young age, the loss is enormous both to the adolescent and to the society.

Heterosexual Relationships

Middle adolescence is the time when friendships with the opposite sex become important. Just as there is a wide variation in the age of onset of puberty, so the time at which the investment in such relationships occurs varies widely among adolescents. In line with their earlier pubescence, girls seem more socially capable in their encounters than boys, who appear shy and awkward in comparison. Boys in contrast have an earlier interest in and need for sexual release, and hence there is a great deal of pressure placed on adolescent girls to cope with the socially awkward but sexually driven boys. Some of this difference in sexual behavior can, of course, be accounted for by social conditioning and mores. But there also appear to be biological differences between male and female sexual development. Although sexual development begins earlier in females, male sexual development is marked by an initial high level of hormone production. In females sexuality increases gradually and levels off later than in males.

From the purely biological point of view, as we have pointed out, heterosexual relationships become a physiological need with the hormonal changes at puberty. But in some families and social groups heterosexual socialization is encouraged in early childhood in the belief that it enhances possibilities for marriage or later social adjustment. In other settings the belief may be that early relationships with the opposite sex encourage later promiscuity or "clutter their minds" and distract from more important interests. There is little evidence for any of these beliefs. However, we do know that much of the turmoil or crisis of adolescence does not exist in societies in which childhood relationships flow naturally into heterosexual relationships in adolescence. In Samoan society, as depicted by Margaret Mead (1950), young children are not inhibited or restricted in their play with children of the opposite sex. As a result they do not face the intense awkwardness that adolescents in our society experience in getting to know the opposite sex.

In our society dating usually begins in middle adolescence. Relating to the opposite sex entails more risks and threats than do previous relationships. The heterosexual relationship is often perceived by the adolescent as a major test of how successful he will be in his adult relationships—Will I be accepted? How do others see me? How successful will I be in a mature role? Will I be successful as a man or woman? Will I be embarrassed or humiliated?—The relatively unformed self is still very vulnerable to failure; therefore heterosexual relationships are hazardous. Adolescents will spend an inordinate amount of time and concern with personal appearance in an effort to deal with their insecurity in a concrete way.

How to handle sexual impulses and demands is a pressing problem. For the adolescent girl the questions are: how far, how much, when, and with whom? Where there are double standards, the conflict is more acute. For the adolescent boy eager to prove his masculinity the fear may be that he will not be aggressive enough, that he will be inept or unsuccessful. Girls may have an additional problem if sex-typing compels them, for the sake of acceptance, to play a subordinate, dependent, and noncompetitive role with boys. Fears and concerns about homosexuality also surface at this time. All these psychological dilemmas are compounded by questions of contraception, venereal disease, pregnancy, and abortion.

The explicit treatment of sex in films and literature results in increased awareness of sexuality and serves as an impetus for sexual behavior; it also brings the adolescent's questions and fears to conscious awareness. But society still helps very little in providing answers or guidance to adolescents, and school curricula dealing with sexuality are, for the most part, skimpy and evasive.

Sexual Behavior and Attitudes

Sorensen (1973) made a comprehensive study of the sexual behavior and attitudes of American adolescents based on a nationwide survey conducted in 1972. The survey included white and nonwhite adolescents from 200 regions of the country and from all economic levels. This study is one of the few that reflect current adolescent sexual mores. The findings are summarized in Table 3.1. We can see from the table that reported sexual activity increases sharply from the 13- to 15-year-old group to the 16- to 19-year-old group. Sexual intercourse had been experienced by 37% of the younger group and 64% of the older group. More boys of the total group (59%) report intercourse experience than girls (45%). This contrasts with Kinsey's earlier data in which 21% of mothers and 45% of fathers born after 1900 indicated sexual intercourse experience prior to age 20. Of the 13- to 15-year-olds, 39% report no sexual experiences (beyond kissing) compared with only 9% of the 16- to 19-year-olds. The study also notes that 58% of the boys and 39% of the girls acknowledged masturbating one or more times. The incidence of masturbation for boys is surprisingly low in comparison with the earlier findings of Kinsey (1948, 1953), who found that approximately 95% of adolescent boys and 33% of adolescent girls masturbated. Sorensen felt, however, that masturbation was underreported in his study. Of all the areas asked about, it generated the most embarrassment, defensiveness, and inhibition. Sorensen states, "There seems to be no practice discussed in this study about which young people feel more defensive or private about than masturbation. Superstition is seldom a factor. Self-esteem, embarrassment, and personal disgust seem to be the major inhibiting factors" (p. 144). This observation is rather interesting in view of the prevailing feeling that the attitudes of the current adolescent population are open and uninhibited with respect to all areas of sexuality. Apparently many of the taboos surrounding masturbation still prevail.

Other prominent findings of Sorensen are that in general the pattern shows greater heterosexual activities on the part of boys than of girls. Also, boys report masturbating more frequently than girls. More sexually experienced adolescent girls than boys also seem to sustain a single sexual relationship ("serial monogamy") while more of the boys move to many different sexual relationships ("serial adventurers"). Most of the adolescents feel that sex and marriage

Table 3.1 **American Adolescents—Sexual Behavior Groups**

	Total	Boys	Girls	13–15	16–19	White	Non-white
Virgins (All adolescents who have not had sexual intercourse)	48%	41%	55%	63%	36%	55%	49%
Sexually inexperienced (Virgins with no beginning sexual activities)	22	20	25	39	9	25	23
Sexual beginners (Virgins who have actively or passively experienced sexual petting)	17	14	19	12	21	20	9
Unclassified virgins (Virgins who for whatever reason could not be classified in the above groups	9	7	11	12	6	9	17
Nonvirgins (All adolescents who have had sexual intercourse one or more times)	52	59	45	37	64	45	51
Serial monogamists (Nonvirgins having a sexual relationship with one person)	21	15	28	9	31	19	14

do not have to go together: 76% of the boys and 67% of the girls agreed with the statement "two people shouldn't have to get married just because they want to live together." Thirty-four percent of the adolescents felt that it is alright for married people to have sexual relations with other people once in a while for the sake of variety, but 45% of the boys and 37% of the girls said they would divorce a spouse for infidelity. At the same time a majority of the adoles-

Sexual adventurers (Nonvirgins freely moving from one sexual intercourse partner to another)	Total	Boys	Girls	13-15	16-19	White	Non-white
Sexual adventurers (Nonvirgins freely moving from one sexual intercourse partner to another)	15	24	6	10	18	11	18
Inactive nonvirgins (Nonvirgins who have not had sexual intercourse for more than one year)	12	13	10	15	10	11	14
Unclassified nonvirgins (Nonvirgins who for whatever reasons could not be classified in the above groups)	4	7	1	3	5	4	5
Current intercourse-experienced (Nonvirgins who have had sexual intercourse during the preceding month)	31	30	33	15	45	24	31
Non-current intercourse-experienced (Nonvirgins who have *not* had sexual intercourse during the preceding month)	21	29	12	22	19	21	20

Source: R. C. Sorensen, *Adolescent sexuality in contemporary America.* New York: World, 1973, p. 122. Reprinted by permission.

cents thought that not to have intercourse before marriage is abnormal and unnatural. Of those adolescents with intercourse experience, 55% said that they did not use contraception with the first intercourse. Among those who did use contraception the most popular methods were birth control pills (one-third of the girls) and withdrawal of the penis (17%). It is not surprising that 28% of the nonvirgin girls have been pregnant.

IDENTITY FORMATION

With puberty, the effort to crystallize an identity and be accepted by one's peers may become a desperate struggle. While sexuality may be a significant driving force of much adolescent behavior, other areas are consciously preceived as more important. The Sorensen report (1973) indicates that independence, learning about oneself, getting along with others, and preparing for the future are dominant concerns (see Table 3.2). All of these concerns are related to the quest for identity.

In many ways adolescence appears to be harder for girls than for boys. Until adolescence, boys seem to experience more numerous and more serious problems in social development. Among those sent to child guidance clinics in early and middle childhood for psychiatric help, boys outnumber girls by three to one. Learning disabilities, such as reading problems, are also much more common in boys. At puberty, however, girls begin to show up at child guidance clinics in about equal numbers with boys.

The case of Janet indicates the kind of disorganization that can occur when the adolescent is unable to achieve a stable sense of self or guidelines for future development.

At 15 Janet had already been experimenting with "ups and downs" (amphetamines and barbiturates) for two years. She was in a school for gifted students but had been truanting a great deal. Her family had hoped she would go to college. But Janet was finding herself increasingly without direction. She didn't see anything she wanted to be, nor could she find any satisfaction in going along with the expectations of her parents. Her parents were in a stable but sterile marriage with much dissatisfaction, especially for Janet's mother. Neither the mother's sexual nor her social needs were being met. In this environment of dissatisfaction and unspoken but deep frustration, Janet found no reason to proceed into adulthood. What had her mother got out of it? In a blind attempt to change her, her parents sent her alone for a summer to Europe, against the recommendations of the psychiatrist. She returned pregnant and later attempted suicide after her family had arranged for an abortion.

Lacking a desirable model for success, Janet could not arrive at a balance between her own expectations and the example of adulthood provided by her parents. Unable to mesh her fantasies about herself with reality, she pursued a course of acting-out in various ways; this carried her to a state of despair and self-condemnation culminating in a suicide attempt.

Table 3.2 Activities Considered Most and Least Important by Adolescents

	Three items most often picked as very important	*Three items most often picked as least important*
All boys	Having fun Becoming independent so that I can make it on my own Learning about myself	Getting loaded and hanging out Having sex with a number of different girls Trying to change the system
Boys 13–15	Preparing myself to earn a good living when I get older Having fun Getting along with my parents	Getting loaded and hanging out Having sex with a number of different girls Trying to change the system/Doing creative or artistic things
Boys 16–19	Learning about myself Becoming independent so that I can make it on my own Preparing myself to accomplish meaningful things	Getting loaded and hanging out Having sex with a number of different girls Trying to change the system
All girls	Learning about myself Having fun Preparing myself to earn a good living when I get older	Having sex with a number of different boys Getting loaded and hanging out Making out with boys
Girls 13–15	Learning about myself Preparing myself to earn a good living when I get older Getting along with my parents	Having sex with a number of different boys Getting loaded and hanging out Trying to change the system
Girls 16–19	Learning about myself Becoming independent so that I can make it on my own Preparing myself to accomplish meaningful things	Having sex with a number of different boys Getting loaded and hanging out Making out with boys

Source: R. C. Sorensen, *Adolescent sexuality in contemporary America.* New York: World, 1973, p. 49. Reprinted by permission.

Throughout childhood the self-image shifts and develops, but by late adolescence it takes on its definitive form. The "Who am I?" is crystallized. This does not preclude later shifts in identity, yet some clear sense of roles and self-concept are important and necessary attributes of the late adolescent. Without a firm conviction of self, the future tasks of early adulthood—occupational and marital choice—are apt to prove exceedingly difficult. Erikson (1963) describes the confusion and anxiety that characterize the adolescent who is not able to achieve a clear sense of identity; he calls this condition *identity diffusion*. The anxiety that identity diffusion generates also makes it difficult to achieve the necessary functional independence from the family.

Occupational Choice

Since adulthood requires a vocation, the choice of life role falls directly in the realm of the identity crisis. "Who am I?" inevitably leads to "What will I be?" Some compromise must be found that mediates between idealistic possibilities and realistic limitations. The adolescent finds it hard to make such compromises. Some never bridge the gap and continue to drift in limbo into adulthood, their lives never taking any clear direction. Commitment means definition and limitation, a step difficult for many to take. Jim's case illustrates this problem:

> Jim's presenting problem when he came for psychotherapy was his inability to settle down to anything. At age 30 he still didn't know what he wanted to do with his life. He had begun college as a pre-med student but then switched to philosophy to the dismay of his family. After his junior year he dropped out and joined the army. Afterwards he returned to school majoring in economics. He graduated and then worked for a stock brokerage firm for two years. He left that because it had been too materialistic and returned to school to study sociology. He obtained a master's degree, then left for New Mexico where he lived in a commune for a year. Throughout this period he lived with a number of women but said he didn't feel committed to anyone.

Surely a technological society poses new problems for the adolescent seeking an occupational role. Few adolescents have the opportunity to try out occupations directly or view them from close up before making a commitment. The situation was quite different in previous generations, when adolescents worked on the farm, in a store or in some other business with a relative, or helped in a parent's craft. Occupations were not a mystery; children and adolescents knew what they were about. When an occupational choice was made, the person had a fair idea of what he was getting into. Today the occupational scene is further complicated by the emergence of new technical fields and related jobs. Even the old professions have become so specialized and infused with technology that they are a mystery to students. These fields do not present adolescents with role models to help them make sound choices. On reflection we might have to take a more understanding view of "floundering," as in Jim's case. Adolescents may need more time because of the changing, unknown, and often confusing nature of occupations as they exist today. We must also recognize that the affluence of many middle-class homes permits adolescents to delay commitments for longer periods of time while their families continue to support them financially. Furthermore, it has become common for adolescents and young adults to seek idealistic pursuits and life styles as a legacy of the revolt against traditional values that erupted in the 1960s. We may need new criteria for determining true inability to make commitments in the light of the realistic complexities of adjusting to the modern world.

Emancipation from the Family

Adolescence is stressful not only to the youngster but also to his family. The adolescent is in the process of becoming an adult, which implies emancipation from the family. Emancipation in this context means being free of direct (and legally total) parental control. Freedom from parental control is desired but also feared both by children and by parents. The parents wonder whether they have adequately equipped their child to participate in an adult society. From the adolescent's point of view there is a certain comfort and safety in being under parental supervision; judgments need not be made and one's ability to express appropriate standards of behavior independently does not have to be tested.

There is also the fear on the part of both that when the son or daughter is no longer fully dependent (at least psychologically) on the parents, there will be a loss of the warmth and affection that has been gratifying to both parents and child for many years. Further, families in our society are frequently separated geographically; hence the prospect of the adolescent's setting up his own family implies the lessening of affectional bonds. In cultures with large extended families living in close proximity this is not such an issue, but in our society a son or daughter may move far away from home. Even if he or she does not, the contacts are likely to be limited.

The prospective loss is probably most acute for those mothers who did not continue other pursuits or develop other sources of gratification as their children approached adolescence. Fathers continue pretty much in their role as providers, but mothers often have a deep sense that they will lose not only affection but also an important role in life.

Of course, emancipation need not be and, for most, is not a breaking of family ties. Rather, it is a change in the nature of the bonds that will continue into adult life between parents and offspring. Parental responsibility for and control over the individual approaching adulthood must give way to personal responsibility and independence.

Our youth-oriented culture places a special strain on the adolescent's relationship with his parents. Parents in their late 30s and beyond, who are often competing with their adolescent children, are particularly sensitive to criticism such as "you're old fashioned" or "irrelevant" or "a has-been." Some parents are embarrassed by their grown-up children. Denying their children's adulthood becomes the parents' way of denying the passage of time and their own aging process. The abrogation of parental responsibilities through a flight into youth can deny developing adolescents the stable models, external controls, and guidance that they need but are so ambivalent about accepting.

THE FUTURE OF ADOLESCENCE

A youth study group under the chairmanship of James Coleman (1973) has examined the problems of adolescence. The report recognizes school as the chief institution affecting adolescents, but one that falls short of helping them to prepare for the future:

> Schools are the principal formal institutions of society intended to bring youth into adulthood. But schools' structures are designed wholly for self-development, particularly for the acquisition of cognitive skills and of knowledge. At their best, schools equip students with cognitive and non-cognitive skills relevant to their occupational futures with knowledge of some portion of civilization's cultural heritage and with a taste for acquiring more such skills and knowledge. They do not provide extensive opportunity for managing one's affairs, they seldom encourage intense concentration on a single activity, and they are an inappropriate setting for nearly all objectives involving responsibilities that affect others. Insofar as these other objectives are important for the transition to adulthood, and we believe they are, schools act to retard youth in this transition by monopolizing their time for the narrow objectives that schools have. In general, the proposed directions of change are intended to break that monopoly through environments that complement schools. (p. 4-2).

The Coleman report makes a number of recommendations for reconstructing the environments of youth to meet their needs more fully. The report suggests reducing the size of high schools to enable youths to have a closer relationship with their teachers. It also recommends the use of educational vouchers to enable adolescents to select from a wider variety of educational experiences and give them greater control over their destiny.

Coleman sees the encouragement of roles other than student as necessary if adolescents are to gain a greater sense of competence and self-worth. This goal could be accomplished by their teaching younger children, by work-study programs, and by part-time placement in other settings such as cultural institutions. Work-study programs and schooling carried out in employment situations would also provide the advantage of more opportunities for interaction with other age groups. Such work programs would require removal of some of the restrictions on hiring youth. These restrictions, while meant to protect adolescents from exploitation, also tend to increase their isolation from the adult world.

Establishing public service programs for adolescents similar to the Peace Corps would provide experience in activities affecting others and would open up opportunities for working in groups toward group goals. Government support for self-governing youth organizations would also provide community service activities and promote a sense of involvement in society.

The Coleman group's recommendations are sensitive to the adolescent's need for independence and active participation in meaningful roles. Some of the recommendations will run into stiff opposition (e.g., lower wages for youth), but the intentions can be appreciated. Adolescents are already beginning to resist the constricting monopoly that school imposes on them. We see emerging a pattern that breaks away from the lock-step of school and works toward a more fluid moving back and forth between schools and other settings. Whether or not the Coleman recommendations are broadly implemented, the pressures will continue for society to come up with more varied roles and real world experiences for the large adolescent segment of the population.

SUMMARY

Adolescence is the transition from childhood to adulthood. The major physiological change is the attainment of sexual maturity. Puberty lasts for from three to five years and occurs on the average in girls two years before boys. With puberty arrive new capacities.

Increased physical strength leads to renewed interest in sports. The ability to reason abstractly develops at this time and makes for interest in searching for higher truths.

In early adolescence, interest in the opposite sex is largely expressed in talk. The chum is an intense relationship that serves an important function in social development. The peer group takes on great importance for the adolescent and supercedes in some respects the influence of the family.

In our society adolescents are separated from both younger children and adults by the school system. As a consequence they have developed a separate culture.

Middle adolescence is a time when friendships with the opposite sex become important. Dating begins at this time, and sexual relations loom as important. Adolescents are now exposed to more explicit sexual material both in school and in the street. Recent data indicate that today's adolescents are more sexually experienced.

By late adolescence, identity formation is taking shape. A clear sense of self needs to be achieved by the close of adolescence. Occupational choice becomes necessary as plans for the future are made. As adulthood approaches, the individual must also loosen the ties of psychological dependency on the family. This process of emancipation from the family is often a stressful one.

If our society is to continue to grow it must provide more adequately for adolescent development. The Coleman Report makes a number of important recommendations for reconstituting the environments of youth to meet their needs more fully.

SUGGESTED READINGS

Blos, P. *On adolescence: a psychoanalytic interpretation.* New York: Free Press, 1962.

Coles, R., and Kagan, J., eds. *Twelve to sixteen: early adolescence.* New York: Norton, 1972.

Jersild, A. T. *Psychology of adolescence.* 2nd ed. New York: Macmillan, 1963.

Miller, D. *Adolescence: psychology, psychopathology, and psychotherapy.* New York: Jason Aronson, 1974.

Muus, R. E. *Theories of adolescence.* 2nd ed. New York: Random House, 1968.

Muus, R. E., ed. *Adolescent behavior and society.* New York, Random House, 1971.

Rubenstein, B., and Levitt, M., eds. *Youth and social change.* Detroit: Wayne State University Press, 1972.

Chapter 4

Early and Middle Adulthood

ADULTHOOD BEGINS at age 18 and spans three-fourths of the life cycle. This vast period is no less marked by change than is childhood, although the changes are usually less dramatic. Physical growth and development stop, but personality change and shifts in life circumstances continue. The timing of these changes is not completely predictable, for unlike puberty with its regular sequence, many of the major events of adulthood occur at quite different periods for different individuals. Marriage may take place at 16, at 40, or not at all, with varying consequences for the course of the individual's development. For purposes of discussion, however, it is practical to think in terms of phases of adulthood: early adulthood (18–30); middle adulthood (30–65); and late adulthood (over 65). In this chapter we will confine our discussion to early and middle adulthood. Late adulthood will be considered in detail in Chapter 6.

WHAT IS AN ADULT?

One of the difficulties of growing up in our society is that no clear demarcation exists between adolescence and adulthood. The word "adult" means full-grown or mature. In effect, it refers to the point at which physical growth has been completed—usually at 16-17 years for girls and 18-19 years for boys. What we consider to be psychological adulthood begins approximately at the same time.

This correspondence is more easily recognized in societies other than our own. In less technologically advanced societies girls and boys between the ages of 16 and 18 take on adult roles in terms of the expectations placed upon them and the responsibilities they assume. The boy takes on a man's job and earns enough to support himself or contribute a man's workload to the family vocation, perhaps as a farm laborer. The girl takes over the duties of a woman in her parents' household and very soon is established in her own household as wife and mother. In agricultural societies a man of 19 and his 17-year-old wife are substantially responsible for their own sustenance (though most likely they live in one of the parental households for a few years). They are young both in years and experience, and they may be immature in some ways, lacking the judgment and skills of older adults, but their position in society is that of man and woman.

The attainment of adulthood does not necessarily mean that an ideal level of adapative psychological growth has taken place. We reach adulthood with a wide variation in individual capacities for responsibility, judgment, and skills. We all meet at some time or other a 30-year-old who is grossly immature in his behavior, lacking the minimal signs of maturity that we expect of adults. Yet this 30-year-old is an adult. What then constitutes maturity?

Maturity

The term *mature* cannot be assigned to specific tasks or behaviors because life situations vary to such a great extent. A young adult may be a student, parent, business person, or laborer. But in spite of these differences in life roles we can identify personality characteristics necessary for effective functioning. These characteristics, which represent a standard for maturity that cuts across all roles, include a sense of responsibility, adequate impulse control, the ability to tolerate frustration, the ability to make plans that can be implemented, the ability to accept differences in others, the capacity to enter into prolonged intimate relationships, and movement toward development and fulfillment of one's potentialities. Let us consider these in detail.

Responsibility.   A sense of responsibility is certainly necessary for the fulfillment of any adult role. To say that a person—whether parent, physician, nurse, secretary, or factory worker—is lacking in responsibility means that the individual cannot be counted on to carry out the tasks that define his or her role. The necessary skills may be present, but if the person cannot be relied upon to use these skills in a consistent fashion that others can depend on, he lacks maturity. Responsibility implies the internalization of standards of behavior that enable the individual to function independently of external supervision or coercion. The truly responsible person will be directed by inner needs and a concern for others.

Controls.   Impulse control is another important hallmark of the mature individual. In fact, immaturity is often most blatantly expressed by impulsive outbursts of anger and frustration that are more usual and, therefore, more expected in childhood and early adolescence. As a person matures, we expect him to channel impulses into more constructive behaviors. This, of course, does not mean that the mature person keeps his feelings and emotions locked inside himself. Overcontrol can be just as immature as impulsiveness and tantrums. Anger, as well as other emotions, is not only appropriate at times but its absence would be maladaptive. Too often we erroneously regard the highly rational, always sober-minded, totally restrained person as mature, when more likely he is a frightened, immature person who is too insecure to allow "weaknesses" to show through. The mature person can let go when letting go is called for.

The style and degree of emotional and impulse expression vary among different social and cultural groups. For example, the French and Italians are considered more spontaneous and outgoing than the English or Germans. Therefore it is impossible to say just how much emotionalism constitutes maturity or immaturity; maturity is always relative to the standards set by the immediate environment represented by the family and larger social group. This relativism of group standards is an issue that applies to all behavior; we will explore the topic more thoroughly in Chapter 13, which deals with social class, culture, and behavior.

Tolerance of Frustration.   The most meaningful goals in life require sacrificing immediate pleasure for long-term gain. In infancy the impulse is to satisfy needs immediately. But in growing up we must learn to postpone gratification for longer and longer periods of time. Whether the activity be attending college, building a business or career, or working on an artistic production, all entail daily frustrations that the mature person can handle. The person with low frustration tolerance gives up easily when the going gets rough, because he is bound to the present and has a strong need to feel comfortable here and now. The mature person has the confidence that he can deal with stress; his future orientation carries him beyond present frustrations.

Planning.   The mature individual is able to plan for himself and others, so that the future is partly mastered by present efforts. Even if the major goal is one's own welfare, planning for future events and implementing the plans as they unfold are marks of maturity. It is the ability to plan and the experience of having plans work out that fortify against frustration.

Accepting Differences in Others.   Almost every area of life in modern society requires working, playing, and interacting with people who are different from ourselves. Differences here refer not only to broad differences of race, culture, and religion but also to needs, goals, values, and styles of life. Almost any group of people, no matter how similar they may appear on the surface, will encompass many differences. Maturity entails accepting differences in others while not submerging or abandoning one's own beliefs and values for the sake of conformity. The mature person has a tolerance for diversity and a respect for individuality.

Intimacy.   Capacity for intimacy is perhaps the most crucial mark of the mature individual, for it implies the presence of other characteristics of maturity. Intimacy requires responsibility, impulse control, the ability to plan, and also the ability to trust sufficiently another human being. Trust is essential because getting close to another person makes one vulnerable to interpersonal hurts. The lack of intimacy draws the person into increasing feelings of isolation and alienation. More so than any other characteristic, the capacity for intimacy is an index of how successful prior development has been in preparing the person for adulthood. Without intimacy the adult is inevitably very unhappy no matter what other sources of gratification are present.

Growth and Fulfillment of Potentialities.   In its highest form maturity means openness to the expansion of self through the pursuit of one's potential for personal development. Some authors refer to this level of functioning as *self-actualization*. The self-actualizing person is flexible, not closed or rigid, and never static but always becoming. Life circumstances do not always allow for maximum development of talents and capabilities, but within whatever constraints exist the mature person strives to reach out and grow.

EARLY ADULTHOOD

In the late teens and early 20s, young adults often feel that they have emerged only part of the way out of their families, and they fear that they will be pulled back in by their own as well as their parents' needs. Many live away from home and are involved in further schooling or are working in new jobs. They are not fully convinced that they can "make it" in the adult world, and they seek moral support in their efforts at independence from their peers and others.

As they proceed into their mid-20s, young adults become more secure; their autonomy is established, and they are more fully engaged in work. Peers remain important to them but are no longer as crucial to the sense of self. They feel they know where they want to go and how they will get there. This is probably the time of greatest self-confidence in one's capabilities; the feeling is that, with a little luck, one can master anything. As 30 approaches, however, this confidence is modified by experience. For many there are feelings of constraint that tarnish the initial glow. The early excitement of a new career may disappear. The sense of being tied down by self-made obligations to spouse and career creates an unexpected uneasiness. The responsibilities that are part of adulthood become apparent. A quest is begun for a way to obtain self-fulfillment within the context of adult obligations.

Role Choice

In the 20s there is a need to move out seriously into the adult world. The teen-age ruminations and gropings for autonomy must be concretized in some commitment to a role or occupation. The commitment may be a tentative one, with "full commitment" postponed until "real" adulthood beyond 30.

Making a commitment does not mean that everyone will choose a job, career, marriage, family, or a house in the suburbs. Choices will depend on each individual's concept of life, family background, peer group influences, and personal psychological strengths and needs. For some, resisting the traditional patterns of early adulthood will be of paramount importance. Thus living in a commune or group, becoming a political activist, or choosing some other life style may constitute the "moving out" of the 20s.

One of the frightening things about selecting a role or occupation is that it runs counter to the need for keeping options open. The conflict between the need for commitment and the need for a sense of freedom can be fierce. Adding to the problem of making choices is the multiplicity of possibilities offered by an advanced technological society. We are exposed to so much and can see so many possibilities that any one choice seems constricting. The family's message regarding what to do may be clear, but other messages conflict. Women's liberation, the counterculture, the sexual revolution, the lure of exotic places and experiences, the steady flow of new discoveries—all say "stay open." But we can tolerate just so much stimulation. Perhaps this is why many young adults pursue their choice of role or occupation with such dedication and determination, shutting out everything else around them.

Occupational Choice

For most the choice of an occupation becomes compelling in early adulthood. Up to this point, the young man or woman may have entertained various possibilities or put off any serious consideration of a career. Most young children go through periods when they are attracted to vocations that represent heroism or excitement: those of fireman, policeman, doctor, nurse. These are especially attractive to the young child because such people appear to be in control of situations or events that are fear-producing: fire, dangerous people such as criminals, and sickness. These early counterphobic choices (counterphobic because they tend to ward off a fear) are rarely the basis for future adult vocational pursuits. But by early adulthood the subtle processes that have defined personality development converge and cohere to yield the person's identity. The crystallization of identity also produces an array of likes and dislikes that shapes the occupational choice. Most important to this choice are such factors as the family, personality, education, and economic circumstances.

Family Role.   The family has a strong influence on occupational choice. It is not simply a matter of pleasing parents; rather, the expectations of the immediate environment tend to shape what one considers appropriate choices. It is very difficult to go against what the social milieu regards as proper. The influence of parents on occupational choice often works in a subtle fashion. Certainly there are instances in which the wish of the parents for a child to be a teacher, nurse, physician, lawyer, and the like has a direct influence, making that choice highly probable. This factor is reflected in the high percentage of physicians' sons (43.6%) and lawyers' sons (27.7%) who choose those professions (Werts, 1966).

A strong identification with a parent encourages a desire to be like that parent. But the identification is often with the parents' attitudes and aspirations rather than with the parents' actual role. The parents themselves may have little education or professional attainment (commonly the case among immigrant groups and the poor) but still have high aspirations for their children, which they reinforce by providing all kinds of enrichment experiences and encouragement. Thus there may be the expectation that the son or daughter will seek a professional career, even though the parents' educational level is minimal. This aspiration then becomes part of the child's self-image. Direct role modeling is more likely in professional homes where children will choose careers similar to their parents' in level and kind. Here again, however, the identification is as much with the aspirations of the parents as with their specific roles.

The presence or absence of immediate role models (parents, relatives, friends, others) will affect a person's ability to identify with and maintain an occupational goal. The person from a poverty background will usually not have family members in professions, business, or highly skilled jobs. Reaching for a college education or professional goal may present great psychological obstacles for such a person; having no models around him, he may feel that his goal is unattainable. Compare this to a boy or girl whose parent is a physician and who has always assumed that he or she would also be a physician, never perceiving any barriers.

The degree of security gained within the family also influences occupational choice. Parents who want their child to be a professional may do all the "right" things to encourage a similar aspiration in the child. But if they do not provide the child with the feeling that he or she can achieve at a high level or be successful, it is unlikely that their goal will be attained. Then there are parents with very modest aspirations who provide so much security and confidence that their children aspire and ultimately achieve beyond the parents' dreams.

Personality. The personality traits that emerge in the course of development also influence career choice. A passive, dependent person may identify with someone who is strong and protective, and make of him a model for life choices. For example, one may strongly desire to be a teacher because of an earlier feeling of having been protected and favored by a teacher. In such instances interests follow satisfaction of personality needs. These needs often run counter to the goals of parents, however. Parents who encourage athletic interests will meet resistance from the unaggressive, noncompetitive child. On the other hand energetic, physically active, socially oriented people will shun occupational choices that they feel will constrain their personality characteristics—"I couldn't be an accountant and sit in an office all day." Of course, a particular occupation is selected by different individuals for different reasons: a career in the military can serve the pseudo-masculine needs of one individual and the dependency needs (i.e., planning, security, and protected life style) of another.

Personality traits also lead us to particular experiences—some accidental—that in turn influence us in making choices. The outgoing social person meets more people and is exposed to more situations that can spark an interest or identification. The more withdrawn person is confined to a narrower range of social influences but may be influenced through such activities as reading or attending plays and movies.

Education. Of course the familial expectations are not limited in their effect to the final occupational choice. The family's attitude toward learning, competitiveness, and social status are important influences during the earlier years. If a child is not encouraged to do well in school or is encouraged to put skills in sports or practical work before academic pursuits, it is unlikely that at 18 he will have the credentials needed for academic success in a profession. The family attitudes toward education are felt even by the preschool child and shape his responses to learning situations.

The quality, richness, and variety of educational experiences offered to children affect the range of choice open to them as young adults. Schools are especially important for children from disadvantaged, poverty environments. In such instances teachers can provide role models and experiences not available in the home, and they can encourage better self-images and higher levels of aspiration. Schools have the potential for discovering and developing in all children talents, abilities, and interests that can have far-reaching impact on their life choices.

Economic Factors. Today, in the United States and in many other countries, resources alone need not deter an individual from electing a field of study or a profession. In the past, education at the college level was open mainly to the middle and upper classes. Now 80% of Americans are obtaining high school educations and almost two-thirds will obtain some education and training beyond high school. Nonetheless, the road to an occupation requiring a lengthy and costly education is very difficult without considerable financial support from families or spouses. Those from affluent families are therefore more likely to pursue such occupations, while the economically disadvantaged will only in exceptional instances struggle against the financial obstacles. This is especially true for a profession such as medicine, which requires a lengthy, expensive full-time education that precludes working during the academic year.

Occupational Choices for Women. The impact of the family and early sex typing of behavior is especially evident in occupational choices for women. Social restrictions for women in the professions are slowly giving way, but family expectations still make certain choices difficult. There is still widespread unwillingness to support extensive vocational training for women other than one that might complement her role as wife-mother. It is, however, becoming both common and expected that women choose an occupation in addition to or other than that of housewife. Although most women will marry (96% marry at least once), today most women work before they are married and continue working until the first child is born. For many women full-time employment is then suspended until the children are grown up, although an increasingly high percentage of women work part-time. The number of women working outside the home increases each year. In 1974 close to 40% of the total work force consisted of women and a large percentage of those were women with small children. As of 1970, one out of three women in the work force had children under the age of 18. Also, recent statistics indicate that women are seeking employment less from economic necessity than to satisfy a psychological need; this is suggested by the fact that the greatest percentage of married working women (52%) come from middle- and upper-middle-class families (*New York Times Encyclopedic Almanac, 1971*). We should point out, however, that most women who work continue to be largely responsible for child care and household chores. This naturally places a tremendous burden—and perhaps punishment—on the working mother and explains why many mothers will return to work only when children and household are more self-sufficient.

In a Harvard University study (Cox, 1970), exceptionally gifted women were shown to take for granted this pattern of stopping work when children were born. As a group, these women, who attended college in the late 1950s, wanted to devote themselves full-time to their houses and children. Though well educated and having the means to return to work if they wished to, they still elected not to do so until after their children were grown up. Other women feel differently and prefer to work outside the home, usually as soon as the last child enters elementary school. If day-care services for preschool children become generally available, more women with young children will no doubt choose to work. Many families desiring the greater income that results when both husband and wife work forego it because there is no means to care for the children in the mother's absence.

There is another factor that determines women's employment outside the home—the accessibility of jobs. The 1970 census demonstrated that the United States now has more people residing in surburban settings than urban ones. A principal reason for this move to suburbia is that it provides a more habitable environment for children. The cities have become the residence of the less affluent, the unmarried, and the childless. However, the city is the place to which the family breadwinner travels for work. Since the breadwinner in families with small children is almost always the husband-father, this leaves the middle-class wife-mother in the suburbs where there are fewer opportunities for employment. Therefore, even if she wants to work, it is more difficult for the surburban housewife to do so.

Nonetheless, it is viewed as increasingly important that a married woman have an education and skills that will enable her to gain employment when she chooses to return to work. The ability to find gratification and a sense of self-worth in work is very important to women, whether they have children or not. The movement of the late 1960s and 1970s to end discrimination against women is likely to make more opportunities available.

Leisure Time. Leisure time is increasing at an accelerated rate. Kreps (cited in Kimmel, 1973) estimates that men born in 1960 will have nine years more of leisure time during their lives than men born in 1900. At the same time, many jobs in a technological, automated society are routine, unfulfilling, and alienating, with little allowance made for individual expression, and as a result many young adults are making their primary investment of time and energy in leisure-time activities.

Until recently the work ethic has been very strong in the United States. The emphasis in child-rearing on preparation for work has been so effective that many adults long for but are unable to use leisure time in a gratifying way. In fact psychotherapists have spoken about the Sunday neurosis, that is, the depression, anxiety, and boredom that seize many adults as they struggle to enjoy themselves on this anticipated day of leisure. A study of middle-class men and women between the ages of 46 and 71 (Pfeiffer and Davis, 1971) provides evidence that society has accomplished an overkill with respect to the work ethic. A large percentage of those surveyed— 90% of the men and 80% of the women—said they would continue to work even if they did not have to and that they got greater enjoyment out of work than from leisure-time activities. Unless these individuals had extraordinarily stimulating jobs—which is not very likely—these results reflect a widespread inability to enjoy leisure time. For many adults leisure-time activities are only superficially a change of pace from work activities; examples are the businessman who plays cards for large sums of money or the person who undertakes tennis with the same fanatic competitiveness that characterizes his worktime activities. One of the important developmental tasks for achieving maturity in the future may well be to learn to use leisure time effectively.

Marital Choice

Another major decision of early adulthood is the choice of marital partner. It is instructive to compare our mode of choosing partners with that of traditional families in India, a society with a joint family pattern. A joint family—one in which more than one generation of married couples live together in one household—is characteristic of societies with agricultural economies. In most of India, the choice of spouse is still made by parents. Since the wife will live in the house of the husband's parents and work in the household under the direction of the senior woman, usually her mother-in-law, the virtues sought in a wife are submissiveness and skills in domestic work. For the husband, high value is placed on family social status and work skills; the latter, in turn, are related to education and family social position. Since the newly married couple will not live separately but share a residence and all income, it is of primary importance that the families, rather than the couple, be satisfied with the union. The couple has a relatively minor voice in the matter.

In our society, newlyweds go off by themselves to establish a household; the choice of marital partners is a matter for the partners themselves to decide. However, many factors influence and limit the choice of mates. The choices are not, as in India, narrowly confined to specific subcastes, yet limits are present, sometimes subtly and at other times quite explicitly.

How do people choose partners? Most marriages are between men and women of similar background: of the same socioeconomic level, the same religion, the same race, the same country of origin. It is opportunity that makes relations possible, and there are simply more opportunities to meet people of the same background because of geographical and social proximity. In addition, many groups have prohibitions about marrying outside the group, particularly when it involves religious differences. There are also prejudices against marrying those of another race or social class. And, finally, people of similar backgrounds more often have similar interests, norms, and expectations than do those of different backgrounds. Thus many factors work toward limiting marital choice: geography, prohibitions, prejudices, and interests. Partners who come from different backgrounds can share their earlier life experiences and have a richer marriage as a result. At the same time, we should note that there is a higher divorce rate among couples from different backgrounds. Not only do such couples have to weather outside pressures from family and society, but, more importantly, they must accommodate two different value systems in working out a common life. Their standards of behavior and their expectations may differ widely owing to their different family experiences.

> Ralph and Annette met while he was spending a year going to school in Europe. They seemed to have similar intellectual interests and educational attainments. They certainly were very much in love and felt themselves ready for an exclusive relationship. They married and soon afterwards returned to the United States. Soon, however, the difficulties emerged. After the honeymoon period of approximately one year, conflict became intense. Ralph, raised in a rather typical Eastern middle-class environment, viewed his wife as a companion who would not change much in her behavior, at least until children were born. She would work, they would share household tasks, and they would both continue their education. Annette's view was quite different. She viewed her work as that of making a home for herself and her husband, and unless they were in dire circumstances, she would not be employed outside the house. These different views were symptomatic of wide divergencies in cultural expectations that for this couple were insurmountable.

Single Living

Most people in our society marry, but some do not, and even those who do marry live in a single state for part of their lives—in late adolescence, early adulthood, after separation or divorce, and after the death of a spouse.

The achievement of intimacy is an overriding problem of single living, perhaps the feature distinguishing it most from the married state. That is not to say that all marriage relationships insure true intimacy. The divorce statistics speak against that conclusion. But in marriage there is always someone—spouse or children—with whom contact can be made, so that feelings of loneliness can usually be avoided. In single living one must constantly initiate or renew contacts and relationships, and another person may not always be available when one reaches out. But living outside a marriage relationship does not necessarily mean loneliness. It just means that intimacy must be worked at more diligently. There is a variety of group living arrangements that can meet the individual's need for closeness with others. Also, many single people living alone work out effective solutions; they have close ties with friends and relatives of both sexes, an active social life, and satisfying professional activities that bring them into contact with others.

Perhaps the greatest stress on single living comes from the prejudices of society. Married friends, relatives, and professional associates tend to shun singles or reserve them for "special" occasions. "Poor" aunt Mary and cousin Charley may be regarded as misfits at social gatherings. Large corporations often expect upper-echelon executives to be married and thus present the "right" social facade. Single people sometimes find it difficult to rent choice apartments, especially if they are women or suspected of being homosexual. But some of these prejudices are diminishing with the liberalization of sexual mores, increased career opportunities for women, acceptance of singles as adoptive parents, and greater openness about homosexuality.

People remain single for as many reasons as those for which they marry. Although most people believe they marry because they are in love or desire children, studies show otherwise. Years later, looking back on their motivations, many men and women admit they married in order to get away from home, or just because it was the thing to do (Sheehy, 1974). Fear of loneliness, the need to escape from decisions about the future, and the wish to feel grown-up are other reasons. In some social groups not marrying carries a stigma that can pressure the most disinclined to seek the social approval of marriage. Also, for women who are uneducated and unskilled, not marrying frequently means inferior status and dependency on one's parents.

Remaining single can also have both positive and negative motives. Some people avoid marriage because they fear intimacy or dependence—just as others marry out of fear of being alone or in order to deny problems with intimacy. Some are scared off by painful memories of their own parents' unhappy marriages. Then there is the fear of responsibility for spouse and children. But in many cases the single person places the primary emphasis on career and views marriage as an intrusion on this goal. A person may, of course, desire marriage but never meet a suitable mate. Finally, we should not overlook the possibility that some people genuinely enjoy the independence and freedom of single living.

Single living or group living away from the family during early adulthood can be an important development experience, even for those who eventually marry. Many people go from the protective custody of the family directly into marriage without ever experiencing full independence or self-reliance; the lack of such experience can prove an additional handicap for those who ultimately lose a spouse through divorce or death. Making it on your own in early adulthood can be an ego-building experience that provides a sense of competence and a realistic assessment of personal strengths and weaknesses. Some young adults on their own discover inner strengths that alter their perspective on life and their relationships with others. Finding you do not need to lean on someone else to survive can affect your choice of a marriage partner.

The socializing opportunities for adults in our society are rather limited beyond the college years. One soon tires of the "singles bars" or the resorts where superficiality is the main currency. Social agencies offer very few opportunities for singles to meet. For divorced women with children the problems are still more complex; aside from the prejudices against divorcees, there are the problems of child support and care. Divorced men generally have an easier time because of their better economic position and their greater opportunity for contacts with the opposite sex. For the elderly, single living frequently presents many hardships, which we will explore in Chapter 6.

MIDDLE ADULTHOOD

Talking about stages of development is always somewhat arbitrary, but it is even more so when we consider the middle adult years—age 30 to age 65. The developmental crises of childhood and aging are predictable, for everyone must contend with the pressures to individuate and later face the inevitability of aging and death. Middle adulthood, however, does not fall into a well-defined sequence of crises; people go through a variety of experiences, but none are universal. Some people reach a level of adjustment at the end of adolescence and do not deviate from it for the rest of their lives; they remain peripheral adolescents or minimal adults. Others experience some but not all of the crises of adulthood. The time at which these crises occur also varies. For example a person may be occupied throughout his 20s with schooling and professional training; another person in his 30s may be absorbed in a particular project (e.g., writing a book, developing a business). Such concentrations of energy can lead the person to bypass or postpone certain crises.

Other types of life circumstances also affect the course of adulthood. For those who live in poverty, the harsh and limiting conditions of life can overshadow and submerge psychological crises. With these points in mind we can approach the middle adult years.

The 30s

For many, age 30 is a turning point, the age at which the generations separate. "Over 30" and "under 30"—this is a psychological barrier emphasized by our youth-oriented culture. As we approach 30, we hear the echoes of our own earlier feelings toward the "over 30s." Now that we have arrived there ourselves, questions must be asked: "Is it worth being over 30?" "Have I made it?"

As 30 approaches, the person's adult life usually takes on a definite shape and direction fashioned by the decisions of the 20s. Skills have been acquired, achievements made, and at least some expectations fulfilled. In the most positive situations the 30s can be gratifying. Success in a job, in love, in marriage, in a family can provide a sense of fulfillment of earlier hopes. Previously there were doubts, struggles, and uncertainty; now there are real achievements. The future can promise better things to come, with greater mastery and expression of potential. Being a full adult also entails rights, privileges, and fulfillments that could not have been attained earlier.

In less successful outcomes there are nagging questions: "Is this what I want to do? or "Why haven't I made it?" Depending on the answers, a person will continue his present course or shift direction. For women who have subordinated personal development to marriage and family, the need for growth is pressing.

Once beyond the shock of being a full-fledged adult, people usually recognize that at age 30 one is still youthful within the adult world. Along with this comes the realization that there is still time for accomplishments, but that decisions must be made. As the mid-30s approach, the hopeful fantasies of adolescence and earlier adulthood undergo the corrective influence of time; depending upon circumstances, this can lead to contentment or to a growing desperation. Psychological disturbances that were only tendencies may become more pronounced. The incidence of depression, anxiety, and other symptomatology (fear, psychosomatic complaints) is high. Ambition may culminate in a desperate effort to "make it"—a businessman takes reckless chances, a professional gives up everything and dislodges his or her family for that "once-in-a-lifetime" job, a teacher undergoes drastic change in life style. Strongly felt disappointments in love and intimacy can result in infidelity, promiscuity, divorce, or quickie marriages of desperation.

For the poor, uneducated, members of minorities who are denied opportunities, these crises of adulthood are luxuries. The passage into maturity is often depressing. The limitations imposed during the most energetic earlier years have come full circle. If doors were previously closed, they are now barred shut. The future shrinks into a monotonous and demoralizing present that holds little hope for change. Individual initiative has no meaning when opportunities and skills are not present. Few constructive avenues are available to deal with the 30s crises when there are no options. Apathy, self-indulgence, or antisocial acts are some of the possible outlets for this frustration and helplessness.

The 40s

The age of 40 is another major psychological landmark in the life cycle—the beginning of middle age. Of course these decade landmarks are artificial, but since they are regarded as significant by society, they come to have a major effect on the individual's self-perception. What does the beginning of middle age connote? The most common stereotypes are that the middle-aged are rigid, they cannot learn new skills, they resist changes in domestic or office routines, and they display narrow or restricted interests. There is, in fact, no objective evidence for these stereotypes (Soddy, 1967), but they do influence the middle-aged individual's opportunities for self-fulfillment. For example, the stereotype that the middle-aged are unable to acquire new skills becomes a self-fulfilling prophecy: the middle-aged are less likely to be given positions in which the learning of new skills is required. This seriously limits job mobility and changes in fields of employment.

Disregarding the stereotypes, however, some definite psychological changes take place during this period. One change is in the attitude toward time. The individual in his or her 40s senses that time is finite, that the life cycle is now irrevocably beyond the halfway mark. This impinging reality often brings with it an exaggerated concern about health. Minor episodes of ill-health bring forth worries about the possible presence of some serious, unknown illness. Any tendency toward hypochondriasis is likely to reach a peak in the 40s.

In this decade, the couple with children is still actively involved with them. It is a time when the children are entering adolescence or early adulthood. As they watch their children begin independent lives, parents have a deeper sense of their own aging. For the woman who has devoted much of her time to rearing children it is an especially problematic period. When the children leave home, her major work—the time-consuming and exhausting labor of creating a suitable growth environment for them—is no longer required. The family is a couple again. The questions such women must face are

"How am I now to derive my sense of being valued?", "Who considers my efforts worthwhile?", "How will I use my time?" Increasingly women answer these questions by seeking full-time employment. If preparations have not already been made, it is a difficult search to find gratifying employment in the mid- to late-40s. Those women with marketable skills are indeed fortunate and suffer least loss of direction and self-esteem.

The changes in the family makeup serve to generate a greater need for the spouse. Marital happiness and contentment continue to increase for most and, with children no longer requiring so much attention, there is a renewed interest in friends and social activities (Gould, 1972).

It is also a period when the more professionally capable or successful individuals are recognized and given positions of more responsibility. Such recognition may also have an adverse effect, when it takes people away from their own work into areas of administration for which they may not be as suited (Vedder, 1967). For instance, a professor of history may be made dean of a college, an administrative position that prevents him from making any further contributions in the field of history. Nonetheless, those who are to reach the top of their fields are now recognized by their colleagues.

Stock-taking. While self-assessment or stock-taking is part of many phases of the life cycle, it has a special significance in the 40s. Since the beginning of this period usually brings the first real awareness of aging, assessing where one is and how much of earlier hopes and aspirations have been achieved takes on great importance. Bühler (1968), a psychologist noted among other contributions for her analysis of the human life cycle, calls the entire period from 45 to 65 the phase of self-assessment.

Most people assess themselves in two major areas. The first is their position with regard to their occupational role. Everyone has dreams of fame, fortune, or conquest, but few can attain these aspirations. In the 40s, the individual may have to come to grips with the fact that occupational or professional attainments are not and probably will not be as momentous as he or she dreamed as an adolescent. For most people, the adolescent dreams have probably already been modified as reality required before the period of self-assessment. If they have remained unmodified, however, realizing the distance between aspirations and attainments may result in crushing disillusionment and loss of self-esteem. For the majority, some disappointment is experienced, but the assessment results in adjusted levels of aspiration that still foster growth without being unrealistic.

The second area of stock-taking is in the field of one's interpersonal experience. For someone who is married and has children, how well he or she has done as parent and spouse is evident by now. The children are old enough to demonstrate by their personality and their achievement whether the parents have provided the environment necessary for adequate psychological development. And as the couple nears or enters the postparental period, the adequacy of each spouse to meet the other's needs is put to its last major test.

For the person who has remained single, the likelihood of marriage diminishes, and the question that arises is whether the chosen life style is proving adequate. For some the answer will be positive; for others the sense of no longer having the option to change will be painful.

The 50s and Early 60s

In the 50s there is often a new sense of psychological well-being. The concern with the finite nature of time that caused anxiety in the 40s has now usually shifted to an acceptance of the fact that the life cycle has an end. There is, however, an increased concern about health, less hypochondriacal now, and more related to the appearance of chronic illnesses in the individual or in his friends. The marital relationship is generally stable and the married couple finds renewed pleasure in social activities. They may begin to enjoy, as grandparents, the pleasure of giving affection to young children without the burden of their care.

For some the 50s and 60s are a time of peak productivity. This is especially true for those in fields requiring high responsibility, experience, and wisdom—judges, industrial executives, religious leaders, and the like. The great German philosopher Immanuel Kant did not reach the peak of his creativity until he was in his 60s and 70s, and for innovators such as Freud, the 50s may represent only the midpoint in their careers.

However, not everyone is in a field that provides an opportunity for continued growth in the 50s. Those whose occupations require physical strength find their work more difficult when their stamina declines and illnesses such as arthritis appear. The 55-year-old painter with recurrent bursitis in his shoulder must continue to work even though the pain restricts his arm movements, and he arrives home too exhausted to enjoy the greater social freedom this decade should bring him.

The problems for women in the 50s and 60s are increased by the fact that a large number of them must face widowhood. The longer life span of women, coupled with the fact that they are generally younger than their husbands, makes it likely that their spouses will die more than a decade before them. Except for those whose profession permits continuing gratification (and their number is increasing), many widows find that society has failed to provide for their psychological needs. Of course it is only in this century that longevity has reached a point where lengthy widowhood is common, but it is important to the large number of widows that we do a better job of integrating them into the social matrix. Those widows who have continued to work outside the family as well as those with marketable skills will have an easier task of constructing an active role after the mourning period.

One way to integrate individuals in this period of the life cycle is to make better use of their experience to improve the communities in which they live. People of this age often display a sense of social obligation and a deep awareness of their roles as citizens and members of the community. These qualities are a potential source of leadership for the revitalization of society.

SUMMARY

Adulthood constitutes three-fourths of the life cycle. In our society there is no clear line of demarcation between adolescence and adulthood. Maturity as an adult represents a standard for effective functioning. Maturity includes a sense of responsibility, impulse control, the ability to plan, the capacity for intimate relationships, and the pursuit of self-actualization.

In early adulthood individuals are still torn between relying on their families and being on their own. As the mid-20s are reached, autonomy is established, and they are fully engaged in working. It is usually a period of great self-confidence which, as 30 approaches, begins to be modified somewhat by experience.

During early adulthood occupational choices must be made. The choice of occupation is influenced by many factors: personality, familial expectations, educational opportunity and experience, economic conditions, and social pressures. Increasingly women are preparing for careers, though many will postpone taking up employment outside the home until they feel that their family duties do not require their full time and attention. The lack of adequate childcare facilities or alternate means of childcare often restricts the personal development of women.

Marital choice is the other major decision of early adulthood. Chief factors in the choice of partners are geographic and social proximity, the latter referring to similarity of socioeconomic level, religion, and race.

Some people opt not to marry, and most people are single for at least a part of early adulthood. Single living can permit concentration on other pursuits, such as a career, that marriage may hinder.

The age of 30 is the beginning of middle adulthood. Adult life at this time has usually taken on a definite shape and pattern. Families are well established, and some occupational achievements have been made. The fantasies of adolescence begin to be modified by the realities of time.

At 40 there is a shift in the individual's attitude toward life. Perhaps for the first time, life is sensed as finite. As a consequence there is an increased concern about health. It is also at this time that stock-taking is prominent. The individual assesses where he is and how much he has achieved of his earlier aspirations.

In the 50s and 60s there is a new sense of psychological well-being. For some, it is a period of their greatest productivity. It is also a time when many women become widows.

SUGGESTED READINGS

Kimmel, D. C. *Adulthood and aging: an interdisciplinary, developmental view.* New York: Wiley, 1974.

Lidz, T. *The person: his development throughout the life cycle.* New York, Basic Books, 1968.

Neugarten, B. L., ed. *Middle age and aging: a reader in social psychology.* Chicago: University of Chicago Press, 1968.

Vedder, C. B. *Problems of the middle aged.* Springfield, Ill.: Charles C. Thomas, 1965.

5

The Family

WE DO NOT KNOW when and how the nuclear family of father, mother, and offspring evolved. Yet we are the heirs of a long history of biological selection and social conditioning that has left us the family unit as the characteristic human social group. Whether we are talking about primitive or modern societies, man exists in families. Therefore, in order to understand human development, we must take account of this universal social force and examine the nature of family life.

Families are the primary context for the child's development and the basic social unit. They have the major responsibility for preparing children to meet the needs of the society of which they are a part. Consequently, the characteristics of the society will shape the structure and functioning of the family. In our discussion of the family, we will therefore want to take into account sociological as well as psychological factors.

THE NUCLEAR FAMILY

The basic family unit, which exists in all societies, is the *nuclear family*, consisting of mother, father, and offspring. In preindustrial societies, nuclear families are commonly combined into multi-generational households called *extended families*. In an extended family, resources such as income and food are pooled, and there is one overall head, usually the oldest male. In the United States and other modern industrial societies, the traditional type of extended family is rare; even when several generations live in one house they rarely pool their resources. Extended families remain prevalent, however, in agrarian societies such as rural India and China.

The nuclear family has four primary functions: sexual, economic, reproductive, and educational. The sexual function consists of the sexual relations and gratifications of the marital couple, which are a required aspect of the marriage itself. Sexual relations outside the marital relationship may be permissible depending on the society, but they are not permitted between other elements of the nuclear family—incest taboos exist in all societies.

The economic function of the nuclear family usually involves a division of labor: one parent cares for the children while the other provides for the family's physical needs. The educational function includes rearing children and imparting to them the knowledge needed for adaptation to their society. (By adaptation is meant the process whereby an organism is modified to fit environmental stresses so as to enhance its chances for survival.) Today, although a large part of the educational function is accomplished by schools, the teaching of norms—that is, standards of behavior—and the providing of role models remain largely family functions.

The Modern Family

In modern industrial societies, conditions exist that are profoundly altering the social life of man: technology is so advanced that people can live and move anywhere at any time; affluence is potentially so great that no one need go without food, clothing, and schooling; birth control methods are so effective that children need be born only as planned for; and destructive capacity is so enormous that man could eradicate himself and all higher forms of life from the earth.

The technological advances are too numerous to catalogue, but some need emphasis. The ability to move over great distances with ease makes neighborhood stability a thing of the past. Families in the

United States move on the average every five years; consequently intimacy is unlikely to develop between family members and neighbors. Knowing that their stay in any one place is likely to be temporary, people are increasingly reluctant to invest in close relationships with neighbors. As a result the nuclear family is becoming more closed in upon itself. The mobility of families also makes an extended family impossible. Grandparents become distant relatives. Older people have a reduced function in such a society.

The mechanization of the household makes the job of maintaining a physically adequate home environment less time-consuming. Less time spent keeping house means more time to do other things. What these "other things" should be becomes the wife-mother's concern as she begins to feel she is not utilizing all her potential skills.

Affluence of the society means that it is no longer absolutely necessary for two people to cooperate in maintaining the family economically. Potentially society can take care of all mother-child pairs, although to what extent it is willing to do so is another question. This greatly diminishes the pressure on the family to remain together because its members would not otherwise survive.

The recent establishment of effective birth control measures makes it possible to control family size, or to choose not to have children at all. Previously, means of limiting conception were highly unreliable. Now marriage without children is a real option for couples.

The modern family is nuclear, relatively isolated, and relatively free from physical survival needs. How will it evolve in order to sustain husband, wife, and offspring?

The Family Developmental Cycle

While we will not be pursuing at any length the concept of the family developmental cycle, it is useful to consider briefly what Duvall (1970) describes as the phases in the life history of a family. She has divided the family life cycle into eight somewhat overlapping stages.

Stage 1—Married couples (without children)
Stage 2—Childbearing families (oldest child from birth to 30 months)
Stage 3—Families with preschool children (oldest child 2½-6 years)
Stage 4—Families with schoolchildren (oldest child 6-13 years)
Stage 5—Families with teenagers (oldest child 13-20 years)
Stage 6—Families as launching centers (from departure of first child to departure of last child)
Stage 7—Middle-aged parents (empty nest to retirement)
Stage 8—Aging family members

In stage 1, husband and wife are concerned primarily with their mutual needs as adult partners in marriage. Their time and resources are focused on their own growth and gratification. In stage 2, there is a shift to providing time and resources for the care of an infant. Priorities change, and some needs of the marital couple are delayed or denied when they conflict with the infant's needs. An uninterrupted night's rest or a spur-of-the-moment night out may have to be foregone with a new infant in the home.

During stages 3 through 6, the allocation of family resources (time, money, emotional involvement) continue to be determined largely by the children. That is not to say that the marital couple's needs are simply neglected—in fact, if they are too much neglected the marriage may not be sustained—but family priorities always must take into account the children's physical and emotional well-being. A mundane example is that of buying clothes. If $100 is available for winter clothing, parents in stage 3 and 4 will most likely provide for their children's needs before they even consider what they will buy for themselves. Not that the parents need be "all-giving," but a central task of the family is to provide for the children.

In stages 7 and 8, the family resources are once again focused on the marital couple. This shift, which occurs after approximately 20 years of child-oriented family life, often constitutes a difficult transition; the partners are much older and established patterns are not easy to alter. But the time, money, and emotional energy now available mean that the couple can gratify needs that have been long denied.

MARRIAGE

Marriage is the socially sanctioned or approved union of a man and a woman and is regulated by the laws, customs, and attitudes of the society. It marks the beginning of a new family and is a major event not only for the individuals involved but for the society as a whole. Since until very recently marriages presupposed children and child-bearing, societies saw the marriage union as the basis for continuing the social system. As the anthropologist Malinowski (1962) stated:

> Human beings, like all higher animals, multiply by the union of the two sexes. But neither conjugation, nor even the reproduction of offspring, is as a rule sufficient for the maintenance of the species. The further advanced the animal in the order of evolution, the longer the immaturity and the helplessness of the young and the greater need for parental care and training. It is thus the combination of mating with parenthood which

constitutes marriage in higher animals, including man. Even in its biological aspect marriage is rooted in the family rather than the family in marriage.

Even though child-rearing is a major function of most marriages, there is a variable period, usually of one to three years, in which the couple live together without children. It is a crucial period of adjustment to constant companionship and partnership. Present indications are that the period before having children is lengthening. Women are finding more job opportunities and greater gratification in working, so that having children is often delayed for several years after marriage. Statistics indicate that the more education the wife has, the longer the time before children enter the family. The reason is twofold: education generally means more job satisfaction as well as greater knowledge and employment of contraceptives.

The state of marriage is characterized by three elements: living together (cohabitation), having sexual relations, and providing mutual support in time of crisis. All these are based on the expectation that the marital relationship will be a permanent one. Today, with the relatively high frequency of divorce, marriage is much less likely to be permanent than in the past, but even those whose marriages end in divorce generally enter the relationship expecting it to last. The Sorensen report (1973) indicates that three-fourths of current adolescents do not want to marry until they are sure of the permanency of the relationship.

The practice of trial cohabitation, common in such countries as Sweden (and more recently in the United States), shows how much weight is placed on the assurance that the couple is compatible for a life-long commitment, even in highly industrialized societies.

There are several reasons for the fact that people need the feeling of permanence in marriage. First of all, marriage involves the birth of children, who need family stability for optimal growth and development. Many couples marry with doubts about having children or with little consideration of the possibility. Yet the fact is that most families do have children—approximately 90% in the United States—and for them the stability of the marriage is clearly desirable.

The need for permanency is also associated with the need for mutual support in time of crisis. The feeling of being able to depend on one's partner is vital to marriage, for security is the most basic of all our needs. This comfort of mutual dependency then, makes marriage a necessary institution for humans; in no other circumstances or relationships is it present to the same degree.

There is a great deal of discussion today concerning changes in marriage, its greater instability, and the need for alternative forms of living. There does appear to be an increase in group living, as in communes, but it is difficult to assess the extent of these innovations because the publicity they receive may be out of proportion to their incidence. We must bear in mind that in all societies there are always a few individuals who develop their own styles of living while the lives and life styles of the vast majority remain unaffected. At the same time we must recognize the importance of experimentation in a changing world. Customs are useful only to the extent that they contribute to effective living in the real world. We do not know what the realities of tomorrow will be, and therefore our customs must be fluid and open to change. We can, however, study the current status of marriage through the data that are available.

Marital Status in the United States

Surprisingly, since the turn of the century the percentage of the United States population living in a married state has steadily increased.

Table 5.1 **Marital Status of the United States Population, 1900–1970**

Sex and Marital Status	Percentage of Total							
	1900	1910	1920	1930	1940	1950	1960	1970
Female								
Single	24.4	24.1	23.9	23.5	24.2	20.0	19.0	12.1
Married	57.5	58.7	59.0	59.6	59.3	63.9	65.6	70.8
Widowed	17.6	16.5	16.4	15.6	14.8	14.0	12.8	13.0
Divorced	0.5	0.6	0.8	1.3	1.6	2.1	2.6	4.1
Male								
Single	32.3	31.9	31.3	30.5	30.7	26.2	25.3	16.5
Married	60.5	60.8	61.4	62.1	62.6	67.4	69.1	77.6
Widowed	6.9	6.8	6.6	6.3	5.4	4.7	3.7	3.3
Divorced	0.4	0.5	0.7	1.1	1.3	1.7	1.9	2.6

Note: Percentage computed for persons 14 years and older for 1900-60; for 1970, percentage is computed for 18 years and older.
Source: Statistical Abstract of the United States, 1971.

As shown in Table 5.1, in 1900 55% of the population over 14 was married. By 1960 this had increased to 68%. In the 1960s the Bureau

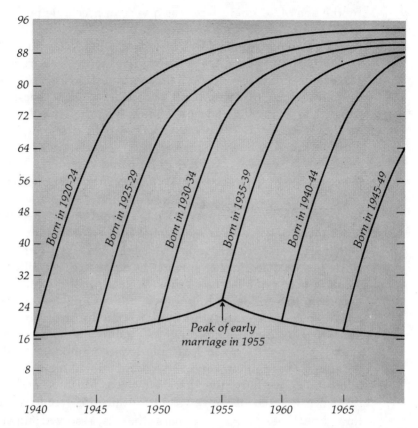

Figure 5.1 **Percentage of Women Born 1920 to 1954 Married by a Given Date (by Midyear)** (Source: *Current Population Reports,* PC-20, October, 1972.)

of the Census changed its reporting to show marital status over 18 instead of 14, so that the figures for 1965 and 1970 are not strictly comparable, but they do indicate the high percentage of married people. At the same time, there has been a steady increase in divorce, although the percentage remains relatively small.

Another useful indication of marriage trends is the percentage of individuals married by a given age. Figure 5.1 shows the percentage of women of a given year of birth married at any designated year. Thus we can see that 94% of women born between 1920 and 1924 (now in their 50s) have been married at least once. And all other age groups of women appear to be heading to a very close approximation of that percentage. There are other interesting features in figure 5.1. The base line indicates the percentage of women married by the age of 20, and there was a very appreciable peaking of early marriages in 1955, when women born in 1935 reached 20. Fully 24% of these women were married, whereas in 1940 and in 1970 only 16% of 20-year-olds were married. Thus marriages are again taking place later. From 1890 to 1955 there was a steady decrease in average age at marriage (for men from 26.1 years to 22.5 years; for women from 22.0 years to 20.1 years). Since 1955 there has been a gradual increase (men in 1971 average 23.1 years at first marriage, women 20.9 years). Although at first glance these differences do not seem great, they concern over 100 million individuals 18 and over and hence represent very substantial changes in social customs.

It seems from the data that more and more people want to marry. What accounts for this trend? One factor is the mobility of the population, which as we have mentioned makes for less intense relations with neighbors, friends, and even relatives. The human need for close ties and intimacy, however, pushes for gratification. One solution is to establish one's own nuclear family, which moves as a unit from one residence to another. Not so long ago a single son or daughter could comfortably live at home most of his or her adult life, working but not needing to establish a separate household. Today parents are much less able to accommodate adult children because moves cannot suit diverse occupational requirements. Young adults also want to live as their needs dictate, and a separate residence is often the only way to attain this freedom. A separate household means an aloneness that is resolved most securely by marriage, although alternatives such as living with a friend or friends are possible.

Another factor that probably contributes to an increased rate of marriage is an exaggerated emphasis on early social maturity, often narrowly defined as heterosexual intimacy. Heterosexual intimacy is certainly a developmental goal, but we tend to lose sight of the great variation in individual rates of development. One result is that the adolescent feels himself under great pressure to "succeed" in heterosexual relations, and they frequently get married in order to demonstrate that they have "arrived." The consequences are unfortunate—the earlier the marriage the more likely it will be unstable and end in divorce.

Divorce

The proportion of first marriages ending in divorce has risen sharply since the 1950s. Comparing women who were in their early 30s in

1955 with women who were in their early 30s in 1970, we find that the 1955 group had 10.5% and the 1970 group had 15.8% of their first marriages end in divorce. It is estimated that by the time the 1970 group of women reach 50 years of age (in the 1980s), approximately one-fourth of their first marriages will have been terminated by divorce (U.S. Bureau of the Census, 1972).

The likelihood of divorce is increased by marriage at a young age, and it is decreased by the presence of children, although children do not prevent divorce—over 60% of all divorces involve children (National Center for Health Statistics, 1973). Divorce rates also vary by region—they are almost three times higher in the West than in the Northeast. State laws with respect to divorce probably account for much but not all of the regional differential. Other important factors are social attitudes and religion.

Interestingly, there is a very high incidence of remarriage among divorced men and women—in 1967 fully one-half of the divorced population under 25 remarried. In fact, they are much more likely to marry than their single (never-married) peers; among those under 25 in 1967, divorced women were three times more likely to marry than their single counterparts, and divorced men six times more so. However, data for 1972 suggest a slowing of the trend toward remarriage (Kimmel, 1974). This probably reflects the increased employment opportunities for women and the liberalization of sexual attitudes and practices. Nevertheless, the reconstituted family with its children from previous marriages has become a common phenomenon in American life.

Marital Roles

In most societies the husband-wife roles are clearly defined—that is, the prescribed behaviors (what is to be done) and the proscribed behaviors (what is not to be done) are spelled out and adhered to with very little modification by the partners. From the standpoint of our own relatively fluid society, we tend to look upon such rigid adherence to role definitions as undesirable. We must bear in mind, however, that the basic patterns of relating that evolve in a society are most often highly adapted to the individual's and the society's survival needs, given the socioeconomic circumstances of their existence. When considering marital roles, therefore, we must not prejudge the form these roles take, but rather assess the degree to which they foster the individual's well-being.

Bott (1957), in what has become a classic study, described two typical kinds of role relationship that she observed among husbands and wives in London: *joint role relationships* and *segregated role relationships.* In the United States, the joint relationship is today the usual one. It is valuable, nonetheless, to compare the two types of relationship in order to gain an historical perspective.

In both types of families there is a basic division of labor, with husbands primarily responsible for supporting the family financially and wives primarily responsible for housework and child care. In both types of families the wife may work and the husband usually has responsibility for certain household tasks. In the segregated family, however, the wife's and the husband's tasks are rarely interchanged. If the husband washes the windows, he always washes them—but he does not do anything in the area defined as his wife's domain. The division of labor is adhered to quite strictly. In contrast, the joint role relationship is marked by a fluid division of labor. Housework and child-care activities are often shared and interchanged.

Differences exist in other areas as well. In the segregated family, decisions are usually made by one member only; for instance, the husband makes all financial decisions, and the wife makes all household decisions. In recreation, each has separate activities— husbands go out with male friends, and wives visit relatives. In a joint relationship, decisions are shared, and there is an expectation that the social activities will also be shared. Recreation means joint recreation.

Is one marital relationship better than the other? Not really. Each serves the needs of the marital couple in their relationship with each other and their circumstances. The segregated relationship is characteristic of the stable "neighborhood" society in which families live for generations in one area. Under such circumstances, men grow up and take on adult roles participating with the same peers at school, at work, and in their recreational activities. Two men working at adjacent desks or workbenches would most likely have had the same first-grade teacher. They played ball in the street together and now go bowling or spend the evening playing cards together. The woman is less likely to continue her earlier schoolday relationships but turns to her relatives for companionship and help. She is confident that if she needs a baby sitter her mother or unmarried sister will come over. They live just a few doors away. They are also there to have coffee with, exchange confidences, and give encouragement. It is expected and not considered "dependent" to have the extended family participate in coping with the everyday problems of living. Husband and wife are definite about their mutual expectations and are confident that their families and friends will provide approval for their responsible behavior.

The joint role relationship, on the other hand, is characteristic of the mobile marital couple. The husband and wife have left their neighborhoods some time ago. Contact is maintained with their families, but visits are relatively infrequent because of the distance. The husband's family may be from one city and the wife's family from another, ruling out a visit with both on the same day. Childhood friends are visited sporadically, but their interests and circles of friends are now quite removed from the marital couple's. The neighbors too are for the most part only friends on a superficial level. It often takes years for intimacies to develop, and these neighbors are not certain that they will be at the same address for a prolonged period of time. The consequence is that the marital relationship must now satisfy many different social needs. Social activities, domestic help, confidences, encouragement, guidance must all be provided by husband and wife; they cannot turn to a range of different friends and relatives. The marital relationship is joint because the circumstances require it. Yet one can readily see that the demands placed on each partner for more varied types of behavior are greater in the joint relationship than in the segregated relationship.

Sexual Adjustment

Sex as a powerful drive or need occupies a central place in the marital relationship. The sexual adjustment of a couple depends on many factors. The primary factor is the strength and security of their affection for each other. Sexual intercourse can be sought solely as a means for physical gratification, but for the couple involved in a lifelong relationship it also serves as a continuing expression of their love and affection. Where the bonds of affection are strong, there will be a search for mutuality in sexual pleasure.

The attitudes brought to marriage from childhood also affect sexual adjustment. When children learn that sexuality is an acceptable and pleasurable aspect of life, they will develop a positive, receptive attitude toward sexual experiences as adults. On the other hand, in a family where sexual matters are taboo and treated with disgust children are likely to experience difficulty in the mutual giving involved in sexual relations.

Further, as in any aspect of relating, sexual adjustment is a process that requires openness of communication and a willingness to learn. Even if two people are sexually experienced, they need to learn from one another what produces optimal gratification. Optimal gratification involves a mutual respect for each other's likes and dislikes as well as a willingness to accommodate to variations in sexual need. Emotional upset, fatigue, illness, and depression can all temporarily diminish sexual desire, and they are usually experienced at different times by each partner. The well-adjusted couple accepts the temporary frustration of one partner wanting and the other partner not wanting intercourse as part of the give-and-take of the relationship. It becomes a problem primarily when the reasons for such temporary shifts in need are not communicated and are misinterpreted as rejection.

Sexual Dysfunction

Sexual dysfunction or incompatability is generally an expression of tensions, basic disagreements, and unresolved conflicts in other areas of daily life. Nonetheless, primary sexual difficulties do arise. Fortunately, now that the discussion of sexual matters is no longer taboo, treatment is available and has a high degree of success.

Impotence. For the man, the major sexual dysfunction is impotence. Impotence is of two main types: inadequate erection, and premature ejaculation. The first type is characterized by the inability either to achieve an erection or to maintain one once it has been achieved, so that intercourse cannot occur. There are numerous possible causes of impotence, but by far the most common is anxiety. The sources of such anxiety vary, and they may not be evident to the man himself. He may be afraid of being unable to perform, or of being genitally harmed, thought inadequate, or made ill; or he may be afraid of doing something sinful. Not infrequently impotence develops in a man who previously functioned adequately when he reaches middle age.

For instance, a man in his mid-40s comes home from a party with his wife. He has been drinking a good deal, perhaps more than usual. He attempts to have intercourse and finds that he cannot develop or sustain an erection. The condition is not unusual at any age when men are intoxicated. At an earlier stage of life, the man would have just tossed it off as a consequence of his drinking, and he would experience no difficulty in future attempts at intercourse. Now, however, he attributes his failure to middle age and a loss of youthful vigor rather than to alcohol. When he subsequently attempts to have relations with his wife, he becomes anxious at the thought that he may fail again, and his anxiety indeed prevents him from maintaining an erection. Fortunately, techniques are available that can effectively treat this common type of anxiety-related impotence.

The second type of impotence, premature ejaculation, is the occurrence of ejaculation before or just as the penis is inserted into the vagina, resulting in the immediate loss of erection. Anxiety and/or excessive precoital stimulation play the major roles, and again techniques developed by specialists in sexual problems have a high rate of success.

Frigidity. In women, frigidity is the most common source of sexual incompatibility. Unfortunately the term is too often used inaccurately. It simply means the inability of a woman to be aroused by sexual stimulation. It does not refer to orgasm. A woman can respond sexually and still not achieve an orgasm. The orgasm is not a necessary end-point for female sexual gratification. As put so well by Masters and Johnson (1964),

> A woman is not necessarily lacking in sexual responsiveness when she does not experience an orgasm. The achievement of an "orgasmic phase" response should never be considered the constant end-all of sexual gratification for the responding female. Many women have never experienced orgasmic release from their sexual tensions and do not need such release. Yet women unable to achieve an orgasmic level of sexual response have frequently been labeled frigid, not only by their sexual partners, but by consultative medical authority as well.
>
> Many women are completely fulfilled sexually by the warm sense of belonging engendered by mutual sexual stimulation. (p. 484).

Lack of sexual responsiveness in the woman frequently has the same source as impotence in the man—anxiety. The anxiety may be generated by early negative attitudes toward sex, fear of pregnancy (now less of an issue because of contraceptives), fear of inadequacy as a woman, and fear of genital harm. Also, anger at the man for other problems in their relationship can readily prevent a woman from responding sexually. Such "overflow" into the sexual area affects men less often, and this difference accounts for a great deal of misunderstanding. An argument, for example, may turn the woman off sexually but not the man.

For many sexual problems, open communication is essential for overcoming the difficulties. Open communication permits both partners to approach the sexual relationship in a manner that may reduce anxiety and the pressure to perform. Under professional guidance, changes in marital sexual responsiveness have a good prognosis. Without professional help, it is not easy because the anxieties are often great, and even the well-motivated couple find great difficulties in shifting out of the old patterns of interaction that are responsible for the incompatibility.

Family Planning

In recent years it has become increasingly common for a couple to plan the exact number of children they wish to have. Although this planning is encouraged by current concern about worldwide over-population, the desire to limit the number of children derives from many subtle and complex social and cultural forces. We tend to regard population control and contraception as recent issues. Actually, they are by no means products of modern technology. Anthropological studies have shown that the desire to limit the number of children in a family is present in all societies. However, the means employed to achieve this end vary widely, ranging from witchcraft to infanticide. These studies also document an extra-ordinary resourcefulness of societies past and present in the prevention of pregnancy despite the lack of "modern" methods. In most societies birth control is left to individual initiative; at times, however, the state has taken an active part in controlling population.

How more advanced societies practice population control is exemplified by France, the Soviet Union, and Japan, all of which have made a conscious effort to plan and control population growth. In the case of France, the goal was to increase the population, whereas the Soviet Union and Japan sought to slow down their population growth.

In France after World War I, experts warned of an eventual disappearance of the French nation, basing their predictions on the fact that since the eighteenth century, despite religious sanctions against the use of contraceptives, there had been a persistent decrease in the rate of population growth. This was all the more alarming since other European countries had experienced a steady increase in the rate of growth over the same period. Through massive government programs—including generous bonuses for each child in a family in the form of support stipends—France has succeeded in reversing this trend over the last two decades.

The goal of the Soviet Union and Japan, in contrast, has been to stunt the growth of ever-expanding populations. As a result of the government effort, most couples in the Soviet Union today elect to have only one child. And in Japan, in spite of the fact that oral contraceptives are not sold and intrauterine devices are not employed, zero population growth has been achieved.

Although from the standpoint of worldwide overpopulation family size restriction is desirable, each couple faces the question of how large a family is optimal. The currently prevailing practice in the United States is to plan for two children. Growing up in such a small family is, of course, different from growing up in a larger family. Indeed, for personality growth there may even be advantages to growing up in a large family; the many personality types and the different relationships present in one intimate group make a variety of demands on the child and provide experiences not available in the two-child family. A two-child family can provide the experience of a brother or a sister, but not of both; it can only provide the experience of a single younger or a single older sibling. The parental investment in and demands for fulfillment of dreams are greater when one or two children must meet these expectations. On the other hand, the more children there are the more the parents' resources, psychological as well as financial, will be taxed. More children also mean a longer period of being "tied down" for both parents, especially for the mother. Each couple must in the end decide for themselves what size family they will have. Government pressures, economic necessities, peer expectations, sources of personal gratification, religious beliefs, and individual priorities all play a part in the decision.

Contraception. In the general sense of prevention of conception, contraception is universally practiced. Among the common methods employed are:

Rhythm method. The rhythm method is the only one sanctioned by the Catholic Church. Conception is avoided by having sexual intercourse at times in the menstrual cycle when the ovum is not fertilizable. The period of safety is approximately four days before and four days after menstruation. Since ovulation may normally be irregular, there is a possibility of a fertile ovum being present even in the period considered as safe.

Coitus interruptus. This method, probably the most commonly employed throughout the world, involves the withdrawal of the penis from the vagina at the moment the male reaches orgasm, and before ejaculation takes place.

"The Pill". Most contraceptive medications taken by women suppress ovulation by their hormonal action. In the absence of

ovulation conception cannot take place. Less widely employed but also effective is the use of postcoital medications, which do not suppress ovulation, but prevent implantation of the fertilized ovum in the womb.

IUD (intrauterine device).   A metal or plastic strip, coil, or spring is inserted into the uterus by an obstetrician and held in place by the pressure the device exerts against the uterine walls. The presence of the small foreign object in the uterus prevents implantation of the fertilized ovum.

Diaphragm.   An elastic ring with a shallow cup of rubber is inserted into the vagina and covers the cervix. Spermicidal jelly placed in the cup is kept against the cervical opening and prevents sperm from entering the uterus.

Condom.   A sheath of thin rubber or similar material placed over the penis prevents the sperm from entering the vagina.

All these methods have some drawbacks: mechanical, medical, or psychological. The rhythm method limits markedly the occasions on which sexual relations may take place; it is also far from "sure." Coitus interruptus is usually unsatisfying for both the woman and the man. The pill is a hormone or combination of hormones and thus carries some danger of cancer (although not shown statistically to be increased) and thrombosis (blood clots). There is also, for some women, an excessive weight gain (actually increased water retention) and some mood change (depression) reported. The IUD has some cramps associated with its use, particularly after its first insertion, and tends to produce excessive menstrual flow. The condom and diaphragm require preparation before intercourse, and therefore are psychologically less appealing to many.

Abortion.   If conception occurs and a woman does not want, or is not ready to have, a child, she now has the option of obtaining an abortion. Since a Supreme Court ruling in 1973, any woman in the United States may legally obtain an abortion in the first three months of pregnancy. Religious beliefs will preclude an abortion for some, but the legalization of abortions will have a profound effect on family planning. In states where abortions were legal before the Court ruling, it was found that married rather than single women with unwanted pregnancies made up the majority of those seeking abortions.

The legalization of abortion will probably have its greatest impact on the poor, who heretofore could not afford the high cost of an illegal abortion. It is also among the poor and uneducated that contraception is least understood and least effectively employed.

Legalized abortion does raise the danger that couples will not be as careful in using contraceptives for family planning. Since an abortion does carry some medical risks (excess bleeding, uterine infection) it should not be considered as a substitute for contraceptives, whose risk is negligible in comparison. Further, most couples experience strongly ambivalent feelings when they must decide whether to terminate a pregnancy by abortion. By clearly planning together how large a family they want and how they are going to regulate their fertility, a couple can usually avoid this dilemma.

Marital Conflict

Conflict is inevitable in marriage, but whether it disrupts the family and impairs its functioning or is resolved depends to a great extent on the mechanisms the couple develop to deal with differences between them. How do marital conflicts arise?

Differences in Values. A major source of conflict between husbands and wives arises from their having different values. Values encompass the norms, standards, and expectations of behavior that are learned as part of growing up in a given family or social group. These values become so much a part of the individual that they go unquestioned, and commonly a person establishes a family assuming that his or her values are necessary ones that will prevail. Some values are widely held and shared, such as honesty, protecting one's children from dangerous situations, working for a living, being reliable, and so on; while some individuals might not implement these values, they will still state that they regard them as important and desirable. Other values, however, are more specific to a given family or subculture and not so universally accepted. In one family, the husband may be expected to be a social companion and confidante of his wife. In another, the wife would think it strange if her husband were never "out with the boys" and wanted primarily her companionship. It may be expected that the husband and wife will have obtained just enough education to equip them for a job in, say, a factory or coal mine, just as their parents had done. In another family, it may be expected that both partners will strive for educational achievement and will continue to work toward job advancement. If a wife places emphasis on educational and professional attainments and the husband, by his standards, is satisfied with his lot as long as the family is provided for, then a basic conflict is in the making. If the husband's standards confine women to the homemaking role ("no wife of mine is going to work") while the wife assumes that she will fill a variety of roles, a serious conflict can arise. The grounds for conflict are endless—and, considering the uniqueness of each individual, inevitable. Nevertheless, compromises will have to be reached; both partners must shift or one partner must adopt or accept the standards of the other. In some instances, neither will shift or compromise. Many couples live for years in a state of conflict, with all the tension and unpleasantness that accompanies it. Other couples just suffer silently, and their conflict never comes to the surface. In these cases the conflict itself may serve the psychological needs of the couple.

Changes in Psychological Needs.   As couples mature and develop, as each partner gains experience, self-confidence, and success, value emphasis can shift. So too with psychological needs. But when these changes occur at different rates and in different directions, incompatibility and conflict will result. If one partner needs to be dependent and the other domineering, the balance will be upset when the dependent one becomes more independent. There are also situations in which the husband initially desires a passive, compliant, and nonthreatening wife but later, when he matures more, wants a more equitable sharing relationship. The following complaint exemplifies such a problem.

> My dilemma is that when I was young and in the Army, I married a Japanese girl. She was alone in the world, very vulnerable, and times were bad.
>
> It is now 25 years later. I dated very little before I met her. She has been a good wife and I have tried to be a good husband. Her deferential attitude, which I found so appealing at one time, has, as I've matured over the years, become irksome. Her lack of independence and her dependence on me has become a burden. I don't feel I can step out of the house for an evening without feeling guilty. She wouldn't complain, but only stoically sit alone.
>
> Now that our two children are grown, we have little in common, except for household concerns. I've given her books to read to see if we could share something intellectual. It hasn't worked. I long for the companionship one looks forward to when one retires, but I dare not retire. What would I do with this good-natured homebody who wants to do nothing but fluff my pillows, till I could scream? (From Dr. Rose Franzblau's "Human Relations" column, *New York Post*, January 14, 1974; used by permission.)

A more common dilemma is that the wife becomes increasingly independent and the husband can't tolerate it. Then the woman feels trapped by her husband's expectations.

> Mr. K. complained that his wife no longer respected him. The first five years of the marriage were ideal. He made all the decisions and she

always asked his advice, even on household matters. Now she challenges his opinions, buys things without asking his advice, has registered for evening courses at the university, and sometimes asks him to give dinner to their four-year-old daughter. Mr. K. was so unhappy that he was thinking of divorce.

In this instance, Mr. K. did not want an equal relationship or an independent wife. It was not what he had "contracted" for.

Sometimes conflict arises because some needs of a couple are compatible but others are not. A couple may marry to satisfy one set of needs only to discover with time that other needs are more important. Thus sexual and security needs are often most important at the beginning of marriage, while intellectual, social, and emotional needs come into sharper focus later. The possibilities for need-based conflict are limitless.

Resolving Conflict. As Haley (1963) has pointed out, one of the issues in the early phase of marriage is the establishment of rules for handling conflict—even if the resulting rule is to avoid confrontation. The need to deal with conflict is universal, and therefore a couple will settle quite early into a pattern that constitutes the rules —often unexpressed—of the relationship. One such rule might be to discuss differences at the moment they arise, with both partners giving a little. Another one might be for the husband to give in on "in-house" matters—care of the children, household purchases, and vacation plans—and the wife to give in on "out-of-house" matters— budget, handling of relatives, and husband's leisure-time activities. The type of issues each family deals with are similar; the rules they set up vary widely, but they must lead to some modicum of effective teamwork.

These rules are for the most part what are called quid pro quo rules (Jackson, 1965). *Quid pro quo* means, literally, "something for something," and essentially a couple explicitly or more often implicitly agrees to exchange certain behaviors. Some implicit rules are destructive and promote dishonesty in the relationship, for example the communication-inhibiting: "I won't criticize you if you don't criticize me." Of course, such "deals" are also necessary for effective teamwork in the context of the personality needs of each partner. Exchanging areas of responsibility in the family can be a constructive quid pro quo.

One way for a couple to diminish conflict is to discuss explicitly their cherished standards and expectations in advance of marriage. They are thus in a better position to evaluate their compatability and the possibilities for compromise. In open discussion a person can discover strongly held views that he or she was unaware of. Values

SELF-AWARENESS EXERCISE

The Marriage Contract

The purpose of this exercise is to help you make explicit your attitudes, values, and goals with regard to the marriage relationship.

Task. *Write your own marriage contract. The contract should cover the following topics:*

1. Employment. What rights, obligations, and freedoms are extended to husband and wife in relation to employment outside the home? The contract should cover the time before and after children enter the picture.

2. Support. What obligations for financial support are required of the husband and wife?

3. Allocation of monies. Joint or separate accounts? Accountability to each other?

4. Children. The contract should spell out your wishes with regard to family planning, obligations and freedoms in contraceptive measures, stipulations concerning abortion, and number of children.

5. Child care. Indicate the role and obligations of husband and wife in child care at different stages of the child's (or children's) development. If both husband and wife will work outside the home, how will this bear on child-care arrangements? Specify methods or orientation in child-rearing, including disciplinary roles of both parents, education, and religious training.

6. Household responsibilities. What are the obligations for household chores when both parties work? When only one is employed outside the home? Will differential salaries affect household responsibilities?

7. Social life. Make provisions for social life in and outside the home, specify joint and separate social activities.

---

and needs often can lie dormant until a situation brings them to the fore. Thus a woman may discover that she wants other roles in addition to homemaking only when the issue confronts her after marriage.

We have designed a Self-awareness Exercise (above) to dramatize the partially unconscious nature of values and their impact on marital conflict. The Self-awareness Exercise calls for your personal involvement.

8. Decision making. *Determine areas of joint and individual decision making, as well as methods for arriving at decisions.*

9. Conflict. *What methods will be employed for resolving conflict? Under what conditions would separation or divorce be considered?*

10. Individual rights, privileges, and responsibilities. *List here any areas not included above in which you would want to specify individual freedoms and responsibilities.*

Evaluation. *After you complete your marriage contract it would be interesting to compare it to the civil and religious contracts that apply to you. Although each state establishes its own marriage laws, the rights and responsibilities legally established for husband and wife are generally as follows (Bair, 1965): "The legal responsibilities of the wife are to live in the home established by her husband; to perform the domestic chores (cleaning, cooking, washing, etc.) necessary to help maintain that home; to care for her husband and children." The wife is obliged to have sexual relations with her husband "as long as his demands are reasonable and her health is not impaired or endangered." The husband is required to "provide a home for his wife and children; to support, protect and maintain his wife and children." It is clear that existing legal marriage contracts do not provide for the mutuality and sharing that has become the theme of many modern marriages.*

What problems do you think you would encounter in actually initiating the contract you have written? How would members of the opposite sex with whom you are close react to your contract? Try out your contract with friends and relatives. How do the marriage relationships you are familiar with stack up against your contract?

CHILDBIRTH
The First Pregnancy

After having the pregnancy confirmed by the obstetrician, the couple begin planning for the changes that will accommodate and provide for the child. During the first few months, the expectant mother may have the discomfort of morning sickness, a transient sense of nausea on arising. Rarely does this become serious enough for medical treatment. The woman may also experience an intensified emotionality, which is probably to some extent physiologically induced. The shifting hormonal balance with its increased progesterone level may well be responsible for much of the change in affect that is experienced by pregnant women. It should be emphasized, however, that for the vast majority of women pregnancy is a time of increased sense of physical and emotional well-being. Many women say they feel their best when pregnant. Some women do experience increased irritability and sluggishness. Again, although psychological response to pregnancy plays a major role in the sense of well-being, the individual's physiological makeup has a good deal to do with it too.

During the first trimester (the first three months) the couple begin their plans and adjust their lives to the new child. If the wife is working—and most women today work in the first years after marriage—a decision must be made as to when she will stop working and for how long. Most couples decide that the wife will not go back to work again at least until the youngest child has reached school age. Most women look forward to motherhood and the full-time work that the mother-wife role will demand. Other women, although they look forward to becoming mothers, do not want to interrupt their occupational endeavors outside the home. They are pulled in two directions by the usually conflicting gratifications of full-time occupational pursuits and motherhood. It takes a stable marriage and a mature woman to choose among the alternative solutions without feeling either "imprisoned" by motherhood or guilty about not devoting all her time and energy to the home. For many women in low-income families there may not even be a choice; a few weeks or months after giving birth they will have to go back to work for financial reasons.

By the second trimester, the decision regarding work has usually been made. If the work is not physically straining, and the woman has the opportunity to rest whenever she feels fatigued, she will be capable of working even in the ninth month. Certainly mothers not employed outside the home work until the labor begins —preparing meals, caring for the children, and maintaining the house. During the second and third trimester, both parents, but especially the woman, engage in a great deal of mental rehearsing. The woman's fantasies revolve around the baby, her thoughts are preoccupied with hopes and aspirations, as well as fears, for the unborn child.

Throughout the pregnancy, the woman normally experiences frequent fears, concerns, and ambivalent feelings. She worries about the effect the pregnancy will have on her figure and whether she will regain her previous shape. She may find the obstetrical examinations embarrassing or even humiliating if they are not performed with care and sensitivity. She is very likely to worry about the health of the fetus. Such a worry is often both a realistic reaction to the fact that there are babies that are born with deformities and an expression of doubts about personal adequacy. Questions such as "Can I give birth to a normal child?" "Am I really a woman?" "Is there anything wrong with me?" arise in almost every woman's mind at least during the first pregnancy, and they foster a heightened concern about deformities. Pregnant women are therefore often hypersensitive to any suggestion that something may not be going right, and they may overreact to the slightest remark by the obstetrician. It is not surprising that the first question that the mother asks the obstetrician after delivery is "Is my baby OK?"

Ambivalence about pregnancy and motherhood is further intensified by a change in the couple's relationship, which frequently takes place after conception. The husband's affection for his wife and his concentration on her as a person may shift to concern for the unborn child and concern for her as the bearer of this child. Often the loss of exclusive attention and love will be deeply felt by a pregnant woman and cause resentment of her state and the unborn child. The change in the sexual relationship initiated by husband, wife, or both partners will also give confirmation to the disruption that pregnancy brings on. Sexual intercourse is sometimes curtailed because the man is turned off by the pregnant woman's changed body or because of fears of danger to the fetus by both husband and wife. The sensed loss of affection when such sexual alienation takes place may not only provoke resentment toward the pregnancy but also fears that the arrival of the child will cause an even greater loss in the relationship.

Pregnancy also places stress on the husband. He may feel left out of the whole process while everyone pays attention to his wife and the unborn child. He may also feel rejected if his wife has less interest in sexual relations.

Although ambivalent feelings will almost always be present during pregnancy, their intensity will be governed by many factors. Some of the more significant of these are the readiness of the couple in planning for the pregnancy, their financial conditions, the maturity of the couple, the stability of their relationship, the degree of self-awareness of each partner, and the nature of their interpersonal communication.

It is apparent that there is a wide range of emotional reactions during this period. The "bliss" that has been traditionally assigned to pregnancy is one side of a very complex experience; as health professionals we must be sensitive to the fact that negative feelings and reactions during pregnancy are as normal as positive ones. Anger, anxiety, depression, and guilt should be expected behaviors of the pregnant woman, who requires understanding and supportive counseling. Health professionals sometimes reinforce the prejudices and stereotyping of society by ignoring, getting alarmed over, or admonishing women for their "immature," "unfeminine," or "abnormal" reactions. Here is one area where we need to implement our knowledge about the complexity of human beings and the normal variety of their psychological experiences.

Delivery

Today most babies are born in hospitals. It was in the 1930s that this practice first accounted for the majority of births (Burgess and Locke, 1945). The advantages are considerable as far as the health of the mother and baby is concerned; the hospital setting makes it easier to prevent potentially fatal infections and to obtain expert care if complications should arise. But the psychological disadvantages are also numerous. A family event is taken out of the home and put into an often depersonalized environment that excludes everyone but the father. Various efforts at overcoming the psychological drawbacks are being tried, including home delivery and rooming-in, in which the baby is kept in the mother's hospital room instead of a nursery after delivery. Another innovation is inviting the father's stronger emotional participation by allowing him to attend the delivery.

The birth of the infant marks the fulfillment of the hopes and burdens of the previous nine months, and the day of delivery is a time of anxiety and relief—anxiety that everything should go well and relief that labor has actually begun. A first labor is an unknown experience, bound to generate considerable apprehension in the wife and husband. Many hospitals hold prenatal classes for couples to help take the mystery out of the birth process. If the woman elects to deliver without general anesthesia, she will also usually take lessons in natural childbirth. These methods range from simple exercises to self-hypnosis. The most widespread method used in the United States is the Lamaze method, which emphasizes breathing techniques to ease the discomfort of labor.

Once the child is born and the parents see that he or she is healthy, there is usually relief and delight. If the child was planned and adequate preparations were made for the baby's arrival, the experience will be dominated by excitement, involvement, and a renewed sense of intimacy between the couple. However, many of the same ambivalences and negative feelings that accompanied the pregnancy will continue after the birth of the child. This will be especially true in situations where there are severe financial problems, an unstable marital relationship, imminent divorce, serious differences over parenting and home care responsibilities, an unwed situation, etc. The woman's fears about her changed role may quickly find confirmation in the demands on her time and energy that the infant makes. She may feel guilty about her ambivalent feelings toward the mothering role and her secret (or open) wishes to be free or involved in a career. The early period of parenting is difficult for many women, because they feel they must live up to the idealized image of the "perfect, all-giving mother." Fortunately, writers such as Angela McBride (1973) are helping to free women from their guilt feelings by effectively portraying the commonness and normality of ambivalent reactions to the parenting role. As McBride indicates, one is probably a more effective parent when he or she accepts the reality of the anger and frustration about the parenting role along with the joy and pleasure.

THE FAMILY WITH CHILDREN

The birth of the first child signals the entrance of the family into a new stage. For the average family with two children born two years apart, the next twenty years in the family's development are marked by the milestones in the growth of the children. The parents, of course, continue to grow too, but the rapid changes in the children's needs define how the family will spend its time and organize and distribute its tasks.

The Newborn

The newborn infant demands full-time care. At first the infant will spend most of its time sleeping, but when it is hungry it will not permit much delay in feeding. Consequently, every three or four hours the parents must be available. Breast feeding is in many respects the easiest means of providing for the infant; it has the advantages of not requiring sterilization of formula, providing the most readily digestible nutrient, and making available some immunity to infection from the mother. Unfortunately, in many hospitals mothers are discouraged from nursing their infants. This is perhaps due in part to the additional time involved in helping a new mother to learn how to nurse, because the inexperienced woman tends to give up quickly if the infant is at first unable to suck vigorously. This situation often occurs with smaller babies. It takes the support and encouragement of the nurse and physician to help the mother coax the small mouth to draw on the nipple. With patience it can always be done. (After all, only recently has the alternative of bottle feeding even been possible.) On the other hand, if for psychological or practical reasons a woman does not want to breast feed her infant she need not feel guilty, because she can communicate the same care and tenderness while holding the baby whether she is bottle feeding or breast feeding. Studies have shown that it is the quality of parenting in general rather than the means that makes for adequate early development.

Family Adjustment

The couple now take on additional roles: they are parents as well as husband and wife. (As parents, they will find that their time is to a great extent regulated by the children. They can no longer decide on the spur of the moment to go to a movie, bowling, or dancing, or to engage in countless other activities that before could be indulged in spontaneously. In fact, the need to plan each activity so as to take into account the age-specific needs of the children—for a period of 20 years or more—is probably the hardest adjustment of parenthood. The gratification that children bring is great, but so are the responsibilities. The young couple will find that in some respects they share more and in some respects less. Rearing the children and recounting the little daily events in their lives make for a new source of pleasure and communication between them. At the same time, they are less free to engage in joint social activities, and they must develop new rules about division of labor. The new father may have to obtain additional sources of income, especially if heretofore his wife's work was an important and necessary contribution to their budget. This may mean less time with his wife at a time when she may need him even more. They may redevelop important ties with their parents, with grandparents supplying some of the much needed relief from the constant demands of the newborn child. An adjustment frequently difficult for the husband is the extent to which the infant becomes a focus of his wife's day. In a well-functioning family, these shifts are expected, and the mother-child symbiosis is an anticipated phase of development.

From Dyad to Triad.   Talcott Parsons and his coworkers analyzed the middle-class family in the United States of the 1940s. They found that the infant forms a basic dyad with the mother until he reaches the age when socialization begins in earnest, at $2\frac{1}{2}$ to 3 years. Up to the age of 2, most of the supervision, nurturing, and guidance is provided by the mother. When a child reaches 3, he is coming into increasing contact with his extrafamilial environment in the form of neighborhood children. At this time, there is a polarization of function; the father comes to represent task demand and the mother functions as maintainer of emotional needs. A similar differentiation of function had been shown to facilitate accomplishment of tasks in small groups other than the family (Parsons and Bales, 1959). The objection has often been made that this functional polarization fosters sexual stereotypes. Actually, there is no reason to assume that the mother could not be the enforcer of discipline and the father the nurturer. Nonetheless, the mother's early relationship to the infant establishes a pattern that apparently makes a later assumption of the task-oriented role difficult, even when she is the only parent as in a father-absent household (Goldstein, 1972).

Nurturing Role

Traditionally, the mother has been the parent primarily responsible for the care of small children. But as the joint type of marital relationship evolves into greater equality for husband and wife, the assumption that women are better suited to child care than men is being questioned. Stated another way, is nurturing behavior socially conditioned or biologically fixed? In Chapter 2 we discussed the early and pervasive role-training patterns for boys and girls. Is the so-called maternal instinct another aspect of this role training? Some people believe it is, and therefore prefer the term *parenting* to *mothering*. Certainly we can recognize individual differences in nurturing ability and inclination. Many of us can cite examples from our personal experience of men who are nurturing and women who are clearly less suited for the nurturing role. However, the anthropological and animal data do show consistent differences in nurturing between male and female. For example, among mammals, the female provides the primary care of the young. Among preadolescent monkeys, the males engage in rough play and clearly aggressive activities with one another but not with young females. The young female monkeys not only do not join the males in rough play but also refrain from the display of aggression among themselves. The juvenile females, however, show a great deal of interest in newborn infants and in grooming activities, behavior not shown by juvenile males. We can question the applicability of these findings to humans since one of the most distinguishing human characteristics is the ability to transcend biology and shape behavior in new directions—for humans biology does not have to be destiny.

Anthropological data, too, clearly identify nurturing behavior as female. In some societies men also participate in nurturing and child care, but nowhere do they perform those tasks to the exclusion of females (Zelditch, 1955). Here, too, questions can be raised about the conclusiveness of these observations since conditions in primitive societies favor sharp role distinctions along traditional lines (hunting for males, child care for females). Modern society no longer necessitates these sharp divisions, and their persistence may be a derivative of the biological and social conditioning and selection that has taken place over hundreds of thousands of years.

We must also make a distinction between the nurturing behavior that children require in infancy and what they require at other periods of childhood. Even if females were found to be more suited to nurturing infants because of the effect of hormones and other factors—and we don't know—there is no apparent reason why males could not also participate in nurturing, particularly after infancy. We would, however, take issue with statements that parenting can be provided by mother, father, or any other "interested adult." One thing that research has convincingly demonstrated is that normal development requires an intensive, personalized, and continuous human relationship with a nurturing figure, particularly during the first two years. Just an "interested adult" will not do. Most institutional settings have interested adults but it has been shown that they cannot perform an effective job of parenting (see the discussion of separation in Chapter 15).

As we move toward greater equality in responsibility for parenting, problems will arise. Many women have decried the burden of parenting that has traditionally fallen almost exclusively on women; this along with other stereotypes has prevented women from fulfilling their potentialities. Betty Friedan (1970) and other authors have dramatically documented the depressing features of the child-care and homemaker role for many women. But, while women are beginning to protest the overwhelming demands of the exclusive parenting role, it is doubtful that men will opt for that role in any great numbers. We can, therefore, foresee many difficulties for couples and families in the years ahead as women seek more varied roles. Alternative life styles will no doubt be a dominant theme of the evolving family of the near and distant future.

The Extended Family and Child Care

Can grandmothers and grandfathers rescue husband and wife from some of the burdens of child-rearing and free them for other fulfilling activities and pursuits? This is one alternative that has been suggested to meet the dilemma of the modern family. It is tempting to look nostalgically back to the times before the Industrial Revolution when the extended family was the norm. But a closer look reveals certain problems with this myth. The extended family has been highly romanticized; prior to the Industrial Revolution few people (except the wealthy) lived beyond the age of 40. See Simone de Beauvoir's (1972) vivid and depressing description of life in those times. The aged grandparents, as we know them, simply did not exist in any great numbers. Only after the Industrial Revolution, with the rise of the middle class and the accompanying improvements in health care, nutrition and pensions, was the life span extended. Child-care helpers before the Industrial Revolution were more likely to be maiden aunts and widows who suffered from the strong prejudices against single women. Their availability was due more to their state of bondage than to any free choice of role.

When writers now talk about the enlistment of the "extended family" in child care, what they really mean is grandmothers. Notwithstanding the "altruism" of "giving them a useful role," this not only implies denigration of the middle-aged and aged (they aren't doing anything useful anyway) but it is also a subtly sexist position. It is doubtful that the liberated woman of age 25 who pursues personal development (which may include family) will wish to return to the parenting role at age 50–65. Grandparents may take a vital interest in the young, but that does not necessitate babysitting while the young parents do the "real fulfilling." We will have more to say about prejudice toward the aged in Chapter 6.

CHILD-REARING

The whole realm of child-rearing practices requires something of a family consensus. The parents must come to some agreement as to what means they will employ to guide their children and foster their development. Volumes have been written on this subject, and we know a good deal, but much remains in the realm of opinion and speculation.

Most theories of personality place primary importance on the early years of life in determining later personality and behavior. The pattern of experiences provided by the parents in the early years is generally the most essential influence on the child. Child-rearing practices are the major vehicle for patterning the child's universe of experience. For the young child, the immediate environment is his universe. The perceptions of this limited world are then generalized to the rest of the environment, forming the basis for expectations in future relationships. How parents interact with their children therefore plays a most crucial role in child development.

Child-Rearing Research

Research on child-rearing has concentrated on two distinct areas. One deals with specific practices such as breast feeding versus bottle feeding, early versus late toilet training, demand feeding versus scheduled feeding, time of weaning, etc. All of these concrete facets of child-rearing practices tend to be influenced by prevailing expert opinion. When breast feeding became associated with forbidden pleasure, late weaning came to be frowned upon. Currently the emphasis is on the importance of intimacy with the mother, and breast feeding and late weaning are recommended by many experts. Parents are very much influenced by expert opinion as well as by the fashions of the time, and they may adopt these practices even though they are contrary to their own inclinations.

In the second major area of child-rearing research, the personalities of the parents are investigated. This research deals with more general or pervasive characteristics of the parents in their interaction with their children: punitiveness, authoritarianism, restrictiveness, permissiveness, and other related qualities. The overall quality of the home environment rather than a specific practice is stressed. Nonetheless, there are undoubtedly relationships between specific practices and overall quality. For example, overly punitive parents are more likely to start toilet training early; on the other hand, the punitive parent influenced by expert opinion may be convinced of the advisability of late toilet training, but the punitiveness may still come through in the manner in which toilet training and other interactions are handled by the parent.

Specific Practices

If specific child-rearing practices are significant for a child's development, then it is reasonable to assume that demonstrable differences can be found in later childhood and adulthood among people raised under different methods. If, for example, breast feeding is presumed to yield greater security and gratification than bottle feeding, then adults who were breast fed as children should be better adjusted and more secure than another group of adults who were bottle fed. The same reasoning applies to other practices. Is this the case? Orlansky (1949) made a comprehensive review of the literature on this topic and found the net results to be inconclusive at best. There was no evidence that specific practices produce a particular outcome. Seawell (1952) reached a similar conclusion.

The most comprehensive recent review of the effects of infant care is reported by Caldwell (1964). She presents charts listing all of the significant studies of infant feeding practices, sucking behavior, and elimination training and their effects on personality. Caldwell concludes: "the breast-bottle dilemma must remain exactly that . . . it is difficult to demonstrate any consistent relationships between oral gratification, defined to include type and scheduling of feeding and time of weaning and either child or adult personality . . ." Only in regard to toilet training is Caldwell able to make a statement of a positive relationship. Children with disturbance of bladder or bowel functioning show a pattern of disturbance in their toilet training, which can be described as early or forceful. But she also points out the crucial deficiency of this research in not demonstrating the absence of severe toilet training among children who do not show bladder or bowel dysfunction.

How can we account for the paucity of significant relationships between child-rearing practices and personality outcome? On the face of it we would expect divergent practices to make a significant difference. An answer suggested repeatedly by researchers in this area is that the complexity of parent-child interactions has so far defied quantified studies. Research that extracts only one dimension of the complex parent-child relationship is not likely to be adequate enough to explain later characteristics. There are always numerous factors present that interact with a particular practice to produce a complex syndrome of events. We have already mentioned that the variations in administering a given practice can be more important than the practice itself. In breast or bottle feeding, the mother's overall attitude of affection or rejection, patience or impatience, and level of tension are essential parts of the feeding experience.

General Orientation

Unlike specific practices, research into the overall characteristics of child-rearing has had somewhat more promising results.

Authoritarian versus Democratic. Authoritarianism as a personality concept was introduced by Adorno et al. (1950) to account for the extreme forms of prejudice manifested by some people.

Prejudiced individuals were found to have certain personality characteristics in common: emphasis on power, adherence to rigid rules, reverence for authority, lack of empathy, need for certainty, stereotyped role concept, and incapacity for honest self-examination. In their intensive studies of authoritarian and non-authoritarian adults Adorno et al. found sharp differences among the subjects in recollections of their parents and their childhood experiences. The authoritarian subjects had childhood memories of victimization by parents, unfair treatment, emotional neglect, a sense of being picked on, and submissiveness to parental authority; the parents were described as strict, distant, and lacking in genuine feeling. Subjects low on scores of authoritarianism had much more favorable recollections of their parents. Fairness, concern, rationally justified rules, and mutual respect were characteristics cited by the nonauthoritarian subjects. Other investigators studied child-rearing practices of parents of prejudiced and nonprejudiced children more directly and arrived at similar conclusions. In a study by Harris et al. (1950) the mothers of prejudiced children had significantly stricter attitudes. Starr (1965) found both fathers and mothers of prejudiced children to be significantly stricter in their child-rearing attitudes than both parents of nonprejudiced children.

Restrictive versus Permissive.   In general the restrictive–permissive dimension refers to the amount of control the parents exert over the child. The failure of much of the research to make a distinction between punitiveness, authoritarianism, and restrictiveness confuses this issue. Also the question of extent of control and permissiveness is crucial. These factors no doubt account for some of the seemingly contradictory findings. Symmonds (1939) showed that parental dominance and submission apparently referred to extreme forms of restrictiveness and permissiveness. The dominant parents used severe punishment, criticalness, and a high degree of control, while parental submissiveness was associated with neglect and inconsistency. The dominated children were found to be insecure, withdrawn, cautious, having difficulty in self-expression; children of permissive parents were described as disobedient, careless, irresponsible, stubborn, rebellious, and independent. In this case the children of both groups reflected maladaptive characteristics. In spite of the haziness in defining restrictiveness and permissiveness, some general trends in the research have been noted. Restrictiveness seems to have an inhibitory effect while permissiveness loosens inhibitions. But neither approach can be associated with consistently positive outcomes. As Becker (1964) states, "restrictiveness while fostering well-controlled socialized behavior tends also to lead to fearful, dependent and submissive behaviors, a dulling of intellectual striving and inhibited hostility. Permissiveness on the other hand while fostering outgoing, sociable, assertive behaviors and intellectual striving leads also to less persistence and increased aggressiveness."

As in the other areas of behavior we have discussed, it appears that one set of variables is insufficient to predict personality and behavioral outcome. Becker, for example, goes on to point out that other variables interact with permissiveness and restrictiveness. Thus the time of life in which the child experiences restrictiveness or permissiveness is important; dependency and conformity are more likely when the mother is restrictive before the child is 3 years of age, while an aggressive reaction is more common when the restrictiveness occurs after age 3. Other complicating factors include the consistency of the parents' methods, whether one or both parents practice the technique, and whether the restrictiveness or permissiveness is accompanied by warmth or hostility.

Birth Order

Alfred Adler, a Viennese psychiatrist and an early associate of Sigmund Freud, was the first personality theorist to ascribe specific personality characteristics to ordinal position within the family. According to Adler, each child by virtue of his ordinal position has a unique experience, and this position influences how the child comes to see himself in relation to others.

The oldest child, according to Adler, will frequently play the role of model or parent with younger children. Because of his original position in the family, the firstborn child can be very sensitive to the idea of being "dethroned." The firstborn longs for the past and has a reverence for rules and authority; having been on the scene first, he has the feeling of natural rights. Firstborns like to exercise power and authority and are therefore sometimes suited to executive or administrative types of positions. The secondborn has the model of someone ahead of him and is therefore very competitive. His inner desire to overtake the older child is expressed in his ambitiousness. The constant striving of the secondborn, according to Adler, makes him more successful than the firstborn. The secondborn has a tendency to replay his sibling rivalry by challenging leadership and authority. Actual studies of ordinal position have somewhat contradicted Adler's view of the second born. For example, one of the more consistent findings is of the greater achievement of the firstborn

(Campbell and Thompson, 1968). This goes along with Galton's observation of the high percentage of firstborns who were fellows of the Royal Society. The least likely to achieve success, according to Campbell and Thompson, is the middle child. These findings, of course, do not refute the observation that secondborn children are more ambitious and competitive than firstborns.

The youngest child of the family, according to Adler, is often pampered and overindulged as a baby. At the same time, the youngest child has many examples to follow and, therefore, he often develops outstanding skills. He is also given to feelings of superiority because of the preferential treatment he is accustomed to receiving.

Since Adler's speculations and clinical observations, researchers have noted the complexities of ordinal relationships. This point is made in a study by Rosenberg and Sutton-Smith (1966), which suggested that boys have an influence on their sisters' achievement but not vice versa. According to another study, mothers were warmer, less restrictive, and less coercive with their second born than with their first born children (Lasko, 1954). Many factors can contribute to how a child perceives his role within the family constellation: the size of the family, the age of the parents, the spacing of the children, sex of the child (e.g., girl followed by boy as opposed to the opposite, or other patterns), role concepts of the parents (e.g., prestige for firstborn son, little status for girls, etc.), the personalities of the parents and siblings, and many other variables. Toman (1969) has presented some of the most detailed work on the variations in ordinal position (e.g., oldest brother of brothers, oldest sister of sisters, etc.). Toman also takes into consideration the ordinal position of the parents (when they were children) in relation to their children of various ordinal positions. So, while ordinal position no doubt contributes to one's world view, we must be cautious about generalizations and stereotypes.

Child Abuse

Child abuse refers to the severe injuries inflicted upon children by their parents or guardians. These injuries may include broken bones, concussions, burns, smashed kidneys, and a host of other physical and psychological injuries. Very often the abused child is under 1 year of age. The incidence of child abuse appears to be on the rise. Harris (1967) estimates that "five infants every hour in this country are injured by their parents."

While more cases of child abuse occur in families of low socio-economic strata, there are occurrences in middle-class and upper-middle-class homes. Among the middle and upper classes the effects of abuse are covered up better, so that it does not come to the attention of hospitals or other authorities. Some of the factors found to be associated with child abuse are divorce, separation, unstable families and marriages, large families with children close in age, economic problems, unemployment, high geographical mobility and social isolation (Spinetta and Rigler, 1972). However, none of these factors taken alone seems to be sufficient to produce child abuse since many parents of similar circumstances do not abuse their children. Steele and Pollock (1968) indicate that a more crucial determinant is a history of child abuse or neglect in the childhood of the abusing parent. As a result of their own earlier deprivation these parents treat their children as if they were older children or adults. This results in a role reversal in which there is the expectation of nurturance, support, and reassurance from their children. The parent becomes frustrated and enraged when the children themselves show dependency needs and seek attention.

The security, dependency, and nurturance needs of children are so strong that they continue to lodge these needs in the relationship with abusing parents. Surprisingly, victims of abuse often want to return to the abusing parent. It is not uncommon for a severely beaten child to say "he's a good father when he doesn't hit me." Such statements taken together with the parents' remorse and promise "never to do it again" can convincingly encourage health professionals to reunite the abused child with the family. This decision can pose dangers to the child since the likelihood of repetition, if the parents do not receive psychological help, is great. Group therapy with the parents and counseling by public health nurses have proved effective in curbing child abuse in many cases (Savino and Sanders, 1973). In any event, a careful evaluation of the family should be completed before plans are finalized for the abused child.

SUMMARY

The family furnishes the context for personality development. Most of each person's life cycle is spent as a participant in a family, either of origin or procreation. The basic family unit of mother, father, and offspring is called a nuclear family. It has four primary functions: sexual, economic, reproductive, and educational. Family life in modern industrial societies has been shaped by the affluence of our technological age, the widespread use of effective means of birth control, and the marked mobility of the population. These factors have led to more options in life style and at the same time made marriage both less stable and more necessary. Mobility limits the depth of friendships and makes the intimacy of marriage more sought-after.

The family developmental cycle is marked by the stages of development of the children. They are the focus of the first 20 years of the married couple's life together. With lengthened life expectancy, more years will actually be spent by the couple together without the children.

Marriage is viewed by all societies as an important institution, largely owing to its child-bearing function. Three elements that characterize the marital relationship are cohabitation, sexual relations, and mutual support. The early task of the couple is to devise rules of working together that are mutually satisfying. Whether they develop a segregated or joint relationship will depend to a great extent on the closeness of ties to their families of origin and childhood friends. Occasional marital conflict is inevitable, and the success of every marriage depends on the couple's ability to develop mechanisms for resolving conflicts.

The sexual adjustment of a couple depends on numerous factors, among these the strength and security of their affection for each other, attitudes learned as children, and a willingness to learn and to communicate openly. The major types of sexual dysfunction are impotence and premature ejaculation in men and frigidity in women.

Family planning is universal and has been with us as long as man knows. Today there are several highly effective means of birth control.

Pregnancy is usually a time of well-being for the woman, although ambivalent feelings are normal and usual. The birth of the infant is marked by relief and delight along with the mobilization of fears and often some anger. The presence of the newborn forces major shifts in the couple's relationship. Feelings of deprivation and resentment by one or the other parent are frequent.

Studies of monkeys and of different human societies indicate that up to the present nurturance of the young has always been provided by women. Current trends in parenting may change this, but who will be the primary nurturer in the future and how such nurturance will be provided are questions only time will answer.

There have been two major approaches in child-rearing research —one focusing on specific practices and their effect on development and the other examining the general orientation of the parents in their child-rearing. Although child-rearing has been the object of much investigation, research has thus far failed to specify consistent relationships between child-rearing practices and personality outcomes. Ordinal position has an important influence on a person's development but generalizations are difficult to make because other factors are intertwined.

The incidence of child abuse is on the rise. In spite of the wish of children to return to the abusing parent we must recognize the dangers to the child if psychological treatment for the parents is not part of the planning.

SUGGESTED READINGS

Anthony, E. J., and Benedek, T., eds. *Parenthood: its psychology and psychopathology.* New York: Little Brown, 1970.

Beach, R. A., ed. *Sex and behavior.* New York: Wiley, 1965.

Bell, N. W., and Vogel, E. F. *A modern introduction to the family.* Rev. ed. New York: Free Press, 1968.

Bell, R. R. *Studies in marriage and the family.* 2nd ed. New York: Crowell, 1973.

Brody, S. *Patterns of mothering.* New York: International Universities Press, 1956.

Burgess, E. W., Locke, H. J., and Thomas, M. M. *The family: from traditional to companionship.* 4th ed. New York: Van Nostrand, 1971.

Duvall, E. M. *Family development.* 4th ed. New York: Lippincott, 1971.

Kaplan, H. S. *The new sex therapy.* New York, Brunner/Mazel, 1974.

Lloyd, C. W., ed. *Human reproduction and sexual behavior.* Philadelphia: Lea and Febiger, 1964.

McBride, A. B. *The growth and development of mothers.* New York: Harper & Row, 1973.

Richardson, S. A., and Guttmacher, A. F., eds. *Childbearing: its social and psychological aspects.* Baltimore: Williams and Wilkins, 1967.

Sears, R. R., Maccoby, E., and Levin, H. *Patterns of child rearing.* Evanston, Ill.: Row Peterson, 1957.

Chapter *6*

Aging

AT EACH STAGE of development, time has a unique meaning. To the child the privileges of adulthood seem far off, if not beyond reach. The adolescent, who must choose a career and make other life decisions, feels time is running out. The young adult feels under pressure to live out his fantasies before it is "too late." In middle age one senses that there is little time left for change if life hasn't fulfilled one's expectations. In all these stages we feel the pressure of time. We respond to this pressure by developing new hopes and aspirations for the next stage of life. For the aged, however, the future is rapidly vanishing, and this produces a fundamentally different perspective. While many elderly people relish the wisdom and the freedom from mundane pressures and demands that this stage brings, they also feel that the future is lost to them, and this change in perception can give rise to major psychological crises.

The process of adjustment to aging is very complex. True, there are natural degenerative processes at work, but these vary on an individual basis. Most of the aged who are physically healthy show vital signs which should not produce significant impairment of functioning. There is, however, a confluence of emotional, social, and physical factors that feed and exacerbate each other, producing impairment for many of the elderly. The aged experience many losses that require reintegration of goals, self-image, and life role. Disengagement from work, lessening of family responsibilities, and the death of family members and friends are all difficult, real crises that tax a person's adjustment mechanisms.

To what extent can the "decline" of old age be markedly reduced or eliminated by understanding, accepting, and treating old age as another psychological crisis period in development (like childhood, adolescence, and adulthood)? What role can social institutions play in fostering positive and productive functioning of the aged? What are the physical, social, and emotional needs and problems of the aged? What is the potential of the aged for continued psychological growth and development? These questions raise issues vital to an understanding of the psychology of aging, and we will explore them in this chapter.

THE NATURE OF AGING

Aging is a process that begins at the moment of conception and ends in death. The organism loses some of its capacity for renewal and longevity with each irreversible change that accompanies growth and development. Most of the changes are very subtle; some of them, however, are easily recognized by all of us. The loss of elastic fibrils in the skin can be seen in the slow progression from the infant's resilient skin to the diminished elasticity of middle age to the wrinkling of old age. At the same time, there is no known time limit on the functioning of any human organ or organ system. The loss of elasticity of the skin makes for greater vulnerability to abrasions and lacerations, but it does not constitute an end to the functional capacity of the skin or the organism it covers. Therefore, we need to make a distinction between aging, which is a continuous process, and old age, the last part of the life cycle.

When is one aged or old? Chronological age does not suffice, as it does at the beginning of the life cycle, to define the last period of life. The point in time when the process of aging limits the organism's functional capacity in a clearly defined way should be labeled old age. This point varies widely with individuals. Some people are aged in their 40s; others do not show evidence of organismic changes even when they are 80. The complex of physical and psychological changes that characterize old age are dependent on the individual's genetic makeup, his life style (e.g., whether he smokes), his life experiences, and his social milieu. Despite such variation, however, it has become customary to define anything over 65 years as belonging to old age. We need to emphasize, though, that this is based more on social factors such as current age of retirement than on the complex of social, psychological, and physical factors that really determine this period of life.

The group 65 years and older is becoming an increasingly significant proportion of our population. In 1900, 4% of the total U.S. population was 65 years of age and over. In 1970, this age group was 10% of the population, amounting to approximately 20 million individuals. Given the older person's greater vulnerability to illness, it is not surprising that about one-third of our hospitalized population consists of persons 65 years and over (Wolf, 1963). Therefore, the problems of aging are the problems of one out of every three patients cared for in hospitals. In nursing homes the majority of patients are 65 and over, as may soon be the case in state mental hospitals.

THE HEALTHY AGED

To speak of the healthy aged is somewhat of a paradox since an organism that has passed into the last phase of the life cycle has an increasing number of organ impairments. At the same time, it is important to recognize that many in the over-65 group show little evidence of what would be classified as illness. In a study (Birren, 1966) that specifically selected healthy aged (mean age 79.8) who were not showing gross signs of organ impairments, an extensive evaluation of their physiological and psychological status showed that such important parameters as cerebral blood flow, cerebral oxygen consumption, and psychological functioning were equivalent to those of normal men in their 20s. Thus, old age does not necessarily mean diminished cerebral function. This finding is crucial, because of all the accompaniments of age diminished cerebral function, whether due to physical or emotional causes, creates the greatest hardship. If the mind is sharp, age does not have to be a limiting condition.

Even though good health is a requisite to satisfaction in life at any phase, alone it is not sufficient. What personal and social factors make for a satisfying life for the physically healthy over 65?

Goldfarb (1961) lists three factors which, with good health, make for high morale: relative affluence, high educational level, and secure social status. Relative affluence frees the aged from fears of being an economic burden on relatives and also assures better services, such as medical and dental care and housing. The concern that many people express for an adequate income in old age, whether from savings, retirement benefits, or investments, indeed has a real basis. The greater the financial security and relative affluence in old age, the higher appears to be the individual's morale. And this factor, though no doubt always important, plays an increasing role today, not only because of increased longevity, but also because of social and family characteristics. When the aged are integrated members of an extended family in which they have a respected role even after they can no longer earn money, income is not crucial. However, in today's mobile nuclear family, the aged are dependent almost exclusively on their own sources of income, and this income must purchase many types of services formerly supplied by the family, e.g., shelter, food, care, and perhaps home nursing. Being able to afford what are crucial services makes the difference between feeling hopeless and helpless and having a sense of mastery and control over the environment.

The second factor contributing to high morale is education. The better the person's education, the better the person can cope with the problems of old age. Education permits development of interests and pleasures that are relatively independent of age and that often are more accessible to the older person, who is no longer under the intense pressure to achieve that younger people feel. The ability to enjoy esthetic experiences in art, literature, music, and the theater is limited only by education, not by age. Further, education often provides skills that permit a continuation of productive work as far into old age as the individual wishes. Physicians, lawyers, nurses, educators, and politicians are not forced to retire at the age of 65. They may find that full-time work is no longer to their liking but that they need to continue their lifetime occupation on a part-time basis in order to maintain their feeling of self-worth and gratification. Education permits such choices and, perhaps most important, the opportunity to choose one's life style instead of having it imposed.

Social status provides another element of security, the security that comes from knowing that one has a place in society. Unfortunately the indigent and the elderly frequently feel that they are social outcasts, of no use and nothing but a burden. As we have already noted, the recently evolved mobile nuclear family provides no status or place for the elderly. The status of the elderly is now more dependent on their functioning in the wider social context. An individual who has been and remains active in local organizations maintains a sense of perspective and self-worth, receiving from others the all-important confirmation that he or she belongs, whether as a member of the local Democratic or Republican party organization, the Knights of Columbus, the Rotarians, or the League of Women Voters.

However, to control the factors that Goldfarb cites—financial security, education, social position—requires planning early in the life cycle. They are realizable for those who have laid the groundwork in the first three decades of their life.

PHYSICAL PROBLEMS

The physical illnesses that befall the aged cannot, of course, be dealt with in detail here. However, we will look at some of the special features of physical problems as they affect emotional well-being and the developmental process of aging.

In old age the organism's capacity to tolerate stress is diminished, and deleterious changes are rapid when illnesses are not quickly overcome. For instance, a fall that results in a femoral fracture may mean invalidism for an elderly person because the strength to mobilize and withstand the pain of using the injured limb is not available. Thirty years earlier the fracture would have meant temporary immobilization, a short period on crutches, and finally complete recovery. In elderly patients, the body is not resilient and does not readily compensate for the injury by using other body parts (in this case the arms and upper body to maneuver on crutches). Often the elderly person, unlike someone younger, cannot force himself to the limits of endurance necessary for complete recovery. The will to live is an all-important and complex psychological phenomenon which varies greatly in different individuals. Many of the aged, feeling that they have less to live for, lose the will to fight for their lives.

Another physical problem of old age is the system-wide nature of many illnesses, which begin to evolve at age 30 or earlier but have their major symptomatic appearance with old age. The most pervasive of the systemic illnesses are those affecting the cardiovascular system. Arteriosclerosis and atherosclerosis are diseases par excellence of old age: hardening of the arteries and the formation of plaques in the arteries are processes that involve decades of change.

By the time the vascular process has proceeded to gross symptomatology the individual is usually in his 50s or 60s, or older. Further, the vascular process is most commonly a general one, that is, most vessels are affected to some extent; therefore the consequences of arteriolar obstruction—ischemia and tissue death—are often present in more than one organ system. For instance, an elderly patient may have as his major presenting symptom coronary artery disease and simultaneously have marginally patent femoral arteries and diminished cerebral blood flow due to narrowing of cerebral blood vessels. When this patient has a coronary infarct with a drop in blood pressure, not only will his heart muscle be damaged but very likely the oxygen supply to the brain will diminish to the point that some tissue loss occurs. The patient will not only have to recover from a heart attack but will also show evidence of organic brain disease, with possible confusion, poor memory, disorientation, and labile affect. Furthermore, since the treatment for the acute phase of the coronary is bed rest, the poor blood circulation in the legs will make bed sores a serious likelihood, and the need for further care will develop.

We should make clear that an individual who suffers coronary artery occlusion in his 40s is not likely to have the advanced, generalized vascular disease depicted for the elderly. An infarct in middle age has a much better prognosis and is unlikely to result in permanent organic brain damage, although if shock is prolonged some acute (reversible) brain damage may result. Many people have suffered serious myocardial infarcts (representing arteriolar disease), recovered, and proceeded to advance their careers. Lyndon Johnson suffered a very serious infarct several years before he became President.

SOCIAL AND FAMILY PROBLEMS

Social and family factors are the major determinants of a relatively happy or unhappy old age. As a society we have not yet arrived at a satisfactory means of integrating the elderly into the larger social process, and individuals must search out their own solutions with little assistance from formal social institutions. The situation is obviously changing. *Geriatrics* (the treatment of the aged) and *gerontology* (the study of the aged) are fields that are attracting dedicated researchers and practitioners.

We have already spoken of the percentage change in the number of persons reaching old age, but let us examine more closely the significance of this change. At the turn of the century, when life expectancy was 50 years, a man could be expected to continue at his work until shortly before he died. Retirement, except for an insignificant few, was not a reality. This meant that a man was performing his occupation, be it skilled or unskilled, throughout his adult life. His work was a contribution to society and a necessity to his family.

What happened when such a man—for example, a grocer suffered a seriously limiting illness such as a hemiplegia (paralysis of half the body) due to cerebral embolism (a stroke)? His invalidism was not likely to be prolonged; in the absence of antibiotics, the vulnerable organism sooner or later succumbed to an intercurrent infection such as pneumonitis. He probably did not take up a hospital bed, his family considering his care their natural responsibility. And, practically speaking, such care was not excessively difficult since in the radius of a few blocks there usually lived near-relatives as well as grown-up children who could help out as needed. In addition, the family business was likely to be maintained by one of the sons, perhaps the oldest, who would continue it after his father's death.

What would happen in similar circumstances today? Our modern grocer sells his store when he is 60. Competition from the larger stores plus the long hours make it increasingly difficult to continue. None of his three sons is interested in taking over the store—having been encouraged to go to college or learn a technical speciality in order to work shorter hours and achieve greater financial security. Two of the sons and a daughter are married, and the youngest son is away at college. The oldest son and the daughter are living with their families in distant cities, and the remaining married son lives in a suburb an hour's drive from his parents.

A year after selling his store, the grocer has a stroke. He is rushed to the hospital in a deep coma and requires intravenous vasopressors to maintain his blood pressure for 48 hours. With good care, and after a brief bout of pneumonia that responds well to antibiotics, he recovers. After three weeks, having received "optimal benefits from hospitalization," he is discharged. His wife wants him home and he wants to be there. After several months at home, however, she shows signs of increasing fatigue and stress, and he is depressed and quarrelsome. The children want to help but all live too far away, and to have their parents live with them is not to their or their parents' liking. What is to be done? If the wife's strength was not under constant stress—that is, if other family members could without extraordinary effort help out in the care of the now invalid husband and father—she might not be overwhelmed. But the family structure does not provide for a situation of prolonged dependency of parents or their integration as useful members. If the wife can no longer cope, then one of the extended care facilities or nursing homes must be sought out. They are expensive, however, and the involved application for government assistance through Medicare will need to be attempted. Leaving the home for a caretaking institution is often better than seeing oneself as too heavy a burden on a loved one, yet it cannot be an optimal solution when the very basis of emotional well-being, intimate relationships with significant others, is disrupted.

PSYCHOLOGICAL ASPECTS OF AGING
Society's Expectations

Aging and *decline* are terms often used synonymously, even though the elderly have frequently produced artistic, political, and social achievements. Picasso, Churchill, and Schweitzer, to name only three renowned examples, continued to make major contributions when they attained old age. Does society's expectation of decline actually contribute to the decline of the elderly? Many of the elderly fulfill society's expectations by interpreting aches, pains, and fatigue as evidence of the expected decline and as a signal to quit. Yet the same individuals might well have interpreted the same discomforts as merely transient a few years earlier in life.

A large number of the elderly participate actively in life. Labor statistics for 1971 showed that more than three million people over 65 were employed full- and part-time. Many more of the elderly work at unreported jobs. As the number of elderly increase to a projected 25% of the population by the year 2000, they will become more vocal in their demands for active productive functioning. At the same time, gerontology research will hasten a change in scientific concepts of the aged. Considerable evidence is already emerging about the more productive and hopeful side of the last phase of life.

Life Review

According to Butler (1964) the aged have a universal need to review their lives. Reminiscing, nostalgia, and story-telling, so frequently observed in the aged, are part of this process. The life review occurs at other landmarks of development—as in adolescence and middle age—but the focus is on the particular problems of those stages. The aged, who are aware of time running out, place great emphasis on assessing their achievements, taking pride in accomplishments, and actually evaluating the meaning and value of life. For many, the life review can result in charting new courses for the rest of life, with a concentration on activities previously neglected or left undeveloped. The here-and-now focus of old age can open up unexplored areas of sensory awareness and feeling. Many elderly people enthusiastically pursue creative and artistic experiences not only as therapeutic diversions but as serious involvements. If a person has a propensity toward guilt and depression the life review can have very negative effects, resulting in despair and withdrawal from life. However, when the elderly person can accept the aging process and openly work through the life review, he can free himself for a productive and gratifying period of life.

Disengagement and Aging

Cumming (1964) has presented a "disengagement" theory to account for the behavioral changes in the process of aging.

Disengagement refers to "a mutual withdrawal or disengagement" between the aging person and others in the social system to which he belongs—"a withdrawal initiated by the individual himself or by others in the system." The onset of disengagement occurs in middle age when the individual perceives the reality of mortality and death. This realization results in the reevaluation of life goals, which in turn produces the rejection of some activities and concentration on others.

One of the most significant characterstics of the disengagement period is the movement away from achievement. Achievement requires a strong sense of a future, a sense that aging works against. The abandonment or narrowing of the achievement motive is likely to cause a crisis, especially in societies where achievement is emphasized and nonachievement is associated with failure. In an achieving society, society itself disengages old people, because its emphasis on youth, production, and competition tends to squeeze them out.

Cumming talks about the freedom that comes with disengagement and the task of coping with this freedom. How a person responds to it will be determined largely by his personality. The outgoing person with initiative will be able to shift and seek new goals in activities consonant with his changed view of life. The more passive, withdrawn individual may be at a total loss when current activities are abandoned.

Levin (1964) questions whether "disengagement is a normal process of narrowing one's energies or an aspect of depression." It is important to evaluate the quality of a person's behavior to differentiate between productive disengagement, which focuses energy on a limited number of activities, and depression, which withdraws energy from most activity.

Behavioristic View of Aging

Behaviorism looks at behavior in terms of discrete stimuli and responses that are bound together by reinforcing events (a detailed exposition of behaviorism is presented in Chapter 10). Applying this theory to the aged, Lindsley (1964) explains that the aged are neglected or avoided because they do not provide social reinforcers for others owing to their behavioral deficits. "Deficit" here means the lack of positive behaviors. Young children, in contrast to the aged, smile, caress, and offer hopes for future gratifications (social reinforcers) to their caretakers. Even young people with illnesses and disabilities can provide some of these reinforcers. Lindsley is obviously referring to the very old and those aged who are infirm or disabled. The large number of relatively healthy aged are certainly capable of a variety of social reinforcers such as attention to and concern for others, socially oriented endeavors, etc. Also, in societies in which the aged are revered, the ability to manifest socially desirable behavior has little bearing on the status of the aged. Therefore, the behavioristic view can only partially account for the negative attitudes toward the aged in our society. For a more complete explanation we must turn to the values and prejudices of society.

Sexuality

Old people are interested in sex, have sexual feelings, and need sexual outlets. Many people like to think of the elderly as completely sexless, devoid of any interest in the subject, yet the continued sexual needs of the elderly should not come as any great surprise. Sexuality is a psychological as well as a physiological need. A person's interest in sex is conditioned early in life, and there is no reason why this interest should not continue throughout life. It is an indication of the prejudice against and denigration of the elderly that qualities of masculinity, femininity, and vigor prized in the young are viewed as shameful when they appear in old people. The "dirty old man" concept reflects this negative view. As in other areas, many of the elderly absorb society's expectations and consequently feel guilty about their sexual urges. Institutions, with their segregation, careful supervision, and discouragement of sexual practices, contribute to the problem. This is unfortunate because it deprives the elderly of an important source of social and physical stimulation.

Men and women of all ages are capable of sexual arousal and orgasm. Masters and Johnson (1966) have emphasized the importance of consistency of sexual behavior for the maintenance of sexual activity in old age. The person who had a consistently active sex life through the early adult years will have a greater capacity for sexual activity in old age. This is contrary to the popular myth of the person using himself up through an early high level of sexual activity.

The male sexual decline is gradual, with the decrement reflected in vigor and intensity of the experience rather than the capacity for sexual activity. Women exhibit no significant sexual decline until about age 60, and even then it is not marked. As Botwinick (1973) states: "For a large number of elderly men and women, sexual relations end only with death." Barring physical problems that may cause impotence, men into their 90s can maintain an erection, though it may take longer and require greater foreplay to achieve. In the later years as in earlier years, male impotence is often caused by anxiety and fear of impotence. While younger men frequently turn to psychotherapy or counseling for help, the elderly will shy away from such help because of guilt—"I'm not supposed to be doing that anyway—what will the doctor think?" Other elderly men interpret their impotence as the expected "decline" and therefore resign themselves to their misfortune.

Because of their often older husband's withdrawal from sexual activity, women cease having sexual intercourse about 10 years earlier than men (Botwinick, 1973). The problem of guilt and shame with regard to sexual feelings is compounded by the fact that women outlive men, making the number of elderly women greater than men. There are just not enough men to go around, and sexual activity outside of marriage is still taboo for most women now comprising the elderly population.

Some authors have suggested that, considering the incidence of masturbation in childhood, adolescence, and old age, it may be the most frequent human sexual experience. Yet masturbation is still shrouded in taboos and associated with infantile behavior. Many institutional settings for the aged chastise the elderly for practicing masturbation and discourage sexuality by denying opportunities for privacy. But the accumulated evidence shows masturbation to be not only a harmless act, but a very important and beneficial one. Especially for the aged, who may have few opportunities for heterosexual relationships, masturbation may be the only possible sexual outlet.

LONGEVITY

Is a person's biological makeup the sole determinant of how long he will live? That heredity undoubtedly has a big role in longevity is attested to by studies of twins and children of long-lived parents; we also find that young mothers have children that live longer, and that women outlive men (Botwinick, 1973). At the same time there are compelling findings suggesting psychosocial influences on longevity.

A case in point is a study of 149 veterans of the Spanish-American War who were an average of 82 years old (Rose, 1964). On the whole these elderly survivors had greater intelligence, more education, and a higher occupational status than the general population of their generation. These three factors, which are interrelated, may have little direct effect but may contribute to higher status and a generally more favorable environment, which enhances survival. Most of the war-veteran survivors came from large families (characteristic of the early part of the century). There was a high percentage of firstborn among these survivors, and many of the other survivors tended to be high in the birth order of their families. The longevity factor inferred here by the researcher was the greater attention and energy supplied by the mother before a large family depleted her. Compared with their peers, a higher percentage of the subjects were married and living with their spouses—conditions that enrich the social environment of the elderly person—and more had worked beyond retirement age, reflecting their greater involvement in life activities.

Other studies of longevity have indicated that impulsive people do not live as long as reflective people and that those actively involved in work and life survive longer. A study of aged psychologists showed them to be unusually vigorous, content, and actively involved in work and other interests (Aisenberg, 1964). Satisfaction in work is one of the best predictors of longevity according to Botwinick (1973). The elderly who maintain meaningful roles live longer. "Meaningful" is the key word here; what is meaningful depends on one's individual outlook. It does not have to be work in the formal sense; for some, active participation in an organization can be meaningful and absorbing, while others may immerse themselves in a hobby or other interest area.

"Time perspective" has been cited as another possible determinant of longevity (Kastenbaum, 1964a). A person whose time perspective extends into past and future with a planned concept of his life may see a variety of satisfactions in life that he can "live for." Also, an extended time perspective does not require immediate gratification for contentment. On the other hand, some institutionalized patients with a narrow time perspective may find sufficient gratification in the structure of their day-to-day existence. But for a large number of people who have a limited time perspective and whose personal initiative is waning, life can seem dreary and purposeless—a state of mind not conducive to longevity.

Kastenbaum has challenged the validity of isolated variables in explaining longevity. He cites evidence showing longevity for persons of relatively low intelligence, poor education, and low employment status. Even some retardates in institutions survive to ripe old ages. He, therefore, phrases the question for longevity research as follows: "How does a person of a certain kind of makeup behave in such a way as to prolong or shorten his life span? Under what conditions, for example, does the bright, high status person survive, and under what conditions perish?" (p. 93).

MENTAL DISORDERS

Individuals over 65 are subject to the full spectrum of mental disorders. There are two disorders however that are especially frequent in the elderly: chronic and acute organic brain syndrome, and depression. How frequent they are is hard to say. Certainly old age does not necessarily mean mental disorder, but mental disorders are known to be most frequent in the elderly. Although the elderly comprise only 10% of the U.S. population, in 1965 they accounted for 25% of mental hospital admissions.

Organic Brain Syndrome

Organic brain syndrome, discussed in detail in Chapter 16, refers to the symptoms that characterize the loss of 'brain tissue. These symptoms, usually found together, are: intellectual impairment (lessening of the ability to comprehend, calculate, and learn); impairment of orientation (not knowing what day it is, to whom one is talking, where one is); impairment of memory; impairment of judgment (going outside on a cold day in pajamas); and lability of affect (marked alterations of mood). The symptoms may be mild or severe depending upon the amount of brain tissue loss.

Chronic brain syndrome is permanent, that is, the brain tissue loss is irreversible. In the aged it is caused primarily by two processes. The first is the vascular disease already mentioned, arteriosclerosis. The hardening of the arteries makes them fragile, leading to hemorrhage when they rupture, and more prone to being blocked by small blood clots. The outcome is loss of blood supply to part of the brain, most often throughout the cerebral hemispheres and on a microscopic level. The second major cause of the chronic organic brain syndrome is tissue breakdown, a process called senile brain disease. The cause of the brain tissue loss is not known, but it appears to be a genetically determined aging process, since the age of onset is similar in families from generation to generation.

Acute brain syndrome is frequently seen in the elderly, and its symptoms need to be clearly recognized. The symptoms are the same as for chronic brain syndrome but the condition is reversible. That is, it represents a temporary state of disorientation and impairment in judgment and in intellectual function. There are numerous possible causes of an acute brain syndrome. It may result from a special susceptibility to a medication (e.g., barbiturate), or it may be a postoperative sequel to anesthesia or transient hypotension. What is important is to recognize the likelihood of temporary confusion and poor comprehension in an aged patient, seek out its causes, and work toward its amelioration. For instance, seeing close relatives or a trusted friend can often help reorient the confused patient and reduce his anxiety enormously, particularly in the postoperative period when transient disorientation can be anticipated and present serious problems (e.g., IVs and catheters torn out, restraints fought).

Depression

Depression is probably the most common disturbance of old age. Fortunately, depression is usually self-limited, although in an appreciable number of cases some treatment becomes necessary. In addition to feeling depressed, sad, or hopeless (depending on severity), the depressed elderly person may suffer from insomnia, fatigue, and lack of energy. Feelings of low self-esteem are prominent. Some degree of depression often accompanies physical illnesses. Each illness seems to say to the elderly person that he is less and less able to care for himself. Illness is seen not only as life-threatening but also as threatening the capacity for independent existence. The dependency that is part of being ill and cared for sets off a more general fear of dependence. The depression that results is often expressed in marked irritability and an unwillingness to participate in hospital and home routines. If the depression is recognized and treated, the irritability and lack of cooperation dissipate and a return to health becomes more likely.

Depression in the aged often mimics senility. The preoccupation with morbid thoughts and guilt for misdeeds supposedly committed many years earlier leads to apathy, withdrawal, and inattentiveness, and these are interpreted as the forgetfulness and lack of interest of senility. Since mental deterioration fits in with the stereotype of the aging process, the physician, family, and patient accept this diagnosis on superficial evidence (though at times even sophisticated tests cannot differentiate depression from organic brain damage). Only when treatment has lifted the depression is it discovered that most or all of the intellectual impairment has been due to depression.

In the severely depressed, suicide is a concern. Suicidal ideas are common even with moderate depression, but fortunately they are acted out relatively infrequently. Among the elderly, however, such preoccupations must be taken very seriously, particularly among males. The suicide rate for white males in their 60s is seven times that for white females. The suicide rate for white females and for nonwhites of both sexes remains almost the same as in earlier decades. The highest suicide rate is among males age 85 and over. Suicide attempts in the over-65 group are usually successful, and there is a good chance that an attempt which fails will be followed by a second successful attempt within two years. Young people often make suicide threats as pleas for attention, sympathy, and help; the elderly more frequently make a determined effort to end life. Suicidal ideas are not always evident in clinically manifest depression or despair—"he didn't seem unhappy or depressed." Therefore even apparently casual references to suicide by the aged, even when depression is not overt, should be taken seriously.

It appears that the life circumstances and personality characteristics of men make them more susceptible to the severer forms of depression. It is certainly true that men rely more on their extra-familial work performance for their self-esteem, sense of identity, and fulfillment, factors that undergo severe stress on retirement. Women's self-esteem has traditionally been more closely related to the internal functioning of the family and the level of gratification they experience in their relationships with others. In fact, a woman's role may actually increase in some respects during the retirement years as there is more involvement with husband, grandchildren, and family. Nonetheless, one would think that the loneliness which is more often the lot of women in old age (since their husbands are likely to die nine years before they do) would take its toll. Perhaps it does, but for some reason women seem to cope with or endure depression better than men and are not likely to resort to suicide.

CARE OF THE AGED
Home Care and Independence

Changing the focus of one's life is a difficult experience at any age. Young people frequently go through periods of anxiety when a significant move occurs, and moving to a new city, or from an apartment into a house, can cause great trepidation. For all of us, maintaining the sameness of the immediate environment gives a sense of familiarity, predictability, and security.

Most old people prefer living at home. The fact that more than 60 % of older people are owners of their own homes indicates that a large number of the elderly are used to being autonomous and independent. For the person who has been independent and self-sufficient, institutional care and hospitalization pose great threats. These feelings are not a reaction peculiar to old age; they reflect the universal need for security and the fear of change. Add to this the reputation of nursing homes and hospitals as the last way-station before death, and the anxieties of the elderly become even more comprehensible.

Choosing where one lives is an important factor in personal satisfaction and constructive living. However, there are circumstances that make institutional care necessary. Living alone requires financial means. Many old people who do not have adequate pensions or other benefits exist at sub-subsistence levels, and the incidence of malnutrition among the aged is very high. A person's basic mental faculties must be intact if he is to survive on his own: he must be oriented to his environment, he must be able to walk, take care of his sanitary needs, manage practical and financial affairs, have access to others when assistance is needed, and have some social outlets.

Some of these factors are less important when the elderly person is living with another person or in a family. Even when there are severe disabilities, home care may be possible if others are able and willing to assist the elderly person to meet his needs. Home care of the elderly does require the availability of medical attention on short notice, and unfortunately such attention is increasingly difficult to obtain. For the future, the expansion of home care for the elderly will probably be dependent on the expansion of nursing services: more public health nurses, visiting nurses, practical nurses, home health aides, paraprofessionals, private practices in nursing, as well as community health programs.

Institutionalization

The decision to institutionalize an elderly person is usually just as difficult an experience for the family as for the elderly person himself. Great tortures of guilt are common, and sometimes these guilt feelings have a basis in fact—when, for example, a parent is not seriously disabled and the family has little reason to resort to institutionalization other than concern for personal comfort and the prejudices of our society against the elderly. Today much of counseling about the problem of institutionalization is directed toward relieving the family's guilt. However, it may be more beneficial to help and encourage a family to accept the care of an elderly person when this is feasible. Attachments to parents run very deep, and when elderly parents are institutionalized without good reasons the resulting guilt can have a disruptive effect on individuals and the family for many years.

There are many instances in which the opposite occurs. Guilt and the sense of obligation sometime lead a family to reject institutionalization of a severely impaired elderly person even though the family is not really able to provide adequate care. Here the issue is not the desire to care for an elderly person but rather the wisdom of the decision. Both adults may work, leaving the elderly person without care for most of the day. Disorientation, incontinence, and severe medical problems may disrupt and damage family life, especially when small children are present. An unstable and delicate relationship between husband and wife can be stretched to the breaking point by the presence of an elderly person. Space limitations and the emotional climate of the home, as well as the relationship between the elderly person and the family members, must also be evaluated. A decision to maintain an elderly person at home should not rest solely on personal and family considerations. The presence or lack of community resources is vital to such a decision. The existence of community recreation programs for the aged, a day hospital, and a well-staffed community mental health center can relieve the family of many burdens, making home care feasible.

Institutional Placement. Except when the elderly person is irrational or disoriented, placement in an institution should not be an arbitrary or externally imposed decision. Discussions should be held and the elderly person should participate in the decision-making process. It is important that the elderly have the feeling of still being part of the family and community. This can be accomplished through arrangements for frequent visits, including brief periods (perhaps occasional weekends) in which the elderly person returns to the family. Butler (1963) recommends keeping open the possibility of the aged person's ultimate return to the community so that placement is not viewed as the final change before death. The fear that elderly people have concerning nursing homes may be justified. Statistics show that one-third of the residents of nursing homes die within the first year, another third within the second year, and that the average residence before death is 1.1 years (Butler and Lewis, 1973). How much of the early demise of patients in nursing homes is due to the anxiety, sense of helplessness, and loss of will to live is difficult to estimate.

Social Services.   The elderly need to be put in touch with social agencies that can provide services to them. This is an area in which nurses can be extremely helpful. Making the elderly aware of community agencies that provide counseling, medical, social, and recreational services can have a significant impact on their lives. Many of the elderly are not even aware of eligibility for benefits (Medicare, Medicaid, Social Security) and do not know how to make applications or inquiries.

Safety.   Accidents are an ever-present danger for the elderly. The majority of all accidents occur to people over 65, and accidents are the third leading cause of death among the elderly. It is necessary to advise families on the possibilities of accident. Homes in which elderly people reside should be carefully assessed in terms of the capabilities of the aged person and the potential hazards within the home. Dangers of falling, slipping, burning, and accidental poisoning need particularly careful scrutiny.

PSYCHOLOGICAL TREATMENT

In spite of the severe conflicts and stresses of old age, the aged rarely show up at community mental health centers or the offices of private psychotherapists. Less than 2% of private psychiatric time is given to the aged (Butler and Lewis, 1973). Prejudice and attitudes toward aging provide some explanation for the insufficient attention to the psychological problems of the aged. Psychotherapists are reluctant to treat the elderly because they anticipate poor results, assuming that the elderly are so set in their ways that change is difficult if not impossible. Actually, since so few of the elderly get into psychological treatment there is little evidence for their supposed unresponsiveness to psychotherapy. Old people themselves are reluctant to seek psychological treatment because they have adopted society's attitude that it is too late to change or that there is no point since they have so little time to live. Kastenbaum (1964b) rightfully criticizes these assumptions. In fact, we do not know how long any patient is going to live. If he lives 15 or 20 years rather than 10 or 5 is help more justified? The function of the helping professions is to help those who seek services, not to determine who should be helped.

There is high status attached to treating young, upwardly mobile, "productive" patients, and psychotherapists who do treat the elderly have a low status (Butler, 1963). Because of our attitudes and values the motives of a therapist who treats or specializes in the aged are suspect, according to Butler. Does the therapist have some morbid preoccupation with death and aging? Is he escaping from the more competitive areas of practice? Butler suggests that positive motives can lead to interest in treating the aged. These include an awareness of the need for such treatment, a positive experience and fond memories of one's parents or grandparents, the rewards of helping a neglected group, and the professional gratification in opening new vistas to people during a difficult period of life adjustment.

Kastenbaum (1964b) sees another motive behind the aversion to treatment of the elderly—fear of the aging process. In dealing with medical or psychological problems of the young, a practitioner can maintain some distance from the disorder he is treating. In the face of the adversity of others we all use varying degrees of denial—"it won't happen to me." Aging, however, is an inevitable process in which we all see our own destiny. Witnessing the decline or disintegration of an elderly person evokes the fear of one's own future. It is not surprising, therefore, to find the aged shunned by many practitioners including nurses, physicians, and psychotherapists.

In the light of this discussion, it is important for the nurse to reflect on her attitudes and feelings about the aged as well as thoughts about her own present and future aging process. To aid you in this task we have designed the Self-awareness Exercise (opposite).

SELF-AWARENESS EXERCISE

The Aging Process

The purpose of this exercise is to bring you to a more personal awareness of the aging process through an examination of possible changes that will occur as you pass through the years of the life cycle.

Task.   *Describe a typical day in your life at ages 30, 40, 50, 60, and 70. In addition to describing the events of the day at each age, from arising in the morning until bedtime, make reference to the following topics:*

1. Attitude toward and goals related to work.

2. Interests and leisure-time activities.

3. Attitudes toward and relationships with people under age 30. How would you project their attitudes toward you?

4. Attitudes toward and relationships with your own children and grandchildren (or the children and grandchildren of friends or relatives if you do not plan to have children yourself).

5. Attitude toward retirement.

6. Involvement in political, social, and professional issues.

7. Major health concerns and precautions.

8. Feelings about physical appearance.

Evaluation.   *What are the significant changes that you portray from age 30 to 70? Is there an age at which the changes appear to be more striking? Which of the descriptions conform to the usual characterizations of the various age periods, and which are different? Do people of the different ages whom you currently know seem to display the characteristics you project for yourself? Has this exercise had any impact on your views of the aging process? Specify.*

SUMMARY

The aging process begins at birth and ends in death. The physiological changes that occur make the aged less resilient and more susceptible to diseases, particularly those affecting the cardio-vascular system. However, for the relatively healthy aged there is no biological reason for a decline in psychological functioning. Many of the psychological problems of the aged are created by society. The negative views of society become a self-fulfilling prophecy, so that the aged quickly interpret aches, pains, and minor illnesses as indications of the expected decline and then behave accordingly.

The need to review one's life is a characteristic of aging. Sometimes the life review results in a revision of life goals and a focus on pursuits that were neglected earlier. The disengagement from some life activities begins in middle age but reaches its height in old age. Sexual interest and activity should normally continue in old age. The frequency and intensity of the experience may diminish somewhat, especially for men, but the need and capacity continues throughout the life cycle. Because of the taboos and myths surrounding sex in old age, many of the elderly withdraw from sexual activity.

Longevity is affected by psychological as well as biological factors. One of the most important psychological factors is involvement in meaningful life roles.

The elderly are subject to the full range of mental disorders. But depression and organic brain syndrome are the most frequent disorders of old age. Depression in the aged poses the problem of suicide. Suicide rates for the elderly (particularly males) are extremely high. Suicide threats of the elderly must always be taken seriously.

Institutionalization of the aged is necessary when chronic problems require constant medical supervision and when the family or community are unable to provide adequate care. There is a great need for expansion of community resources in order to help the aged maintain their independence outside of institutions.

A self-awareness exercise was presented to call attention to the problems of aging.

SUGGESTED READINGS

Botwinick, J. *Aging and behavior.* New York: Springer, 1973.

de Beauvoir, S. *The coming of age.* New York: Putnam, 1972.

Butler, R. N., and Lewis, M. I. *Aging and mental health.* St. Louis: C. V. Mosby, 1973.

Kastenbaum, R. *New thoughts on old age.* New York: Springer, 1964.

Chapter **7**

Dying and Death

DEATH HAS BECOME an alien, secret experience in modern society, concealed in its natural course much as sex was a century ago. In the latter half of the nineteenth century, sex was a taboo subject, not to be publicly discussed or admitted, although of course the population continued to grow (presumably as the result of sexual relations) even in the most Victorian communities. Death, on the other hand, was not as taboo then as it is now, primarily because people died at home. There was no attempt to hide the fact of death; it could not be hidden because the moment of dying, like the moment of birth, dominated the family and household. Neither event could be relegated to the "not thought about" because they took place in the home, with family and friends as accustomed participants. Now birth has been moved to the hospital, reducing its physical hazards but creating serious, still unresolved psychological difficulties. So too with dying, which now generally takes place in a hospital or nursing home—the physical gains are real, but we have all lost psychologically. Today, unless one's profession requires it, a person can go through life without ever observing the process of dying. Children are often shielded from any knowledge of death, and thus an important part of reality is denied them. At the same time, of course, such behavior makes them sense the taboo nature of the subject.

The consequences of this distancing are most unfortunate for all of us. Major technological advances often disrupt long-standing, basic human adaptations so severely that we are left to wonder whether the advances are worthwhile. Such is certainly the case when we look at what has happened to our attitudes and behavior with regard to death.

In this chapter we will explore the psychological aspects of dying and death. We will consider reactions to the anticipation of death, the role of fear in attitudes toward death, reactions of young and old people to the thought of death, the needs of the dying patient, family and social problems of survivors, problems connected with the dying child, the role of grief and mourning, and problems of nursing care involving the dying patient and his family.

PSYCHOLOGICAL ASPECTS
Reactions To Death

In her book *On Death and Dying* (1969), Elizabeth Kubler-Ross lists five stages in the psychological process of dying. She labels them: (1) denial and isolation, (2) anger, (3) bargaining, (4) depression, and (5) acceptance. Not everyone goes through all these stages. A person may not move beyond denial or one of the other stages.

Denial. When terminally ill patients first become aware that death is approaching—in terms of months or days, as the case may be—their most common reaction is denial. This defense against human mortality—"it can't happen to me"—is a coping mechanism that almost all of us use at some time. Among the terminally ill, the reaction is the same whether they are told of the approaching end or they become aware of it themselves.

Perhaps the most tragic aspect of dying, and something we can all help change, is the collusion of silence that is unfortunately so common to the natural end of life today. There has developed such a sense of dread of telling the dying of their condition that family, friends, physicians, and nurses often avoid any indication that they are witnessing a fatal illness. When Dr. Kubler-Ross undertook to locate dying patients for her study of patients' reactions to death, she was told by nurses and doctors that there were no terminally ill patients in their hospitals. She finally had to locate the dying patients by their physical appearance. The denial of death runs very deep in our society.

Anger. Most people pass quickly from denial to anger. As with denial, the anger stage varies greatly both in duration and intensity with the personality of the individual. The anger takes two forms. The first is leveled at others for not having done enough. Such feelings are hard for family and helpers to cope with, but irrational guilt or counteranger will not achieve the goal of relating to the dying person. Realizing that the anger is not truly generated by outside events but arises from the inner anxiety of facing the end makes it possible to deal with it appropriately. The best course is to help the patient in coming to grips with the anxiety, as well as to listen and respond appropriately in those areas where the anger may be justified.

Bargaining. The stage of anger is in many instances followed by a period in which the dying person behaves as if he is bargaining for life. If he does not die then he will do something very important for his family, society, or some needy individual. It is a temporary pretense that perhaps he can still influence his life through his behavior, as he did when he was more active and healthy.

Depression. The fourth stage is depression. Kubler-Ross distinguishes two types of depression in the dying: *reactive depression* and *preparatory depression.* Reactive depression refers to the feelings of sadness and loss connected to external circumstances. A mother is sad because she will not be able to care for her young children; a husband feels guilty for not leaving his elderly wife with what he considers adequate income. These important and real problems of life's never-quite-finished business may cause a great deal of distress. Words of advice and a helping hand from clergy, friends, or family, as well as from health professionals, can aid enormously in resolving or facing these problems.

Preparatory depression, on the other hand, is the natural sadness that the dying feel as they contemplate the loss of all that is significant and loved. This sadness is appropriate and should be respected. Trying to cheer up an individual who is undergoing this universal human experience is not advisable.

Acceptance. The final and fifth phase of dying is that of acceptance. The individual is no longer depressed, and a sense of peace or tranquility emerges. Interest in life as well as in the living diminishes; there is a gradual withdrawal and turning inward as physical weakness progresses. Death becomes a natural playing out of the life cycle.

Informing the Patient

In the process of avoiding what is of course the dominant thought and reality of the last days or months, family, friends, and—unfortunately—health professionals often avoid the dying person altogether. The rationale for not speaking of issues that are uppermost in the dying person's thoughts is that it would be too painful for him. "He couldn't bear knowing," is the usual statement. This assumption has been seriously questioned, since it has been shown that the vast majority of people want to be told what their condition is. Most important, the dying want to be able to talk of their concerns, their memories, and their thoughts with the people who are important to them. Instead, they are forced to join in the silence for fear of hurting others, who are obviously fearful of their own reactions.

In fact, the reluctance to speak of death with the dying is largely due to our anxiety about how we would handle the emotions generated in us, the physically well, during such a dialogue. Would we become tearful, be forced to talk of subjects that make us uncomfortable, be asked questions we are not able to answer, or be asked for solace that we don't know how to provide?

Like so many fears that stem from irrational sources, it is the anticipation of an unknown discomfort that fosters the silence. In reality, talking of dying is not the unbearable discomfort that we anticipate. On the contrary, it tends to be accompanied by a sense of relief and increased tranquility in the family and the dying individual.

The question most often asked is whether the last illness should be labeled as terminal by family and physicians when they have such knowledge. Most often, patients want to know, but many physicians are opposed to this. The disparity between the medical profession and patients on the issue of informing about impending death is best indicated in a study by Pearlman et al. (1969).

Reviewing the literature on the topic, they found that "69-90% of the physicians, depending on the specific study, favor not telling the patient. In contrast, 77-98% of the patients want to know."

Recently it has become the consensus among mental health professionals that the dying have a distinct psychological advantage in facing death if they are told of their condition "officially." The manner in which the dying are told of their state is crucial. It should be in private (not during morning hospital rounds with a group in attendance) and clearly stated. The patient should be permitted to use whatever means of coping he requires. The reaction may be marked denial, anger, apathy, relief, or tranquility. If the patient wishes to deny resolutely that he is seriously ill, he should be permitted to do so. But he should have the choice. He should not be forced by a conspiracy of silence to deny overtly in order to save others from discomfort while he suffers privately.

Anxiety in Health Professionals

It is a readily observable fact that even health professionals whose work brings them repeatedly to the bedside of the dying tend to distance themselves from the terminal patient. Like anyone else, the nurse needs to protect her psychological stability. Repeated confrontation with death on the wards is an enormous psychological drain.

Coping with death can be overwhelming, particularly for the nursing student. Quint (1967), who studied nursing training in relation to the dying patient, found little in the way of structured experiences to guide the student. Yet the nurse's first encounter with death has far-reaching consequences in setting her style of relating to dying patients. Quint sees a need for graduated exposure to death and dying in a context of supportive help from instructors and supervisors. Part of the problem is that nurses are not held accountable for verbal and emotional interaction with patients to the same extent that they are held accountable for technical procedures. Quint recommends that the nurse's first encounter with death take place in a geriatric ward, with pediatric experience coming much later. She also stresses the importance of experience with post-mortem body care.

One technique of insulating against the pressure is to be uninvolved or detached. Some nurses report that their patients never talk about death, but closer observation reveals that many of these nurses do not encourage such discussions. If we are really to humanize the process of dying, perhaps nurses need more support services to help them deal with their reactions to death and their problems of interacting with patients, particularly dying patients.

One of the problems in nursing care for the dying is that many nurses define their role exclusively in terms of saving lives and aiding recovery. The death of a patient is often perceived by the nurse as a repudiation of her usefulness. But this is not the case. The nurse's role is to help the patient to the best of her ability. Easing suffering and meeting the psychological needs of the dying patient are as much *positive* nursing functions as is the saving of lives. Consciously, of course, most people acknowledge the need to provide care and comfort to the dying. After all, it has always been the responsibility of the health professional not only to heal but to make the lives of the patients as comfortable as possible. No time requires more sensitive help than the final stage of life. Why, then, the distancing?

Kastenbaum and Aisenberg (1972), who have provided a comprehensive study of the various aspects of death, cite three main sources of our need for distancing. First is the sense that the dying person is somehow socially inferior. In our achievement- and youth-oriented society, weakness, failure, and old age itself are signs of inadequacy to be looked down upon. Second, and perhaps the most generally crucial factor, is the fact that most of us, professional and lay, do not know what to do or say when dealing with a dying person. Appropriate behavior is not in our response repertoire because nobody has given us adequate instruction or provided opportunities to learn how to give comfort during this final stage of life. Third is inner perturbation; that is, we experience fear or discomfort in the presence of the dying person because his dying brings to the surface our own fears of dying or of facing death.

Fortunately, dying and death are no longer hidden away as subjects in medical and nursing schools. Increasingly, formal lectures and discussions cover these topics. It still rests within the clinician, however, to overcome the sources of his own reluctance to serve dying patients in a way that will meet more fully their psychological needs in the final weeks and days of living.

Fear of Death

Cases of accident victims and others facing "imminent" death provide insight into the role of fear in relation to dying. Hunter (1967) reports the case of a 34-year-old nurse who had a severe reaction to penicillin and thought she was about to die but, in fact, recovered. In the moments before unconsciousness she experienced intense fear, but this passed quickly, yielding to a number of other reactions: sympathy for her husband and related thoughts about their relationship; a last struggle against death, followed quickly by a passive resignation devoid of fear in which death was welcomed; a flashback of scenes from her childhood accompanied by pleasant feelings and vivid images; and a euphoric state of happiness. This final feeling of bliss was so intense that she resented regaining consciousness in the emergency room of the hospital. It is interesting that fear did not dominate her reactions.

Other investigators have made similar observations. In an extensive study of near-death incidents Kalish (1969) found that most of the subjects did not stress fear in their reactions; thoughts about other family members were most common and a small number experienced flashbacks. Concern for the grief of others, as opposed to fear of the end of personal existence, is even prevalent in the thoughts of the elderly. In the case of patients who are actually dying, depression seems to be more prevalent than overt fear.

Kastenbaum and Aisenberg discuss the difference in the way the young and the old react to death in terms of two opposing orientations: overcoming and participating. In the first instance, common among the young, the person views death as a sign of personal failure and as an external menace that needs to be overcome to protect one's integrity. The participatory attitude, associated more frequently with the old, sees death as part of an internal process that includes fulfillment, satisfaction, and at-homeness with one's environment. In our society, however, the overcoming orientation seems most prevalent. Jackson (1969) cites a California study in which the majority of people surveyed did not regard death as a reality of man's mortality but rather as an illness to be dealt with through medical research. This view extends even to the medical profession. According to Jackson, physicians tend to think of death in terms of accidents, and their language demonstrates this—"cerebral accidents," "circulatory accidents," and "coronary accidents." In the United States, according to Kastenbaum and Aisenberg, the emphasis on achievement and fear of failure encourages the overcoming orientation.

This ethic of achievement is more prevalent among the young, and this perhaps explains why the elderly exhibit less fear of death than do the middle-aged or adolescents. In view of the greater participation and acceptance of death found among the elderly, Kastenbaum asks: "What is the effect, then, of our usual gambit of avoiding or denying the reality of impending death for the elderly and ill? Does this not reject a vital aspect of the person who has entered into a participatory relationship with his own demise? Love me, love my death." Popular intuition assigns a strong fear of death to the elderly, and this assumption is used as an excuse for avoiding the topic of death with the aged. Actually, acceptance is much more the rule among the elderly. It appears that the elderly are compelled to work through their feelings about death because their life situation makes death a personal reality. For younger adults denial and avoidance result in a high level of fear and anxiety. Adolescents seem to have the greatest fear of death; their doubts about succeeding in life (symbolic death) magnify their fears of not becoming adults.

An orientation to death does not suddenly occur in old age, when the individual is shocked by the reality of the end. Concern about death as the end of life begins early, first emerging in early childhood and changing in emphasis at each succeeding stage of life. By old age most people have worked out some kind of adaptation to death.

Change of Affect

A number of investigators have independently reported a puzzling phenomenon that frequently occurs in patients shortly before death. Some change in the patients' feelings is manifested that suggests a premonition of imminent death. The change is sometimes inconsistent with the patient's usual manner of behavior. Withdrawn and uncommunicative patients may express a desire to talk to someone. In some cases, the patient was reported to show sudden terror in his facial expression. Although the physician perceived no essential change in the physical condition, the patient would die within a few days. Dr. Ursula Thunberg, in a case presentation made at a staff conference at Downstate Medical Center, New York, has described a similar change of affect occurring in dying children 24 to 36 hours before death. Entirely unresponsive children have thanked her and other children have reacted with anger at expressions of hope ("You will get better") just prior to death. At the other extreme are cases reported by Kastenbaum and Aisenberg in which danger of death was perceived by the physician but the patients were not particularly anxious. An unusual rate of recovery in such cases has been observed. While these reports have a mystical quality there may be a biological mechanism signaling something drastically wrong when the person is near death.

Terminal Drop

A terminal drop in cognitive functioning, reflected in declining scores on intelligence tests, has been found to occur preceding death. Botwinick (1973) cites the case of thirteen elderly men studied by R.

W. Kleemier in which the four who died first showed the greatest decline in test scores. Jarvik and Falek (1963) obtained similar results for the earlier dying twin of twin pairs; the most discriminating tests were Vocabulary, Digit Symbols, and Similarities. Jarvik and Falek state: "Persons who showed a critical loss on all three of these tests had a significantly higher mortality rate than did subjects with a critical loss on less than two tests." This decline can precede death by a few months or several years. Whether or not the terminal drop is psychological in origin or based on a more general physiological deterioration as death approaches needs further clarification. Jarvik and Falek believe that the critical losses are due to "circulatory changes which lead to death within a five-year period."

Grief

Expressions of grief are natural reactions to loss and death. Grief can be expressed in many forms and can include deep sighing, crying, feelings of weakness and fatigue, insomnia, poor appetite and nausea, preoccupation with memories of the deceased person, feelings of strangeness and unreality, restless pacing, inability to concentrate or persist in organized activities, irritability, anger, and guilt. Some people are less overt in their expression of grief and become withdrawn and introspective in their preoccupation with the loss. All these symptoms of acute grief are normal reactions to death even among those who were highly rational prior to grieving.

The shock reaction in grief, according to Blank (1969), is a defense mechanism that protects the mourner from being overwhelmed by his feelings. The shock or anesthesia provides some distance from the emotionalism of grief. Sudden, unexpected loss usually results in more acute grief reactions than loss after a prolonged illness in which there has been painful suffering before death.

In addition to the normal grieving process, loss has a personal meaning that plays an important role in individual reactions to death. The range of such meanings is very great: abandonment, a sense of one's own mortality, overwhelming guilt at not having done enough for the deceased person, the empty feeling of loneliness, and others. Because of the personal nature of loss it is not possible to make any objective assessment of how deep grief should be on the basis of the actual relationship between the deceased person and the survivor.

Since the grieving process is necessary for effective restructuring of life after a loss, Klein and Blank (1969) are opposed to heavy sedation, which interferes with the mourning process. Because persistent insomnia can produce other complications and make the mourner increasingly vulnerable to physical and emotional stress, they recommend minor tranquilizers to aid sleep. In *agitated depression,* a much more serious and pathological grief reaction, the mourner focuses on himself rather than on the lost person. According to Klein and Blank, "The person suffering from agitated depression is preoccupied with himself, his own feelings of mental pain, emptiness, powerlessness, and often has no ability to cry or mourn." Overwhelming feelings of guilt, self-debasement, and suicidal thoughts also commonly occur in agitated depression. In such cases Klein and Blank advise using the major tranquilizers and major antidepressants that have proven effective with these conditions.

Children's Grief. Children have fewer psychological resources for dealing with death than adults. The shock of losing a loved one will, therefore, often be met with extreme defensive measures aimed at warding off the intolerable feelings. Children will sometimes refuse to accept the fact that the loved one is really dead. Statements such as "she's just sick" or "she'll come back" with regard to the deceased person reflect blatant denial. In some instances the child will have hallucinations, claiming he has seen or heard the deceased. The child may also deny the event by acting as if nothing has happened, continuing usual routines and making no references to the death. But in school he may appear more anxious, depressed, and withdrawn (Felner and Stolberg, 1974). Some children will react to death with apathy and detachment in an effort to insulate themselves from all feelings.

In a study of children's reactions to the assassination of John F. Kennedy, Harrison et al. (1967) found some typical denial reactions. One of the hospitalized children, for example, laughed when the bugler in the television coverage of the funeral hit a wrong note; in another incident some children protested when a party scheduled for the evening of the assassination was cancelled. It is interesting that the hospital staff in these instances reacted to the children's behavior with moral indignation. Harrison et al. suggest that hospital personnel as well as other adults expect children to manifest adultlike grief in the face of death regardless of their developmental levels. This study helps to point out the need for nurses to recognize the internal struggle of the child confronted with death and not to be misled by his superficial behavior.

Delayed Grief. Sometimes the grief reaction is delayed. According to Lindemann (1944), the delayed or postponed reaction is most common when the loss occurs at a time when important tasks have to be completed or when the focus is on giving support to and attention to others. Lindemann gives the following example of a 17-year-old girl who lost both her parents and her boy friend in the famous Coconut Grove fire. She herself was burned seriously.

> Throughout her stay in the hospital her attitude was that of cheerful acceptance without any sign of adequate distress. When she was discharged at the end of three weeks she appeared cheerful, talked rapidly, with a considerable flow of ideas, seemed eager to return home and to assume the role of parent for her two younger siblings. Except for slight feelings of "lonesomeness" she complained of no distress.
>
> This period of griefless acceptance continued for the next two months, even when the household was dispersed and her younger siblings were placed in other homes. Not until the end of the tenth week did she begin to show a true state of grief with marked feelings of depression, intestinal emptiness, tightness in her throat, frequent crying, and vivid preoccupation with her deceased parents.

Anticipatory Grief. Anticipatory grief frequently occurs when there is the expectation that someone will die of an illness or injury. The anticipatory grief helps the person detach himself from a loved one as a protection against the expected shock reaction at the moment of death. The process can sometimes backfire in cases where there are remissions prior to demise. Knight and Herter (1969) report cases in which emotional conflicts, particularly anger, arose because the survivors had already worked through many detachments from the dying member of the family. Anticipatory grief can occur not only in illness but in cases of separations during war when a wife believes her husband has died: "On arriving home, he discovered that his wife did not love him any more and wanted a divorce. In such instances it was often found that the wife had mourned the potential loss of her husband so effectively that she actually emancipated herself from her ties to him."

THE DYING CHILD

While the topic of death is usually associated with old people, the fact remains that fatal illnesses also strike children. The death of a child is especially painful for all involved. In the case of the elderly, death is expected and on some level recognized as inevitable. Fatal illness in childhood is always a great shock and a difficult event to absorb. The grief in these cases can have a devastating effect on family life and make the final days of the dying child more painful than is necessary.

Children's Fear of Death

Children of all ages have a fear of death but it is manifested in different forms at different ages. Natterson and Knudson (1960) divided children's fear of death into three age periods: up to five years, five to ten years, and ten years and older. In the youngest group the anxiety over separation from the parents was the most severely manifest reaction. The five- to ten-year-olds expressed intense anxiety over painful medical procedures. The oldest group showed the strongest manifest fear of death. These varied reactions fit in with what we know about the conceptual development of children (see Chapter 11 on Jean Piaget). Separation anxiety is present in all the children but the fear of death per se is dependent on the development of a sense of reality.

Parental Reactions

The child's adjustment to the hospital in the case of terminal illness is very much in the hands of the parents as well as the hospital personnel. As is generally the case with hospitalization of children, the terminally ill child's adjustment is related to his level of anxiety and his reaction to separation. Preparation and supportive handling of the child during the admission process is the most effective means of facilitating adjustment. This is easy enough to recommend, but in practice the intense emotions surrounding the event reduce the parents' ability to function constructively. The denial, grief, anger, and guilt that parents experience immobilize them and prevent attention to the child's real needs. Supportive service, including the sensitive intervention of the nurse, are essential in these cases.

Natterson and Knudson discuss three stages of parental coping with the impending death of a child. Denial characterizes the initial phase. In the intermediate stage the situation is comprehended and there is a focus of energy on hopeful possibilities—new medication, "the best doctor in the field," and so on. Some of these hopes are realistic and some magical thinking. Anger may be part of the intermediate reaction. Parents may accuse the hospital staff of not doing enough or not having the "miracle" doctors or the "miracle" drugs. In the terminal stage, the inevitability of the child's death is accepted.

For young parents, coping with the death of a child is made more difficult by the fact that modern society protects its members from the death experience. Goldfogel (1970) points out that the impending death of a child may be a young parent's first personal encounter with death. A group therapy experience with other parents of dying children has been found helpful. Not only does the therapeutic situation permit an outlet for bottled-up emotions, but it also helps the parents get beyond the denial stage by encountering other people who are going through a similar experience.

The parents' psychological well-being is usually enhanced when they can actively participate in their child's care. Caution must be exercised, however, to see that this is not overdone to the detriment of parents and child.

Sometimes, when parents have worked out much of the anticipatory grief over the impending death, they may show increased attention to other children on the ward. This should not be misunderstood as rejection of their own child.

Parents may have difficulty in handling practical matters that they can ordinarily manage with ease—caring for other children, scheduling time, providing family health care needs, and many routine concerns. The nurse can be helpful in offering practical guidance during the period in which the parents are overwhelmed with grief. After-care contact with the family following the death of a child has also been suggested (Ford 1972). There is ample evidence that unresolved grief can produce psychological disturbances in families for long periods of time. A skilled nurse or social worker who had contact with the family during the dying process could extend an already established relationship to help the family work out the shock reaction. Such after-care is much needed, but our society must progress in its willingness to pay for humane treatment before this is realized on a broad scale.

Nurses' Reactions

We have already spoken about the avoidance tactics consciously or unconsciously used by nurses as defenses against facing the dying patient. These same feelings operate more intensely when the patient is a child. Goldfogel (1970) gives a very honest account of her reactions to a dying child and his mother, a reaction that is probably very typical:

> to defend myself against these feelings [anxiety], I began to spend shorter and shorter periods of time in direct contact with both the patient and his mother. I withdrew . . . I realized that, in a sense, I was experiencing some of the same feelings of grief that Mrs. C. had experienced. My with-

drawal from the situation was my way of attempting to deny the reality of the prognosis: "If I'm not able to see him dying then it isn't going to happen."

If the nurse is to be helpful to the patient and his family in cases of terminal illness, she must come to grips with her own emotional reactions. This is not to imply that understanding and acceptance of feelings about death and dying will make emotional anguish go away. The emotions will always be there. But openness paves the way to our helping the patient and his family rather than becoming immobilized by our own conflicts.

Reactions of Others

Denial, we have noted, is a typical initial reaction to death. The social supports for this denial are massive—lack of experience with death, the placing of death in the hands of professionals, the emphasis on our technological ability to overcome almost any obstacle, the decline in religious affiliation, and so on. Yet the person experiencing a loss is forced by circumstances to face death. Parents of dying children have fewer opportunities for total denial because of their immersion in the death process from the onset of the terminal illness to the moment of death. For others—relatives, friends of the family—denial and avoidance is easier to achieve. They frequently stop visiting the parents after the death of the child. The parents of the deceased child in most cases have worked through their grief and feelings about death, and are ready and willing to talk about their child's death as part of the grieving process. Friends and relatives believe they are protecting the parents from further upset, but in fact they are inflicting further loss by indulging in their own anxieties. Nurses can help remedy the situation by counseling friends and relatives who visit the hospital on the need for continued contact with the family after the child dies.

Informing the Child

Most children suffering from terminal illness know or sense the life-threatening nature of their condition. Avoiding the issue of death may give solace to the parents, but it will most likely cause agony for the child. Fond (1972) illustrates this point in discussing the case of a 14-year-old girl who died of a malignant tumor. Although the nurses followed the mother's instructions not to talk to the girl about dying, the girl gave indications of knowing. She was pleasant enough when the family was present but would cry and manifest depression when alone. She played the parents' game of silence to protect them but was deprived of an outlet for her real agonizing feelings. Green (1967) cites another case of a child knowing:

> On the day Larry died he asked the intern to hold him and said he was afraid to die and that his doctor should promise to come anytime Larry needed him. The intern was astounded, wondering how long this 4-year-old boy had known that he was dying. When Larry died 24 hours later in a coma his parents reassured themselves by saying Larry had not known he was dying. The intern and his supervisor knew this was not true, but agreed that it was intolerable for the parents to realize that their only son had sensed his own approaching death.

Fond recommends telling siblings about the impending death of their brother or sister, because fantasies are usually far more frightening than reality. Also, a sibling may feel vaguely responsible for his brother's or sister's death. Talking truthfully can dispel many of these irrational feelings and short-circuit unrealistic fantasies, thus helping to bring about meaningful grieving. In line with this, visiting the dying sibling should also be encouraged.

While honesty and openness are most beneficial to the child, it is best for the parents to make the final decision of whether or not to tell the child of his impending death. Informing the child against their wishes can lead to an emotionally harmful atmosphere that is damaging to all concerned. Also, the parents should be given the opportunity of being the informants. The nurse can be very helpful in preparing parents for the kinds of questions the dying child and siblings might ask and the possible responses.

Maintaining the Terminally Ill Child

Many terminally ill children are able to ambulate and appear more or less normal when they are not having a serious attack. Should such a child be kept in the hospital? While normal functioning (including school and playmates) is beneficial to the child's emotional state, there are definite psychological and medical risks. The emotional reactions of family members and friends may be morbid and anxiety-provoking, negating any advantages. There is also the risk of sudden relapses and the need for emergency medical treatment (which may not be quickly available). Some drugs, such as corticosteroids, are immuno-suppressants, and make children dangerously (sometimes fatally) susceptible to common illnesses. Nevertheless, if parents are willing and able to handle contingencies, home placement can be an emotionally important and gratifying experience for the entire family. Even in the hospital the child should dress and engage in normal activities to the extent possible.

Death of a Newborn

Stillbirth or death of an infant soon after delivery is an extremely emotion-laden event. Not only is it likely to be the young parents' first direct experience with death, but it is also a great trauma, coming so unexpectedly upon the joyful anticipation of birth.

Zahourek and Jensen (1973) have studied twenty-five cases of infant mortality in the last trimester of pregnancy. Their insights and recommendations have great relevance for nursing intervention to help with the grieving process. To prevent a prolonged period of shock and disbelief, they suggest confronting the mother with the reality of the infant's death, maintaining at the same time a sympathetic and empathetic relationship. This, of course, requires time, patience, and the willingness to listen. Zahourek and Jensen also raise questions about the practice of excessively medicating the mother when a stillbirth is recognized by the delivering physician. The mother's unconsciousness during the birth, they feel, contributes to the disbelief reaction. Some mothers want to see the baby's body and others do not. While the mother's wishes should be followed, the authors emphasize the need for preparation since the mother may not have seen a dead body before. "It is vital to ask the mother whether she has ever seen a dead body, to have her express her expectations, and to correct misconceptions. Preparing the mother for the altered skin color, stiffness, and coldness can prevent some of the initial horror of touching a dead body."

Another factor that seems to feed disbelief and denial is the difficulty that the mother frequently experiences in finding out about the cause of the infant's death. In many cases the mother is discharged before the autopsy is performed, but the authors cite instances in which bureaucratic entanglements prevent even the nurse from learning the cause of death.

Not knowing may reinforce a guilt reaction of self-blame ("It must have been my fault"), or accusations between husband and wife ("It must have been your fault because there were so many stillbirths on your side of the family"), whereas knowledge of the cause of death can help parents realistically assess the risks involved for future pregnancies.

Zahourek and Jensen stress the need to respect the mother's method of grieving. Loud outbursts of crying upset many nurses, which results in the unnecessary use of tranquilizers. Grieving is an essential part of working through a loss. Interruption of the process can only serve to increase guilt feelings and inappropriate interpretations and thus lead to prolonged suffering. Finally, they advise that patients who have marked reactions to the loss but do not have outside supports to provide comfort (e.g., no husband or family) be referred for psychological help.

EUTHANASIA

Should life be maintained and preserved under all circumstances? When there is no hope for survival or improvement should a patient who wishes to die be required to suffer agonies of pain? When a patient has deteriorated to a subhuman level should the medical staff keep him "alive" as long as possible? When patient, family, and physician agree on the futility of continued existence should mercy killing be considered a crime? These questions embody the moral, ethical, and legal dilemmas of euthanasia. They are dramatized for the nurse when she participates in the "death watch" of a terminal patient kept alive by the marvels of modern medicine.

The question of euthanasia or mercy killing is one that is debated all over the world. Nowhere is the practice legal; in Uruguay it is a crime, but the courts can omit a penalty; in Germany and Switzerland there are reduced penalties (Fletcher, 1973). The distinction has been made between positive and negative euthanasia. In positive euthanasia the physician, patient, or someone else does something directly to help the patient die. Negative euthanasia entails doing nothing to help the patient stay alive, for example, not administering a drug that could maintain life. According to Fletcher, negative euthanasia is a common, although unofficial, practice. "Every day in a hundred hospitals across the land decisions are made clinically that the line has been crossed from prolonging genuinely human life to only prolonging subhuman dying and when that judgment is made respirators are turned off, life perpetuating intravenous infusions stopped, proposed surgery canceled, and drugs counter-manded." Fletcher, who is a former Dean of St. Paul's Cathedral in Cincinnati, Ohio, argues that negative euthanasia (letting the patient die) is moral acceptance of euthanasia but essentially "superficial, morally timid, and evasive of the real issue. . . . It is harder morally to justify letting somebody die a slow, and ugly death, dehumanized, than it is to justify helping him to avoid it." Yet Fletcher recognizes the psychological (and legal) problems involved in active participation in euthanasia.

As medical technology advances, with the concurrent ability to sustain life "endlessly" at minimal levels of existence, the question of euthanasia will become more pressing. Still, a number of issues will have to be resolved. How shall we define hopelessness and uselessness of existence? What safeguards will be built in to protect patients and prevent abuses? What role will the patient's wishes play? Perhaps the time will come when people will carry cards indicating the conditions under which their life should be terminated—much in the way instructions for organ donation is currently given. In view of the feelings of dying patients the question of euthanasia will have to be faced squarely. Here is one expression of the problem:

An Old Man's Prayer

Pardon me, doctor, but may I die?
I know your oath requires you try
As long as there's a spark of life
To keep it there with tube or knife;

To do cut-downs and heart massages,
Tracheotomies and gavages.
But here I am, well past four-score,
I've lived a life-time (and a little more).

I've raised my children, buried my wife,
My friends are gone, so spare the knife.
This is the way it seems to me:
I deserve the dignity . . .

Of slipping gently off to sleep,
And no one has the right to keep
Me from my God: when the call's this clear
No mortal man should keep me here.

Your motive's noble, but now I pray
You'll read in my eyes what my lips can't say
Listen to my heart! You'll hear it cry:
"Pardon me, doctor, but may I die?"

—Bob Richards

(From the *American Journal of Nursing* 73 [April 1973], p. 675. Used by permission.)

SELF-AWARENESS EXERCISE

The Obituary

Because the health professional must deal directly with death and grieving, a personal awareness of death must be worked through. The following self-awareness exercise calls attention to the reality of death as each person's personal destiny. It also demonstrates how awareness of death can result in a reassessment of life and life goals.

Task. *Write your own hypothetical obituary. Include in the obituary age of death, manner of death, and achievements (professional and social).*

What were the main focuses of your life? What would you want to be remembered for most? What were the outstanding values and principles which were exemplified in your life? Was your life satisfying or frustrating?—in what ways? What tasks or goals, if any, were left unfinished? If fate gave you the choice, what kind of death would you prefer? What circumstances would you like to surround you in your last hours?

Evaluation. *What were your reactions to undertaking this exercise? If you were uncomfortable can you explain the reason (or reasons) for the discomfort? How did you feel about life goals while looking at them from the vantage point of death? Did the task lead you to question any aspects of your own current life? If so, explain.*

SUMMARY

Death has become an alien experience in modern society because it largely occurs in hospitals or other institutional settings where the family is shielded from its full impact. The distance of the death experience feeds an atmosphere of taboo and denial that shrouds the topic.

There are generally five stages in reactions to impending death: (1) denial, (2) anger, (3) bargaining, (4) depression, (5) acceptance. In spite of the tendency for family and professionals to avoid the subject of death with the dying patient, research indicates that the dying not only want to know about their condition but want to talk about it with sympathetic and understanding listeners. Avoiding the dying patient and denying him opportunities to discuss his impending death leads to increased patient suffering. Studies of persons "retrieved" from death show that fear is often not the most prominent or persistent reaction; concern for survivors (spouse, family, etc.), flashbacks, and even euphoria have been found to occur. Fear of death appears to be more intense in adolescence and middle age than in old age, with adolescents showing the strongest reaction to the thought of death.

Grief and mourning are normal reactions to death. It is essential for grief to be expressed for effective working through of a loss. Major tranquilizers can inhibit normal grieving and therefore should be avoided except in pathological reactions.

The death of a child is an especially painful experience for all concerned. Children's attitudes toward death vary, depending on their developmental stage. The dying child usually has some awareness of his condition and, therefore, it is not advisable to avoid the topic with him. Some tragic cases have been reported of children knowing about their terminal status but suffering privately. Death of a child usually has a disruptive effect on family life that needs psychological attention.

Mercy killing (euthanasia) will become a more pressing issue of professional concern as our capability for maintaining minimal states of life increases.

SUGGESTED READINGS

Kastenbaum, R., and Aisenberg, R. *The psychology of death.* New York: Springer, 1972.

Kubler-Ross, E. *On death and dying.* New York: Macmillan, 1969.

Kutscher, A. H. *Death and bereavement.* Springfield, Ill.: Charles C Thomas, 1969.

Neale, R. E. *The art of dying.* New York: Harper & Row, 1973.

Quint, J. C. *The nurse and the dying patient.* New York: Macmillan, 1967.

Zeligs, R. *Children's experience with death.* Illinois: Charles C Thomas, 1974.

Part ***II***

Theories of Development and Behavior

IN PART II we will introduce you to theories of human behavior and development. We will begin by discussing the nature and importance of theories in psychology, considering ways to look at and evaluate theories. Chapters 9-11 are an overview of three major theories of development: psychoanalysis, behaviorism, and the developmental psychology of Jean Piaget. Each is strikingly unique and represents a school of psychology, and all three are presently thriving with large numbers of followers. After presenting the major concepts of each theory we indicate how each theory may be applied to nursing and health-care situations. The final chapter of Part II reviews the major concepts of other currently important social theories of personality.

In the present state of development of psychology and psychiatry, it is not easy to find theories that satisfy everyone. At the same time, it is important to know where the emphasis of each theory lies and the ways in which each can help you deal with the multitude of human problems that will confront you in your professional life.

It is also important to be familiar with theories of behavior, because the nursing and health-care literature makes frequent references to them, a great deal of research is based on theories, and theories stimulate our thinking and research in new areas. But most important is the fact that when we are conscious and explicit about theory, the consistency of our professional functioning is increased, and we are in a better position to select concepts from a variety of useful theories.

Chapter *8*

Psychological Theories

"WHY DO I have to know about theories of development and personality? I have to deal with real situations and real people." This familiar cry assumes that theories have little to do with practical matters. The theoretician is often thought of as removed from reality and dabbling in an irrelevant world of abstractions and fantasy. Some practitioners will be heard to say, "I don't believe in theories —I just use common sense and what works for me." Such statements can be heard from nurses, teachers, counselors, and other professionals who specialize in human relations. Despite these protestations, a closer scrutiny will show that even the opponents of theory use theoretical concepts. All practitioners have their pet theories. In fact, it is difficult to work effectively in human relations fields without some sort of theory.

When we speak of formal psychological theories, however, we are using the term in a more exact sense. A formal psychological theory is a general, logical, and coherent system derived from scientific observation of human behavior. It postulates patterns of behavior that can be verified by others through further observation and research. Once a theory is demonstrated to have a certain validity, we can draw upon it to explain and organize our own observations of human behavior and to make predictions of future behavior.

THEORIES AND NURSING

Without theoretical principles guiding our professional functioning, our methods would be quite disorganized and inconsistent. Perhaps the nurse or teacher or counselor does not have his theory well thought out or well articulated—but it is there. How do we know it is there? All we have to do is to observe the language and behavior of the practitioners in their professional functioning with patients and clients to know that they are operating from some theoretical framework. A certain pattern in their behavior, attitudes, and style will be noted that can be translated into an implicit theoretical view. Let us take a look at an example to make this point clearer.

Interpreting Patient Behavior

On a ward in a municipal hospital we notice that Mr. Pearson, a 78-year-old man who is recovering nicely from a gall-bladder operation, is hoarding food and stealing small items from the hospital. He is soon to be transferred to a long-term nursing home. Although he has two married daughters and a married son, they feel it would be too much of a burden to care for their father. Mr. Pearson is a widower whose wife died eight months earlier. He had been a very successful businessman. When he retired two years ago he had considerable financial resources including large real estate holdings and stocks in major corporations.

What hypotheses would you formulate about Mr. Pearson's behavior? Agreed that any speculations based on the limited information presented would be risky. Nevertheless, it is possible to make tentative speculations that would later be checked out against more data. In fact, speculations may be useful in leading you to certain information. Here are a few possible explanations for his behavior. Do you think these are plausible interpretations? Which one, if any, do you prefer?

1. Hoarding food represents, on a symbolic level, a quest for security, which Mr. Pearson feels is slipping away. After all, he was a very active man until only two years ago, he lost his wife recently, and now he must face the prospect of a nursing home.

2. He is preoccupied with a fear of death and holding on to things is an unconscious attempt to hang on to something permanently.

3. Stealing is an expression of anger against the authorities, who, he feels, are ganging up on him to put him away.

4. Unconsciously he may want to embarrass his children, with whom he is angry for not taking him in after he had helped provide them with affluent lives.

Most students of human behavior would agree that the above interpretations make sense, and any of them could be the case. You can probably think of other interpretations along the same lines. There is nothing startling or unusual about these interpretations. They are typical of a host of similar explanations for a wide range of behavioral manifestations. The essential element in this type of interpretation is the implication of unconscious or symbolic processes. The patient's behavior is seen as caused by factors consistent with his history, perceptions, and personality. To most of us such interpretations would seem plausible if not obvious. How many times have you implied unconscious forces in explaining the behavior of another person?

Theory, "Common Sense," and "the Obvious"

Common sense is not as common as we sometimes think. Rather sophisticated theories may be lurking behind the "obvious." What makes us feel that common sense is common is a lengthy process of learning or indoctrination that makes the current theories part of us. A hundred years ago the interpretations offered above would have been considered strange. And, if you were living at that time, you would not have thought of them. We are all products of our own times. There is nothing common or obvious about the speculations concerning Mr. Pearson's behavior. They are inferential and very much dependent on current popular theoretical notions about personality.

Many researchers have called attention to how the "obvious" changes periodically. Martha Wolfenstein (1955) has written about the changes that have occurred in child-rearing practices, using the *Infant Care Bulletin* of the U.S. Department of Labor as her main source. The *Infant Care Bulletin* is an annual publication addressed to the general public, and its views and recommendations are good reflections of the popular theories of the moment. Dr. Wolfenstein focuses her discussion on two main periods: 1914 and 1942-45. In the earlier period (1914) the child's impulses and pleasure seeking are viewed as dangerous. Thumb sucking and masturbation were particularly singled out for attention. Both, according to the 1914 bulletin, should be eradicated as early as possible since they represented pleasures considered to be manifestations of the child's "sinful nature." It was also thought that the child's pleasure seeking could get out of hand and "ruin the child." Consequently, a variety of mechanical and physical restraints were recommended to parents for preventing infants and older children from engaging in thumb sucking and genital stimulation. Eating, play, and any other form of pleasure and self-indulgence were seen in the same light as thumb sucking. Amazingly, parents were told not to play with their children for fear of harming the children's "delicate nerves."

In the 1942-45 period the concept of the child had changed radically and therefore the recommendations were quite different. Impulses were no longer regarded as dangerous. In a complete turnabout, parents were told to make play a part of all activities. Not only was there less fear of impulses, but the child's physical activities were now tied to his need for exercise and motor development. Auto-erotic (self-stimulating) activities were no longer overshadowed with dire consequences. Contrasted with the stoical and self-denying concept of motherhood in 1914, the 1942-45 mother is allowed to find enjoyment in play, breast feeding, bathing the child, as well as all other interactions with the child. Compared with the 1914 danger of "titillating" the child, the mother in 1942-45 was given the mandate to have pleasure in her child-rearing interactions.

Sunley (1955) discusses some of the techniques of child-rearing recommended by the "maternal associations" that were popular in the United States in the early nineteenth century. Their fundamentalist theological view saw the infant as "depraved and evil in nature." The goal of child-rearing was, therefore, to subjugate the child's nature to the "good" authority of the parent by "breaking the child's will." Sunley describes an article in an 1834 issue of *Mother's Magazine* in which a mother proudly reported how she broke her daughter's will. The 16-month-old girl refused to say "dear mama" upon the father's command. She was then whipped and commanded repeatedly until she finally obeyed. Today such treatment would be called cruel; the parents might even be charged with child abuse. Yet in 1834, if you adhered to a certain view of the child and his nature, the behavior of the parents in this incident would have seemed not only reasonable but praiseworthy. If you had come along suggesting a more permissive and tolerant approach, the parents might have been horrified; and, within their belief system, their reaction would be consistent and comprehensible. Even parents, it seems, operate according to theories they may not be aware of, and this makes it difficult to argue about child-rearing techniques with them. Although most modern parents do not subscribe to techniques like "breaking the child's will," there are still wide differences in the way parents conceive of the child. What is "obvious" may be different for a middle-class parent, a low socioeconomic parent, a highly educated parent, a religiously orthodox parent, a parent from a rural area, a parent from a primitive society, and so on. It is important for the health professional to keep this fact constantly in mind. But more essentially, in order to make use of your awareness of variations in the conception of the child, you need to be familiar with the range of theories about children and human development.

EVALUATING THEORIES

Now that we have seen that theories are not only important but almost inevitable, we have a number of tasks before us. With an attentive eye we can discover the implicit theory by which a professional is operating, even if he is unable to tell us himself. If he is aware of his theory, then the descriptive process is of course easier. After spelling out the theory we might relate it to a larger complex of theoretical concepts. In doing so we can then elaborate on other dimensions of the point of view. All this is fine and part of the functioning of the trained health professional. But now we come to a more difficult task. Description of a theory may be straightforward, but evaluation is complex. How good is the theory? Should you accept it or reject it? Should you use it? The answers to these questions require knowledge about the nature of theories. Merely looking at the surface doesn't help very much; often theories sound quite convincing as rational arguments. We get into a dilemma, however, when completely opposite points of view sound equally plausible.

For example, consider the question of how to organize a play area for young children in pediatrics. One group might argue that "Children have natural interests and enthusiasms for learning. When they are unhampered and given the opportunity of freedom of expression children function best." Therefore, the play area should have little structure, and the children should be allowed and encouraged to move freely with minimal adult direction. "In this way," the argument might continue, "the greatest amount of creativity and individual expression will be obtained." Sounds good and convincing! But another group may say the following: "Young children have personality structures that are fluid and still developing. Therefore, they need structured environments to help them organize their behavior in a goal-directed manner and to prevent their distractibility from interfering with effective functioning. By maximizing their focus and attention through structure, children develop interests and discover their own abilities; in an open situation the young child's natural distractibility might prevent such interests from coming to the surface. Once the child develops emotional strength and inner control he will be able to cope with open situations more effectively by generating structures from within." This argument also sounds good. Yet one proposal calls for structure and the other for the opposite. How frequently do we hear such rationally convincing arguments and accept them without questioning further? Sometimes it is a good idea when confronted with rational arguments to try to develop an equally convincing argument that states the opposite. The results are often surprising and can alert you to the fact that the issue in question is much more controversial and disputable than one side would have you believe. In addition to common sense being not so common, we must now state that the sense part is frequently not good sense. In Science, argumentation cannot substitute for fact. We therefore need some systematic method for evaluating theories. The professional should be able to ask questions that go to the heart of the theory and its assumptions. After scrutinizing the theory, one should be able to take a stand based on solid principles, not because "it sounds good."

There are many criteria for evaluating theories. Establishing the "goodness" of a theory is no simple matter. This is especially the case regarding theories of personality and human behavior. The task is not to determine which theory is "correct." Theories are rarely completely correct—or, for that matter, completely wrong. Considering the short history of the science of behavior, dating only from about the turn of the century, theories about human behavior are likely to be in an early stage of evolution. It takes science a long time to accumulate enough facts and observations to make up a theory that is advanced and all-encompassing. In the absence of a large body of facts to build upon, theories that seem to be broad in their scope are likely to be daring stabs in the dark. Still other theories that stick very close to the "available facts" will be much narrower in their scope.

Some of the early Greek philosophers, speculating on the nature of the universe, showed some of the same daring that the fledgling science of psychology displays today. The Greeks had comparatively few valid facts about the universe, but nevertheless they tried to leap from their sparse observations to theories about the workings of the entire universe. Thus Thales concluded that the universe was basically water, Heraclitus saw fire as its core, and Anaxagoras gave "number" a central role. Perhaps the behavioral sciences, in which theorists place their bets variously on "sexual drives," "habits," or "cognitions" as the ultimate chief explanations of human behavior, repeat this primitive pattern of too much theorizing too soon on too grand a scale. On the other hand, faulty as they may be, theories do generate research that establishes fact. These facts, in turn, serve to develop more adequate theory.

Applicability

Users of theories will naturally differ in their needs. The applied worker, such as the nurse, physician, counselor, or teacher, has needs different from the experimental scientist, and these will play an important role in choosing a theory. The experimentalist may be caught up in constructing neat logical structures that are put together in a hierarchical fashion. We may even marvel at his theories. At the same time such theories may not have anything constructive for the nurse, let's say, who wants to know how to deal with the patient who is manifesting a postoperative depressive reaction. The applied worker's need for practical application may lead the practitioner to select less complex theories because they can be of immediate help.

Formal Considerations

Clarity of Concepts. Are the terms of the theories clear and comprehensible? Sometimes theories are couched in confusing technical terms that do not have specific meaning. This creates a communication problem. You may not be sure what is meant by certain terms since various people may use them differently. Some researchers feel that terms such as ego, self, and unconscious fall into the "vague" category since they are used by different people to mean entirely different things. However, some theorists prefer to use "flexible" concepts because they leave room for growth and development.

Research Evidence. Does the theory have a body of evidence to support its assertions, or are the conclusions based on speculation and questionable data? Are conclusions drawn from observations of a sizeable number of subjects? Have findings been confirmed by different investigators? Solid research findings can increase our confidence in a theory. They can also confirm applications of the theory in areas that are of interest to us. Whether research pertains to animals or humans is of relevance. If the theory is based solely on animal behavior we would want to examine this evidence closely. Is there any assurance that the results of the animal research also apply to humans? If so, why hasn't human research been carried out? There may be good reasons, but nevertheless, the questions ought to be asked when evaluating a theory.

Does It Make Sense? Human behavior is a subject that touches us all in a personal way. We all have a large reservoir of experience against which to evaluate behavioral theory, and we can usually relate the theories to something in our own histories and experience. Does a theory in question fit in with our experiences at all? While it is difficult to put sufficient distance between ourselves and our histories to evaluate notions bearing on these experiences, our personal reactions can have merit. A theory in chemistry or physics may be quite foreign to us, but behavior is not.

Consistency. Do the concepts of the theory fit together in a logical pattern? Are there inconsistencies and contradictions? A theory with too much internal confusion may be too primitive for serious consideration. The ideas may be interesting but need further development before we would think of adopting them.

Range. Does the theory address itself to a wide range of behavior? Does it relate to the problems and topics that are of value and interest to us? Even if the theory does not have great practical application in the areas of our special interest, does it tell us anything about these areas? A theory that can predict how fast rats will run a maze, or another one that can explain dreams, may be sound theories, but do they relate to a wider and more inclusive range of behavior that fits our needs?

Fruitfulness. In science it is not as important to be right at any given moment as it is to move in the right direction. The discovery of fact and the development of good theories take a long time and entail many mistakes and stumbling. In the long run, a "poor" theory may be very useful and important in generating research and thinking about problems. A theory may have *heuristic* value, meaning that it stimulates ideas and leads to further discoveries.

Science is replete with this heuristic value of theories. In psychology, for example, behaviorism grew as a reaction to the earlier introspective psychology, instinct psychology, and psychoanalysis. Gestalt psychology arose in protest against behaviorism and other schools. Conflict and confrontation in the scientific sphere are healthy and usually lead to useful constructions. A theory that can stimulate such an intellectual arena, even though it is ultimately rejected, is a useful theory. To recognize the usefulness of a theory it is sometimes necessary to detach ourselves from our immediate and pressing practical professional concerns.

SUMMARY

A theory is a set of concepts that organizes observations, provides an understanding of observations, and makes relevant predictions possible. Theory is important for the health professional because it is the basis for consistency of behavior and procedures. We illustrated how theoretical concepts are unavoidable in dealing with human behavior. Even what is often passed off as "common sense" on closer examination turns out to be theoretical assumptions. Since there are many conflicting theories of human behavior that lead to different courses of professional action—we gave the example of various ways one might go about setting up a play area for children—guidelines are needed for evaluating theories. Six areas were emphasized in making such evaluations: clarity of concepts, research evidence, sense, consistency, range, and fruitfulness.

SUGGESTED READINGS

Brody, B. A., and Capaldi, N. *Science: Men, methods, goals.* New York: W. A. Benjamin, 1968.

Davies, J. T. *The scientific approach.* New York: Academic Press, 1965.

Killeffer, D. H. *How did you think of that? An introduction to the scientific method.* New York: Doubleday, 1969.

Madden, E. H. *The structure of scientific thought.* Boston: Houghton Mifflin, 1960.

Sarton, G. *A history of science.* Cambridge: Harvard University Press, 1959.

Chapter *9*

Freudian Psychology and Psychosexual Development

THE HISTORY OF scientific ideas is filled with examples of "accidents" leading to great discoveries. Considering Sigmund Freud's eminent contribution to our thinking about human psychology, it is startling to realize that he arrived at the study of the mind by accident. As a young physician at the University of Vienna's Physiological Institute in the late 1870s, Freud was far removed from psychology. Only after his prospects for an academic position in physiology looked dim did he reluctantly move into clinical medicine in 1882. It was the repeated contact with hysterical illness in his medical practice that drew Freud's attention to neuroses and the nature of mental functioning.

Today, so many of the terms introduced by Freud have filtered into everyday language that almost everyone seems to be a Freudian to some extent. *Unconscious, Oedipus complex, repression,* and *super-ego,* are just a few of the terms that crop up in ordinary conversation. Many laymen know about Freud more directly through the treatment method of psychoanalysis, which is based on his theory. Many schools of personality and psychotherapy, although not strictly psychoanalytic, still derive a great number of their concepts and techniques from psychoanalysis. Even the social and interpersonal theorists (Chapter 12) who are gaining popularity today have a link with Freud's pioneering work. Some of these theorists have deemphasized or rejected certain of his concepts while developing or extending areas left unexplored by Freud. But Freudian psychology remains the main point of departure for discussions of personality theory.

Popular notions of psychoanalysis and psychotherapy have overemphasized the importance of some Freudian concepts. Consequently many people think of Freudian psychology in terms of "the couch treatment," dream interpretations, sexual conflicts, and free associations. Yet Freudian psychoanalytic psychology is much more than a therapeutic technique or the exclusive concentration on particular problem areas (e.g., sex). *Psychoanalysis is basically a comprehensive theory of human development.* As such, it is important in our discussion of Freudian psychology to clarify the main principles of this developmental theory. Freudian theory is not easy to grasp in its totality, but Rapaport and Gill's analysis (1959) provides a useful approach for understanding the complexities of the theory. According to this analysis, Freudian theory falls in to five types of concepts or points of view: adaptive, dynamic, economic, structural, and developmental.

ADAPTIVE CONCEPT

Behavior, in Freud's view, has an overall goal of adaptation. By adaptation Freud means the organization of behavior in such a way as to gratify impulses. Impulses refer to instinctual drives associated with sexual and aggressive behavior and feelings. In infancy, the behavioral patterns available to the child for adaptive purposes are quite limited and inadequate. Consequently, the infant and young child are frequently in a state of frustration. The development of higher and more varied forms of behavior is necessary for the growing child to achieve adaptation. The child must learn to manipulate the environment in order to get the things necessary for gratification of impulses.

Adaptation is one of the features that permeates all behaviors, both normal and pathological. Sometimes, in immature or pathological behavior, the adaptive aspect is difficult to see. From

Freud's point of view, pathological no less than normal behavior is adaptive in intent. The difference is that the maladaptive person perseveres in more primitive forms of adaptation that do not yield full gratification or mastery of the environment. Take, for example, the whining, complaining person, who sometimes succeeds in getting attention but whose relationship with others is quite limited. He cannot vary his behavior to meet changing situations. In his early environment, whining and complaining may have been the only way he could get the attention of his parents. His behavior therefore may have been initially adaptive—but later on, it is poorly adaptive. In a similar sense, extremely pathological behaviors may be adaptive efforts to adjust to pathological situations. A child in a severely disturbed family may learn to shut out much of his environment in order to survive. But if he continues "shutting out" in a school environment, he may be unable to learn.

DYNAMIC CONCEPT

"Dynamics" refers to the energy force behind behavior. Behavior needs something to get it going and to keep it going—some motive force—and a theory of behavior must explain what motivates behavior. Freudian theory sees one force as driving all behavior from birth to old age. The energy source is called the *libido* or life force, and its goal is reduction of tension—the *pleasure principle.* The libido is tied up with the instinctual (physiological) drives. Release of these drives results in a reduction of tissue irritation, or tension, which is experienced as pleasure. The form that behavior takes in seeking pleasure or reducing drives may shift in each stage of development, but the quest for release from tension is always present.

In a civilized society there are rules and restrictions governing the expression of instinctual drives. While the infant in all cultures may seek impulse gratification in the most direct and primitive manner, society soon intervenes to teach him the prescribed form of expression. For example, in a puritanical society an adolescent seeking sexual gratification may have to go about it in devious and limited ways. On the other hand, in some primitive societies there are fewer restrictions on adolescent sexual behavior, and therefore gratification is sought directly.

Freud believed that restrictions on the expression of impulses were necessary for the evolution of highly developed forms of civilization. Without restrictions, he felt, psychic energy would not be available for sublimation into intellectual and creative activity.

In his early formulation, Freud separated the instincts into the *ego instincts* and the *sexual instincts*. The ego instincts included behaviors necessary for self-preservation, such as eating, safety, mastery of the environment, etc. The sexual instincts, in Freud's expanded conception of sexuality, applied to behavior necessary to the survival of the species; reproduction and associated behaviors. Later, Freud combined the two separate instincts under *eros*. Libido was then viewed as the instinctual energy available to eros, which in turn consists of the self-preservation and sexual instincts. The sexual nature of the libido was established.

The death instinct, another dynamic concept, was introduced in Freud's later writings. In *Beyond the Pleasure Principle* he postulated the existence of a death instinct, *Thanatos*, which worked in opposition to eros (the life instincts). The death instinct presumably had the self-destructive aim of returning the organism to an inorganic state. Most analysts rejected the death instinct as Freud presented it. But there has been wide acceptance of the aggressive aspects of what Freud termed the death instinct. Aggression is viewed as a primary instinct that can work with or against libidinous strivings. For example, when effectively integrated into strivings for success, aggression can enhance behavior. But aggression turned inward can hamper the individual's strivings.

The libidinous energy of eros is focused on different *erogenous zones* of the body at different points in development. The mouth, anus, and genitals become, successively, the focal points of stimulation as development proceeds. Thus, sexuality in Freudian psychology extends to all periods of development from birth onward. His theory of infantile sexuality describes the transformations of the libido during childhood. We will examine this theory in greater detail when considering the developmental point of view.

ECONOMIC CONCEPT

According to the economic point of view, there is a limited but constant supply of energy (libido) available for psychic functioning. Psychic energy cannot be destroyed, only changed. When energy is used for one purpose, the amount available for other purposes is reduced. A person may invest so much of his psychic energy in protecting his self-esteem that he may not have energy for more productive functions. One of the goals of psychoanalysis is to free the energy bound up in pathological behavior, so that the patient can function more effectively. It was because of the economic principle of psychological functioning that Freud viewed the delay of impulse gratification as necessary for civilization to advance. When direct expressions of impulses are the accepted mode, the person has little need to develop skills for mastery of his environment. In this analysis it is the invention of substitute and disguised forms of gratification that carries societies to advanced levels. The ability to channel gratification in creative ways (sublimation) is the highest form of personal expression in Freudian theory.

STRUCTURAL CONCEPT

Freud conceived of mental life in terms of three major structures: *id*, *ego*, and *superego*. The structures are a way of conceptualizing aspects of human functioning. Calling the id, ego, and superego structures does not mean that these entities have a concrete locus or existence in the brain. They are *hypothetical constructs* or useful fictions that have explanatory value. They help us organize human functioning and think about people in a way that is not obvious but nevertheless meaningful. Psychoanalysts have collected a great deal of data to support the usefulness of conceptualizing behavior along the structural lines described by Freud.

Nature of Structures

Two features should be kept in mind when thinking about structures: their design or architectural properties (as hypothetical entities), and the energy source that drives the structure. Knowledge of these two factors will tell a great deal about a given structure, in the same way that the design of a car and the nature of its energy source can tell you the manner in which the car will operate and the limits of its operation. The design of the car will lead you to expect it to move in some ways but not in others—you would not expect a car to fly, for example. The design of a boat, on the other hand, would lead you to other conclusions.

The design properties of Freud's three structures are crucial aspects of their functioning. They tell a great deal about the nature of behavior, which is always mediated through the id, the ego, and the superego. All three generally function at one time, but one of the structures will usually dominate a given behavior pattern. The qualitative aspects of a person's behavior will indicate which structure of his personality is dominant.

The energy source of all behavior in Freud's system is always the same—the libido or life force. The discharge of energy is always the goal of behavior (pleasure principle). But the three structures have different means of achieving the goal of pleasure, i.e., impulse release.

The Id

The id is the most primitive structure of personality. It is the reservoir of the instincts. The id cannot delay discharge of energy; therefore when behavior operates through the id it is impulsive and often inappropriate. The id seeks discharge of its energy—that is, it moves the person to act, whether or not an object or situation that can gratify the impulses is present. The id has no communication with the real world and therefore operates independently of reality. Thus the infant, who is primarily id, screams when hungry and begins to suck even though the nipple or bottle is not present.

The design of the id is simple. Energy goes in and is discharged immediately. The id is a relatively undifferentiated structure, and thinking that operates through the id is characterized by illogic, condensation, and symbolism. This type of thinking is sometimes referred to as *primary process*. Dreams exemplify primary process mechanisms. The content of dreams is frequently very confused and symbolic, with the order of events reversed and other elements of primitive thinking present. During sleep, the higher level controls are relaxed, permitting more primitive mechanisms to come to the fore. Some psychotic states exemplify the confused primary process thinking characteristic of the id. There are also positive aspects of the primary process. This can be seen in the condensation, symbolism, and abstraction of metaphors in poetry as well as expression in other arts.

The Superego

Society and the family prescribe that certain behaviors are acceptable and others taboo. The superego is the structure that embodies the values, customs, prescriptions, and prohibitions that a person internalizes in the course of his development, and that limit the free expression of impulses. The limitations are determined by the particular culture. Some cultures impose severe restrictions on sexual behavior, while others permit open expression of sexuality. Similarly, in some families sex may never be discussed, while other families are quite open about it. In some societies respect for elders is mandated and transgressions treated as severe offenses; other societies merely lament that the young are disrespectful. The examples could go on and on—but the point is that mores are relative. Whatever the culture, the individual must coordinate the impulsive demands of the id and the prohibitions and restrictions of the superego dictated by his particular society. The superego is not all "don'ts," however; just as important are the prescriptions or dictums of good behavior. These are epitomized in the ego ideal of each of us—what we would want to be like if we could. This ego ideal often involves such attributes as goodness, magnanimity, strength, and wisdom.

The superego functions in opposition to the id. The id wants to let go, while the superego strives to hold back. Violations of the superego's prohibitions lead to guilt and anxiety. Sometimes, because of repressive childhood training and a repressive culture, a person's superego is so severe that very few avenues are left open for him to obtain gratification of his impulses. Even minimal expression of impulses will cause intense guilt feelings that can pervade all his behavior. Impulses, however, must ultimately be expressed in some form. The more limited the possibilities for gratification allowed by the superego, the more extreme, devious, or pathological will be the individual's way of getting around it. Sometimes psychotic break-downs or bizarre behavior occur because of the desperate efforts of the individual to break through his internalized prohibitions. When energy is "dammed up" for a long time, it may finally come out in an explosive and uncontrolled manner. For example, a very mild-appearing, friendly, and overly nice person might suddenly go berserk and commit rape, murder, or some other antisocial act. No doubt you have read about such incidents in the newspaper. It is difficult to understand these occurrences without taking into consideration the dynamic interplay of psychic structures introduced by Freud.

The Ego

The ego has mechanisms that enable it to make a realistic assessment of the environment. This assessment is essential for healthy functioning. In fact, Freud stated the goal of his therapy in terms of ego development—"where id was, there ego shall be." Unlike the id, the ego does not discharge energy impulsively but is capable of delaying discharge until an appropriate object or situation exists that can reasonably be expected to yield gratification of impulses. The delaying aspect of the ego renders behavior more adaptive and mature. Because the ego has contact with reality it can mediate between the id and the superego, directing the person to situations that can release impulses, but in a way that is acceptable to the superego.

Depending on the nature of the person's superego, the demands of the id, and the strength of the ego, the ego's task will be more or less difficult.

The action of the ego can be likened to that of a periscope: it scans the environment and exercises reality-testing. In testing reality, the ego processes of memory, attention, concentration, and logical thinking are activated to make an assessment. The ego is searching for an appropriate source of gratification that will be acceptable to the id and superego. There is a delay or binding of instinctual energy as the ego utilizes its structural characteristics. Thus the young boy who hurts himself may not cry until he sees his mother. On the other hand, if his culture makes it taboo for boys to show pain, he will have to find some other way of achieving nurturance and comfort. The adult who is hungry finds a restaurant; he does not scream like the infant. Some people, however, do act in infantile and impulsive ways. Observation of such behavior is important in assessing the relative strength of the person's ego and the person's level of development. Illness and disability tend to bring out the more infantile behavior of people; it is important for the nurse to note the quality of the patient's behavior in order to assess ego strength.

Structures and Psychological Adjustment

Freud's structural view of mental life portrays the individual in a constant state of tension, striving to find some workable compromise among divergent "pulls." Adjustment in this scheme is always a tenuous and delicate balance of forces. There is no pure state of mental health but rather a continuous struggle by the individual to maintain his stability. Psychological adjustment is an active process in which the individual copes with his outer and inner worlds.

Mechanisms of Defense

Defense mechanisms are behavioral techniques devised by the ego to ward off anxiety. Anxiety arises, in the Freudian model, when unacceptable impulses break into consciousness. On a manifest level, the anxiety associated with the breakthrough of unacceptable impulses may be experienced as a loss of self-esteem. For example, the person who finds himself having "bad sexual thoughts" in violation of his high moral standards not only experiences the physiological symptoms of anxiety but also a devaluation of self (i.e., loss of self-esteem). A similar situation may occur with the pacifist who is overcome with rage and has a temper outburst. It is the job of the defense mechanisms to prevent these disruptive feelings from emerging by keeping impulse expression in line with the person's moral standards (superego). People vary in the extent to which they are vulnerable to anxiety. These differences are based on early childhood experiences, culture and family mores, and individual levels of maturity. Anxiety and defensive action will be high for individuals raised in environments where sexual and/or aggressive expression are considered taboo. In less repressive environments, the ego's job of defending against impulse expression will be easier since more avenues will be open for transforming impulses into acceptable behaviors.

As we discuss the various defense mechanisms, we must keep in mind that we all use defense mechanisms and need them for survival. But when they become extreme they distort reality and prevent us from functioning effectively. Psychological well-being requires gratification of impulses, but exaggerated defenses inhibit gratification and lead to symptoms and adjustment problems.

The type of defenses a person uses and the degree to which they are manifested become very important in the diagnosis of psychopathology. The person who quickly blames others, rationalizes his faults, denies his feelings and impulses, or displaces his feelings from one situation to another is utilizing mechanisms of defense. The most commonly used defense mechanisms are:

Repression. In repression an unacceptable thought or impulse is put out of consciousness. A simple example is that of forgetting the name of someone whom you dislike or with whom you are angry. The name is conveniently repressed so that the unpleasant or unacceptable anger associated with the name does not have to be experienced. Repression is also evident in persons with rigid and narrow life patterns that seem devoid of instinctual drive representation. Such people may be totally unaware of any sexual or aggressive thoughts or feelings. Their constricted life styles help maintain repression by keeping them away from stimulating situations. Repression can also be inferred when a person does not experience sexual or aggressive thoughts or feelings at a time when they are appropriate. This can sometimes be seen in psychological testing, when a patient is shown a picture that is suggestive of sexual ideas and is asked to make up a story about the picture. If no sexual associations or connotations are given, repression is very likely taking place.

Repression is basic to all the defense mechanisms. But repression alone is sometimes not sufficient to keep impulses out of consciousness. Then, other mechanisms for transforming or disguising the impulses are invoked by the defensive apparatus of the ego.

Repression must be distinguished from *suppression*. In suppression one is aware of one's unacceptable impulses but makes a conscious effort to direct attention away from them.

Denial. As the name of this defense implies, the person denies the presence of feelings and impulses that can be assumed to be present. People who manifest excessive guilt about sexual and aggressive feelings will often deny that they have such feelings at all. Denial can also be represented in wish-fulfilling fantasies and behaviors that help a person escape from existing realities ("He's living in a dream world"). While denial is usually unconscious, a person can also make conscious efforts of denial. For example, by avoiding unpleasant situations and topics we try to deny them out of existence. Denial, like repression, is a pervasive defense mechanism that is an aspect of most of the other defense mechanisms. When we put an impulse out of consciousness or disguise it, there is always an element of denial operating.

Denial is a defense mechanism that is found prominently in the behavior of hospitalized patients. A patient's need to deny his illness may sometimes be so great that he will do things injurious to his health.

Regression. In regression, the individual who is under stress invokes behavior that was successful at an earlier stage of development. Thus the older child, when frightened, might cry and seek nurturance from his mother as he did when he was a small child. The adult who becomes very helpless and dependent when anxious may also be exhibiting regression. Sometimes, under the pressure of exams, students will revert to oral behavior (overeating) and dependency (an inability to do anything for themselves). Some regressions are only temporary and situational, while others are deeper and more enduring.

Reaction Formation. When this mechanism is used, the person manifests the opposite of his true impulse. Reaction formation protects the person's ego, keeping unacceptable thoughts and feelings out of consciousness by disguising them. The person who cannot accept his own anger may, in situations that evoke aggression, act in the most benign, friendly, and apologetic fashion. The underlying feelings will, however, sometimes slip out in subtle and "accidental" ways. The compulsive person who must be super clean and orderly may be defending against an unconscious impulse to be messy.

Projection. Projection takes place when a person attributes his feelings and attitudes to others. A person who feels guilty about sexual impulses, for example, may constantly perceive others as provocative and "disgusting." The person who perceives himself as the "nice guy" but who quickly or frequently attributes hostile motives to the people around him is often projecting his own repressed impulses. By attributing the "bad" impulses to others the self-esteem of the ego is protected.

Rationalization. We will often rationalize our own behavior when we make mistakes, in order to minimize or negate the errors. Rationalization is a very commonly used defense. One type of rationalization entails the reinterpretation of our own unacceptable behavior in order to present ourselves in a more positive or more favorable light. Statements such as "it was the only appropriate thing to do when he implied that about me" and "my affair with his wife really strengthened their marriage" are examples of rationalization. Explaining failure, as on an exam, by saying, "I wasn't feeling well" can be another rationalization to protect self-esteem. Rationalization is also frequently used to defend against feelings of envy; when beaten out for a higher position, the loser might rationalize with "that job is no good anyway" (sometimes referred to as "sour grapes" reasoning).

Isolation. In isolation—sometimes called isolation of affect—the person's impulses come into consciousness, but the feeling usually associated with the thought or act is cut off from awareness, that is, isolated. An example of isolation is the case of a person who has an obsessive, destructive thought such as killing or harming someone without any accompanying feelings of anger or hostility. People who experience no emotional reaction to emotionally stimulating situations may also be manifesting isolation. In extreme pathological cases of isolation a person may commit an act of violence in a cold and detached manner, unaware of any feelings.

Undoing. The mechanism of undoing entails an act that attempts to cancel out an unacceptable, unconscious wish. Ruth Munroe (1955) gives the example of a woman who had a compulsion to pick up stones on the road "lest someone should be injured." In her dreams and associations, this woman showed a strong death wish concerning her mother. Her compulsion was an unconscious effort to undo the hostile and aggressive thoughts that were trying to gain access to her consciousness.

Displacement.   Sometimes people will transfer feelings or attitudes from their original objects to some other object or situation. For example, the person unable to express anger toward a parent may vent the anger against other authority figures. A person feeling guilty about masturbation may develop a hand-washing compulsion in which the manner of washing clearly resembles the masturbatory act. In these examples of displacement, the original objective is disguised. Nurses encounter displacement when patients respond to them as if they were the parent, spouse, or significant other.

Sublimation.   Sublimation is the most adaptive, productive, and desirable defense mechanism. The defense of sublimation requires the transformation of basic aggressive and sexual impulses into creative expression and activities useful to society. When impulses are repressed, the defensive process draws from the limited psychic energy, thereby reducing the amount available for constructive activities in the external world. Sublimation is the most economical use of energy, because it requires the harmonious functioning of id, ego, and superego. Freud viewed the highest expressions of human beings in the arts as well as other fields as examples of sublimation. Any kind of productive work or socially constructive behavior embodies sublimation.

Defenses and Normal Behavior

While reading about the defense mechanisms you no doubt examined your own behavior to see if they were present. If you have found examples of them it is not necessarily an occasion for alarm. Let us remember that defenses are an aspect of the healthy, well-functioning ego and a very vital and necessary part of all behavior. Within the Freudian scheme defenses are necessary to prevent impulses from emerging in a crude and primitive form. Defenses are basically adaptive mechanisms in that they permit the expression of impulses in a way that is compatible with the rules of society or one's individual values. Defenses become pathological when they are so extreme that they block the expression of impulses and result in behavior that is maladaptive and causes pain and suffering to the individual. In evaluating psychological adjustment Freudian-oriented psychiatrists and psychologists will examine the nature of a person's defenses and the extent to which they are adaptive or maladaptive.

The Unconscious

Freud conceived of three levels of mental functioning—conscious, preconscious, and unconscious. Consciousness refers to the perceptions (including thoughts and feelings) that are in our immediate awareness. Preconscious ideas can readily be made conscious when we make an effort to retrieve them. For example, if you concentrate you may be able to recall certain events from your childhood or of that trip to Spain you took five years ago. But for the moment you may only be aware of reading this sentence; at this time the other ideas are preconscious. Unconscious perceptions, on the other hand, are not available to consciousness. They cannot be easily retrieved because the defense mechanisms keep them unconscious for self-protection.

Discovering the realm of unconscious mental life and behavior was one of Freud's great contributions. While others before him had suggested that behavior had unconscious aspects, it was Freud who made the concept an essential feature of his theory of the mind. To Freud all psychological events have unconscious elements. A person may give one explanation for his behavior, but in psychoanalysis it will be found that there are other dynamics tying his behavior to long-forgotten events and experiences that contribute to the web of unconscious motivation. Examples of the unconscious are not difficult to find. We have all experienced "slips" of the tongue and sudden insight into the "real" reasons behind a particular behavior. Freud documented evidence for the unconscious in *Psychopathology and Everyday Life* (1951).

The unconscious is not confined to any one aspect of mind but is a part of all the structures. Thus id, ego, and superego all have unconscious elements. The id impulses are largely unconscious but become conscious when they break through the defenses. Many of the ego's contacts with reality are conscious, but fantasy production and the dynamic process of defense are largely unconscious. Similarly there are components of the superego that are unconscious and conscious; a person may be aware of his moral precepts but unaware of how they interact with the other structures of personality.

The greater the degree of conflict and repression in the course of a person's development, the greater will be the need to relegate perceptions to the unconscious. As we will see when we talk about the application of Freudian theory and the technique of psychoanalysis, making aspects of the unconscious conscious is an important part of the therapeutic reconstruction of psychoanalysis.

DEVELOPMENTAL (GENETIC) CONCEPT

Development, in Freudian theory, proceeds through a sequence of stages corresponding to the changing manner in which gratification or pleasure is sought. The stages are called *psychosexual stages.* The term "sexual" here should not be confused with the commonplace usage that refers to sexual intercourse or other adult expressions of sexuality. Freud conceived of all pleasure-seeking as basically sexual in origin, in the sense of going back to the same energy source, the libido. Libido expresses itself differently in infancy (sucking) than in adulthood (sexual intercourse). Freud fell into great disrepute in his own time because of his use of the term "infantile sexuality." His Victorian colleagues could only think of sex as genital sexuality. The idea of "pure" infants and children having sexuality was repugnant. Nevertheless, viewing sexuality as a continuous process from birth through adulthood has explanatory and predictive value within the Freudian framework.

Each developmental stage proposed by Freud focuses on a particular problem or crisis. The outcome of these crises in the first six years of life determine a person's personality characteristics in adulthood.

Oral Stage (0–2 Years)

During this period pleasure centers on the mouth; the child's chief means of gratification is through sucking. This stage is characterized by the child's taking gratification from the outside. Disturbances during the oral stage can lead to a variety of personality characteristics and problems having to do with security and nurturance. The person who has not received sufficient gratification during this period can develop an "oral personality," characterized by dependency and the constant seeking of attention, affection, and other forms of nurturance from others. Like the infant, the oral person demands and takes love from others but is unable to give love. Sometimes his needs are overwhelming and insatiable. Another type of reaction to deprivation or frustration during the oral stage is rage. Later manifestations of this reaction can be seen in "oral aggression." The oral-aggressive person is easily frustrated, very demanding, often verbally abusive of others, and in general difficult to please.

Anal Stage (2–4 Years)

Autonomy is the central task of the anal stage. Pleasure during this period centers on elimination processes. Prior to the anal stage the child could eliminate freely without restrictions. Now, when the toilet training begins, he is suddenly asked to control himself. Since pleasure is associated with uninhibited release, this new demand for acquiescence to rules produces a crisis of autonomy versus conformity. The child wants his independence but fears the loss of parental love and approval.

A variety of resolutions are possible. Personality characteristics derived from this period can result in disturbed relationships with authority, ranging from extreme conformity to extreme rebellion. "Anal personalities" are frequently compulsive, ungiving individuals with latent hostility; they are often openly hostile to authority, very challenging in a defiant manner, and condescending toward those weaker than themselves. This type of anal personality takes pleasure in breaking rules and regulations and in being messy in personal habits. These behaviors are reenactments of the child's earlier efforts to defy his parents during the anal stage.

The child who is made to feel guilty about his wishes for autonomy during the anal stage may manifest other characteristics. Fearing the loss of parental love in retaliation for his defiance, the child may, as a reaction formation, become a super conformist. In his behavior the super conformist does the opposite of what he would really like to do. This type of anal personality may follow rules and regulations to their ultimate details, be compulsively neat and orderly, follow well-regulated and rigid routines, and in many respects lead a narrow and circumscribed life.

Phallic Stage (4–6 Years)

During the phallic stage, pleasure centers on the genital area. Boys become aware of the penis and girls of the vagina and clitoris, and they may masturbate actively because of the pleasurable sensation from the genital erogenous zone. Children become keenly aware of sexual differences during the phallic stage, and the problem of sexual role identification is central.

Children test out their newly perceived sexuality on those closest to them. Boys therefore become attracted to their mothers (Oedipus complex) and girls to their fathers (Electra complex). These incestuous desires and fantasies are usually more unconscious or implicit than conscious, manifesting themselves in a desire to possess or have an exclusive relationship with the parent of the opposite sex. As a consequence the child has feelings of rivalry, competition, and hostility toward the parent of the same sex. The conflict is successfully resolved when the child identifies with the parent of the same sex. In this manner the child achieves a sense of masculinity or femininity and gives up the incestuous object choice.

In the course of the Oedipus complex the paramount fear for boys is punishment through castration by the father. Castration anxiety prompts identification with the aggressor-father. In identifying with the father and giving up the incestuous object choice (the mother), the moral component of personality (superego) emerges; identification entails the adoption of the standards and restrictions represented by the father. In Freud's word, the superego is the "heir" to the Oedipus complex.

The course of sexual development is somewhat different for girls than for boys, according to Freud. The boy's early attachment to the mother flows naturally into the Oedipal strivings but the girl must shift attention from the mother to the father. This is not so easily accomplished and many girls persist in the attachment to the mother. Freud places great weight on the anatomical differences between girls and boys in accounting for female sexual development. According to Freud, when girls become aware of their lack of a penis they conclude that they have been castrated. As a result girls feel inferior (penis envy). It is this assumed depreciation of the female that paves the way for the girl to reject her mother and turn to the father. The mother becomes a rival when the girl desires to posess the father. The girl also replaces the wish for a penis with a wish for a child. This complex series of events leads to female identification as the girl takes on what Freud believed to be the necessary passive female role. But, since girls already feel castrated, there is no powerful reason for quickly resolving the Electra complex; mother cannot do harm comparable to the castration that boys fear from fathers. Consequently, the Electra complex lingers longer than the Oedipus complex and it inhibits moral (i.e., superego) development.

Freud's Victorian views, which assigned inferior status to women, have little support in present-day psychoanalysis. The social theorists and ego psychologists have placed heavy emphasis on human relationships in sexual development; role models, education, self- and interpersonal awareness take the foreground over anatomical differences. Fortunately, Freud's overall theory does not hinge on male-female sexual differences, and revisions can readily be made to incorporate more recent insights.

Later problems of homosexuality, heterosexual relationships, competition, and ambitiousness are associated with the phallic stage. Preference for older men or women in heterosexual relationships may represent the lingering Oedipal wish for the parent of the opposite sex.

People who freeze up in competitive situations may have unresolved guilt associated with the rivalry with the parent of the same sex; competing may have incestuous overtones that make the person stop himself before consummating the competitive wish. One interpretation of homosexuality views it as the inability to identify with the parent of the same sex during the phallic stage. The person who relishes "love triangles" may be reliving an unresolved Oedipus complex. These are just a few of the many personality characteristics that can stem from the phallic stage.

Latency (6-11 Years)

The latency period is characterized by relative quiescence. There are no new developmental crises during latency; it is a time of integration of earlier psychosexual stages and of development of ego skills for mastering the environment. During this period the child's attention is turned outward to his environment. Since there are no new conflicts, this period is regarded as ideal for education. The child is very responsive to learning and is eager to acquire new skills. The attitudes of the family and society determine whether the latency period is used to best advantage. If society invests in its young and has meaningful roles for its children and preadolescents, the enthusiasm and energy of this period can be harnessed in a beneficial and productive way. If, on the other hand, childhood is regarded as a meaningless custodial period, then a crucial opportunity for the personal development of individuals, and in turn society, may be lost.

Genital Stage (11-16 Years)

The genital stage is coincidental with adolescence. This period is marked by the surge of genital sexual development. There is the appearance of secondary sexual characteristics including pubic hair, development of breasts in girls, the descending of the testes in boys, the advent of menstruation, and an increase in the internal secretion of sex hormones. For boys frequent erections and nocturnal emissions may occur. In girls the vaginal area and clitoris in particular become more sensitive to stimulation. Active sexual fantasies and masturbation are commonplace during this period.

The person at this stage is physiologically ready for mature sexual behavior. In fact, he must in some way deal with his heightened sexual tensions. In the Freudian view, the energy must be expressed. The manner of sexual expression at this time establishes the pattern for adult life. The genital period is the culmination of all the stages that precede it. If the crises at the earlier psychosexual stages have not been successfully mastered, remnants from those faulty resolutions will be manifested in adult sexual activities, interpersonal relations, and work life. Some of the potential fixations from earlier stages have already been mentioned: the man or woman who seeks dependent and nurturant relationships (oral remnant), the person who needs to dominate in love relationships (anal remnant), the person who likes to "steal" partners from others (phallic-Oedipal remnant) are three typical genital-stage patterns that are carryovers from earlier stages.

EGO PSYCHOLOGY

At its inception Freudian psychology concentrated primarily on the internal conflicts of the individual in his struggle with the demands of instinctual drives for impulsive expression. This was consistent with early Freudian theory, which regarded the infant as all id (impulses) and saw the controlling or reality-oriented ego as nonexistent at birth and evolving slowly with maturity. Modern Freudian psychologists and psychiatrists have rejected this view of development and have given much more importance to the ego. Ego psychology asserts that the ego, with all its mechanisms for potential adaptation to the real world, exists from the start of life.

Initially the ego is "conflict-free." It is only when conflict arises in the course of development that the ego becomes distracted from focusing its energy on productive involvement with the outside world to deal with the conflict. The greater the amount of conflict the more engulfed the ego becomes in dealing with intrapsychic tension, thereby lessening its ability to exercise conflict-free functioning. With this altered view of the ego, Freudian psychology has shifted its concern from the impulses to the social world and the way in which the individual interacts with his environment to achieve psychological adjustment or adaptation and gratification.

Recognition of the ego as a primary structure has called attention to motives other than sex and aggression. The ego displays a real interest in the world, and the person obtains satisfaction from the exercise of ego functions. Curiosity, mastery, and self-actualization enter as strivings in their own right. The social theorists, who are discussed in Chapter 12, have contributed many of the concepts basic to ego psychology.

APPLICATION IN NURSING AND HEALTH CARE

At this point you have probably realized that Freudian ideas have shaped some of your perceptions of other people. Since Freud based his work on studies of people with emotional problems, his ideas have been extensively applied to the understanding of pathological functioning and behavior under stress conditions. In your professional life you will meet people in the throes of crises both physical and mental. Therefore Freudian psychology can be an important part of your professional equipment, and throughout this book there are references to its application. In illustrating its application here, we will emphasize certain broad areas of the theory.

The Unconscious

Freudian psychology teaches us not to be misled by the obvious overt behavior of patients. From the Freudian point of view there is more to the person than what immediately meets the eye. The nurse, in striving to understand patients and design a mode of relating to each of them, needs to explore the meaning of behavior with care. What is the meaning of anxiety, fear, dependency, hostility, friendliness? How much of the patient's behavior has a realistic basis and how much a neurotic origin? Sometimes it is tempting just to take behavior at face value and look no further. After all, one might argue, doesn't the search for "hidden meaning" destroy the simplicity, honesty, and spontaneity of human relations? Frequently the health professional must undergo some hard experiences before recognizing that helping a patient may require a sophisticated understanding of behavior and attention to unconscious needs. For example, it may be tempting to give in immediately to the dependency strivings of the patient and bombard him with support, encouragement, and affection. However, if these needs have deep roots and gratify infantile longings, the patient may regress into a passive state of increased demands that eventually destroys his relationship with the nurse and slows his will to recover. Aggression is another case in point. The patient who enters a relationship with the nurse expressing anger, hostility, and criticism can put off the nurse who is guided by her "honest" reactions. If you are attacked, the natural response is to defend yourself and to retaliate. But in this instance, the genuine reaction is clearly inappropriate and nonprofessional.

Stages of Development

The developmental theory of Freud calls our attention to the relationship of present behavior to earlier psychosexual stages. The residue of the stage of development at which the person's behavior is largely rooted serves as a screen through which he interprets his experiences. For example, under stress or frustration the oral person will feel insecure, dependent, and enraged, based on his adjustment to stress at the earlier period. The person with unresolved anal stage problems may perceive stress in terms of the weakness he associates with the earlier pressure to conform. Therefore, he may become rebellious, defiant, or superconformist, as the case may be. For the person whose development is lodged primarily at the phallic stage, stress may be a signal of the danger associated with forbidden wishes and the punishment feared in relation to those wishes. In recognizing the predominance of a stage-specific reaction pattern, the nurse can adjust her behavior accordingly. The anal patient who is sensitive to feelings of weakness can be given a greater feeling of control by including him in the decision-making process. The oral person may need a great deal of reassurance, sympathy, support, and individual attention. The guilt and fear of the phallic-stage person may be lessened by reassurance of a different type; making explicit that he is liked and accepted by others and that he is not responsible or to blame for his situation (i.e., not being punished) speaks directly to the unconscious fears guiding his behavior.

These brief vignettes are only a few suggested applications of knowledge about stages of development. In actual health-care situations the nurse will have to guide her responses by the momentary cues given off by the patient. But awareness of the stage phenomenon can enable the nurse to address herself appropriately to dynamics that are present but not obvious.

Defenses

It is important to recognize and respect a person's defenses, as Allen V. Wheelis (1954) illustrates in the following case. The patient happens to be a nurse.

Jean S. had been head nurse in the pediatric department of a small hospital. Highly regarded by her colleagues, she was a very con-

scientious nurse whose dedication to the job went beyond the specified duties. She would often voluntarily work overtime checking on
various children. Her mental problems, resulting in hospitalization,
developed after the following incident:

> Three months previously she had returned to the hospital at midnight
> because of her concern for a child critically ill with diphtheria. She stood
> by his bed for half an hour or more closely observing him. Presently his
> labored breathing became faint. She sent the student nurse to get the
> resident. In the ensuing delay the child's breathing stopped entirely.
> Cyanosis became marked. She opened the tracheotomy set which was at
> the bedside, took out a scalpel, and incised the child's neck. "Blood was
> everywhere. I cut too far. His trachea was so small and slippery I'd get
> hold of it and then lose it in all that blood!" A few minutes later the
> resident arrived and with some difficulty completed the operation. The
> child died the following morning at 9:30, Jean having remained
> continuously with him. She was not censured for her act; indeed several
> of her colleagues commended her for her brave attempt. She, too, felt
> that she had acted rightly and subsequently was aware of no sense of
> guilt. Nevertheless, it was immediately after the death of this child that
> her symptoms began. (p. 124)

Feelings of inadequacy in her professional as well as in her social life,
along with feelings of depression and anxiety, began to overwhelm
her. She worried continuously about the patients she was caring for
and would cry without any apparent reason. Jean hospitalized
herself voluntarily—but the hospitalization lasted only three days.
At the end of this time she checked herself out, saying that she was
lonely and that her husband needed her.

In discussing the case, Wheelis emphasizes the errors that were
made in treating Jean. In the course of treatment, various insights
relating to destructive impulses were uncovered. As they were presented, however, they only served to agitate the nurse more, and this
led to her checking out. Wheelis points out that the patient would
have ultimately been able to tolerate insight, but her anxiety needed
to be diminished and her defenses strengthened so that insight could
be achieved under conditioning that would enable her to integrate
the insight. Furthermore, Jean had shown a previous pattern of
compulsive defenses—that is, a pattern of highly organized
scheduled tasks that served to keep threatening impulses from consciousness in her everyday life. The lack of structured activities at
the hospital tended to increase Jean's anxiety, because she could not
exercise her usual compulsive pattern of behavior. Wheelis suggests
that the hospital should have given her a nurse or a companion to

help her get into her usual style of functioning. If these and a few other measures had been taken, Wheelis believes, the patient could have been treated with slow doses of insight to help her make a good recovery.

Hospitalization can disrupt a patient's usual mode of adaptation, resulting in a breakdown of defenses. The sensitive nurse must be alert to a patient's defenses and attempt to create conditions that allow the patient to function most effectively. Patients who cannot muster their characteristic defenses will experience intense anxiety, which may be detrimental to their prognosis and recovery. We have already indicated how anxiety can impair recovery from all kinds of illness.

Catharsis

In psychoanalytic treatment catharsis has a particular meaning, referring to the release of emotion inhibited by early conflict. In a broader sense, catharsis means the release of emotional tension in general. Tension often works in a circular fashion, generating more tension, which in turn can magnify a person's problems and create new ones. Emotional release is an important component of effective mental functioning. Patients have different styles of releasing tension. Some can do it through creative activities, while others may get angry, explosive, and abusive; some may cry or yell for help. It is important for the nurse to recognize a patient's need for catharsis and not to overreact to emotionalism. Sometimes the nurse may have to help a patient express his feelings in order for catharsis to take place. Once tension has been released through catharsis, a patient may be able to take distance from his problems and develop more realistic reactions. We are all familiar with the positive effects that accrue from "crying it out" or "getting it off my chest." Sometimes patients need reassurance that, in "letting go," they have not lost face or respect.

SUMMARY

Freudian psychology is a comprehensive theory of human development. Many people are familiar with this school of psychology through its clinical treatment method, called psychoanalysis. Freudian theory of personality consists of five types of concepts: adaptive, dynamic, economic, structural, and developmental. The goal of all behavior in Freudian psychology is pleasure or tension reduction. The organism is seen as initially impulsive in its quest for pleasurable gratification, with delaying controls developing over time as a more effective means of achieving its goal. Human motivation is both unconscious and conscious, with the unconscious aspect given primary importance. The libido or life force that energizes behavior is mediated through the three structures of personality—id, ego, and superego. The id contains the instinctual drives and functions impulsively. The superego embodies the prohibitions of society and the family, placing restrictions on the impulses of the id; it also embodies the person's ego ideal of what he would like to be. The ego is the structure that assesses reality and, therefore, moderates between the impulsiveness of the id and the restrictions of the superego by finding realistic methods of compromise. Defense mechanisms are an important part of the ego's functions. Defenses ward off anxiety and protect self-esteem. Modern Freudians have focused their attention more on the ego in relation to the social environment than on conflicts arising from sexual and aggressive drives. Illustrations of applications of Freudian psychology to nursing and health care were given in the relation to the unconscious stages of development, the defense mechanisms, and catharsis.

SUGGESTED READINGS

Fancher, R. E. *Psychoanalytic psychology: The development of Freud's thought.* New York: Norton, 1973.

Freud, S. *Civilization and its discontents.* London: Hogarth Press, 1930.

Freud, S. *A general introduction to psychoanalysis.* Garden City, N.Y.: Garden City Publishing, 1943.

Freud, S. *Psychopathology and everyday life.* New York: Mentor, 1951.

Munroe, R. L. *Schools of psychoanalytic thought.* New York: Dryden Press, 1955.

Chapter 10

Conditioning, Behaviorism, and Behavior Modification

CONDITIONING, behaviorism, and behavior modification are all aspects of one basic approach to human behavior—the psychology of learning. As in other areas of psychology, learning psychologists have differences as well as similarities. In this chapter we will present the major points of view that have influenced modern learning theory and some of the techniques now gaining popularity.

The learning-theory approach to behavior has its roots in the work of Ivan Pavlov (1849-1936) on the conditioned reflex. Although Pavlov was more interested in the activity of the cerebral cortex than in a theory of learning, other psychologists saw in the conditioned reflex the basis for understanding human behavior. Beginning in the 1920s, American psychologists extended Pavlov's work and developed more elaborate techniques and concepts of conditioning.

Today, conditioning approaches to human behavior problems are attracting a great deal of attention. The learning-theory method of changing behavior does not require overhauling the entire personality, and it has always had a certain appeal because of its direct, practical bent. Behavior modification techniques are finding a wide variety of health care applications, as we will illustrate at the end of this chapter.

CONDITIONING
Conditioned Reflex

In the conditioning process, a previously neutral stimulus acquires the ability to elicit a response that was tied to another stimulus. Pavlov demonstrated classical conditioning in his famous experiments with dogs. A dog naturally salivates when presented with meat. The relationship between the stimulus, meat, and the response, salivation, is called a reflex. The reflex involves an unconditioned stimulus and an unconditioned response. Both stimulus and response are called unconditioned because the relationship is guaranteed, that is, a biological given. Salivating when food is placed on the tongue, blinking when a puff of air is blown on the eyelid, and all other reflexes are part of the biological makeup of the organism. The responses do not require learning.

Pavlov introduced a neutral stimulus—a bell—simultaneously or slightly before the presentation of the meat; he found that eventually, after repeated trials, the dog would salivate to the bell without the presence of food. Since bells do not ordinarily produce salivation, the dog's salivation to the bell alone is a learned response that is acquired through the conditioning arrangement.

Figure 10.1

Meat—Unconditioned stimulus (US) ⟶ Salivation—Unconditioned response (UR)

Bell—Conditioned stimulus (CS) ⟶ Conditioned response (CR)

It is easy to see from Figure 10.1 why conditioning is sometimes called *substitution learning*. The conditioned stimulus (previously neutral stimulus) substitutes for the unconditioned stimulus in eliciting the salivation response. Once a conditioned stimulus-response (S-R) association is established, the conditioned stimulus can be used as if it were an unconditioned stimulus to obtain *higher order conditioning*. Thus a light can be paired with the bell, ultimately resulting in the dog salivating to the light.

Conditioning involves other relationships more complex than the brief and simple model presented above. For example, the conditioning relationship will be influenced by the time span between the introduction of the conditioned stimulus and the unconditioned stimulus. Let us suppose there were a delay of three seconds between the bell ringing and the presentation of the meat; later, when the bell alone is presented, there would be a three-second delay before the dog would salivate. This is known as delayed conditioning. Other factors, such as the frequency of pairing of the conditioned stimulus and the unconditioned stimulus and the intensity of the conditioned stimulus, would also affect the nature of the conditioned response.

Pavlov conducted his experiments in a soundproof laboratory equipped with special apparatus. In a natural environment conditioning is somewhat more difficult to obtain. There may be many noises and other distractions (incidental stimuli), which may make it difficult for the animal or person being conditioned to discriminate the stimulus that is to be learned or substituted.

CONDITIONING AND HUMAN BEHAVIOR

John Watson was the first American psychologist to see, in Pavlov's experiments, a key to all of human behavior. It seemed to Watson that even the most complex and sophisticated human behaviors were merely conditioned responses that had developed over the course of time. According to Watson, all human beings are born with a set of reflexes—or, as he referred to them, "squirmings." These "squirmings" are acted upon by the environment so that, as in Pavlov's experiment, new stimuli come to elicit them. As more and more conditioned responses emerge, the complex behaviors of the adult come into existence. On the surface it might seem that the complex emotional, intellectual, and social behaviors of the adult are far removed from reflexes and that behavior is too varied to be accounted for by the simple set of reflexes present at birth. Watson recognized this apparent incongruity and countered with the following argument: Given even 100 "squirmings" at birth, the possible combinations of these 100 responses are phenomenally large. All the various combinations of 100 responses would be represented by 100 factorial. To compute 100 factorial you multiply $100 \times 99 \times 98 \times \cdots \times 1$. The result, as Watson points out, "is a colossal, stupendous number. If any human being possessed 100 factorial responses, he would have so many that he could not run through his repertoire of responses if he lived to be as old as

Methuselah" (Watson, 1928). In his humorous and flamboyant manner Watson also cited the area of language behavior:

> You think you use almost a limitless number of words. As a matter of fact, few of us adults use more than 8,000 words. Most of us get along on less than 2,000, many get along on 500–800 words. Society in America as we have it today calls upon us to possess such a simple set of adjustments. Our accomplishments, even our words and sentences, are so limited and stereotyped that you can pretty well predict what the majority of men and women are going to say and do in most situations. We are so stupidly uninteresting. (Watson 1928, pp. 33–34)

Instrumental Conditioning

After Watson, learning psychologists began to emphasize another form of conditioning called instrumental conditioning. Instrumental conditioning requires the person or animal to do something before the reward or reinforcement is introduced. In other words, the correct or desired response must be made, then some reward follows. In one type of experiment demonstrating instrumental learning, rats must press a bar before pellets of food are released; the rats must learn to make the correct response in order to be fed. This is quite different from Pavlov's dog, which did not have to do anything in order to be fed, the food being part of the experimental arrangement. Most modern learning theorists view instrumental learning as playing a far greater role in human behavior than the classical conditioning of Pavlov.

Other Characteristics of Behaviorism

Reinforcement. Reinforcement is the single most important concept of modern behaviorism and learning theory. Most of the techniques of behavior modification and behavior change are based on reinforcement. Essentially, reinforcement is any stimulus that increases the probability of a response occurring. If, for example, we note that when a child is given candy after making a certain response he tends to repeat or learn that response, we say the candy was a reinforcement. In the case of the rats who must press a bar to obtain food, the food is reinforcement. Some behaviorists speak of reinforcement as something that the person or animal desires or finds pleasurable; other theorists try to avoid identification of reinforcement with feeling states and prefer to define it in terms of a stimulus that results in learning. The effect of reinforcers on behavior has been investigated in many controlled studies. Reinforcers are not restricted to concrete things such as candy or money but also include verbal stimuli such as praise and social stimuli such as interest in and attention to the person. Often reinforcement involves a combination of different types of stimuli.

"What You See Is What You Get."   The emphasis in behaviorism is on observable behavior. The person consists of the sum of his behaviors, i.e., of what he does. Processes that cannot be directly observed are, to the behaviorist, fanciful and nonscientific constructs. From its inception behaviorism strived to place psychology on a solid scientific footing. In its effort to do so it wanted to rid itself of the subjectivity and speculation that had previously characterized philosophical psychology. Like the physical sciences, it wanted to deal with data that could be experimentally observed and manipulated. Observable behaviors fit that bill. In turn, the behaviorists ridiculed terms such as conscious, unconscious, ego, mental ability, and will power as unscientific and in the same realm as terms like "soul." To the behaviorist, the person is his behavior and nothing more.

Learning Is Automatic.   In learning to salivate to the sound of a bell Pavlov's dog had very little to say about the matter. Given the context of the experiment, conditioning took place automatically. When a response is reinforced a sufficient number of times it will automatically occur. Behaviorists reject implications of inner processes of motivation or goal direction that are supposed to supersede external and observable conditions. In fact, concepts implying elusive unobservable internal structures are flatly rejected by behaviorists. The conditions of learning are maintained and controlled by factors external to the organism. What we often refer to as motives, desires, goals, and so on are, according to the behaviorists, nothing more than habitual learned patterns that are stamped in by external conditions. In short, purpose, goals, choice, and any other notions of unobservable inner forces are, in the behaviorists' view, illusions.

External Control of Behavior.   It is the reinforcers, according to modern behaviorists, that control, guide, and maintain behavior. Since reinforcement is associated with an external stimulus, motivation for behavior is outside the person. The environment acts on the person and the person responds to the environment. This is in contrast to other views that ascribe a more active role to internal forces in the individual. For the behaviorists the only behavior that can occur consistently is that which is called forth by stimuli and then reinforced by environmental events.

Learning Is Linear and Quantitative. Figure 10.2 represents development from childhood through adulthood in two ways: by a straight line and by a broken line. Behaviorism would correspond to the straight line (Model A). In this model there is little basic difference between the child and the adult. The adult has more complex (i.e., a greater quantity of) learned habits than the child but the units of behavior (habits) are the same. Development, then, is a process of getting more of a unit which is there from the start. John Watson's prescription to parents in his book on infant and child care to treat children "as though they were young adults" is an expression of the *linear, quantitative* view of development.

In the second, broken-line model (Model B), development is seen as occurring in distinct, qualitatively different stages (this "stage" model will be discussed in greater detail in Chapter 11, in connection with Jean Piaget).

Child ——Adult

Model A

Figure 10.2

Child — — — — — — — — — — — Adult

Model B

Environmentalism. The behaviorist's position is one of extreme environmentalism. He places great stress on the environment as determining behavior and development. Heredity and biological factors play a small role (except in cases of obvious biological defects). Watson was very definitive and unhedging in his statements on the environmental point of view. In *The Ways of Behaviorism* (1928) he states:

Conditioning—nurture not nature . . . (p. 28)

Give me the baby and my world to bring it up in and I'll make it a thief, a gunman or a dope fiend. The possibility of shaping in any direction is endless. (p. 35)

Placing its faith in the environment, behaviorism has always held out great hope for changing behavior at any time in a person's life. If behavior is initially shaped by experiences (the environment), new experiences could presumably be introduced to reshape behavior. Extreme environmentalism rejects any notions of inherited talents, abilities, interests, goals, or purposes. All of the latter are determined by experience. The behaviorist position in this regard is a very optimistic one. It attributes great plasticity to behavior and suggests equality of possibilities among all humans, given equality of opportunity. Any notion of a fixed personality or fixed intelligence is rejected by behaviorists.

Behavior Is the Problem, Not Just a Symptom. In the area of pathological or problem behavior, the behaviorist differs sharply with those "dynamic" psychologists who stress internal conflicts. To the behaviorist, deviant behavior *is* the person's problem; such behavior is not regarded as merely a symptom of some other, possibly hidden or unconscious, problem. Since the behaviorist accepts nothing beyond what he observes, i.e., overt behavior, his therapeutic efforts are directed toward changing the overt behavior rather than solving "invisible" conflicts.

Opponents of behaviorism have argued that merely changing a segment of undesirable behavior or removing a symptom will result in substitution of another undesirable behavior or symptom. However, Bandura (1969) has pointed out that symptom substitution occurs only when faulty or incomplete conditioning procedures are used. He emphasizes the need not only to remove the reinforcing conditions that are maintaining the undesirable behavior or symptom (which would lead to extinction of the response) but also to reinforce alternate desirable behavior. Under these conditions, he maintains, positive behavioral changes will be enduring, and symptoms will not recur or be substituted by new symptoms.

Learning versus Personality

As we have seen, behavioristic theories are frequently referred to as learning theories because of their environmental emphasis. Behavior, according to this view, is acquired or developed through experience, i.e., learned. Theories that are called "personality" theories characteristically talk about entities or structures within the person that are independent of experience. Internalized structures proposed by personality theories are also attributed motive force of their own apart from immediate environmental influences. For example, the statement "John hit Robert because he has an aggressive personality" suggests some force within John that directs him to certain behaviors. Behaviorists, on the other hand, do not like to use concepts such as personality, which they see as implying a sort of "little man" within each person that guides and directs behavior. Rather, they prefer to describe the environmental conditions that guide and direct observable behavior. From the point of view of the behaviorist, John is aggressive because there are certain specific stimuli that elicit and maintain his aggressive behavior; apart from these conditions there is no aggressive personality.

The difference between personality theory and learning theory, then, is one of preferred concepts of development and behavior, not one of scope or objective. Both theories can deal with the totality of human functioning or with limited areas. The designation "learning theory" or "personality theory" only gives a clue as to the type of concepts employed. The learning theories of Watson and B. F. Skinner strive to explain all behaviors (including emotional, social, intellectual, pathological, and normal) in terms of behavioral principles. Freud's personality theory has the same goal but approaches the task with different methods and concepts.

B. F. SKINNER AND BEHAVIORISM

B. F. Skinner is the spiritual leader of the modern behaviorist movement. After John Watson, behaviorism fell into relative disuse as a practical approach to behavior problems and psychopathology. The dominance of psychoanalysis in psychopathology overshadowed behaviorism from the 1930s through the 1960s. Yet during the same period behaviorism was very much alive and well at universities in the field of experimental psychology. Such distinguished theorists as Edwin Guthrie, Clark Hull, and Kenneth Spence, as well as B. F. Skinner, were prominent and active. Unlike John Watson, however, who had from the outset applied behaviorism to everyday problems of living such as enuresis, thumb sucking, phobias, and other maladaptive behaviors, the leading behaviorists who followed him concentrated on laboratory studies of animal learning until the 1960s. Only in the field of education was behaviorism actively applied, because of the relevance of learning theory for the acquisition of academic curriculum skills. (It may be that the close association between learning theory and "school learning" has contributed to the misleading dichotomy between learning theories and personality theories.) But the diligent and persistent work of behavioral researchers over the past forty years has now enabled behaviorism to return to the arena of the study of human behavior with more sophisticated and comprehensive concepts and methods. B. F. Skinner's work stands as the major theoretical foundation upon which modern behaviorism has been built.

Two Types of Conditioning

Watson viewed all behavior in terms of classical, Pavlovian conditioning. But Skinner found classical conditioning too limited to account for all behavior. While he recognized that classical conditioning did apply to some behaviors, there were many in which unconditioned stimuli could not be discerned. It seemed to Skinner that there are many behaviors that are "emitted" by the organism and that "operate" on the environment. The specific stimuli that elicit these emitted behaviors are unknown. Skinner called these *operant* (as opposed to *respondent*) behaviors. In respondent behavior the stimulus eliciting the behavior is known. Respondent conditioning follows the principles of classical conditioning as described by Pavlov and Watson. But operant behavior, which is the more typical type of behavior, follows different principles of conditioning. Examples of operant behavior are talking, aggressive behavior, and social behavior. In all of these cases we cannot specify the stimulus or stimuli related to the behaviors; we can only note that the behavior is emitted. Operant conditioning is very much like instrumental conditioning. The organism is rewarded when he "emits" the desired response and this results in the learning of that response, i.e., increases the probability of the emitted response recurring under the same conditions.

Controlling Operants

Skinner is not too concerned with the stimuli behind operants. Since operant behavior can be brought under control through external reinforcement it is not important to determine the stimulus or stimuli that originally elicited an operant. In general, Skinner is not very interested in underlying processes. In Skinner's science of behavior, inferred processes are unnecessary as long as behavior can be controlled through the manipulation of observable stimuli.

In his research with pigeons Skinner has demonstrated how the control of operants works. Pigeons typically peck. This pecking behavior is operant in that it is emitted by the pigeon and operates on the environment. The specific stimulus related to pecking behavior is not clear. Nevertheless, Skinner found that he could control the pigeons' pecking behavior through the use of positive *reinforcement.* By giving the pigeon a pellet of food after the pigeon had pecked in a designated place, he was able to increase the probability of the pigeon's pecking at the same spot. Through the manipulation of various *schedules of reinforcement* Skinner found that he could get a high degree of control over the pigeons' pecking behavior. In the same manner behaviors could often be shaped in a desired direction. By arranging the conditions of reinforcement Skinner found that he could shape behavior to a remarkable degree. Even highly improbable behaviors (improbable in the natural environment) could be consistently elicited.

Operant Conditioning and Human Behavior

Most human behavior, according to Skinner, is in the operant category. As such, these behaviors are subject to *contingencies of reinforcement*. It is the conditions of reinforcement that will control and direct operant behavior. If you want to change an operant behavior it is necessary to change the contingencies of reinforcement—you must withdraw the reinforcement that is maintaining the behavior or reinforce an alternate desired behavior. In this view, Skinner is as optimistic as Watson in his confidence in the almost limitless possibilities for shaping human behavior and human society. Skinner's view is clearly expressed through Frazier, one of the characters in his novel, *Walden II* (1948), which depicts a utopian society based on the science of learning:

> "Now," Frazier continued earnestly, "if it is in our power to create any of the situations which a person likes, or to remove any situation he doesn't like, we can control his behavior. When he behaves as we want him to behave, we simply create a situation he likes, or remove one he doesn't like. As a result, the probability that he will behave that way again goes up, which is exactly what we want." (p. 259)

Punishment and Learning

Punishment is popularly considered the opposite of reinforcement. This conception of punishment is an error, according to Skinner:

> "The old school made the amazing mistake of supposing that the reverse was true, that by removing a situation a person likes or setting up one he doesn't like—in other words by punishing him—it was possible to reduce the probability that he would behave in a given way again. That simply doesn't hold. It has been established beyond question. What is emerging at this critical stage in the evolution of society is a behavioral and cultural technology based on positive reinforcement alone. We are gradually discovering—at an untold cost in human suffering— that in the long run punishment doesn't reduce the probability that an act will occur." (p. 260)

In his research Skinner found that punishment does not result in the unlearning of an undesired response but merely a *"suppression in the rate of responding."* A patient who, let's say, is denied reading material as a punishment for not following hospital routine may capitulate. It may appear on the surface that the patient learned something through punishment. Actually, however, when the nurse isn't around the patient will very likely revert to his previous behavior. Similarly, the punitive practices of a conquering army may make people submit to their wishes. But the submissiveness can only be maintained through the continuance of a high level of punishment. The victimized do not learn to love their masters, and their behavior usually changes when direct threat is removed. The adage "don't turn your back on your enemies" is a statement of the ineffectiveness of punishment for learning.

Skinner's principle, then, with regard to reward and punishment is to elicit and reward desired behavior and to avoid the use of punishment. He simply finds punishment ineffective in the long run.

BEHAVIOR MODIFICATION
New Techniques

In addition to reinforcement, behavior modification specialists have developed other techniques for changing maladaptive behavior, which are derived from learning theory. Some of these techniques combine several behavioral principles.

Token Reinforcement. In token reinforcement the direct application of reinforcers is delayed through the use of tokens. Tokens are awarded when the desired responses are made. After a specified number have been accumulated, these tokens can be redeemed for the actual reinforcers. For example, patients can be given tokens for manifesting desired behavior such as cooperation, neatness, socializing, pursuing interests, and so on. These tokens can later be turned in for privileges. Token reinforcement has been applied effectively in ward management problems. (A more detailed example will be given at the end of this chapter.)

Shaping. In this technique reinforcement is used to condition successive close approximations of some desired behavior. The technique is particularly useful in cases of disability, where a desired behavior or motor activity is not part of the repertoire of the person because of his disability. For example, it is possible to shape the fine motor coordination of a child suffering from cerebral palsy by reinforcing the closest possible approximations until the terminal behavior is achieved. Shaping is frequently a painstaking process that requires a great deal of patience and careful observation of the person's behavior to locate the approximations. But in the end it is possible to condition behaviors that were not thought possible of achievement.

Relaxation.   In relaxation therapy the person is presented with fear- or conflict-inducing stimuli while in a relaxed state. The relaxation is incompatible with and comes to replace the anxiety or fear reaction usually associated with the stimulus. In using this technique, stimuli related to but somewhat removed from the actual fear-inducing stimulus are presented in sequential form until finally the actual target stimulus is presented to the person in this relaxed state. Both fantasy and in vivo forms of relaxation procedures are used. In the fantasy form the patient is asked to imagine various fearful situations. Thus the person afraid of flying in airplanes may at first be asked (while in a state of relaxation) to imagine himself looking at a picture of an airplane in a magazine. This is less threatening and more removed from the fear-inducing situation than the thought of flying in an airplane or even the act of actually approaching an airplane. The in vivo approach is similar but involves real situations and behavior. Accordingly, the patient may first be shown a picture of an airplane, but ultimately he is asked to go to an airport and look at airplanes, walk on them, and finally attempt to fly on one. The same sequence of *desensitization* to an anxiety-producing stimulus can be applied to a feared medical procedure or situation (e.g., the operating room).

Aversive Conditioning.   In aversive conditioning (sometimes called counterconditioning) a painful stimulus is presented simultaneously with a maladaptive response. For example, to help a person stop smoking, a nausea-producing substance might be placed on the tip of the cigarette. As a result the person trying to stop smoking associates smoking with nausea rather than pleasure. Aversive conditioning has also been used in the treatment of homosexuality. In such cases presentation of a homosexual stimulus or fantasy is accompanied by a shock or a nausea-inducing stimulus. Again the undesired behavior is eliminated through its association with an unpleasant or painful stimulus. The fact that "punishment" seems to work in this type of clinical application may perhaps be explained by the person's desire to eliminate an undesired behavior.

Implosion.   In this type of treatment the patient is given massive exposure to the threatening or fear-inducing stimuli. In one experiment utilizing this technique, female college students who were afraid of rats were exposed to a one-hour tape recording describing in the most gruesome detail rats attacking and biting people. Oddly, after the implosion therapy session the students were able to handle a rat more easily than a comparable group of students not exposed to the therapy. However, conflicting results are reported on the outcome of this therapy and therefore it should be handled cautiously (Bandura, 1959).

Flooding.   This technique is related to implosion but is slightly different. A fearful stimulus is presented in a massive dose but there are no adverse consequences. In this procedure, the subjects who fear rats might be repeatedly exposed to rats without anything happening to them. As a result the subjects give up the fearful association to the object. In implosion, outcomes that the person might never have imagined, such as rats ripping flesh, are introduced. This is quite different from the innocuous conditions of the flooding method.

Assertiveness Training.   Behavior problems frequently stem from a person's passivity and inability to express or seek gratification for his needs. In this technique the person is trained by means of conditioning techniques to behave more assertively. Assertiveness training is a slow process of reinforcing minimal manifestations of assertiveness and working toward more overt and complete expressions. First the patient may be required to make small demands and assertions for which he is praised by the therapist. Later he is required to carry his assertiveness over to social situations.

APPLICATION IN NURSING AND HEALTH CARE

Changing Apathy in a Hospital Setting.   Schefer and Martin (1966) have shown how the systematic use of reinforcement by nurses and psychiatric technicians on the ward of a mental hospital reduced the "apathy behavior" of schizophrenic patients. Since apathy is a frequent reaction to hospitalization in general, the study methods have potentially broader application.

Forty female patients who had shown varying degrees of apathy were randomly divided into two groups. The experimental group was given token reinforcement for desirable behavior while the control group was not. For the control group, nurses were instructed to "treat patients in a way in which you would treat patients before you ever heard of the analysis of behavior" (i.e. behavioral analysis). The target behaviors to be changed were personal hygiene (including showering, manicuring, brushing of teeth, combing of hair, use of cosmetics), social interaction (saying good morning, playing cards with another patient), and adequate work performance (carrying out household chores such as emptying wastepaper baskets, vacuuming, and wiping tables). Brass tokens were used as the reinforcers. These tokens could be used by the patients for acquiring the daily needs and luxuries, such as food and recreations, operating TV sets, etc. The experimental group had to emit the desired behaviors to get tokens. For the control group the tokens were free. The results showed a significant reduction of apathy scores for the reinforced group.

Ward Management.   Taylor and Persons (1970) report the effective use of behavior modification of some typical patient behavior problems found in ward management. Citing three cases in a physical medicine and rehabilitation center the authors illustrate the effective use of positive reinforcement in changing patient behavior. The first case was that of a 22-year-old quadriplegic patient who had been injured a few months earlier. The patient expressed the desire to go to college as a way of compensating for his handicap. The staff raised serious doubts about the feasibility of the goal, since the patient had shown a low level of motivation in physical and occupational therapy as well as other signs of a lack of persistence. To prepare him for university activities a behavior modification program was instituted aimed at increasing the amount of time he spent reading. Social attention was the reinforcer used in the program. The entire staff was instructed to comment on the patient's reading and to engage in social interaction with him when he maintained or increased his reading. During the ten weeks of the program there was a sharp increase in the amount of time the patient spent reading. At the beginning of the period he read for less than 30 minutes per day, whereas at the end of the training the average reading time per day was 3 hours and 9 minutes.

In another case reported by Taylor and Persons a 54-year-old housewife with multiple sclerosis was a serious problem on the ward because of her chronic and bitter complaining. This behavior alienated her from other patients as well as the staff. In fact, the staff was so affected by her behavior that a drop in the quality of her treatment was noted. The strategy for behavior modification in this case was twofold: to make the patient aware of the frequency of her complaining and to reinforce noncomplaining behavior. The patient was given a wrist counter to record the number of times she complained during the day. The staff also recorded the frequency of complaints. In addition, the staff was instructed to use social reinforcement in the form of interaction with the patient when the patient was not complaining but to keep interaction to a minimum when she complained. This twofold strategy brought about a dramatic decrease in complaining behavior. Even the other patients began to respond more favorably to her.

In a third case behavior modification was used to reduce dependency behavior in a patient. The patient was a 37-year-old man who was quadriparetic as the result of an automobile accident. The staff feared he would not make much progress in rehabilitation because of his extreme dependency. The social history showed that he had already been extremely dependent and in psychiatric treatment prior to his accident. He preferred to talk about his "many and varied psychiatric complaints" rather than work positively on his rehabilitation. Instead of traditional psychotherapy, which the staff thought would increase his dependency and keep him from focusing on rehabilitation, behavior modification was prescribed. The program consisted of withholding attention when the patient dwelled on his psychiatric complaints but actively responding to him (social reinforcement) when he talked about other topics such as progress in occupational therapy and physical therapy. Again the results were striking. At discharge psychological testing showed that the patient "improved in terms of self-confidence and self-esteem, was less preoccupied with his physical problems, less depressed, less dependent, had a better sense of identity, was less obsessive and ruminative, was in better touch with reality, and was more sociable." Staff ratings of the patient also showed marked changes in psychological adjustment and independence.

Modifying Physiological Functions. Behavior modification techniques have even been called upon for retraining of physiological functions. In a study by Wright et al. (1969) two infants were able to return to normal breathing following tracheostomy with the application of reinforcement principles. Prior to the use of behavior modification the infants could tolerate less than five minutes of breathing without the artificial assistance of the cannula. In both cases there was no physical reason why normal breathing could not be reinstated. According to the authors, decannulation (removal of the cannula) following tracheostomy is important since the patient can become totally dependent on the cannula. They state that addictions lasting as long as twelve years have been reported. The isolation associated with cannula dependence can lead to various degrees of physical, emotional, and intellectual retardation, and in some instances death.

In introducing the behavior modification procedure the authors first instructed the nurses to note the conditions that provided the infants with the greatest amount of gratification. One infant was found to derive gratification from "moving about in his walker, his bath, tender loving care and other social contacts, and from contact with toys and other objects." The second patient derived pleasure from "tender loving care and other social contacts, and from contact with toys and other objects." Next the cannulae were occluded for three periods a day. During these periods the patients were reinforced with the preferred gratifications. When breathing through the cannulae the infants were isolated except for essential care. Over the three weeks of the behavior treatment the cannulae were increasingly occluded from three minutes on the first session to 36 hours by the 21st day. Decannulation was then performed. Over the subsequent nine months no complications or distress were reported. Here is an instance in which the hospital staff used behavior modification to remediate a problem that could escalate into many medical and psychological complications.

SUMMARY

Behaviorism has its roots in the pioneering work of Ivan Pavlov on the conditioned reflex (classical conditioning). John Watson, an American psychologist, later developed a theory of behavior based entirely on the conditioned reflex. Behaviorism from its inception placed great emphasis on the environment as shaping the individual; innate or biological processes have been minimized. Later behaviorists, notably B. F. Skinner, changed the focus of behaviorism to instrumental conditioning (operant), in which the organism must make a correct response before it gains the reward. The reinforcement principle has evolved as the most important one in behavioral control and change. Modern behavior modification specialists have developed a host of techniques to change maladaptive behaviors. The techniques discussed in this chapter were token reinforcement, shaping relaxation, aversive conditioning, implosion, flooding, and assertiveness training. Applications to nursing and health care were illustrated in cases of changing apathetic behavior, gaining patient cooperation in rehabilitation, and retraining a physiological function after surgery.

SUGGESTED READINGS

Bandura, A. *Principles of behavior modification.* New York: Holt, Rinehart and Winston, 1969.

LeBow, M. D. *Behavior modification: a significant method in nursing practice.* Englewood Cliffs, N.J.: Prentice-Hall, 1973.

Lazarus, A. *Behavior therapy and beyond.* New York: McGraw-Hill, 1971.

Skinner, B. F. *Walden II.* New York: Macmillan, 1948.

Skinner, B. F. *Beyond freedom and dignity.* New York: Knopf, 1971.

Chapter *II*

The Developmental Psychology of Jean Piaget

JEAN PIAGET'S interest in psychology dates back to 1920, when he obtained a position in the Alfred Binet Laboratory in Paris. In working on the standardization of items for a reasoning test, he was struck by the kinds of wrong answers that children gave. Certain patterns of thinking seemed to be present, which Piaget set out to investigate. Although originally trained in biology, from that time onward he was a psychologist. More than half a century later we have the fruits of his labor—some 25 books and 150 articles.

Piaget's approach to development is sometimes referred to as *genetic epistemology*. This term expresses Piaget's concern with the origins of man's mental functioning and his understanding of the world around him. As such, the focus is on the intellectual structures of mind and how they evolve and function.

The newborn infant, in Piaget's view, comes into the world with a primitive set of reflexes that provide limited responses for survival. These reflexive behaviors are initially rigid and stereotyped, allowing little variation to meet changing circumstances, but they evolve into highly complex structures that enable the person to manipulate symbols and deal with his environment in a highly flexible and varied manner. The nature of this hierarchy of mental structures, culminating in formal logical processes, is the essence of Piaget's theory.

BASIC CONCEPTS
Characteristics of Development

A number of principles in Piaget's conception of development apply to the overall characteristics of development. In spite of the specific changes that occur in the course of development from birth to old age, these *invariants*, as they are called, are always present in some form.

Stage Concept. Development follows a sequence of stages and each stage has unique characteristics. More advanced stages do not totally replace earlier, more primitive ones, but incorporate and build upon them. The order of these stages of development is invariant, that is, it always follows the same sequence. Piaget does not insist on a specific time for each stage, but he does give general guidelines. The age at which a stage begins can be influenced by individual differences, experience, and culture.

Organization. Mental functioning tends toward meaningful and coordinated organization of behavior and mental structures. New mental structures that emerge in the course of development do not exist in isolation but combine with other structures to yield more complex organizations. Thus, reaching behavior soon integrates with looking behavior to form a more complete, organized, and effective unit.

Adaptation. All mental functioning is adaptive in its aim. Mental development progresses in response to the increasing demands of the environment. Consequently, more and more complex structures must be devised by the individual to satisfy the adaptive motive. At every level of development adaptation can be seen. The biologically given reflexes present at birth provide only minimal adaptation. Sucking, breathing, blinking, and other reflexes are the basis for survival, given a supportive environment. But these reflexes are rigid and inflexible and therefore cannot meet the complex demands of the environment. For adaptation to take place, the child must develop new behaviors or *schemas.* Schemas are the mental representations of behavior. The need for adaptation continues throughout development.

Equilibrium. The concept of equilibrium is closely related to adaptation. Once a new behavior emerges it restores a balance or equilibrium in the person. He can now handle the environment in a more effective or adaptive manner. But until the individual reaches the highest level of development, new behaviors will only be temporarily effective in establishing equilibrium. New demands will arise that will be beyond his ability for the moment. These demands will create disequilibrium, requiring the person to develop further in order to re-establish equilibrium.

Assimilation and Accommodation. These two processes are also related to adaptation. In order to establish adaptation through equilibrium, new response patterns must be tailor-made to deal appropriately with incoming stimuli. Such new patterns represent accommodations to the environment.

Initially, stimulation is taken in or assimilated through the existing mental structures (schemas). At the reflexive level, stimuli can only be assimilated in terms of the rigid structure of the reflex; reflexes do not allow for variation in response. When accommodation takes place, a new structure will emerge to take in stimulation in new, more differentiated ways. Assimilation and accommodation are, therefore, reciprocal processes that feed each other in the service of adaptation and equilibrium.

Landmarks of Development

Landmarks of development consist of significant additions to the child's behavioral repertoire; they are signposts of maturation and growth. Piaget specifies a number of such landmarks.

Coordination of Sensory Stimuli. Initially the infant perceives his world in a fragmented manner. Reality for the newborn is a vague, global mass of unrelated incoming stimuli. One of the developmental tasks for the infant is to integrate the various inputs in order to create a stable, organized, and objective understanding of reality. The sound of pouring water must become integrated with the visual perception of the water pouring so that the sensory events can be perceived as part of a unified experience. Similarly with touch, smell, taste, visual images, and auditory input of any experience. The mental structures or schemas related to each of these initially separate sensory experiences must become integrated and unified.

Object Constancy.   For the adult, reality is not a fleeting, transient, stimulus-bound experience. When you leave your house in the morning you know that it is there even though you are not immediately perceiving it. We know that friends, relatives, loved ones exist although we are not presently with them. The fact that we carry reality around with us seems to be an obvious and unquestioned part of our experience. Yet this is not the case for the very young child, for whom object constancy develops slowly. At first things only exist for the child when they are directly perceived. For example, the child under about age 2 will not search for an object that is hidden. Here is an example from Piaget's research, reported in *The Construction of Reality in the Child* (1954):

> Laurent's reaction to falling objects still seems to be non-existent at 0;5 (24) [5 months, 24 days]: he does not follow with his eyes any of the objects which I drop in front of him.
>   At 0;5 (26), on the other hand, Laurent searches in front of him for a paper ball which I drop above his coverlet. He immediately looks at the coverlet after the third attempt but only in front of him, that is, where he has just grasped the ball. When I drop the object outside the bassinet Laurent does not look for it (except around my empty hand while it remains up in the air). (p. 14)

In this example Laurent did not look for the object when it was removed. Piaget also points out that "peek-a-boo" is of great interest to small children because of its developmental relevance to object constancy. The possibilities for complex behavior are quite limited without the advent of object constancy. Its appearance, therefore, is a milestone in the individual's development.

Use of Symbols.   The ability to represent reality in some shorthand way also greatly enhances human functioning. Not only does symbolism free the person from immediate ties to reality by enabling him to "carry the world around" with him, but it also permits and stimulates the formation of new constructions through the manipulation of these representations. Object constancy is the beginning of symbolism, because it implies mental representation of reality. But simple one-to-one representation is quite limited compared with the more abstract representation that emerges later on in development. Symbols can become highly telescopic and personalized. For example, a complex idea can be represented by a visual image for one person and by a word for another. Language is a very important type of symbolism that develops. The emergence of symbolism permits language development and language feeds back upon symbolism by promoting greater mental development.

Focus on More Than One Aspect of Experiences. Typically children below age 7 cannot solve problems that seem simple and obvious to older children, adolescents, and adults. Piaget's *conservation* experiments have attracted much attention because they dramatically demonstrate stage differences in mental functioning. The general principle involved in all the conservation experiments is the constancy of objects and experiences in spite of superficial transformation. In the conservation of continuous quantity the child is asked to judge whether or not water poured from a short wide beaker is the same or more after being poured into a tall narrow beaker.

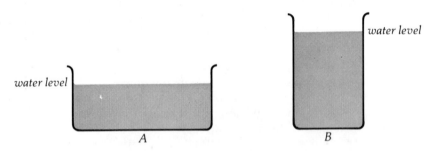

Figure 11.1 **Conservation of Continuous Quantity**

The child observes the experimenter pouring the water from A into B. Simple enough. Yet most children under age 7 are unable to recognize that B has the same amount of water that was originally in A. Children 7 years and older can usually solve the problem easily. The younger child believes there is more water in B because the level of the water is higher. Seeing the process reversed and repeated does not help.

The reason for the young child's difficulty with the problem is his inability to focus on more than one aspect of a situation. He is overly impressed with the immediate perceptual data (the level of the water) and cannot simultaneously relate other information and observations. In contrast, the seven-year-old can reverse processes mentally and focus on many aspects of a situation. Advanced cognitive functioning requires these abilities. In our everyday experience things constantly change and yet remain the same. A person wears different clothes, changes his hairstyle, is seen in different settings, and yet he is the same person. For a sense of stability in the world the child must see that many apparent transformations are only superficial.

Mastery of Egocentrism. Egocentrism reflects a problem in self-world differentiation and a corresponding overemphasis on self. In Piaget's theory, egocentrism is one of the invariants that is present throughout development. But egocentrism manifests itself in different forms throughout the developmental sequence. Each stage of development introduces a different aspect of egocentrism. The earlier forms are primitive and need to be mastered for the most advanced cognitive functioning to take place.

In the earliest stage of development, egocentrism is manifested in the child's inability to differentiate between himself and objects. Experience forms one undifferentiated mass in which subject and object are not distinguished. Later the child distinguishes between himself and others and other objects but confuses his thoughts with the thoughts of others and believes in the superiority of his own thoughts.

To illustrate, David Elkind (1970) cites the example of the 7-to-11-year-old-child who erroneously concludes that because he's correct about some things he must be correct about everything. The assumptive realities used at this age, according to Elkind, lead children to jump to conclusions that they will not reverse even when confronted with contradictory evidence. At still a later age, during adolescence, the child has overcome the earlier egocentrism but then cannot fully differentiate between idealism and realistic possibilities and limitations. The hypothetical realities of pure justice, pure love, pure idealism, and so on that the adolescent is able to construct frequently dominate his thinking, making him contemptuous of the real world. The adolescent also misjudges his own concerns to be the concerns of others.

METHOD OF INVESTIGATION

Most of Piaget's insights have been based on informal methods of observation and experimentation. His early major works were derived from painstakingly detailed observation of his three children Laurent, Lucienne, and Jacqueline. At times Piaget would intervene with experimental variations of the child's natural behavior. For example, if he noted the beginning of searching behavior, he would conceal objects in different ways and record the child's response; or if the infant grasped an object he might vary the position of the object and then observe the coordination capability under the differing conditions. In studying the content of children's thinking Piaget developed an informal clinical method. Rather than asking the child highly specific questions he would ask more open-ended ones such as "How did the moon come about?" He would then proceed with further inquiry, using the language of the child's response in a nondirective manner to gain insight into the child's beliefs. With the clinical method the questioning in each instance might be quite different.

Piaget's naturalistic, informal, and intuitive method is not the rigorous, hard-nosed type of research with predetermined, highly controlled experimental conditions. It is related to the informal observation that we spoke of in Chapter 1 as most suitable for nurses in observing patients. The fruitfulness of Piaget's informal method shows how powerful the technique can be in developing hypotheses. While it does not have the large number of subjects or precise repeatability necessary for making immediate generalizations, it has the advantage of flexibility and unrestrained observation that are favorable for discovery. More recently, Piaget and his associates as well as other investigators have tested out and confirmed many of his hypotheses using large samples and controlled experiments.

STAGES OF DEVELOPMENT

There are four major stages of development: sensorimotor stage (0–2 years), preoperational stage (2–7 years), concrete operational stage (7–11 years), and formal operational stage (11–15 years).

Sensorimotor Stage (0–2 Years)

During the first stage of development the child's functioning is confined to actions related to immediate sensory experiences. The child responds only to objects and events that are present, i.e., within his perceptual field. He has not yet achieved symbolism or mature object constancy and therefore his repertoire of behavior takes place in the sensorimotor sphere. Nevertheless, the child's behavior does develop. Beginning with simple schemas that remain very close to the biological reflexes present at birth, through successive accommodations to the environment, the child's behavior becomes increasingly complex. At the end of the sensorimotor stage,

Sucking, grasping,

the child's developmental progress in terms of the emergence of new schemas has prepared the way for the leap to the next stage. Six substages make up the sensorimotor period. Their main characteristics follow.

Substage I (Birth to 1 month).   Behavior during this period centers on the biologically given reflexes, which serve the adaptive function by providing the basis for survival. But even within the first month these reflexes undergo changes that reflect the infant's experience. At first the infant manifests only *functional assimilation.* He repeats reflexive actions such as sucking even when he is not hungry. Soon this functional assimilation becomes *generalized assimilation* when the infant extends the sucking reflex to a wider range of objects than just the breast or bottle and includes objects that are suckable but not nutritive. He also develops *recognitory assimilation;* for example, when hungry, the infant demands the breast or bottle and will not accept substitutes. He also responds to cues related to the bottle or breast, demonstrating primitive anticipation, even if it is on a purely rote, conditioned learning basis.

Substage II (1-4 Months).   The *primary circular reaction* characterizes substage II; the infant strives to repeat interesting events that initially occurred by chance. The events at this substage are related to the infant's own body. Thumb sucking is a good example of a primary circular reaction: it first occurs when the hand is accidentally placed near the mouth; repeating it, however, is difficult for the substage II child because some rather complex coordination is involved. While at first the infant only brings his mouth to the thumb, he eventually learns to bring his thumb to his mouth. This develops over many trials. When accomplished, it advances the infant by introducing a new organized schema involving the coordination of a number of movements and discriminations. Primary circular reactions such as thumb sucking are enjoyable because they serve functional and generalized assimilation.

During substage II the infant will begin to look for the things that he hears. Auditory and visual aspects of the same experience become coordinated. This coordination of sensory experiences is the underpinning for the establishment of the permanent object, which will be accomplished later.

Substage III (4-10 Months).   The *secondary circular reaction* occurs in substage III of the sensorimotor period. This reaction is similar to the primary circular reaction but involves events somewhat removed from the infant's own body. Interesting events that are accidentally produced in the environment are repeated by the infant; for example, by chance the infant makes an object hanging in his crib swing. In reproducing this event the infant's curiosity extends to a wider arena and he must coordinate many schemas in order to reproduce actions consistently.

Primitive causality is implied in both the primary and secondary circular reactions through the connection the infant makes between his participation and the effect that is produced. Primitive thought appears in substage III in the form of what is called the *abbreviated schema*. For example, the child may kick his foot or swing his arm in reaction to objects that he has swung. This abbreviated schema is not true thought, because it is not internalized or representational; it still occurs in terms of action.

During this period the infant will begin to search for an object that has disappeared, indicating that he has developed further in establishing *object permanence*. During this same period, if the infant drops an object he can anticipate where it will come to rest, again suggesting the beginning of object permanence.

Substage IV (10-12 Months). In this substage the previously acquired secondary reactions are extended and combined to deal with new situations. In the case where an infant removes a barrier to obtain a desired object, he applies schemas already in his repertoire but now uses them in combination as means toward a new goal rather than ends in themselves. These *coordinations of secondary schemas* that characterize substage IV are more flexible than preceding behaviors.

Object constancy progresses during this substage. The infant can follow the simple movement of objects. If, for example, an object is hidden, he will look for it in the right place. But if the movements of the object are complex, involving many displacements, he will merely look for the object in the place where he last found it.

The child's ability to imitate also improves during substage IV.

Substage V (12-18 Months). The *tertiary circular reaction* is exhibited in this substage. The child seeks out novel events rather than merely reproducing events that occur accidentally. Thus the child moves out further into the environment. In turn, this opens up a whole new world of experience. He also varies his approach to novel events. For example, if a child finds dropping an object interesting he will drop it from various positions and heights, noting the variations; he will behave similarly when pushing or swinging objects.

Imitation improves still further in this substage. While previously his imitation was confined to behaviors that were part of his repertoire, the child can now imitate behaviors that he himself has never performed.

Object constancy again advances, and now the child can follow complex displacements of objects. But he is limited to following displacements only when he can see them. If an object is concealed in a closed hand and then put in different places with the object being hidden in the last place, the child cannot correctly guess where the object is. To do so he would have to infer that the object is in the closed hand, an operation he is incapable of at this substage. Invisible displacements require symbolism and thought, which are acquired on a higher level and not yet developed.

Stage VI (18 Months-2 Years). The beginning of thought is the hallmark of this substage. The child gives evidence of the beginnings of mental representations of events and thinking about problems. Rather than groping with new problems on a trial-and-error basis, the child will seem to think about problems, and he will sometimes come up with solutions in a sudden and apparently insightful manner.

Deferred imitation, which appears at this time, is another form of behavior suggesting mental representation. The child will imitate an event that occurred previously, perhaps days before, indicating that the event was carried in the child's mind in some fashion. Previously imitation would only occur in the presence of the model.

Invisible placement can also be inferred by the child during this substage. This implies not only object permanence but also the presence of thought. Thus when Piaget hides a pencil in his hand and successively places the closed hand under three different objects, Jacqueline at 19 months looks for the pencil under the last object. According to her behavior, Jacqueline knew of the pencil's existence even though she could not see it, and she was able to use thought to infer where it would be located.

Preoperational Stage (2-7 Years) *Symbolic*

In making the transition from the sensorimotor to the preoperational stage the child enters a qualitatively new realm of functioning. Sensorimotor behavior is slow and confined to specific and limited events that must be dealt with one at a time, and the *now remembers past.*

Information gathering

child is tied to the plane of action in a here-and-now world. During the preoperational period the child progresses to the symbolic and conceptual plane. Behavior comes to be guided by mental representations and internalized thoughts rather than purely by sensory and motor events. Symbolism, which develops during this period, not only improves the quality of the child's functioning but it also enables him to do more things faster in his environmental encounters; with symbolism the child can represent many things quickly and can handle many events. The preoperational child is, however, still only on the threshold of "intelligent" behavior. Advanced cognitive functioning is represented during the preoperational state only in rudimentary forms.

Symbolism. In the preoperational stage a mental event comes to stand for something in the real world. The beginnings of symbolism are inferred by Piaget from the activities of the child. In symbolic play, for example, the child may treat a handkerchief as if it were a pillow. The child's behavior indicates that he must have an internalized representation of the actual pillow. Similarly, in deferred imitation the child repeats an event that previously occurred many hours or days before, demonstrating the presence of symbolism. Since the event imitated was not taking place at the time the child repeated it, there must have been something mental that stood for the event. Deferred imitation increases rapidly during the preoperational stage.

Language Development. The preoperational child begins to use language in a symbolic fashion. Words are no longer just pure imitations of sounds; now they are used to stand for things. But language does not become truly communicative and socialized until the end of the preoperational period. Initially, words are used egocentrically through the *monologue* and *collective monologue*. In the monologue the child uses words in an idiosyncratic fashion with no intent to communicate. The words may express a wish fulfillment, as when the child tells an object to move, or the words may be part of the child's ongoing activities and intertwined with them. The collective monologue is similar to the monologue but involves two or more children. Children may be playing side by side but not really communicating. Although language behavior can be seen taking place among these children, closer examination will reveal a lack of communication much of the time.

Reasoning and Causality. The child in the preoperational stage

no problem solving before 6 years

cannot engage in true inductive or deductive reasoning. He makes a number of faulty attempts at reasoning and explaining causal relationships. One of the more primitive types of reasoning is called *syncretism*. In syncretic reasoning the child relates independent ideas in one confused global mass; any one element of this mass can be cited as a cause for any other element merely because they are perceived as belonging to a global unit. Sometimes the preoperational child will use the language of reasoning, but it is merely a learned association between two events. For example, in the statement "It is raining and the garden is wet" the child connects the two events because he has learned that they go together but he really doesn't understand the causal relationship. In another type of reasoning at this period, the child's egocentricity dominates. He might say "It must be Tuesday because I ride my bike on Tuesday and I want to ride my bike." The child's wish in this case leads to a faulty conclusion. Another type of reasoning closely related to this egocentric one is *juxtaposition*. In juxtaposition the child expresses isolated ideas without any attempt to tie them together; the child may enumerate related ideas but not provide any links. In *transductive reasoning*, which is another type associated with the preoperational stage, the child moves from the particular to the particular, often reaching faulty conclusions. When Piaget's daughter concluded that it wasn't afternoon because she didn't have her nap, she was exhibiting transductive reasoning. Sometimes preoperational children using various modes of faulty reasoning will reach factually correct conclusions—demonstrating that correctness can never be used as the sole index of logical reasoning.

Rules and Moral Development. At the beginning of the preoperational stage the child does not understand rules very well. In playing games he often makes up rules, changes rules, and does not play cooperatively. His primary concern is with winning. Once the child understands rules, he believes they are absolute and unchangeable—there is only one right way. From about 4 to 8 the child's concept of right and wrong is governed by what Piaget calls *moral realism*. In one type of problem the child is asked questions such as, "Which child is naughtier, the one who breaks 15 cups accidentally or the one who breaks one cup on purpose?" The child in the moral realism phase focuses on the actual amount of damage and considers the breaking of 15 cups the greater crime. He is invoking the absolute rule that breaking is bad; therefore more is worse. It isn't until the end of the concrete operational period that the child develops *subjective morality* and begins to consider the intent of behavior in arriving at moral judgments. The development of subjective morality is tied to many other cognitive advances. The child must be able to focus on many aspects of situations, he must have an awareness of other people's feelings and motives, and he must come to realize that rules can vary.

Concepts of the World.   Three types of beliefs are expressed by preoperational children in relation to natural events:

Realism.   The child's confusion of psychological and physical reality is expressed in his belief in the physical reality of psychological events. Thus, the child may believe that a dream actually takes place in his room; "Last night there was a train in my crib." He may confuse thinking and speaking and will consider the name of an object as a real part of the object.

Animism.   The child attributes life and purpose to objects such as the sun, moon, and trees. These objects are described as expressing feelings, purpose, and motives.

Artificialism.   The child believes that the purpose of all objects and events is to satisfy human needs. In the statements "There is water because people get thirsty" and "There is night so we can go to bed," artificialism is reflected in the child's belief that a purposeful relationship exists between humans and all the things that surround them.

Limitations of Preoperational Functioning.   *Egocentricity, centration,* and *inability to reverse processes* limit the functioning of the preoperational child. His *egocentricity* works against development by removing the possibility of self-criticism. The child views his thoughts and views as the best possible. He cannot take the other person's point of view into account and is therefore insulated from a need to make new accommodations. He can assimilate events into his existing schemas without the need of making new accommodations. This can be seen most clearly in the child's play, in which he shapes the world to his own needs rather than shaping his behavior to the demands of reality. Ultimately however, constant pressures from the environment create the need for adaptation and lead the child to new accommodations.

Centration maintains the preoperational child's focus on limited aspects of the environment. He perceives only the most salient characteristics of stimuli and does not explore all facets of objects or situations. One typical experiment demonstrating centration requires the child to compare rows of objects, in which six objects may be spread further apart than nine objects (see Figure 11.2-A).

The preoperational child believes there are more objects in the row of six, because he focuses only on the length of the rows and does not at the same time consider other data.

The preoperational child is further limited by his *inability to trace processes backwards*. Thus when a line of objects is lengthened, he cannot mentally reverse the process to see that it contains the same number of objects as before (Figure 11.2-B). The lack of reversibility renders a degree of rigidity and inflexibility to the preoperational child's thinking. The same centration impedes the child's ability to perform other conservation tasks successfully.

A   B

Figure 11.2. **Centration.**   *building block for abstract thinking.*

                                              6-12
Concrete Operational Stage (7-11 Years)   *conservation -*

During this period the child is freed from many of the limitations of the preoperational stage. In giving up the preoperational ego-centricity the child is able to raise his functioning to a higher plane. Many of the aspects of concrete operational functioning have already been implied in discussing the limitations of the pre-operational stage. Therefore we will cite only the highlights of the advances.

Thinking and Reasoning. Centration no longer dominates the child. He can simultaneously consider different facets of a situation. Consequently many problems that he could not solve previously are now mastered. He can manipulate symbols, conserve and reverse processes mentally; his thoughts are no longer dominated by immediate perceptions, and he can therefore think things out. These advances open up a whole world of logical operations that were previously closed off.

Ordering (Seriation). During the concrete operational period the child improves in his ability to see ordinal relationships and order events in a hierarchy. In one seriation problem the child is presented with stick A, which is slightly shorter than stick B. Then stick A is taken away and the child is presented with sticks B and C, in which B is slightly shorter than C. The child is asked to state the relationship between A and C. The preoperational child can see that A is shorter than B and B shorter than C, but in the absence of A he cannot state the relationship between A and C; the concrete operational child can solve this abstract problem dealing with concrete objects.

Classification. The child's ability to classify matures during the period of concrete operations. When presented with wooden beads of which 18 are brown and 2 are white, both the preoperational and the concrete operational child can classify them along single dimensions of color and color versus wood. However, when asked whether there are more wooden or brown beads, the preoperational child will say there are more brown beads. He is dominated by the immediate sensory experience of brown; the concept of wooden is more abstract and he cannot consider it at the same time. The concrete operational child, who understands classes and subclasses, easily solves the problem.

Time. Up until the concrete operational stage the child has no real concept of past and future. During the sensorimotor period reality is the experience of an enduring present. As the child acquires the ability to represent events mentally and to recall events that happened over a wider span of time there is a vague sense of things lasting and having a temporal order. The preoperational child will use the language of time such as "last week" and "next year," but he will not have a precise concept of what these statements mean. "A long time ago" could very well mean the previous day. The preoperational child's confusion of age with size is another example of the limited concept of time prior to the concrete operational period. The preoperational child will say that the apple tree is older than the smaller pear tree even when he is told that they were planted at the same time. The concept of time takes on fuller meaning when the concrete operations of reversibility, seriation and decentration (the focus on more than one aspect of experiences) are acquired. The concept of time will not reach its full fruition until the formal operational period when the abstractions of "history" and "the future" become meaningful constructs.

Language and Social Behavior. During this period, the child's language and play become more socialized and cooperative. Initially his play still retains some egocentric characteristics, but he is able to perceive the other person's perspective and therefore can manifest cooperation. Language becomes more communicative and socialized.

Formal Operational Stage (11–15 Years) *12 – adult* *abstract thinking make deductions.*

The stage of formal operations is the last stage of cognitive development. Cognitive structures do not advance after this stage in Piaget's conceptual framework.

The adolescent in this stage can deal with problems not related to current or real situations. He can solve purely abstract and verbal problems without the presence of actual referents. While the concrete operational child can solve seriation problems involving objects that he can see and manipulate (as in the stick problem), he cannot solve an abstract seriation problem like the following: "Edith is fairer than Susan; Edith is darker than Lilly. Who is the darkest of the three?" The problem presents no difficulty for the formal operational child. In this last stage the child can think scientifically. He can utilize assumptions in his thinking, formulate hypotheses, construct theories, and engage in systematic experimentation. If a problem requires an assumption contrary to reality it puzzles the concrete operational child but not the formal operational child. A problem that begins with the statement "Suppose rain were dry" would be perfectly comprehensible to the formal operational child and he would be able to reason accordingly. The formal operational child can relate to the pure structure of an argument, independently of the specific content. While the concrete operational child has risen above his immediate perceptions in his ability to see many aspects of the situation, his problem-solving is still tied to concrete events. The formal operational child is much more flexible in his thinking. He can manipulate many concepts simultaneously and he can mentally anticipate a variety of possible outcomes. Reality becomes one subclass of the larger class of total possibilities.

The Pendulum Problem. The pendulum experiment illustrates Piaget's approach to studying the characteristics of the thinking process during this period. The child is presented with a pendulum consisting of an object hanging from a string. He is asked to determine which factors affect how fast the pendulum swings. In solving the problem the child deals with four factors: the length of the string, the variations in the weight of the object hanging from the string, variations in the height of the pendulum, and variations in the force with which the pendulum can be pushed. At the preoperational stage the child functions in a random fashion and his reasoning is faulty. The concrete operational child functions in a much better way, but there are still shortcomings in his approach. He may test out certain relevant contributors to the speed of swinging, but he does not approach the problem in a systematic way. The activities of the formal operational child on this task show a truly systematic approach incorporating scientific methodology. He tests out all possible combinations of the factors while systematically making careful observations and drawing correct logical conclusions.

Idealism and Social Behavior. The adolescent's abstract abilities are applied to the social sphere as well. His ability to perceive possibilities beyond reality is the foundation for the idealism that characterizes adolescence. The adolescent will frequently become a champion of many idealistic causes without being able to understand realistic limitations. Focusing exclusively on the world of the possible, he may become very critical of adults and authority figures for not exemplifying the ideal to which he is devoted. The adolescent may criticize his parents for their level of education, lack of optimum success in life, and their acceptance of limitations. His egocentrism is incorporated in the excessive power and validity that he extends to the world of the abstract. It is only over time and through life experience that this egocentrism wanes and becomes integrated into a more balanced harmony with reality.

APPLICATIONS IN NURSING AND HEALTH CARE

The greatest application of Piaget's work is in dealing with children, from infancy through adolescence. Additional applications may be found in cases of older patients who show regressions caused by psychological disturbance or organic injury and in cases of senility, where earlier modes of thinking and mental functioning may predominate.

Answering Children's Questions

David Elkind's (1974) discussion of children's questions can be very instructive to the nurse working with children. The child at age 3, according to Elkind, begins to ask questions. The earliest questions are about the names of things. The child is fascinated by the observation that everything has a name. The nurse should bear this in mind and not read more into a child's question than he intends. A young child who asks "What's that?" pointing to a wound or disability may be more interested in the label than in a detailed physiological explanation.

True questioning begins at about age 4. The child wants to know the reason for almost everything around. Examples given by Elkind are "What makes you grow up?", "What makes you stop growing?" "Where do babies come from?", "How come mommies have breasts and daddies don't?". At this stage the child believes that everything is made for the sake of humans (artificialism). Therefore, detailed explanations can go over the head of the 4-year-old and miss the point of his question. Merely to give a cause may be sufficient to meet a child's need at this period. Simply to state "That's the way people are made" or "God planted the seed" are answers that, depending on the child's background and family beliefs, Elkind finds appropriate. Questions about death also arise at about age 4. Here too, Elkind recommends being factual without being explicit. Since the child is concerned with the purpose of death, explanations such as "to make room for others" or "when someone dies we don't see or talk to them" are adequate at this time. To explain death in physiological or philosophical terms may be the imposition of an adult point of view that exceeds the child's level of development. It would be well for the nurse, before giving explanations to children, to explore the kinds of explanations they find acceptable. This can be done by asking the child similar innocuous questions. In this manner the nurse can learn the kind of answers that are meaningful to the child.

Questions about the physical world start at about age 5 to 6. Elkind tells the story of his 5-year-old son asking if they will come to the end of the earth if they keep driving. At first Elkind was tempted to give a precise response; but then, realizing that he could not convey the idea of a world without a beginning or an end because the roundness of the earth is too abstract and not directly observable, he came up with the following: "When you come to the end of the land there is water, and when you come to the end of the water you arrive at some more land."

At about age 6 children's questions begin to resemble adult questions. Elkind calls our attention to the importance of taking children's questions seriously and answering them.

Explaining Routines

In explaining rules and regulations the nurse should also be aware of the person's level of abstraction and his concept of causality. Young children accept rules when they are explained concretely and when a reason is given. The reasons, as we have already indicated in discussing children's questions, do not have to be highly detailed or precise. The young child merely wants reasons and the assurance that the rules come from an authoritative source. The situation might be quite different with adolescents. The adolescent with his newly acquired hypothetical deductive capability may question reasons and rules in a playful if not challenging way. He will frequently reject authority and will question the rationale and logic of rules.

Providing Appropriate Stimulation

Piaget's theory has application to other areas of health care with children. Recognizing a child's need for appropriate stimulation at each stage of development, the nurse can organize play materials and the child's environment accordingly. In the sensorimotor period the child should have objects to exercise his sensorimotor schemas. There should be things of interest to see, hear, and touch. Objects that permit hand-eye and other coordination should also be available. The nurse working with children must be a careful observer and note levels of development and emerging mental structures. After assessing the child's level, the nurse can then provide stimulation to exercise evolving mental structures. As we have noted, the child has a need to use his newly acquired mental schemas (process of functional assimilation); the exercise of these schemas promotes further cognitive development.

Perception of Reality

The nurse familiar with the cognitive stages of development will find it easier to differentiate between a 4-year-old's fabrications and his actual perceptions of reality. The same goes for children of other ages. Reality, as we have seen, means different things at different stages of development.

Environmental Changes

For the child who is unable to conserve, i.e., see minor changes or transformations as insignificant and superficial, slight variations in ward conditions can cause emotional upset. For example, the rearrangement of a bed or other changes of furniture and apparatus on the ward can be confusing for the preoperational child (2-7 years) and the sensorimotor child (under age 2). They may feel that everything has changed. Shifts in staff can have a similar effect. Of course older children can differentiate between minor and major changes and are able to maintain a sense of "sameness" when there are relatively minor variations. But older children and adults under stress may revert to earlier modes of cognition and, therefore, overreact to changes. The nurse must be alert to the possible cognitive origins of some emotional reactions.

SUMMARY

Piaget's theory of development traces the origin of mental structures (genetic epistemology). Mental development proceeds through the individual's active interaction with his environment. New structures (schemas) develop as the existing ones cannot meet the complexities of the environment. Starting with biologically given reflexes, development at its highest level can ultimately achieve symbolic processes and hypothetical-deductive capability. The overall characteristics of development (invariants) are the stage concept, principle of organization, adaptation, equilibrium, and assimilation and accommodation. The four stages of development are: sensorimotor (0-2 years), preoperational (2-7 years), concrete operational (7-11 years), formal operational (11-15 years). These stages always follow the same order but their age of occurrence will vary individually. Application of Piaget's concepts will be greatest in relation to children and adolescents but also pertains in states of adult regression and organic brain pathology. Some examples of applications in nursing with children were given with reference to children's questions, explaining routines, providing appropriate stimulation, perception of reality, and effects of environmental changes.

SUGGESTED READINGS

Elkind, D. *Children and adolescents.* New York: Oxford University Press, 1974.

Flavell, J. H. *The developmental psychology of Jean Piaget.* Princeton, N.J.: Van Nostrand, 1963.

Ginsberg, H., and Opper, S. *Piaget's theory of intellectual development.* Englewood Cliffs, N.J.: Prentice-Hall.

Piaget, J. *Six psychological studies.* New York: Random House, 1967.

Piaget, J., and Inhelder, B. *The psychology of the child.* New York: Basic Books, 1969.

Chapter *12*

Social and Interpersonal Theories

IN THIS CHAPTER we will present several schools of thought that have influenced our current views of human behavior. So many individuals have made significant contributions to the field of human behavior that it would be impossible to give due recognition to all in this introductory text. Therefore, we have selected six theorists who have offered comprehensive and systematic theoretical innovations. For coverage of other modern approaches, many excellent books are available. For example, Hall and Lindzey's *Theories of Personality* (1970) provides a valuable overview of the topic of personality. Other important references are indicated under Suggested Readings at the end of the chapter.

The first five theorists discussed are Erik Erikson, Harry Stack Sullivan, Alfred Adler, Karen Horney, and Erich Fromm. All are called social theorists because of their common high regard for the importance of the social environment in shaping the personality of the developing individual. They all move away from looking at the individual in isolation. For the social theorists, the individual is in dynamic interaction with the social environment and, therefore, cannot be studied apart from that environment. The humanist school of psychology, represented mainly by Abraham Maslow, will be introduced because it is so much akin to the social theorists and is making a distinct contribution to current discussions of human motivation.

We do not attempt to describe these theories in their entirety, but rather to outline the major concepts that have had the greatest impact.

ERIK ERIKSON

Erik Erikson is basically within the Freudian camp, but he has emphasized the social aspects of development. Whereas the main thrust of Freud's writings is toward problems of impulse expression and the pathology resulting from the "damming up" of instinctual drives, Erikson has been much more concerned with the integration of the person with the social institutions of his culture. As such, Erikson has been responsible for moving psychoanalysis away from an almost exclusive preoccupation with the internal conflicts of the individual to a consideration of the impact of the social world.

The Eight Ages of Man

In his theory of the Eight Ages of Man, Erikson (1963) traces the critical periods of ego development in relation to the environment and society. Each of these ages centers on a crisis of alternatives, with the outcome having a far-reaching effect on the unfolding of the person's life.

1. Basic Trust versus Mistrust. The social trust of the infant is established in his relationship with his mother. The manner in which the mother provides for the child's needs will affect his feelings of regularity, comfort, and equilibrium. If the mother-child relationship during infancy is a gratifying one, the infant will make his first social achievement: "his willingness to let the mother out of sight without undue anxiety or rage, because she has become an inner certainty as well as outer predictability" (p. 247). The feelings of trust and/or mistrust established in infancy will be projected on the environment and thereby set the pattern for the person's sense of security in the social world throughout his life.

2. Autonomy versus Shame and Doubt. The developing child must come to grips with the conflict between "holding on" and "letting go"; this problem pervades many facets of the child's functioning. It begins with muscle maturation but then extends to other areas. Whether we are talking about rage, muscular activities, or bowel control, the problem of autonomy comes to the fore. "Shall I let go or hold back?" is a constant crisis for the child at this stage. To permit mastery of the problem of autonomy, the social environment must provide ways for the child to express himself without excessive punishment, but at the same time it must offer firm control so that the child does not become overwhelmed by the anarchy of his own impulses. Lack of societal control can lead to disorganized ego development. Excessive control yields strong inhibition. Both over-control and under-control lead to doubt about one's capacity to cope and feelings of shame about one's strivings. "From a sense of self-control without loss of self-esteem comes a lasting sense of good will and pride; from a sense of loss of self-control and a foreign over-control comes a lasting propensity for doubt and shame" (p. 254). Social order embodied in the laws of society provides the individual with the possibility of balancing the need for autonomy and the need for limits and control.

3. Initiative versus Guilt. Initiative is necessary for all human activities in every stage of development. We must mobilize our energy and move out into the environment in order to be productive and to achieve a sense of fulfillment. Striving for initiative can easily become attached to early sexual and aggressive motives. If these early impulses are severely punished or locked in conflict, guilt comes to replace expression. In turn, the guilt can come to pervade all efforts at expressing initiative. Sibling rivalry, unresolved Oedipus complex, and castration anxiety are frequently the dynamics behind inhibitions of initiative. In adulthood the denial of initiative can be expressed in psychosomatic ills, limited aspirations, impatience, or "showing-off" (as an overcompensation). Society, according to Erikson, can help enhance initiative by providing activities, roles, and institutions that can replace the heroes and goals of the person's childhood fantasies. The adolescent and adult, no less than the child, need opportunities to make "conquests" for confirmation of the effectiveness of initiative. Job opportunities, socialization outlets, possibilities for competition and success are some of the societal supports for initiative.

4. Industry versus Inferiority.   In this period identified with latency (age 7 to 11 years), the normal child sublimates his aggression and unrealistic, grandiose strivings; he establishes identity through real accomplishments. In developing a sense of industry, the child extends his ego to include his fields of interest, the tools of work and study, and the products that result from his diligent efforts. The child must be educated by adults and society to enhance the exercise of industry and to prepare him for the ultimate separation from the family. There must be opportunities to learn and do things with others. If the child feels inadequate or ill-equipped compared with others he may be "discouraged from identification with the tool world." Advanced technological societies pose special problems for this stage because its roles are vague and its tools often inaccessible to the young.

5. Identity versus Role Confusion.   In adolescence the task becomes that of integrating the roles and skills of childhood with the demands of the adult world. Occupational choice becomes crucial. Where there have been feelings of inadequacy and poor sexual identification in the past, role confusion will result. The adolescent with role confusion will flee from the conflicts of this stage. Most adolescents form cliques and crowds that serve to submerge the individual and thereby alleviate the identity crisis. Society plays an important role in the identity crisis of adolescence. A society that can offer meaningful roles for adolescents and appeal to their ideological bent will enhance identity and reduce role confusion. To the extent that opportunities are denied, distant, or unclear, withdrawal from the social world will be encouraged.

6. Intimacy versus Isolation.   Erikson defines intimacy as "the capacity to commit [oneself] to concrete affiliations and partnerships and to develop the ethical strength to abide by such commitments even though they may call for significant sacrifices and compromises" (p. 263). The self-abandonment required for intimacy can be a great threat to those with weak egos. The young adult who escapes from intimacy moves into a state of isolation. Heterosexual love is an important part of intimacy. Where intimacy cannot be achieved there are distortions in sexual relationships with the attendant frustration associated with incomplete gratification. The potential for intimacy is not only an individual matter but also in the hands of society. There must be traditions, customs, and opportunities favorable to the achievement of intimacy.

7. Generativity versus Stagnation. Generativity "is primarily the concern in establishing and guiding the next generation . . ." (p. 26). It is one of the developmental landmarks of the mature adult. Generativity requires working and giving but is not necessarily embodied in the act of having or raising children. In contrast to generativity are self-indulgence and self-concern, which lead to stagnation. All social institutions to some extent incorporate the generative drive.

8. Ego Integrity versus Despair. Ego integration is a somewhat philosophical concept as discussed by Erikson. It reflects a feeling of faith in individual existence, civilization, and the continuity of life. Ego integrity is the mature adult's reward for mastering infantile needs. In achieving ego integrity the individual attains an "at-homeness" with himself, his place in the social order, and the life cycle. Each culture has a unique style of ego integrity related to its institutions and its historical place. But there are commonalities in ego integrity; as Erikson put it, "a wise Indian, a true gentleman, and a mature peasant share and recognize in one another the final stage of integrity."

HARRY STACK SULLIVAN

The interpersonal emphasis of Harry Stack Sullivan's theory is perhaps best expressed in his definition of personality as "the relatively enduring pattern of recurrent interpersonal situations which characterize a human life" (Sullivan, *Interpersonal Theory of Psychiatry*, 1953, p. 111). Thus, the interpersonal situations current and past are the subject of study and analysis in Sullivan's approach. Many of the concepts of interpersonal psychiatry are based on Freud's work, and Sullivan recognized his debt: "Needless to say behind all this phase of [interpersonal psychiatry] are the discoveries of Sigmund Freud" (p. 16). Nevertheless, Sullivan quickly moves away from an interpretation of behavior based on biological strivings or internal struggles among opposing structures (id, ego, superego) to focus on the relationships of the child with significant others in his environment. It is these interactions, according to Sullivan, that shape the personality structure of the individual. At every point along the developmental continuum, social acts and situations are the determinants of personality development. Sullivan (1953) explicitly expresses his aim in the following quote: "I came to feel over the years that there was an acute need for a discipline which determined to study not the individual human organism or the social heritage but the interpersonal situations through which persons manifest mental health and mental disorder" (p. 18).

The *self system* is one of the most important constructs in Sullivan's theory. The self system refers to the sense of "me" or "I." It includes all the projections, feelings, and beliefs that one has about oneself. Anxiety emanating from the infant's insecurity in the parent-child relationship is what gives rise to the self system. The self system emerges out of the need to ward off anxiety—its basic function is to insulate from the anxiety of interpersonal hurts. "The self system is thus an organization of educative experience called into being by the necessity to avoid or minimize incidents of anxiety" (p. 165). By establishing *security operations* the self system is able to protect itself from threatening anxiety. While having the positive effect of lessening tension, the self system accomplishes its security operations at a cost to the individual's social functioning. Defensiveness works against honest and open interpersonal relations. Once a style of interpersonal relating based on security operations comes into being it tends to persist since it has worked in the past. The prospect of changing behavior exposes the self system to the very danger it exists to defend against—anxiety.

Very early experiences of the infant with its mother determine the nature of the self system by establishing the *interpersonal vulnerabilities*. The mother who does not respond to her infant with "tenderness," i.e., warmth and responsiveness to the child's needs, will, through an empathic flow between mother and child, generate anxiety in the infant. A mother who is outrightly rejecting and punitive can convey to the infant the "personification" of the "bad mother" and the "bad me." Personifications are enduring internalized images of self and significant others; they become incorporated into the self system and are then generalized to other interpersonal situations, even when inappropriate. The person who easily feels rejected and inadequate may be projecting the "bad me" personification. To the extent that the person's personifications are distortions, they result in continued distortions in interpersonal relations in all areas of life.

Although the security operations and personifications of the self system are established early, the individual is still open to change. New interpersonal relationships hold out the possibility of altering existing personifications and modes of relating. In this view, the individual is regarded as highly malleable and therefore open to change at any time.

The child is most vulnerable to intense anxiety during infancy, when the protaxic (vague and undifferentiated) mode of cognition pertains. During this period of global perceptions the child can easily be overwhelmed by exaggerated reactions from his parents. For example, a mother reacting with horror to the infant's *zonal play* with genitals, anus, or feces may produce *uncanny emotions*. These uncanny emotions, which are similar to dread or "otherworldly" feelings, have a disorganizing effect on the self system and in turn lead to inhibition in the quest for gratification in childhood and later on in adulthood. The uncanny feeling will return when the child—and later the adult—engages in activities that have an actual or a symbolic relationship to the earlier situations that produced the uncanny feeling.

Sullivan believes that the human is basically social rather than aggressive or destructive. He attributes what appears to be *malevolence* (destructiveness) in children to a lack of tenderness in their early interpersonal relationships and the infliction of pain by the mother. Malevolence and aggression are, therefore, viewed as coverups for the underlying need for love and tenderness. Only when the child does not get love and support does aggression develop. You will recall that for Freud aggression is primary; for Sullivan it is a secondary reaction.

Sullivan describes six stages of development: infancy, childhood, juvenile era, preadolescence, early adolescence, and adolescence. In each of these stages he emphasizes the social needs and forces that characterize and shape the stage.

The methodology of interpersonal psychiatry also reflects the social character of the theory. The therapist is not, as in the Freudian system, a distant, uninvolved observer of the patient. On the contrary, he is actively involved as a *participant observer*. The psychiatric interview (meaning anything from one interview to long-term therapy) is a social act in which the therapist relates to the patient while maintaining his professional acumen. The therapist must ultimately make formulations that can be communicated in such a way that the patient can make use of them in his life situation.

Transactional Analysis

Transactional analysis is related to the interpersonal approach of Harry Stack Sullivan. As a specific theory it was developed by Eric Berne (1964). Recently, transactional analysis has been popularized by Thomas A. Harris in his book *I'm OK—You're OK* (1969).

Harris explains that within each of us there are actually three people or selves—the Child, the Parent, and the Adult. Each one of these represents an indelible recording of early childhood experiences based on transactions with parents and significant others in the environment: "Continual observation has supported the assumption that these three states exist in all people. It is as if in each person there is the same little person he was when he was three years old. There are also within him his own parents. These are recordings in the brain of actual experiences of internal and external events, the most significant of which happened during the first five years of life. There is a third state different from these two. The first two are called Parent and Child, and the third, Adult" (pp. 17-18).

The Parent part includes all the do's, don'ts, supports, affections, and conflicts recorded from the interaction with parents. It is all the data recorded from observing the parents. Many of the unexplained "instinctive" rules of living, prejudices, and compulsions are the Parent part speaking out.

The Child in us includes the recordings of helplessness, inadequacy, and frustration that occur inevitably because of the child's dependent position. Childhood experience accumulates a large number of "Not OK" feelings. These Not OK feelings are unavoidable because of the necessity of giving up pleasure in the civilizing process. The Child recordings are predominantly recordings of feelings because early experiences occur at a time before we have developed an adequate vocabulary. To offset the Not OK feelings are all the positive feelings of warm, supportive, and stimulating transactions. However, Harris states, "Our observations both of small children and ourselves as grownups convince us that the Not OK feelings far outweigh the good feelings. This is why we believe it is a fair estimate to say that everyone has a Not OK Child" (p. 27).

The germination of the Adult begins at about 10 months of age, with locomotion and the ever-increasing ability to master the environment. The Adult can mediate between the different selves by using logic, skills, and experiences of success to update and contradict the Child and the Parent. The Adult injects reality data to reinforce the OK feeling. Problems arise when the Adult part is undermined during the early years. The growing child is vulnerable and the emerging Adult is therefore easily thwarted. A weak Adult self allows greater expression of the Child and Parent selves than does a strong Adult.

Harris gives many examples of the transactional games adults constantly play to relive early transactions. In these games the Child and Parent dominate. We will present more details of transactional games when we discuss therapy techniques in Chapter 17.

ALFRED ADLER

Adler was an early associate and follower of Freud, but he worked out independent views of development. He disagreed with Freud on the importance of aggressive and sexual drives in shaping human personality. Social interest, Adler believed, was at the core of human functioning. He was critical of Freud's position that social interest is a secondary development of the individual as a more effective means of achieving pleasure. For Adler, social interest is primary, and therefore uncooperativeness, lack of mutuality, and poor human relationships—all aspects of social interest—serve as indices of faulty development. In normal development, a socialized, empathetic, and sensitive orientation to the human environment is a natural unfolding of human potentiality. Social interest becomes thwarted when development is impeded and dominated by conflict.

Early in his career, Adler was impressed with the compensation people made for physical defects or weaknesses. Demosthenes, who stuttered, became a great orator; Theodore Roosevelt was physically weak and sickly in childhood but became an athletic and robust adventurer. Everyday life is filled with similar examples of compensation. Ultimately, Adler extended the model of physical organ inferiority and compensation to the psychological realm. He thought that inferiority feelings in infancy were inevitable because of the child's relative position of helplessness and the many achievements needed for mastery of the environment. *Striving for superiority* is the means by which the individual attempts to overcome his feelings of inferiority. In normal development, striving for superiority is not a quest for personal power at the expense of others, but the fulfillment of one's potentiality for productive and creative living in a social context. Looked at in this way, superiority is not a pseudo-masculine, superman image. It is only when the child's environment exploits and intensifies his state of helplessness that exaggerated and pathological forms of seeking superiority evolve into enduring life patterns.

Each individual develops a style of life that embodies his unique striving for superiority. If the parents and siblings are rejecting and unloving, a child may develop great needs for personal power to compensate for his pervasive feeling of inferiority. This "inferiority complex" (a term coined by Adler) can suppress the inherent social feelings of the child, leading to hostility and self-interest. An accepting and secure environment, on the other hand, distracts the child from his feelings of inferiority and helps him concentrate on developing skills and social relationships that contribute to positive growth and a humanistic life style.

Unlike Freud, who emphasized the unconscious, Adler had great faith in consciousness and rationality. His therapy, therefore, consisted of talking directly to the patient. He believed that if the therapist constantly points out the faulty style of life in present and past behaviors, the patient will alter his goals and effect significant changes. Goals play an important role in Adler's psychology because the future orientation of the person is a driving and guiding force in life. It is not only the past that influences behavior but also the future, represented by aspirations and goals. Therapeutic efforts toward behavioral change in the Adlerian scheme are multi-dimensional, working on past, present, and future.

Social interest, feelings of inferiority, striving for superiority, and goal orientation are the major themes of Adlerian psychology.

KAREN HORNEY   *Horni*

Karen Horney, another early adherent of Freudian psychology, broke with Freud over the issues of the instinct theory and female psychology. For Horney, *basic anxiety* is the central dynamic of human functioning. Development is the process of relating to and coping with this basic anxiety. The early mother–child relationship is a key factor in the amount of basic anxiety that will be present; this relationship can intensify or reduce the basic anxiety. The greater the basic anxiety, the greater the need to use distorted and maladaptive behaviors in coping with life. Conflict, for Horney, is not an inherent part of the person but is rooted in the social environment. An early environment that gives love, warmth, security, and respect will produce a child and adult who is relatively conflict-free. Neurosis develops when a child's basic anxiety is intensified by an unloving, hostile, and rejecting early environment.

Horney listed ten neurotic needs that result from high levels of basic anxiety: (1) the neurotic need for affection and approval, (2) the neurotic need for a partner who will take over one's life, (3) the neurotic need to restrict one's life within narrow borders, (4) the neurotic need to exploit others, (5) the neurotic need for power, (6) the neurotic need for prestige, (7) the neurotic need for personal admiration, (8) the neurotic need for personal achievement, (9) the neurotic need for self-sufficiency and independence, and (10) the neurotic need for perfection and unassailability. Later Horney classified these needs under three headings: moving toward people, moving away from people, and moving against people. The normal person integrates these three orientations, using all of them at different times. Appropriate flexibility is the signpost of normality. The neurotic emphasizes and perseveres in one of the orientations that he manifests in exaggerated and inappropriate forms. Thus the neurotic, in moving toward others, may establish only dependency relationships in an effort to squash his anxiety and insecurity. The neurotic who moves against people may do so only in hostile and aggressive ways, again hoping to eliminate the imagined and projected sources of his anxiety and insecurity. The neurotic who moves away from people may completely isolate himself, giving up hope and faith in the possibility of achieving support, love, or security from others. Neurotics continue their faulty adjustments because they can never quite achieve the desired feelings of security or the removal of their intense basic anxiety.

Another point of departure from Freudian psychology was Horney's rejection of Freud's conceptualization of female psychology. Underlying Freud's view was the assumption that women suffered from "penis envy" and an associated sense of inferiority based on the feeling of having been castrated. Horney felt that Freud's conclusions were speculative and largely the reflection of Victorian male attitudes toward women. She very ingeniously showed (Horney, 1926) how the popularly held Freudian view of female sexuality closely resembled the ideas that boys have about girls (see Table 12.1).

While the starting point for Freud's analysis is the girl's reaction to the boy's penis, Horney gives primary attention to the female anatomy. The young girl, according to Horney, is absorbed in her own body and sensations—she does not initially envy boys. Only when guilt and anxiety over sexual feelings arise does the girl "flee from femininity." The desire for maleness—or symbolically, the penis—is a secondary reaction to this flight. Frigidity, for example, occurs not because of an unresolved wish for a penis, but because of the repression of female sexual desires. Other sexual difficulties may arise because of specific past traumas in relation to menstruation and other early sexual experiences. The interpersonal relationships within the family in early childhood govern the woman's later sense of well-being both sexually and otherwise. Horney rejected Freud's emphasis on penis envy and the supposed feeling of inferiority due to the lack of a penis. The roots of feminine psychology, according to Horney, are in basic anxiety. But women must also contend with the lack of confidence that they acquire in our male-oriented society.

ERICH FROMM

Fromm, too, is critical of the exclusive importance that Freud gives to biological motivation (i.e., frustration, pleasure, and instincts that Freud assumed to be the driving forces in life). The social

Table 12.1 Comparison of Ideas of Female Sexuality

The Boys' Ideas	*Our Ideas of Feminine Development (i.e., Freudian Ideas)*
1. Naïve assumption that girls as well as boys possess a penis.	For both sexes, it is only the male genital which plays any part.
2. Realization of the absence of the penis.	Sad discovery of the absence of the penis.
3. Idea that the girl is a castrated, mutilated boy.	Belief of the girl that she once possessed a penis and lost it by castration.
4. Belief that the girl has suffered punishment that also threatens him.	Castration is conceived of as the infliction of punishment.
5. The girl is regarded as inferior.	The girl regards herself as inferior. Penis envy.
6. The boy is unable to imagine how the girl can ever get over the loss or envy.	The girl never gets over the sense of deficiency and inferiority and has constantly to master afresh her desire to be a man.
7. The boy dreads her envy.	The girl desires throughout life to avenge herself on the man for possessing something which she lacks.

From Karen Horney, "The Flight from Womanhood," *International Journal of Psycho-analysis*, 1926, 7, 327. Used by permission.

environment, according to Fromm, shapes the needs and personality of the individual. Society can even create new needs that are more powerful than the biological ones. The need for individuality is one such social creation. Making his case for the importance of social forces, Fromm traces the evolving human personality through different periods of history. Starting from a oneness with nature during his earlier primitive existence, man has moved in the direction of greater and greater individuality. In the first stage man is very much part of his physical world, not perceiving himself as a separate entity. This unity with nature provides a sense of security by affording protection from loneliness and isolation, but at the same time unity with nature denies individuality and freedom. During the Middle Ages man grew away from his identification with nature, achieving his identity through membership in social institutions such as the church, social group, or guild. Status at this time could not easily be changed, so that a person who was a peasant could not rise in the social order. If your father was a tailor you would most likely become a tailor as well. Life was static and the choices open to individuals were limited; people spent their lives in a very narrow sphere. The Industrial Revolution broke down the rigid class lines of feudalism and encouraged the growth of individuality. The new capitalism enhanced individuality through its emphasis on competition, individual initiative, and other characteristics of an open, competitive system.

Along with individuality or freedom came feelings of loneliness and helplessness. The security of unity with nature is lost as man separates and differentiates himself. Neurosis, in this view, consists of traits developed to cope with the loneliness of isolation. Some people need to "escape from freedom" while others relate to their anxiety more productively. Masochism, sadism, destructiveness, and conformity are the neurotic techniques of interacting with society. All of these techniques are efforts to overcome the sense of weakness, inadequacy, and loneliness of life in the modern world. The masochist submits to the power of others in order to submerge his own anxiety through the identification with power. Sadism is used by some to gain a feeling of power but it is really an effort to deny the underlying feeling of weakness. Destructiveness is a more extreme form of sadism; the person in this case must destroy in order to eliminate what he imagines is giving him the feeling of helplessness. Destructiveness, however, does not work because the feeling of weakness continues to reside within the person. Conformity is the most commonly used form of escape from freedom. By erasing differences between self and others the person strives to eliminate his feeling of loneliness and helplessness. The creative solution to the crises of individuality, according to Fromm, comes through recognizing the problem of loneliness and then relating to the world in a productive and loving manner.

HUMANISTIC PSYCHOLOGY

Humanism is an important movement within contemporary psychology, most closely associated with the names of Carl Rogers, Abraham Maslow, and Rollo May. The humanistic psychologists have a strong link with the social theorists. Both emphasize social rather than aggressive or destructive motives at the core of human existence. But the humanists go further in detailing the uniqueness of human strivings and potentialities.

Man demonstrates in his own nature a pressure toward fuller and fuller Being, more and more perfect actualization of his humanness in exactly the same naturalistic, scientific sense that an acorn may be said to be "pressing toward" being an oak tree, or that a tiger can be observed to "push toward" being tigerish, or a horse toward being equine. Man is ultimately not molded or shaped into humanness, or taught to be human. The role of the environment is ultimately to permit him or help him to actualize his own potentialities, not its potentialities. The environment does not give him potentialities and capacities; he has them in inchoate or embryonic form, just exactly as he has embryonic arms and legs. And creativeness, spontaneity, selfhood, authenticity, caring for others, being able to love, yearning for truth are embryonic potentialities belonging to his species-membership just as much as are his arms and legs and brain and eyes. (Maslow, 1968, pp. 160-161).

Maslow proposes a hierarchy of needs in the following order: physiological, safety, security, belongingness, affection, respect and self-respect, and self-actualization. Self-actualization, the highest form of human expression, cannot be vigorously pursued unless lower needs are met. Unfulfilled needs lead to frustration, aggression, and violence, which prevent a person from having self-actualizing experiences. Yet it is in the process of self-actualization that the person becomes truly human:

We may define [self-actualization] as an episode, or a spurt in which the powers of the person come together in a particularly efficient and intensely enjoyable way, and in which he is more integrated and less split, more open for experience, more idiosyncratic, more perfectly expressive or spontaneous, or fully functioning, more creative, more humorous, more ego-transcending, more independent of his lower needs, etc. He becomes in these episodes more truly himself, more perfectly actualizing his potentialities, closer to the core of his Being, more fully human. (p. 97).

The humanists take issue with personality theories that are based on deficiency motivation. The deficiency-motivated person is driven by deficits of one sort or another. The behaviorists assume that biological needs and their gratification comprise the cycle of drive, behavior, and reinforcement. When biological drives and tensions are reduced, the organism returns to a state of equilibrium. This equilibrium or quiescence is considered the goal of behavior in deficiency motivation theory. Psychoanalysis is another deficiency motivation theory because of its preoccupation with impulse gratification and defense; the person constantly seeks gratification (equilibrium) of sexual and aggressive impulses, and defenses are invoked to prevent the primitive expression of the impulses from emerging into consciousness and behavior. For the humanists these deficiency-oriented theories leave out the most important part of being human. Reduction of tensions may apply to biological needs and to the behavior of disturbed people whose basic needs have been frustrated, but for healthy people self-actualization supersedes the gratification of needs. The self-actualizing person acts upon his environment and does not simply react to biological or environmental stresses or pulls. The self-actualizing person is inner-directed. In being truly human a person seeks goals, exercises will-power, overcomes obstacles, and is creative in a continuous sequence of growth and development. Rather than settling for mere gratification or equilibrium, the self-actualizing person seeks activity and involvement that carry him to higher, not lower, levels of tension and excitement.

The humanists, in their diligent attention to human potentialities, have been an important force in directing all personality theorists to reassess their conceptions of human motivation.

SOCIAL THEORIES AND NURSING

The theories outlined in this chapter are of special interest to nurses because of the basic interpersonal and social nature of nursing and health care. Nurses interact with people not only in the one-to-one relationships with patients, but also in the broader contexts of hospital, family, and community. The social theories give great encouragement for the potential power of social forces to effect real changes in individuals. The nurse can, therefore, through expert handling of interpersonal relationships, be a catalyst for growth experiences in clients. Also the nurse's attention to the social forces within the hospital and community can be used to organize influences to work toward patient rehabilitation and growth. Humanistic psychology adds an important dimension to nursing practice in its attention to human potentialities. The humanists remind us that growth and development are possible throughout the life cycle, that humans can always overcome obstacles. The task is to tap the self-actualizing core that is present in everyone.

SUMMARY

The social and interpersonal theorists emphasize the influence of the social environment on human development. Interpersonal relationships in early childhood are among the most important social determinants of personality formation. Each of the theorists presented has a somewhat different focus. Erik Erikson stresses the interaction of Freud's psychosexual stages and ego development with the child's social world and the institutions of society. Harry Stack Sullivan's interpersonal theory of psychiatry draws attention to the importance of interpersonal relationships in the first few years of life for shaping the person's self-system and style of relating to others. Transactional analysis has extended interpersonal theory to show how childhood experiences within the family become internalized into three types of representations—Child, Parent, and Adult—which then affect all our behavior and relationships. For Alfred Adler it is the infant and young child's perception of weakness and helplessness (feeling of inferiority) in relation to others and the world around him that becomes the central motive force of life. Karen Horney is concerned with basic anxiety arising from the early mother-child interaction and its bearing on orientations toward the social world (moving toward people, moving away from people, and moving against people). Erich Fromm's theory stresses man's feelings of loneliness and alienation in a technological society and their impact on evolving personality patterns both historically and individually. Humanist psychology has directed the attention of personality theorists to a broader concept of human motivation and human potentialities.

SUGGESTED READINGS

Ansbacher, H. L., and Ansbacher, R. R. *The individual psychology of Alfred Adler*. New York: Basic Books, 1956.

Erikson, E. H. *Childhood and society*. New York: Norton, 1950.

Fromm, E. *Escape from freedom*. New York: Farrar and Rinehart, 1941.

Hall, C. S., and Lindzey, G. *Theories of personality*. New York: Wiley, 1970.

Horney, K. *New ways in psychoanalysis*. New York: Norton, 1939.

Maslow, A. H. *Toward a psychology of being*. New York: Van Nostrand, 1968.

Munroe, R. L. *Schools of psychoanalytic thought*. New York: Dryden Press, 1955.

Sullivan, H. S. *The interpersonal theory of psychiatry*. New York: Norton, 1953.

Part *III*

Social and Situational Influences on Development and Behavior

THUS FAR WE have viewed people principally from the "inside looking out," concentrating on the dynamics of the individual personality acting in the world. But for a full understanding of human behavior we need to take an "outside" view as well, and see how social and situational factors shape development from birth onward.

At the most general level, human beings are formed by the societies into which they are born. We have already discussed social factors in connection with personality theorists in Chapter 12. In Chapter 13 we examine the concepts of culture and social class, considering how people are affected by different social structures and value systems. We also discuss the implications of these differences for health care personnel, who must be able to understand and help other people whatever their background.

In Chapter 14 we turn our attention to situational influences of a more specific kind, but of particular significance for those in the health care field: the effects of illness, hospitalization, and disability on behavior. Here we discuss how different people—men, women, children, the aged—react psychologically to these special circumstances, and how they can best be helped by those responsible for their care.

The inclusion of a chapter on intelligence may seem somewhat surprising here, since we commonly think of intelligence as a "fixed" element in the individual's makeup. Yet intelligence develops through a complex interplay of social and biological factors. We consider these factors in Chapter 15, as well as some of the problems involved in defining and measuring intelligence.

Chapter *13*

Culture, Social Class, and Behavior

ACCORDING TO Erich Fromm, "social character has the function of molding human energy for the purpose of the functioning of a given society" (in Maccoby, 1967). Looked at in this way, the cultural characteristics of a society have a decisive role in shaping the behavior of the individual. For the nurse, culture is an important area of study because of the very nature of our society. We live in a multicultural setting composed of many cultures and subcultures, and nurses come into contact with all segments of society. In this chapter we will look at a variety of these influences on behavior, including cultural traditions and social class differences.

Culture leaves its mark at such an early age that we sometimes come to view our own beliefs, attitudes, and values as the only right or "normal" ones. The whole question of what is normal in behavior cannot escape a cultural analysis, and so we will emphasize the cultural basis for many of our own cherished values and assumptions.

Culture intersects with health care through the conditioning of a host of attitudes and behaviors with regard to illness, authority, the body, life, and death. Examples will illustrate how the understanding of cultural differences can be harnessed to help patients and improve health-care delivery.

TWO CULTURES

To set the stage for this excursion into culture and behavior let us take a look at some differences between two primitive tribes that have been extensively studied by Margaret Mead (1939).

The Mundugumors are a tribe of head-hunters living in the jungles of northeastern New Guinea. From early childhood the Mundugumor is trained to be aggressive as preparation for his role as a warrior. For the Mundugumors head-hunting is a mode of behavior that is not questioned; on the contrary, it is highly prized and praised. A Mundugumor adult male revolted by head-hunting would be an outcast in his society. He would undergo ridicule and find life very difficult. However, you are not likely to find many mild-mannered Mundugumors. The child-rearing practices of this tribe are such that the valued characteristics are likely to be developed.

Rejection for the Mundugumor child starts even before birth. Children are unwanted and pregnancy is an occasion for the husband to become angry at his wife. In Mundugumor society sons do not become part of the father's social constellation, so that a man has no heirs; further, sons are trained early to defend their mothers against their father and to abuse the father. Thus the possibility of the woman giving birth to a son signals the beginning of the father's decline. The woman is equally distressed by her pregnancy, since it increases the likelihood that her husband will abandon her or take another wife. It is not surprising to learn that infanticide is commonplace among the Mundugumors. The child is placed on his own early. Weaning is a harsh process of rejection in which the child is pushed away from the breast that he seeks. There is no intimacy or coddling. Prohibitions against other relatives are taught early and the child learns a long list of other "no's." Thus the child is prepared for the brutal aggressiveness, distrust, and hostility that characterize Mundugumor society.

The Arapesh are another tribe living on the northeast coast of New Guinea just about 100 miles from the Mundugumors. They are a tribe of very mild people who shun violence and favor cooperative social activity. To the Arapesh aggressiveness is very undesirable, and an aggressive, destructive Arapesh would be ostracized. If an Arapesh showed an inclination toward head-hunting his fellow tribesmen would be horrified. Unlike the Mundugumors, who live in isolated and secret huts in the bush, the Arapesh live in clusters of villages. Cooperation is the term that best describes the behavior of the Arapesh. All of their activities, whether planting, hunting, or building a house, are cooperative and communal. "The men spend over nine-tenths of their time responding to other people's plans. . . ."

The characteristics of the Arapesh are firmly established in their child-rearing practices. The Arapesh child is a wanted child except in unusual circumstances such as famine. Boys are most preferred, being considered "the joy and comfort" of the parents' old age. Nursing is an activity in which both mother and child delight—much different from the quick abrupt breast feeding of the Mundugumor children—and suckling continues until age 3 or 4. Weaning is a slow, patient process of teaching the child to eat more solid food. When Arapesh women have to wean a child early because of a new pregnancy they feel guilty. Both husband and wife share in the caring for the new infant. If the woman has urgent things to do, the father will gladly take on the domestic chores. Parents are extremely tolerant and uncritical with their children. Babies are never left unattended, and there is always human warmth and contact nearby.

From early childhood the Arapesh learn to trust and love everyone around. There are many surrogate parents and the children learn to address everyone as if he were a relative. In this society, in which sharing is so commonplace, sharp distinctions in relationships are unnecessary. It is also not unusual for children to visit with relatives for weeks at a time. It is no wonder that the Arapesh have a safe and secure image of the world. The intimacy and warmth that dominate the child's environment set the stage for the friendliness, generosity, and cooperation that characterize Arapesh society.

DEFINING "NORMAL"

Which tribe is more normal? Is one group more disturbed or deviant than the other? If you venture to answer these questions by naming one of the tribes, you are making a value judgment.

No doubt you do not care for head-hunting. Head-hunting would be deviant, maladaptive, or pathological in most societies. But the fact that head-hunting is the *norm* in Mundugumor society illustrates an important principle with regard to the definition of deviant behavior: It cannot be absolutely defined or described. Deviancy or abnormality is always relative to a particular set of circumstances, and any effort to impose an absolute definition is an expression of the values of the individual, group, or society—that is, preference based on a particular sociocultural experience.

The problem of defining deviance would not be difficult if we were living in a completely homogeneous society. But not only do societies differ from each other, they are also pluralistic—that is, the members of a particular society hold different values as a result of national origin, race, education, income level, religion, age, sex, and other factors.

Certainly these variations exist in most Western urbanized societies. Each subcultural factor can give rise to beliefs and values embodying different notions of what is normal. We can see conflicts arising from these different notions every day. What is considered quite normal in Greenwich Village may seem as outlandish as head-hunting in rural parts of the country. Young people view the behavior of older people as "uptight" and highly constricted; older people say that the youth culture is impulse-ridden. To agnostics and atheists, orthodox religious people may seem primitive and misguided. The middle class rejects lower-class values, while the middle-class work ethic is currently under attack from many quarters. Clearly, if any one group were asked to specify a set of behaviors that were considered normal, the list would be highly biased and filled with value judgments.

In spite of the difficulties of defining normality, deviancy, or pathology, it is necessary, especially in a health-care setting, to assume some working definition. We cannot promote positive mental health without a concept of normal; and given a concept of normal, a definition of abnormal will be implied.

How would you define normal? Compare your definition with those given by a group of college students:

1. "If you have a lot of friends and get along with everyone, you're normal."

2. "I guess you're normal if you don't do freaky things like flip out on drugs or sleep with everyone."

3. "A normal person doesn't get too excited or nervous about things. He can handle things."

4. "Normal means not different."

5. "If you don't get bad feelings like tense or very down."

6. "A normal person doesn't feel guilty about things like sex."

7. "You do what you want as long as you don't hurt anybody."

8. "Normal is following the teachings of the church—the straight and true life."

9. "You do the right things, get married, get a good job, have a family, and join community groups."

10. "Acts of violence like murder or rape or doing bizarre things aren't normal."

These informal definitions, which typify frequently heard, off-the-cuff remarks about normality, imply the major points of view about the nature of normality. The *average* concept of normality is suggested by definitions 1, 4, and 9. Item 8 reflects the *authority* concept of normality. The *symptom* concept of normality is expressed in items 2, 3, 5, 6 and 10. We will now discuss these concepts in more detail.

Definition by Average

In this usage "average" refers to what most people are doing or what is typical behavior. Extreme behavior deviating from the average in either direction would then be considered abnormal. This definition is clearly stated in number 4 above, "Normal means not different." The statement says that you are normal if you conform to the behavior of most people or the average person. Some sense of "average" behavior is probably the definition most commonly used by laymen.

Conformity lends a degree of security to many people, and the belief that "everyone" is doing something often produces the compelling feeling that it is OK. But there are problems with this way of defining "normal." We have seen in the discussion of tribes in New Guinea that what is normal and average in one place is not so in another. Consider, for example, a woman who has always lived in a neighborhood where most people are of similar background. This experience may have given rise to a strong belief that everyone thinks, feels, and behaves as she does—or that she thinks, feels, and behaves like everyone else. She may always have observed, in this neighborhood, that a woman's role consists of getting married young, having children in quick succession, cooking meals, caring for the children, and later marrying them off. This pattern may have occurred with such regularity and consistency that she feels this is the way things should be—i.e., normal. The saddest lot seems to be that of the girl who doesn't get married by age 19. A problem arises when the woman meets other women with different experiences who reject the exclusive homemaker role, regard women as equals of men, and desire to pursue careers (even with families). Such women challenge the traditional sex roles and do not hesitate to compete with men in every area of life. If the traditional image of the woman is normal, what of this other view?

Such clashes are commonplace in our society, in which we find great diversity in modes of living. Average, therefore, is not a statistical average that takes into consideration the whole range of possibilities. Rather "average" usually means what we have absorbed from a limited experience in a particular social group. Our personal notion of normal or average may be quite different from that of someone living in another region or even just a few blocks away.

We may try to rationalize our personal concepts of normality by seeing others as abnormal. Thus the women's liberationist is called "a man-hater, lesbian, anarchist, angry, domineering, and sick." In time, however, the women's liberation view may have a strong impact and the concept of what is normal for women may change. Consequently, the average concept is unreliable as an index of normal behavior because the concept of average changes from time to time and differs from group to group and society to society. The changeability of "average" behavior has been clearly evident in the last few years with regard to hairstyles for men. A hairstyle first regarded as a symbol of defiance or social protest—even perhaps the occasion for being fired from a job or being suspended from school —looks perfectly "normal" several years later.

The "average" concept runs into trouble even when we take cultural relativism into account. It may seem "normal" for Mundugumors to engage in murder and brutality because that's what they do and they are a small isolated group living in a far-off place —would we be so generous in calling similar behavior "normal" if it became typical in an advanced country? There have been times in history when typical behavior in Western countries took such a direction. If typical is normal then we are deprived of the right to call those behaviors and those societies sick.

There is another problem with the "average" definition of normality. A person may perform all the typically normal behaviors and conform to the prescriptions for social adjustment—e.g., marriage, family, getting along with others, holding a job—and still suffer inner turmoil and conflict. Surface appearances do not always reflect a person's feeling state. Yet personal fulfillment is very much dependent on the way we feel. The "average" concept leaves little room for individuality. Definition number 7 ("You do what you want as long as you don't hurt anybody") suggests a more individualized approach, but it does not give sufficient guidelines.

Definition by Symptoms

Symptoms are commonly used in medicine as indices of pathology. Physicians expect diseases to be accompanied by observable physiological deviations. Sometimes the symptoms are very slight manifestations that require specialized instruments and diagnostic skill to detect, but the assumption is that symptoms and pathology go together. Is this the case with human behavior and personality disorders? In other words, are people with no symptoms of personality disorder therefore normal, and vice versa?

Some experts consider the symptom requirement for psychological malfunction inadequate. Thomas Szasz, a prominent psychiatrist, opposes applying the physical illness model of pathology to personality disorders; according to Szasz, this model erroneously implies an absolute reference point for mental health (Szasz, 1960). For example, in the physical area a body temperature of 98.6° is considered normal, and significant departures from this absolute reference point represent illness, which will be accompanied by symptoms. In psychological functioning, however, there is no such reference point for absolute health. Psychological norms, as we have seen, are so influenced by culture and our immediate environment that wide variations in human functioning can be "normal" under particular circumstances. At the same time there are personality disturbances that are not characterized by such prominent or disabling symptoms as anxiety, depression, phobias, uncontrolled behavior, etc. Even people who experience relatively high anxiety levels and frequent depression can sometimes function effectively. We might also point out that behaviors highly prized in some societies are designated symptoms of pathology in ours—for example, trance states and seizures have high status in many primitive societies.

According to Szasz, the symptom definition of mental illness falsely leads to the view that mental health is a passive state. The person who has a 98.6° temperature may be healthy physically, but the mentally healthy person must work actively to maintain his healthy state by the ongoing process of coping effectively with the problems of living. There is no clear sailing in psychological adjustment.

The freedom-from-symptoms definition of normality also runs into conflict with the average concept. Consider the recent, and extensive, mental health study conducted in midtown Manhattan, in which 75% of the people interviewed had symptoms of anxiety. High anxiety would seem to be the norm in American urban society.

Other research on so-called normal people also raises questions about the symptom-free definition of normality. In a study by Golden et al. (1962) fifty males of about age 14 were selected from all ninth graders in the Minneapolis public schools on the basis of the lack of pathological indicators as shown by psychological testing. Twelve years later these "normal" males were studied in depth by psychological tests, structured psychiatric interviews, social histories, and interviews with their wives. Results showed that all of the 50 subjects with the exception of 5 would still, at the later date, be considered emotionally healthy. Their married lives were stable with no separations or broken marriages. The men tended to idealize their wives and the wives, with one exception, were content with their husbands as stable, responsible, dependable individuals. However, some of the findings were not so encouraging. These "normal" men were found to have little imagination and generally limited interests and social activities. They indicated limited educational and vocational aspirations for themselves and also for their children.

Apparently normality in the conventional sense is achieved by stunting the more creative aspects of life. Perhaps in a highly complex, technological world the lack of anxiety or problems represents an insensitivity to the environment. Vitality and a deep involvement in life may entail a degree of anxiety, uncertainty, and instability. To sit, so to speak, on a fire and be perfectly complacent may be a denial of reality rather than normality.

Definition by Authority

Appeal to an authoritative source for a definition of normality is reflected by student definition number 8, "Normal is following the teachings of the church—the straight and true life." While the behaviors favored by various philosophies and religions are frequently humanistic and socially oriented, this is not always the case. Philosophies are sometimes at odds. Citing authority also brings us back to the contradictions of cultural relativism. The authorities among the Mundugumors, after all, prescribe head-hunting. The prescriptions of the authorities in a communal atheistic society may be different from those in a new industrializing nation as well as from those of an advanced capitalistic society. The fact is that there are many authorities, some religious and some secular. The prospects for a universal standard does not seem likely in a highly diverse, multicultural world.

Resolving the Dilemma of Definition

If there is so much confusion and controversy surrounding the definition of normality and pathology, how can nurses and other health-care professionals be expected to use these terms and apply them in practice? The solution to this dilemma is suggested by David Mechanic (1962). In a study in a New England mental institution Mechanic examined the reasons why patients came to the hospital. Some were self-referrals, others were brought by friends or relatives; in either case someone decided that serious pathology was present. But what these patients and their families regarded as "sick" varied greatly depending on social class, the lower and middle classes holding different views. In this instance, as Mechanic points out, the professional controversy over definitions of pathology played a very small role, since all the patients appearing for admission were admitted. In practice, then, deviancy is defined by social groups.

These implicit social definitions have a certain validity since they reflect the norm of the environment in which the individual must work and live. In a low socioeconomic environment, for example, quitting a job and remaining unemployed for a long period of time may be acceptable behavior. A long history of poverty has a demoralizing effect, often lowering a person's level of aspiration and producing apathy. A person with such a background who quits a job without giving substantial reason may arouse the anger of his family, and they may think of him as "lazy" or "inconsiderate"—but not "sick" or "crazy." Yet in a middle-class environment the same behavior would probably alarm family and friends and might be the occasion for seeking professional help. Similarly, in poverty cultures, violence is a more common part of everyday life than in the middle-class environment. Consequently outbursts of temper, beatings, and threats may be characterized by one group as "he is a mean person," or "he gets excited easily," while in another sub-culture any marked physical agression is regarded as a sign of serious disturbance. Of course it is not possible to draw simple stereotypes, and each case must be fully evaluated. For a clinician it is necessary to explore a person's behavior in the light of his inter-nalized values and customs. Ultimately, "normal" can only be defined in terms of the individual—what constitutes adaptive, gratifying, and productive behavior in the light of the person's own internalized values and customs.

From the point of view of health-care professionals it may not always be essential to define psychopathology. In most health-care situations it is not important to put labels of pathology on patients. In dealing with a person as a person, the main task is understanding. The nurse should be able to describe the patient's behavior and then understand it. In this way, a strategy can be worked out for relating to the patient and encouraging behaviors and attitudes conducive to recovery and general health. (For a full discussion of psychopathology, see Chapter 16.)

CULTURAL PATTERNS

The cultural background of the individual should always be considered when trying to understand behavior—not only unusual or strange behavior but all behavior. At the same time, one must exercise caution, avoid jumping to conclusions and/or stereotyping. It may be true that broad cultural patterns can be associated with different groups, but these general patterns are often caricatures that have little bearing on a particular individual. Each individual's experience is unique. And, as we have noted, even among fairly homogeneous groups various subcultures can be found. Therefore, never assume that the cultural patterns reported by investigators are directly applicable to a patient who belongs to a particular group. Instead, treat the stereotyped pattern as a hypothesis to be checked out against the knowledge that you yourself acquire about the real patient.

National Character

There has been considerable speculation and research on traits that typify people from different countries. Madariaga (1967) described the Englishman as the man of action, the Frenchman as the man of thought, and the Spaniard as the man of passion. Others have called the English cold, Americans friendly, American women independent and domineering, Swedes and Danes generous, Italians and French romantic, and Germans dependable and efficient. Some of these comments are based on casual observation but there have also been some more probing studies.

Maccoby (1967), analyzing the Mexican national character, described the Mexicans' lack of faith in authority as stemming from centuries of exploitation. The Mexican, he says, cannot believe that an official would place the people's needs before his own. Maccoby also discusses the "machismo" of the Mexican male, i.e. a compulsive need for masculinity that conceals a more basic need—"their wish to be fed and cared for by women." There are other characteristics that Maccoby points to: "Mexico is . . . a land where creative talent abounds . . . both men and women seek liberty and a peaceful life."

Hiroshi Minami, a Japanese psychologist, writing on the psychology of the Japanese (quoted by Haring, 1967), cites submission to power as a common characteristic of Japanese. The status consciousness of the Japanese makes them uncomfortable in social situations unless they know the status of others with whom they have to relate; given the status, they know how to behave. Haring (1967) emphasizes the burden that obligation places on the Japanese. Favors and kindnesses must be returned; if they cannot be returned, anxiety results. As a result of this sense (and fear) of obligation and responsibility to others (called *giri*) the Japanese can quite innocently engage in nudity and bathing with the opposite sex without there being sexual overtones. Even casual sexual involvement would set off the anxiety-provoking sense of obligation.

Sundburg in 1914 cited the Swedish talent for building large-scale organizations but also referred to a lack of psychological feeling and interest; Myrdal more recently attributed the Swedish reasonableness in politics and social action to their "detachment and lack of deep involvement with others" (in Carlsson, 1967). According to Hendin (1964), who studied suicide in Scandinavia, Swedish men are preoccupied with work, career, and money.

Dhirendra Narain (1967), writing on the modern Indian national character, stresses the history of enslavement and the caste system in accounting for some of the characteristics that he notes. The presence of foreign rule during much of the past has created an attitude of dependence and lack of assurance: "a great amount of initial enthusiasm may be shown but it soon dissipates. At the collective level, faith in objectives is proclaimed, but the requisite amount of sustained effort is not forthcoming." According to Narain, "there is a great patience but little perseverance." Supression of intense emotions is another characteristic cited by Narain. Strong emotions are too threatening to be allowed into consciousness. Therefore, when the usual controls break down, extreme emotional outbursts are likely to occur.

Despite such observations of national character it is quite another matter to be confronted with a particular German, Spaniard, Italian, Indian, Mexican, or any other ethnically identifiable person. It would be unreasonable to expect all persons of a particular nationality or ethnic group to fit a stereotyped pattern. On the other hand, you should not be surprised if some of the national characteristics do appear. In other words, be ready for them and consider the possibility of those characteristics showing up. There have been sufficient reports in the nursing literature on misunderstandings of a patient's culturally determined behavior to necessitate alerting the nurse to this important area.

Health Care

Frances McGregor, in her article "Uncooperative Patients; Some Cultural Interpretations" (1967), states: "One cannot underestimate the tenacity of cultural patterns and the hold they have on patients even when health is at stake. Such things as ethnic and social class background and religion are all sources of different responses to illness and treatment; the violation of health requirements by many patients stems from these differentials. Unless the nurse learns to think in cultural terms just as she learns to think in psychological terms she will continue to be baffled, if not exasperated. . . ." McGregor presents three cases that illustrate the importance of cultural interpretations of patient behavior. In one case a young adult patient with coronary artery disease was found, soon after admission to the hospital, out of bed and looking out the window. He was reprimanded by the shocked nurse. This did not seem to be at all effective since the next day he was found looking out the same window a number of times. The nurses were particularly shocked by his behavior because it placed his life in danger. This "strange" behavior was explained when it was discovered later that the patient, a devout Moslem, was required to pray looking toward Mecca five times a day. In his value system his life was secondary to his religious practices. When the patient's bed was placed facing the direction of Mecca he no longer left his bed.

In another case a Swedish patient refused offers of all sorts of services that would have made him more comfortable after his surgery. He would just say "No thank you" when offered such things as water, juice, and back rubs. His behavior seemed strange indeed, especially when his wife reported that her husband had complained to her about not receiving the very services the nurses had offered. This "strange" case was cleared up at last when a Swedish nursing student explained to the other nurses about Swedish etiquette. It is considered polite in Sweden to refuse offers of food and attention until they are offered a number of times. The patient quite naturally was insulted when the offers of the nurses were not repeated.

The third case deals with an elderly female patient of Czechoslovakian background. The woman had both legs amputated as the result of a peripheral vascular disease. She was generally uncooperative in her treatment program, complaining that the staff was "punishing her, bossing her around." But the patient's smoking was a particular problem. Nicotine in the blood causes constriction of peripheral blood vessels, and a continuation of smoking could have worsened her illness; yet reprimands and threats simply did not work. Of course a variety of psychological explanations of her behavior could readily be hypothesized, i.e., smoking supplied oral gratification, represented hostility, indicated possible suicidal tendencies, etc. McGregor, however, analyzes the patient's behavior in terms of Martha Wolfenstein's report on typical child-rearing practices and early experiences of Czechoslovakian children. According to this analysis, Czech mothers manipulate reward in such a way as to give children the feeling of receiving unfair treatment. In retaliation the children often rebel by doing the opposite of the mother's wishes. According to Wolfenstein, coercion, demanding, and commanding will often fail with Czechs because of this need to resist what is perceived as irrational authority. Acting on the basis of this cultural explanation, the nurses ceased giving orders to the patient in question. Instead of threatening, they merely advised her on the dangers of smoking and then left cigarettes around, placing the responsibility on the patient for her own health. The technique worked, and the patient shortly became more cooperative and cut down significantly on her smoking.

Leininger (1967) describes a nursing situation in which cultural differences led to a misunderstanding. A nursing student noticed a lovely 3-year-old Mexican-American child sitting with her mother in an outpatient clinic, and she began to praise the child's beauty and appearance. The mother became restless and uncomfortable while the compliments were being offered, so the nurse, assuming that the mother did not understand her, repeated the praises. A few moments later when the nurse was called away, the mother quickly gathered up her things and left the clinic with the child. The student nurse had failed to understand the beliefs of Mexican-Americans. Admiring the child without touching her is casting an "evil eye" on the child. Believing that the child was under an evil influence, the mother sought treatment for the child from a native practitioner. The misunderstanding was further emphasized when the student later explained that she usually did not touch a strange child until she had first talked to the mother and child. While this may be appropriate decorum in many communities it was the wrong thing to do with the Mexican-American mother and child.

In all these cases, the cultural interpretation proved to be valuable. But again we must emphasize the difficulties in applying purely cultural interpretations. The cultural aspect of the person must be considered among the universe of other influences on personality and behavior. There are no foolproof cookbooks that can assure you of the right interpretation in a given case. As a clinician the nurse must put all the pieces together each time in a unique configuration to account for the individual who is her patient.

Pain

Cultural orientations play an important role in perception of pain. Just as culture selects preferred personality characteristics, so does it influence reactions to pain. In fact, many of the personality characteristics associated with different reactions to pain may be an aspect of culture. For example, a culture that induces high anxiety in its members may predispose them to greater experiences of pain while cultures that do not allow for very much expression of feelings are likely to produce people who do not give vent or recognition to painful experiences. In some cultures it is perfectly acceptable to express pain and to seek comfort and reassurance from others. In other cultures expressions of pain are frowned upon. It is therefore not surprising to learn in a study by Schultz (1971) that 10- and 11-year-old American boys said "they felt brave" when they had pain. Our society expects boys to play a certain role and they pick this up very early.

The cultural influence on reactions to pain is potently illustrated by Basu (1966) in her observations of patients in India:

> Their reaction to pain is freely shown by groaning and crying. Some try self-control by prayers and religious rituals. There is a deep dependency role played by the sick on the family concurrent with the family's willingness to accept a great deal of the responsibility for care and support. Thus the apprehension of pain experience seems to be lessened in the presence of the family members. Faith and passive dependence on God seem to ease the tension associated with pain, and the pain is expressed by invoking God's name. (p. 232)

Blaylock (1968), in his review of the literature on cultural influences on pain, reports some interesting findings. In one study, prizefighters, American Indians, and blacks showed less reaction to pain than the average white urban person. Black patients in a Southern hospital, in another study, tended to deny pain and were reluctant to request pain relievers. A study of patients of Jewish, Italian, and "old American" (i.e., long native ancestry in America) origin revealed that the Jews and Italians were emotional and seemed to experience more pain than the "old American" patients. The latter were unemotional and showed little overt expression of pain. Another study reported by Blaylock found a lower threshold for pain among black, Italian, Russian, and Jewish patients than among northern Europeans. However, these finds are by no means universal, as indicated by another study showing no differences in the threshold for pain for all normal subjects. (We will discuss the psychology of pain further in Chapter 13).

SOCIAL CLASS
Child-rearing Environment

In discussing the differences between the two New Guinea tribes we stressed the importance of the early child-rearing environment in molding cultural characteristics of the individual. Recent research along these lines has consistently turned up two factors that differentiate middle and low socioeconomic homes: the extent of parental interaction and communication with the infant and young child, and the organization of the home environment. Middle-class children typically come from homes where their early life is stable, with routine patterns that enable them to develop more organized patterns in relation to all behavior and activities throughout their lives. In low socioeconomic environments, where poverty and demoralization due to limited opportunities lead to desertion, stress, and social disorganization, children frequently do not develop the same ability to organize their behavior. Left on their own or to the dominant influence of the peer group at a very early age, these children have difficulty following routines or organized activities with prescribed rules, and sometimes their behavior may appear impulsive and erratic. In this regard the presence of family life appears to be more important than social class. Eleanor Pavenstedt (1965) studied children from a "very low" socioeconomic group and an "upper-low" socioeconomic group. On the surface there appeared to be many similarities among the children of these two groups. They often lived in the same neighborhoods, and they seemed to dress equally well. Upon closer examination, their family life and behavior revealed sharp differences. The upper-low-class children in the study came from stable homes where both parents were in the home. Parents were very concerned about their children and about the need to train them in order to prevent delinquent behavior. Separation of parents and children was rare, and there was generally a strong sense of family. The apartments in this group were clean and well cared for, although there was no reading material apart from magazines such as *True Love*. Movies and visiting with family were the only social activities. In contrast the very low-class group was disorganized. "Separation, desertions, abandonment and divorce and neglect of children are commonplace." Crime and frequent contact with law enforcement and other agencies were also common for this group. Most lived in projects, while the other group lived largely in flats or three- and four-family houses. Apartments of the very low-class group were chaotic. "Dishes were found everywhere and the smell of urine pervaded the place. . . . diapers were changed infrequently." There was no consistency or routine, and the activities of the group were characterized as "impulse determined." Little supervision was provided once the children played outdoors.

Oscar Lewis (1966) coined the term "culture of poverty" to depict the characteristics that he found common to the poor in many different countries. In his studies of the poor in Mexico, the United States, and Puerto Rico he found a "strong feeling of fatalism, helplessness, dependence and inferiority," as well as "weak ego structure, orality, and confusion of sexual identification . . . a strong present time orientation with relatively little disposition to defer gratification and plan for the future, and a high tolerance for psychopathology of all kinds." It is the despair and oppression of the poverty environment that nurtures these characteristics. Since the nurse will meet many people from the "culture of poverty" in hospitals, clinics, and community health services, she must be familiar with their characteristics, beliefs, and attitudes in order to make health-care delivery effective.

Health Care

Social classes and their related values can have a strong impact on the type of health care a person selects. Milio (1967) found marked differences in the prenatal care activities of lower-class and middle-class pregnant women. The middle-class "future" or planning orientation, along with middle-class confidence in experts and familiarity with bureaucratic structures (e.g., hospitals and clinics), leads middle-class pregnant women to seek good prenatal care. The values of the middle-class women fit in well with the assumptions and requirements of what Milio calls the "prenatal care system." On the other hand, the lower-class emphasis on immediate gratification, preference for peer advice rather than expert advice, focus on immediate well-being as opposed to long-range planning for health needs all militate against lower-class women seeking good prenatal care. These differences were found even when low-cost clinic care was readily available. In order to make health care and nursing effective, Milio stresses that "quality of care cannot be separated from the form in which care is given." Health care for the poor must take the lower-class value system into consideration.

Crisis intervention techniques have proven most successful with lower socioeconomic patients and families because of the "here-and-now" quality of this type of intervention (Anguilera, 1970). In crisis intervention, relief of the immediate symptoms and environmental stresses is sought. Sometimes there may be as few as six sessions in the crisis intervention program. The emphasis on immediate relief as opposed to the long-term goals of other psychotherapy fits in well with the needs and perceptions of the low socioeconomic family.

Brinton (1972) compared the value priorities of nurses and low-income mothers with reference to health care. The study was prompted by the fact that over 60% of mothers failed to keep appointments for follow-up health care in a pediatric clinic program sponsored by the Seattle County Health Department. The lack of patient cooperation was particularly striking since the mothers selected had infants with high-risk conditions, and taxi fare to the clinic was provided. Brinton was interested in exploring the value area for possible explanations of the parents' behavior. Quite interestingly, she found that the mothers ranked health as high on their priority list as did the nurses. But nurses and low socioeconomic mothers mean quite different things by health. Ability to function at even minimal levels was considered "well" by the mothers. This concept is very different from the concept of health held by nurses. Perhaps this gap in outlook explains in part the failure of the parents to keep appointments. Too often we assume that preventive care and the more subtle manifestations of health problems are everyone's concern; this is not so. In understanding such differences in concepts of health, nurses can communicate better with low socioeconomic families and educate them on the importance of overall health care. It might do well to illustrate to low socioeconomic families the concrete effects on daily life that poor health care can produce. Also, health care in poverty areas would be enhanced by community-based facilities that reach out to families and maintain easily accessible, comprehensive, and personalized services including preventive community nursing.

DIVERSITY WITHIN GROUPS

Whether we are talking about Italians, Jews, Irish, Catholics, blacks, or any other ethnic, religious, or racial group, we must not lose sight of the diversity that each group encompasses. Within each group are young, old, first-generation Americans, second-generation Americans, males, females, educated, uneducated, those maintaining old-world ties, those rejecting old-world values, orthodox religious, atheists, rich, poor, and an endless number of other factions. In short, there is no such thing as a homogeneous cultural group. As a matter of fact, it has been found that people of different cultural backgrounds who live in the same area have more in common than people of the same cultural background who live in different places. Rokeach (1960) found that Jews, Catholics, and Protestants living in large cities shared more attitudes than did rural and urban members of the same religious affiliation. Although members of a cultural group may be prone to manifest certain behavioral characteristics, those characteristics will be tempered or altered by a large number of influences. This makes the nurse's job of understanding behavior more difficult. There are no simple guidelines in the area of human behavior; we can only recommend sensitivity, open-mindedness, and the exercise of sound clinical judgment.

Of course it is impossible for the nurse to be familiar with the beliefs and practices of every culture and subculture. Even professional sociologists and anthropologists cannot claim to have achieved that feat. But it is necessary to be thoroughly versed in the concept of culture and its possible effects on behavior in general and health care in particular. The nurse should also make every effort to learn about the characteristics of culturally different groups in the community in which she works.

SUMMARY

The cultural environment represented by the family and society shapes the behavior of the individual in significant ways. The dramatic impact of culture was illustrated through a description of two vastly different neighboring primitive tribes in New Guinea. Cultural differences among groups emphasize the difficulties in defining "normal" behavior. The three most commonly applied definitions of normality are: the average concept, the symptom concept, and the authority concept. All three definitions are problematic because they embody particular cultural values that fail to take into consideration the variety of adaptive human behaviors. In practice formal definitions of normality carry little weight since the cultural group defines normal or acceptable behavior for its members. Thus middle-class and lower-class conceptions of what is normal differ.

The concept of normality as culturally relative is essential to the nurse, who must understand behavior of patients in a multicultural society. Cultural characteristics of patients often have a bearing on adjustment to the hospital or clinic, and attitudes toward health, illness, and rehabilitation. Socioeconomic class values have particular relevance to health care, as illustrated in the description of prenatal care behavior of mothers from low-income families. It is important for health professionals to gear health-care delivery to the "present orientation" of low socioeconomic groups and their need for community based, nonbureaucratic facilities. While general cultural characteristics may apply in some instances, each individual must be evaluated in the light of the many influences and variables that determine behavior.

SUGGESTED READINGS

Benedict, R. *Patterns of culture.* New York: Penguin, 1934.

Bullough, B. *Poverty, ethnic identity, and health care.* New York: Appleton-Century-Crofts, 1972.

Clark, K. *Dark ghetto.* New York: Harper & Row, 1965.

Lebra, W. P. *Transcultural research in mental health.* Hawaii: East-West Center (University of Hawaii), 1972.

Leininger, M. M. *Nursing and anthropology: two worlds to blend: culture factors in nursing care.* New York: John Wiley, 1970.

Lewis, O. *The children of Sanchez.* New York: Random House, 1961.

MacGregor, F. C. *Social science in nursing.* New York: Russell Sage, 1960.

Mead, M. *From the south seas: studies of adolescence and sex in primitive societies.* New York: Morrow, 1939.

Chapter *14*

Illness, Hospitalization, and Disability

ILLNESS, hospitalization, and disability have varying psychological effects on individuals. The common factor in these experiences is that they evoke a basic threat to the individual's security and stability. This threat can be one of the most terrifying of human experiences. Consequently, it is essential for nurses to be aware of the nature of these experiences, their variety, and the diversity of their effects, and to apply this knowledge about the patient's inner experiences in order to help lessen the painful emotional consequences.

While we usually make a distinction between minor and serious illnesses, and between those with poor and excellent prognoses, from the psychological point of view the person's own perception of his illness or disability is the most important factor. The physical and emotional components of illness become inseparable parts of a unified experience. Some patients with minor illness react as though they were suffering from a terminal illness, while other seriously ill patients react with relative calm and a strong determination to get well. It is the individual's personality that largely determines his reactions to illness and disability. The factors that play a central role in this regard are the defense mechanisms and the person's self-image. It is therefore important in assessing the patient's response to his illness or disability to understand his personality needs and unique perceptions.

REACTIONS TO PAIN

The psychological component of pain has been known for centuries. Aristotle, for example, did not classify pain as a sensation but rather as a powerful emotion. To say that pain in a particular case is psychological does not minimize the severity or reality of the person's experience of the pain. Psychologically based pain can be as intense or more intense than physical pain and is frequently indistinguishable from it.

Pain is the most frequent concomitant of illness. It is one of the symptomatic manifestations that health professionals must contend with constantly in providing patient care. Pain is sometimes intense, with an identifiable physiological basis. At other times the nurse will have difficulty interpreting the meaning of a patient's expression of pain. Lishman (1970) quotes Montaigne (sixteenth century) in a passage that captures the psychological aspect of pain: "We feel the cut of the surgeon's scalpel more than ten blows of the sword in the heat of battle." The anxiety surrounding a medical situation can intensify the perception of pain and render it more "painful" than greater wounds incurred under other circumstances. We can see this phenomenon when children (and adults) respond with great distress to simple medical procedures such as injection, although when outside the doctor's office they may endure greater physical insult with little reaction.

Experimental psychologists have noted individual differences in the perception of kinesthetic sensations. Psychophysical experiments have shown that individual thresholds for perceiving increases in pressures to a part of the body vary greatly. What is still unclear and controversial is the basis for these differences—is it biological or psychological? If biological, can the thresholds be modified by psychological factors? On the psychological side, findings have shown that extroverts have higher pain thresholds than introverts;

low-anxiety people have higher thresholds than high-anxiety people; the pain threshold is lower in states of fatigue than in states of alertness; neurotics have lower pain thresholds than normals; and hypochondriacs have very low pain thresholds (Lishman, 1970).

The effectiveness of conditioning techniques tends to favor a psychological explanation of some pain. When Pavlov, for example, conditioned dogs to expect food after a painful stimulus, they did not show a pain reaction to that stimulus. The psychological component in pain perception can also be inferred from the pain-relieving effects of hypnosis (Mastrovito, 1974). Also suggesting the psychological origin of some pain are reports of "phantom" pains (i.e., pain that is felt in a limb or part of the body no longer present or functional). Weinstein et al. (1964) report that phantom pains occur in a large number of patients following mastectomy or limb amputation, and in paraplegics. However, phantom pains have also been explained neurologically. The interaction of psychological and physiological factors in pain is illustrated in biofeedback techniques in which patients control physiological functions associated with pain (e.g. brain waves) through psychological measures such as concentration, relaxation, and meditation (Siegele, 1974).

Neurological factors play an important but not yet fully understood part in pain sensation. A number of theories have been offered to explain the role of the brain. One theory proposes that specific receptors, pathways, and areas of the brain are involved; another cites a mass-action summation or patterning within the brain. Still another proposes a "gate control" phenomenon (Melzack and Wall, 1965). That the brain is involved can be seen in cases of pain reduction following surgical lesions of the lateral spinothalmic tract or portions of the thalamus; other surgical procedures have also proven effective with some patients (Drakontides, 1974). Electrical stimulation of peripheral nerves (Gaumer, 1974) and dorsal column stimulation (Goloskov and LeRoy, 1974) are some other physical methods that can reduce pain. And, of course, a variety of drugs that act on the nervous system produce pain relief (Drakontides, 1974). Also, Petrie (1967) has identified three types of individuals according to the way each perceives pain and sensory stimulation—augmenters, reducers, and moderates. Petrie associates each of these types with a particular biological makeup that produces psychological characteristics. For example, reducers (having a high tolerance for pain and sensory stimulation) are more athletic and physically active than augmenters, who rely more on verbal behavior and do better in school work. Augmenters avoid sensory stimulation while reducers suffer when subjected to monotony, isolation, and restricted activity.

Altering Pain Perception

Although the final word is not in on the nature of pain, many studies have indicated the possibility of altering a patient's perception of pain through attention to his psychological needs. The perception of pain can be influenced by one's attitude toward a wound. If, for example, a soldier in a dangerous situation, fearing death, escapes with a serious injury, his perception of the pain related to that injury may not be great. On the other hand, a less serious wound received under ordinary circumstances, in which the wound itself is the focus, may generate intense pain. Beecher and Boston (1955) compared soldiers wounded at the Anzio beachhead in World War II with civilians subjected to surgery. The soldiers, viewing their wounds as the end of the war for them and a return to safety, were cheerful and optimistic. The less dramatic civilian wounds generated more anxiety. Only 30% of the soldiers requested morphine 7 to 12 hours after being wounded while 83% of the civilians requested a narcotic. Also, the pain experienced by the soldiers was less severe even though their wounds were more massive.

Blaylock (1968) reported a number of factors that can reduce reaction to pain: group pressure, reassurance, giving the patient a reason for the pain, specifying when the pain will end, distractions, and hypnosis. He stressed the nurse's role in reducing patients' perception of pain by talking to them about their pain and discussing ways of reducing it. However, he also emphasized the importance of the nurse–patient relationship. When nurses merely told the patient about the pain-reducing effect of a drug that was being administered, in the absence of other interactions with the patient, there was no pain reduction. Lishman (1970) describes studies that indicate that patients undergoing surgery perceive pain differently depending on pre- and postoperative discussions and instructions. When patients are told about the pain they will have, its location and duration, they show less post-operative distress and require fewer pain-relieving drugs than patients who are not so advised.

Studies of the *placebo* effect have also called attention to the psychological component in pain perception. Every nurse is familiar with the incredible pain-reducing effects sometimes induced by the administration of substances that actually have little or no influence on the specific pain the patient is experiencing. However, the patient's belief in the efficacy of the substance (or procedure) eradicates or reduces his perception of pain. As a matter of fact, 30% of patients get significant relief from pain with the use of placebos (Beecher and Boston, 1955). Evidently pain, far from being inevitable or invariant, can be very much influenced by nurses' activities and procedures of ward management.

REACTIONS TO ILLNESS
Sense of Threat

The threat posed by illness, hospitalization, and disability is experienced on an emotional level as anxiety. Anxiety in turn evokes the characteristic defensive reactions of the individual (see the discussion of defenses in Chapter 9). Denial is a commonly used defense mechanism in illness. A person who uses denial may act as if he is not ill at all—this can be very dangerous if it prevents him from getting the appropriate care that he needs. For a coronary patient who refuses to be bedridden or restricted in his activities, denying that he has had a heart attack ("It was just exhaustion"), can have a fatal outcome. We must be wary of mistaking denial for courage. The danger posed by denial is highlighted in a study by Caron (reported in McDaniel, 1969) in which first-time cardiac patients using denial were excessively disabled one year later compared with patients who showed early recognition of their condition.

Some denial can be useful in helping a patient cope with the trauma of his illness. Since defenses are essential to the individual's sense of stability, the nurse should try to assess the degree to which the patient's reactions are exaggerated defenses that are dangerous to his health and the extent to which they are helpful constructions for bridging a difficult period of adjustment. When defenses do not endanger recovery, it is best to encourage the patient to follow his usual coping behavior patterns since they are likely to work best for him. Remember, the main goal is to help the patient mobilize his resources toward physical recovery, not to cure his deeply rooted emotional conflicts.

Depression

Depression is another common reaction to illness and disability. The symptoms of depression include loss of interest in surroundings, feelings of hopelessness, slow speech and retarded physical movements, reduced appetite, somatic complaints, introversion, self-debasement, and slowed or impaired thinking. The grief expressed in depression due to illness often resembles that expressed over the loss of a loved one through death. Patients may show some or all of the clinical manifestations of mourning to varying degrees for different lengths of time. Wright (1955) sees a positive function in the mourning reaction to illness in that it reflects the patient's awareness of his condition, thus paving the way for the incorporation of the illness or disability into the patient's self-image and altered goals. At the same time, McDaniel (1969) reports: "The recent literature contains many statements relating the least favorable disease course and frequent exacerbations in cardiac disease, multiple sclerosis, tuberculosis, rheumatoid arthritis, diabetes and malignancy to depressive symptomotology and stressful life situations." Whether or not depression ultimately aids or hinders the rehabilitation process depends, no doubt, on the intensity and duration of the depressive reaction. During its prominent phase depression certainly has an inhibitory effect on recovery and rehabilitation. Depressed patients do not put out the energy and involvement required for rehabilitation; they often have a hopeless attitude toward the prospect of recovery and require great amounts of success to motivate them.

Self-Image

How an individual views himself and his role in life will have a major effect on his response to illness and disability. The person who perceives himself as strong, independent, and self-sufficient may react unfavorably to the dependency associated with illness and disability. Here too, defenses are important. If, for example, the patient's self-image of independence is a *compensation*, or a disguise for underlying feelings of inferiority, illness may be extremely difficult for him to deal with. Ordinary life situations provide such an individual with opportunities to avoid experiences that confront him with his inferiority feelings; he covers up, boasts, or uses some other flamboyant behavior—or even real achievement. Yet illness and disability are inevitably accompanied by feelings of weakness that he may not be able to tolerate. Such patients have a difficult time facing their incapacity. In contrast, a patient whose self-image of independence and confidence is on a more solid footing can deal with illness with the same determination and mastery that he has always applied to life situations.

As previously mentioned, employing defensive reactions does not mean that a patient will not be able to cope—defenses can be harnessed to work in a positive and productive fashion. For example, the patient whose superficial appearance of independence really covers up feelings of weakness can be encouraged to overcome his illness or disability by representing his recovery as an extraordinary feat that everyone will recognize, and for which he will be admired. In other words, it is possible to find ways of encouraging patients that are consistent with their defenses, self-image, and personality needs.

Patients who prior to their illness or disability had a self-image of dependence and weakness can pose other problems for nurses. These patients may too readily accept their "sick role" or incapacitated state and show little motivation for recovery and rehabilitation. The attention they receive from the nursing staff, family, and friends may be a kind of infantile nurturance they had always wanted but had difficulty obtaining in everyday life. Illness can provide the dependent person with a plausible basis for exacting long-sought-after "mothering" from everyone in his environment. Unlike the patient who uses the mechanism of denial, these patients can *regress* to an earlier level of functioning and, rather than minimize their discomfort, they will exaggerate it.

Cultural Factors

Cultural factors also play a role in a person's reaction to hospitalization. A culture that emphasizes independence—individual success and control over the environment—can make the relatively passive and dependent condition imposed by illness intolerable. On the other hand, some cultures teach that the person has little control over the environment. The fatalistic attitude derived from such cultures can render patients passive, apathetic, and detached. In this regard, religious beliefs should not be overlooked since they have an important influence on a person's attitude toward life, death, and illness. Frequently a priest, minister, or rabbi can be an important aid to the nurse in meeting the health-care needs of patients. However, patients should be prepared for visits from the clergy. We have in mind a not so seriously ill patient who was convinced he was going to die when a priest unexpectedly showed up in his room.

As is the case with all behavior, no specific predictions can be made with respect to cultural influences. The person who for cultural reasons seeks independence can also be motivated to overcome his illness or handicap, and one whose culture teaches fatalism can be an excellent and cooperative patient who places complete trust in his physicians and nurses. We cannot emphasize too strongly the need for nurses to use the patient's characteristics, be they emotional or cultural, to help him move in a positive direction.

Reality Problems

Not all of a patient's concerns and reactions are emotional. Often an illness or disability gives rise to real problems in the patient's life. Therefore, in assessing the patient's functioning it is necessary for the nurse to know as much as possible about his life situation.

What kinds of problems are reality problems? Worry about finances, business management, family stability, or status on a job, for example. Everyone lives within a different set of life circumstances, and these circumstances have real impact on a person's life. If a hospitalized young mother has small children at home with no close relatives nearby, her worries would have a foundation in reality. Another person whose business depends on his presence may have similar concerns. Sometimes anxieties that stem from real sources have a snowballing effect. They add fuel to the person's more emotional reactions. Often there is intertwining of the reality and emotional problems, making it difficult to see where one begins and the other ends.

Conditions That Intensify Problems

The very nature of the hospital situation contributes to certain kinds of problems. Being bedridden, with activities limited, the patient can dwell on problems and emotional reactions. Illness and disability intensify awareness of internal processes—processes that go unnoticed in a healthy state. This can can escalate the emotional reactions of the brooding, suppressing type of patient. Other patients who are outgoing and need a high pace of activities can get very tense and bored with hospitalization. Still others may be prudish and react with intense anxiety to standard hospital procedures that require exposure of the body, especially in the presence of doctors and nurses of the opposite sex.

The stresses and anxieties emanating from various sources may be relatively minor when viewed in isolation, but when combined with the patient's more central stresses any one of them can be "the straw that breaks the camel's back." This observation becomes important when considering how to deal with extreme emotional reactions of patients. In order to return the patient to relative stability it may not be necessary to solve all his problems or even his most important problem (this may be an impossible goal for the nurse). Reducing the relatively minor sources of stress can often take the edge off sufficiently to allow the patient to cope effectively with his remaining difficulties.

Hospitalization and Sensory Deprivation

McDaniel (1969) suggests that emotional distress including depression, anxiety, peculiar sensations and feelings, and even hallucinations may be due to the isolation and lack of stimulation associated with prolonged hospitalization. It is certainly well known in experimental psychology that prolonged sensory deprivation in normal subjects produces behavioral aberrations.

Closer to the area of illness and disability, Mendelson et al. (1961) reported the reactions of normal subjects who were placed into a tank-type respirator that duplicated many of the restrictions imposed on polio patients when placed in respirators. Movement of limbs was inhibited and the subjects were unable to see their own bodies. After only a few hours under these conditions, subjects reported intense anxiety and hallucinations. The authors related these results to the hallucinations that have been reported among polio patients. While polio is not the widespread disease it once was, there is a host of disorders and disabilities that impose various degrees of sensory deprivation and isolation on patients.

Transient psychotic states have been reported to occur under medical conditions that require isolation, silence, and darkness (Solomon et al. 1961). Extensive cardiac surgery, hemodialysis, and many other procedures submerge the patient into an unfamiliar world devoid of the usual basic sources of stimulation.

McDaniel's point on this subject (1969) is well taken and is of particular importance to nurses: "Limited mobility and severely restricted sensory stimulation may combine to produce behavioral disruptions that can interfere with treatment and rehabilitation objectives, but are typically ascribed to very nebulous concepts such as 'dependency' and 'lack of motivation'."

SEPARATION

Separation from family, friends, and loved ones is an inevitable offshoot of hospitalization, disability, and serious illness. Reactions to separation are rooted in the very early experiences of the child with respect to feelings of security within the family. The insecure child clings to his parents and doubts his ability to survive independently. Each individual revisits and grapples with separation fears at various times in the course of growing up (e.g., when starting school, leaving home, taking a first job). Bad early experiences with separation make a person more vulnerable to later separation experiences, but general immaturity can also arouse separation anxiety. Any threat to one's security can reawaken earlier fears of separation. For the hospitalized patient separation may be represented not only by the physical act of separation but also symbolically in terms of loss of functions and the fear of death. Illness also promotes a heightened awareness of self that links up with the separation anxiety residing within all of us. As would be expected, separation has its most dramatic effects on children; however, it occurs in more subtle forms in adolescents and adults as well.

It is important for us to take a close look at extreme reactions to separation in childhood in order to gain an appreciation of the powerful unconscious forces that are unleashed when separation fears are tapped by illness, hospitalization, and disability.

Effects of Separation on Children

The observation that infants deteriorate when they remain long in institutions is an old one. At one time, when most institutionalized children came from the poor, the indigent, and the ill in our society, deterioration was assumed to be related to "bad heredity." With the emergence of the environmental point of view in the twentieth century, the experience of separation and its impact on development has been given a psychological interpretation. Systematic research on this topic is fairly recent, dating from the 1930s. Perhaps the best known and most influential of the early group of studies were those done by Spitz (1945, 1946). We made mention of this research in Chapter 2 but will now return to it because of its bearing on our understanding of separation and illness.

Spitz compared 69 children raised by their mothers in the nursery of a penal institution with 61 children in a foundling hospital. The major difference in care at these two settings was that in the nursery the infants were fed and cared for by their own mothers while the foundling hospital children were cared for by nurses with a ratio of six nurses per 45 infants. In the foundling hospital the babies lacked human contact for most of the day. Although the foundling children initially had higher developmental quotients than the nursery children, the situation was reversed by the end of the first year; the nursery children had progressed, and the foundling children showed marked deterioration and regression. Also, from the third month on the foundling children were highly susceptible to infection and a variety of illnesses; almost one-fourth of them died after a measles epidemic. In a follow-up study two years later, the foundling children were found to be markedly retarded in their overall development (speech, vocabulary, weight, and height). In contrast, the nursery children showed normal overall development and not one had died.

The behavioral observations of Spitz give us some insight into the extreme psychic trauma brought on by early separation. The main reactions were crying and protest, which then moved into a withdrawal phase that became more and more profound. Eventually, many of the infants became isolates who shunned human contact. In the advanced stage, the infants became apathetic, passive, and depressed. A frozen expression was common. According to Spitz, a crucial point is reached at three months of separation. If by that time the mother-child relationship is not restored, permanent damage will result.

Children who are exposed to early separation from their mothers develop in later life what John Bowlby called the "affectionless character." They cannot form meaningful human relationships and, in general, lack feelings for other people. Many other investigators have confirmed the main observations of Spitz (Hoffman and Hoffman, 1964).

Object Relationships. It appears that children develop early attachments to their mothers (or early nurturing figure) and need a constant object relationship with such a person for normal development to take place. Even the best institutional care cannot meet the need for a constant object relationship with the exclusive intimacy and spontaneous responsiveness that the parent-child relationship embraces. Real parenting is never bound by a nine-to-five schedule, changing shifts, vacations, holidays, or shifting employment. It is doubtful that institutional care can ever meet infants' needs for constant nurturing.

An interesting study by David and Appell (1961) points to another complication in meeting the emotional needs of institutionalized children. In their study, the nurses who were assigned individual infants to care for were found to hold back emotionally. This behavior was interpreted as a defense against the anticipated separation from the children under their care. In other words, the nurses didn't want to get too involved for fear of their own hurt that would occur at the time of separation of the child from the institution. However, other studies have demonstrated how nursing and institutional care, when molded to the special needs of the separated infant, can reduce some of the negative effects of the separation experience (Freud and Burlingham, 1944; Prugh et al, 1953; and others).

Time of Separation. There has been some dispute about the age at which the most severe separation reactions occur. Much of the research stresses the period between 6 months and 3 years of age, the important factor being the child's ability to have a clearly perceived relationship with the mother. This, no doubt, varies on an individual basis in terms of the child's ability to discriminate the mother as a distinctive totality from other persons in the environment. At the upper end of this age group the effects of separation may depend on how advanced the child's state of development is at the time of separation. If he has developed relatively mature cognitive structures the effect is likely to be less severe than when development is at a less mature level.

Contradictions and Problems. As in other areas of developmental research, the problems arising from separation are more complex on closer examination than they appear at first. Recent research has emphasized some of the complications. Yarrow (1964) points out that the early studies on separation dramatized the possible effects of separation but did not focus much on the discrepancies. Not all children suffer extreme reactions and even fewer actually die (especially since the increase in immunization programs and the introduction of antibiotics). Those who do not suffer serious consequences are of special interest since they may give clues to the nature of the effects of separation and ways of reducing the effects. Some follow-up studies of children separated at an early age have also shown the impact to be variable. For example, the study by Bowlby et al. (1956) examined children between the ages of 6 and 14 who were hospitalized for tuberculosis for a long period of time prior to the age of 4. While many of these children did show signs of withdrawal and aggressiveness, their symptoms were not very marked and they did not have difficulty in establishing peer relationships.

The question arises about the source of reaction to separation. Is it the separation per se, or are other factors that occur at the time of separation the effective agents? Separation does not occur in a vacuum. The circumstances that accompany separation can be more or less traumatic. The sudden death of a parent, rejection by a parent, separation because of illness, forcible removal of the child because of abuse, are all events surrounded by many possible additional traumas that may have greater effect on the child than the separation itself. It is likely that each set of events will have a different effect on the child's reaction to separation. Also, what happens after separation can be of consequence in the child's reaction.

The type of institution or foster home, the type of care, the presence or absence of other family members, the presence or absence of a mothering-type figure can all be significant. Of course, the age of the child at the time of separation and the prior relationship with the parents are also of vital importance.

Separation Through Hospitalization.   The effects of hospitalization usually have carry-over to the home after the child is discharged. Robertson (1953) studied children immediately after hospitalization. He noted both anxiety about losing the mother and hostility toward the mother. Some children regressed in such areas as toilet training. Robertson suggests that the separation effects of hospitalization may leave a vulnerability that can be activated later in life. Therefore, we can see that some of the factors pertinent to separation in general apply to short-term hospitalization.

Especially for the preoperational child (Piaget's stage, ages 2-7) who cannot differentiate between past, present, and future, the issue of short-term versus long-term hospitalization or separation may be meaningless. For such a child, separation is separation. Therefore it is not surprising that the age of the child when hospitalized proves to be most crucial. The early childhood years—6 months to 7 years— have been found to be the most sensitive period for hospitalization. In a study by Prugh et al. (1953) of 2- to 12-year-old children, the most severe reactions occurred in children 2 to 3 years of age, and reactions decreased as age increased. These researchers found that in the 2-to-4-year-old group, crying, screaming, and panic were common and there were many instances of somatic complaints. Depressive reactions, regression, eating problems, school disturbances, thumb sucking and rocking were also common among this group. In the 4-to-6-year-old group, depression, homesickness, withdrawal, and masturbation were less frequent than with the younger children. But somatic reactions and phobias were frequent. Children in this group tended to deny their dependency needs by covering up feelings of loneliness and displays of crying. However, the presence of other symptoms indicated their fear. There were also less frequent manifestations of overt aggressive behavior among the 4- to 6-year-olds. All types of symptoms were less frequent for the 6- to 10-year-olds except withdrawal, which was very common. Compulsive behavior, obsessive fears of death, denial, and rationalization appeared frequently in this group of children.

Prugh et al. (1953) go on to discuss the different reactions of children between the ages of 2 and 12 to hospitalization in terms of specific problems associated with different stages of development. The child under 3 is immature and dependent and therefore interprets separation from the mother as punishment or desertion. At the Oedipal stage (4-6 years), the child is vulnerable to feelings of guilt and therefore perceives the medical procedures as punishment that will damage him. Thus the anxiety at this stage is more a symbolic castration fear than fear of separation per se. The older child is struggling with the problem of internalizing his behavioral control mechanisms and is therefore threatened by the loss of control implied by his anxiety and fears. The more highly developed and varied reaction patterns of the preadolescent will yield such exaggerated defensive maneuvers as obsessions, denial, rationalizations, and other sophisticated ways of dealing with the separation situation.

While ward management can go a long way in reducing severe reactions to hospitalization, Prugh et al. stress the need to prepare children for the experience of hospitalization. Also, parents frequently intensify the adjustment problems of their children through guilt reactions. They may visit compulsively and cling to their children; some avoid talking about departure time during visiting, and others will visit infrequently or not at all because of guilt and anxiety (Prugh et al, 1953).

There is much a hospital and nursing staff can do to ease the child's adjustment to hospitalization. Sensitizing nurses to developmental problems is most important. Liberal visiting hours with sleep-over arrangements for parents of younger children can be a great help, as well as organized activities that are age-appropriate. Other services include making psychiatric and psychological consultation available to the staff and providing counseling and social work service for parents.

Finally, children will benefit from as much individualized care as is possible.

Separation and Adolescents

For the adolescent, hospitalization and illness place further stress on the already existing identity crisis. Typical of adolescence are grandiose fantasies about future conquests and achievements. The adolescent is absorbed in idealism and is very threatened by realistic limitations. This process is constructive up to a point in helping the adolescent test the limits of his possibilities in life. But beneath the surface of the adolescent's fantasies are doubts about his abilities and fears of not succeeding. Illness, hospitalization, and disability are realistic factors that can feed the despair to which adolescents are vulnerable. Any possibility of deformity or damage to physical appearance are especially anxiety-provoking. Adolescents are very self-conscious of their appearance and overestimate its importance in achieving success in life. Moreover, physical appearance is closely associated with sexual relationships, an area of anxiety and self-doubt for the adolescent. Independence is another adolescent need that is threatened by illness. Torn between the drive to be an independent adult and the fear of leaving the dependency state of childhood, adolescents will frequently appear super-independent to cover up the dependency strivings that are still present. It isn't until the adolescent gains confidence in his new independent role that he can accept and give vent to his dependency needs. Illness, hospitalization, and disability all thrust the adolescent into the feared dependency state that he seeks and at the same time wants to escape from. Fuszard (1969) quotes Anna Freud, who has captured the hospitalized adolescent's dilemma:

> Adult patients who, while healthy, feel certain of their independence in body matters can, during physical illness, permit themselves to return temporarily to the state of a helpless infant whose body is under other people's care and jurisdiction. It is impossible for the adolescent to accept nursing in the same spirit. For him to have attained a measure of physical independence from the adult world and to have personal control over his own body is a great developmental achievement which he prizes highly, and is reluctant to renounce. (p. 426)

The hospital can mobilize the independence strivings of adolescents by treating them in an adult manner. Some techniques of fostering the adolescent patient's independence are allowing him to take a greater role in the diagnostic and treatment process, letting him help plan his own care, giving him a degree of control over his activities, and including him in family conferences.

Hospitals that do not have special adolescent wards may find it difficult to meet the adolescent's needs. In many hospitals, adolescents are placed on pediatric wards or with adult and elderly patients. In the pediatric ward the adolescent may be threatened by being identified with small children. On adult wards the illness of older patients can arouse anxiety and the age gap can make the adolescent feel like a child. Surprisingly, many hospitals do not have special adolescent facilities. By 1965 there were only 59 adolescent clinics and inpatient facilities in the United States (Fuszard, 1969). A statistic for the same year showed that in England only one in 200 adolescent patients were in adolescent wards, with the largest percentage being in adult wards (Green, 1968).

Privacy is an important consideration in the treatment of

adolescents. The self-consciousness of the adolescent is particularly intense with regard to exposure of genitals. Self-consciousness is heightened by the physical changes that are taking place. Not only is there fear of sexual inadequacy that nudity arouses but also the anxiety of stimulation by the opposite sex. Adolescent boys are often fearful of having an erection in the presence of a female nurse. Adolescent girls are also easily embarrassed. Byers (1967) cites the case of Jean, a 14-year-old adolescent hospitalized for rheumatic fever:

> Jean's refusal to permit more than one physician to examine her at any one time persisted throughout her hospitalization. She clutched her pajama top, making it impossible for anyone to listen to her heart from the front of her chest. Although the medical staff was very impatient with this behavior, Jean held her ground and, I might add, won the battle. In a firm independent tone she exclaimed, "I'd just die having all those doctors see me. There are at least five of them and some are so young." (p. 33)

Separation and Adults

Although the literature on separation is almost exclusively about children's separation problems, many adults experience similar anxieties. This is especially true when regression is aroused by threatening and stressful situations such as illness and hospitalization. Just as 6- and 12-year-olds may suppress some of their fearfulness because of a need to be independent, many immature adults may have intense separation anxieties that they are unable to express openly. Separation anxiety in adults is most likely to show up in disguised forms.

Hospitalization may be the first experience of separation from family, even for adults. While in everyday life these patients are able to submerge their fears of independence by placing themselves in dependency relationships at home and at work, the hospitalization experience suddenly casts them on their own. In such cases the nurse may note apathy, withdrawal, somatic complaints, exaggerated expressions of pain and anger, and other indications of emotional stress that we have previously met in observing separation in children. The difference here would be the adults' greater ability to rationalize, deny, and project, all of which tend to conceal the basic separation anxiety. Often these exaggerated behaviors diminish once the patient begins to feel more familiar with the hospital and the staff. The quick recognition of dependency can be used to advantage by the nurse to facilitate the adult patient's adjustment to the hospital. Embarrassment is another factor that inhibits adults from admitting their separation anxieties and feelings of loneliness. These patients can be helped by the nurse's recognition and acceptance of their feelings in a supportive relationship.

Community-Based Treatment

One obvious way to avoid separation problems in adults as well as children is not to hospitalize, except when absolutely necessary. In recent years there has been a movement away from institutional treatment to community-based outpatient clinics with comprehensive home visiting services along with accessibility of health professionals to maintain patients in their normal environments. This is an excellent innovation in health-care delivery that will not only improve patient care but will also widen the role of health professionals, as it emphasizes working with the entire family on prevention and rehabilitation. Programs can be set up to treat even chronic patients within the community so that continuous hospitalization with its debilitating effects is not necessary. Runyan et al. (1970) have reported on the successful use of neighborhood clinics staffed by public health nurses to provide care for stabilized chronic-disease patients. The nurses make changes in therapy and provide symtomatic treatment for minor complaints as well as serving other health-care functions. It is to be hoped that community-based health-care delivery will get wider support and funding in the future. For the moment, however, most of us have to contend with the multiple problems of institution-based patient care.

CHRONIC ILLNESS
The Single Person

Not everyone has a family available in times of illness and crisis. Single people without families, those who are living far from home, those alienated from their families, widows and widowers without families, the aged, and many others have no family to call on when illness strikes. Feelings of separation, loneliness, and isolation will be most acute for such people. Unless there are friends who will take the place of family, a sense of alienation may intensify the person's condition. The prospect of dependency with no one but strangers to help can evoke long-forgotten abandonment and separation fears. The presence or absence of community resources for integrating the chronically ill makes a big difference in the rehabilitation and the psychological stability of people without families. In most instances, however, family will play some role in an individual's chronic illness and disability.

The Chronically Ill Parent

Few generalizations can be made about the role of the family in chronic illness. Each case is unique with a unique configuration of psychological forces. There are differences in the type of illness, the extent of disability, the prognosis for rehabilitation. Also, whether the chronically ill person is a child, adolescent, adult, aged person, or the mother or father of a young family will determine differential effects on family life. In the case of a chronically ill parent, the emotions evoked by the impact of chronicity are often suppressed. Family members usually have ambivalent feelings, wanting to help the disabled person on the one hand and on the other hand feeling hostility toward him for disrupting things. Many times the anger will be suppressed, but the guilt reaction for having such "bad feelings" remains. Actually, ambivalence is an expected and normal reaction to chronic illness of a parent, for which patient and families should be prepared. Unfortunately, the breakdown of communication that is likely to occur when guilt and denial are present leads to further deterioration of an already fragile emotional climate. The following factors contribute to the emotional stresses of chronicity, especially in a family with small children.

Finances. If the father is the chronic patient, the effect on finances will be most severe. The family will have to cut back drastically on all expenditures if the father is unable to return to work, or if he can only return to a limited extent. Even when there is extensive medical insurance, the medical expenses mount and are another drain on resources. In many cases disability of the father may ultimately cause the family to go on welfare, an outcome that can be devastating to a family that has prided itself on independence. The financial impact of disability can truly wreck a family. The mother may return to work, but most women who have been primarily homemakers will earn considerably less than their husbands did. Thus the strain on finances will still be great.

Role Change. Chronic illness of the husband or wife inevitably results in a revision of roles and relationships within the family. How well the adjustment to these changes proceeds depends a great deal on the couple's previous roles. If the change is a radical one—for example, the formerly dependent wife-mother must now become independent—the change can be severely resented. On the other hand, many women blossom when they are required to be more independent. Sometimes the role change required is just an extension of what preceded the disability (e.g., a dependent man or woman simply becomes more dependent).

The changed roles infuse into all areas of life and can be the basis for a rising tide of resentment, which can then intensify other conflicts. Work, household chores, social planning, care of the children, etc. may all fall on one of the partners. A woman who has little previous work experience may now be overwhelmed by the dual job of breadwinner and homemaker. The husband who now has to work harder to cover the increased expenses of disability or child care may resent the absence of a normal family life to reward him for his efforts. Many of these feelings are irrational but they are always there and must be dealt with.

Revision of Goals. Plans for the future must also be revised when husband or wife becomes chronically ill. That house in the suburbs, trip to Europe, small business, and college for the children may all have to be discarded. Since people are closely identified with their goals as the driving force in their lives (even though the goals are not achieved in many cases), the loss of goals has a very depressing and demoralizing effect. The process of establishing new realistic goals is a long one.

Sex. Closely related to role change are the myriad problems in sexual relationships that occur along with disability. Here again the specific nature of the disability will play a large role in adjustment. The patient on hemodialysis may be only mildly affected in sexual functioning while the paraplegic may be more so. In all instances of apparent difficulties in sexual relationships, much depends on the flexibility of the couple and their willingness to explore new ways of achieving sexual gratification. Sometimes sexual problems arise because one of the partners must play an unfamiliar role in order to achieve sexual gratification. For example, the husband who has been a passive sexual partner may now, as the healthy partner, have to play a more aggressive and initiating role, something he may be unable to do. A similar role may have to be adopted by the previously passive wife whose husband becomes disabled. One partner may also resent the necessity of the other one taking a more active role and may therefore prefer to cut off the sexual relationship.

One of the partners may be turned off sexually by the other's disability. This may be particularly true when sexual characteristics are affected by an illness or disability, as in the case of mastectomy. To prevent the attitude of repulsion from surfacing, sex contacts may be shunned. Sometimes there is the fear that injury will result from sexual activity. For example, the wife of a patient who has suffered a cardiac infarct may be afraid that her husband will have a heart attack and die during intercourse; the patient may have a similar fear. Perhaps the greatest impediment to sexual activity is the feeling of being unmasculine or unfeminine due to an illness or disability.

Psychological barriers that interfere with the resumption of sexual relationships can usually be overcome by understanding, insight, and open discussion. Sometimes counseling or psychotherapy of one or both partners is necessary to break down the barriers to communication. The health professional trained in interpersonal relations can help couples in the area of sexuality through discussions while the patient is in the hospital or after he has returned home.

Neglect of Other Family Members. The conflicts and stress resulting from disability disrupt the usual pattern of family life and can lead to the neglect of children. Sometimes the parents will be so overwhelmed with the shakeup of their existence that the needs of children will be overlooked, and home care and other practicalities neglected. Here is an area where the extension of the health professional's work to the entire family can be very important. The problems of disability extend beyond the identified patient.

Institutionalization. Institutionalization should not be considered unless there is a real threat to the disabled person's life or when necessary care just cannot be provided at home. Otherwise the presence of a disabled parent will help the family members work out their feelings toward each other and help them develop new plans. Institutionalization often, by its distance, maintains denial and prevents realistic planning.

The Chronically Ill Child

Usually the chronic illness of a child does not have the pervasive effects on family life that the chronic illness of mother or father does, but in some cases the effects can be severe. Variables such as the nature and prognosis of the disability are important in this regard.

The terminally ill child (although he may have years to live) will place different stresses on the family than does a child with stabilized paralysis or blindness. Nevertheless, the strain on finances, revision of roles, and neglect of other family members can still occur. Also, guilt from vague feelings of "What did I do wrong?" and ambivalent feelings of love and anger may also be present. The guilt factor is a big problem for other siblings, who must deal with their normal feelings of rivalry toward a sibling who is chronically ill. From the other side, the chronically ill child may use his disability to manipulate the parents and achieve a competitive advantage over his siblings. The net result can be a breakdown of communication while, on the surface, everything looks fine.

The Chronically Ill Aged

We have already discussed facets of the problem of chronic illness in the aged in Chapter 6. Therefore, we will only cite some of the prominent effects of such illness on other family members. Ambivalence with guilt feelings occurs in these cases in addition to the possible drain on financial resources whether the elderly person is living at home, with one of his children, in an extended family, or in an institutional setting. Sometimes the chronic illness of the elderly person awakens feelings of sibling rivalry among his children. They may compete over who is doing more or nothing for "mama" or "papa" with the outcome of hostility and alienation among the siblings and their families. Also, when the elderly person is living within the extended family the love-hate syndrome will have the usual negative effects on communication and result in a tense, conflict-ridden environment.

DISABILITY

All disabilities strike at the core of the person's self-image and security. However, different disabilities bring specific crises into focus. In this section we will briefly review some major surgical procedures and disabilities that health professionals come in contact with, and outline the prominent psychological problems associated with them.

Mastectomy. The removal of a woman's breast in the surgical treatment of breast cancer is always intensely anxiety-provoking. First is the woman's fear that she will die. Facing this possibility is similar for anyone with a potentially fatal disease. In addition, however, the breast has a dual meaning for the woman's sexual identity; it is part of her sexual attractiveness and symbolizes her mothering capacity. The younger the woman, the more intense the adjustment problem is likely to be. The adjustment will also depend on the extent of the emotional security provided by her family (parents, husband) and friends, as well as her earlier personality development.

Hysterectomy. The removal of the uterus signals the end of reproductive potential for the woman. Postmenopausally this capacity is no longer present so the psychological distress is often less than with mastectomy. However, it often causes a sense of incompleteness and of not quite fully being a woman. This sense is increased if the ovaries are also removed, even though sexual responsiveness is dependent on neither uterus nor ovaries. An added concern is that the woman may believe that she has cancer even if that is not the case. Death anxiety then needs to be coped with.

Coronary Occlusion. Following a heart attack the struggle to regain normal functioning is often beset by maladaptive psychological mechanisms. Frequently, the patient denies the serious stress of his illness and, since his cooperation in recovery is crucial, this denial can be fatal. Depression is also common, as is to be expected in life-threatening illness. More specific to cardiac disease is the occurrence of psychological invalidism. This type of disturbance, an unrealistic obsessive concern with cardiac symptoms, can lead to invalidism for the remainder of the individual's life even if the heart function returns to normal.

Epilepsy. The patient with epilepsy often reacts to his illness with shyness and withdrawal. Most epileptics are not seriously handicapped by their illness once medications have brought the seizures under control. Still, the feeling of being different and at times of losing control tend to impart feelings of shame and inferiority that need to be actively combatted by family and professionals.

Cerebral Palsy. The child or adult with cerebral palsy is frequently subjected to depression and self-doubts. Because his physical awkwardness is a public source of embarrassment, he will tend to withdraw and isolate himself. This unhappy result precludes his enjoying the rewards of work and personal relationships that his usually normal intelligence allows him. A further complication is that the muscular coordination frequently affects the face and mouth, making communication both by words and facial expression problematic.

Diabetes.   The patient with diabetes faces a lifelong therapeutic regimen. The idea that his life depends on careful attention to medications and diet are common sources of depression, denial, and rebellion. Especially in the chronologically or emotionally immature individual the restrictions placed by diet, by testing of urine, and administering of insulin are met with anger and attempts at "doing the opposite." In adolescents, this problem is especially prominent since the age-appropriate rebellion against authority and striving for independence is hampered by the life-or-death necessity of conforming to an "imposed" treatment regimen.

Blindness.   Of all our senses, sight is the most important to our sense of well-being. Without sight we are always dependent on the good will of others for our physical safety and care. This extreme dependence is the most difficult aspect of the adjustment of the unsighted individual. There are many gratifications that do not require vision, including friends, music, certain types of work, and so on, but to enjoy these opportunities the blinded patient must come to terms with the dependency that to some extent will be lifelong.

Deafness.   The deaf individual lives in a private world that requires special efforts on his part as well as others to bridge. The fact that he is excluded from much that is communicated around him makes him especially susceptible to feelings of suspiciousness. The hard-of-hearing are also prone to feelings of depression and irritability due to the isolation their handicap may induce.

Stroke.   Brain damage resulting from blocking or bursting of a cerebral blood vessel may lead to any number of different disabilities from mild and transient speech difficulties to hemiplegia and aphasia (loss of the ability to speak). Such cerebrovascular accidents most often, but not exclusively, occur with advancing age. When the immediate fear of death subsides, there is often a sense of depression and despair at loss of independent functioning. A feeling that others will see one as weak or intellectually failing (even if no deficit exists) leads frequently to withdrawal and social isolation. For rehabilitation to succeed these tendencies must be combatted by firm and kind insistence on an active life by professionals and by family.

SELF-AWARENESS EXERCISE

Disability

The purpose of this exercise is to give you a personal perspective on disability through an imagined identification with a specific disability.

Task. *Let us assume that you have suffered paraplegia as the result of an accident. Your rehabilitation has proceeded to the point where you are ready to return home and resume "normal" life activities.*

Now, describe in general terms how the paraplegia will affect you. What impact will it have on feelings about yourself, aspirations, current activities, social relations, and interest areas? Be specific in relating these questions to your actual current life situation.

Next, list your schedule of activities for a typical week, including weekends. Make the schedule as detailed as possible. Social as well as academic and professional activities should be covered (perhaps last week's schedule or plans for next week would be clearest in your mind). Now go back over the schedule and in each instance indicate how the paraplegia will affect each event. Indicate the effect it will have on your activities, feelings, and relationships, and on the attitudes and feelings of others with whom you interact.

Evaluation. *What impact has this exercise had on your understanding of disability? Compare your reactions with those of other students. What similarities are reported? What differences? How can you account for the differences? Can you make any generalizations about the probable emotional impact of disability based on this exercise?*

SUMMARY

Illness, hospitalization, and disability pose threats to the individual's security needs. Responses to this threat vary in accordance with personality strengths and needs. The severity of psychological reactions is often unrelated to severity of actual illness. The experience of pain is both physical and psychological. Emotional needs will affect the intensity of the patient's experience of pain. The nurse–patient relationship as well as specific procedures can be instrumental in reducing a patient's perception of pain.

Denial and depression are two common reactions to illness. Denial can be dangerous when the patient refuses to recognize the presence of a serious illness. Severe depression is detrimental to rehabilitation by making the patient immobilized and unwilling to participate in his recovery. Sometimes depression can be positive in that it signals the patient's awareness of his condition.

Self-image is another important determinant of reaction to illness, hospitalization, and disability. The person with an exaggerated self-image of independence may react strongly to the passivity imposed by illness. On the other hand, overly dependent patients sometimes slip too willingly into the "sick role" and magnify and prolong their dependency. In helping the patient adjust to illness, hospitalization, and disability it is important for the nurse to direct needs in a positive direction in the service of rehabilitation.

Many emotional and reality problems contribute to the patient's state of stress. In reducing some minor sources of anxiety it is sometimes possible to bring the patient to the point of effectively coping. Separation anxiety also contributes to the stress of serious illness. Separation effects are greatest in young children. Institutionalized children who are separated from their parents at an early age show persistent physical, emotional, and social problems later in life. Adult reactions to separation are usually less extreme but are manifested in a host of emotional upsets. Separation anxiety is a threat to the independence strivings of the adolescent.

In chronic illness the necessity for changes in relationships, goals, and finances places great stress on the whole family. Chronic illness has a particularly disruptive effect on family life when it strikes a parent with young children. Disability requires a reorientation of the patient's self-image. Various disabilities evoke specific psychological crises, of which some examples were given.

SUGGESTED READINGS

Blumberg, J. E., and Drummond, E. *Nursing care of the long-term patient.* New York: Springer, 1971.

Hammar, S. I., and Eddy, J. *Nursing care of the adolescent.* New York: Springer, 1966.

Melzack, R. *The puzzle of pain.* New York: Basic Books, 1974.

Petrillo, M., and Sanger, S. *Emotional care of hospitalized children.* Philadelphia: Lippincott, 1972.

Wright, B. A. *Physical disability, a psychological approach.* New York: Harper & Row, 1960.

Wu, R. *Behavior and illness.* Englewood Cliffs, N.J.: Prentice-Hall, 1972.

Chapter *15*

Intelligence

THROUGHOUT THE life cycle, intelligence exerts an important influence on the course of development. How others view us, how we view ourselves, the degree of mastery and competence that we achieve in the environment, and the opportunities that are open to us, all bear a relationship to intelligence and intellectual development. As adults we constantly apply the concept of intelligence in our interactions with others. How many times have you said something like, "I like Carol, she's very sharp"; or "Bill doesn't catch on to things quickly, he's somewhat dull"; or "John is so bright—look at the way he handles people"; or perhaps, "Sally knows how to get what she wants, she's a smart girl." The examples are endless. Not only do we constantly make evaluations of intelligence but we take these evaluations seriously and often make important decisions based on them. Yet these informal estimates are usually intuitive, subjective notions that have questionable validity.

Considering the important role intelligence plays in our lives, it is worth exploring some of the work that has been done to identify and assess intelligence. Some of the prominent questions about intelligence are: Is there a universal definition of intelligence? How is intelligence measured? Can intelligence increase throughout the life cycle? Are there inborn limits to intellectual development? Do our experiences affect how intelligent we become? Is creativity a part of intelligence? We will address ourselves to these questions in this chapter.

THE MEASUREMENT OF INTELLIGENCE
Defining Intelligence

Edwin Boring, a famous experimental psychologist, once attempted to put to rest the confusion over defining intelligence by stating, "Intelligence is what the tests test" (Boring, 1923). In fact, *there is no one definition of intelligence.* Since our formal estimates of intelligence are based on intelligence test scores, intelligence is defined by the particular items on a given test. Some tests of intelligence measure largely verbal skills such as reasoning, vocabularly, comprehension, and abstract thinking. Other tests include, along with the verbal, nonverbal measures such as perception, mechanical tasks, and rote motor skills. Some intelligence test experts believe that personality characteristics are an important part of intellectual functioning; thus in their definition of intelligence such factors as motivation, persistence, attention, and concentration are included.

One approach to defining intelligence suggests that intelligence is related to satisfactory adaptation to the environment. According to this definition, those who can survive best and succeed in a given environment would be considered more intelligent than those who could not survive or succeed. The continuum from low to high intelligence according to this concept would depend on measures of adaptation. Defined in this manner, intelligence becomes a relative rather than an absolute concept. Since different environments and different cultures require different characteristics for success, the definition would vary. For example, agricultural societies and advanced technological societies require different skills for adaptation.

Another method of circumventing the confusing term *intelligence* is to find what a given test of intelligence can predict. If a person does well on a particular intelligence test, what can he do well in real life? Stated in more technical terms, with what do the test scores correlate? (Correlation is discussed more fully in Chapter 19.) We know, for example, that children who do well on the Stanford-Binet Intelligence Test tend to do well in school. This is no great surprise since the Binet test is made up of verbal items that are analogous to school tasks and activities. On the other hand, the Wechsler Intelligence Test can predict more accurately how a person will do in general life situations because it includes measures of manual and manipulative skills as well as verbal skills. By concentrating on the purpose and application of a test we can get away from the problematic term "intelligence" which can mean different things to different people.

Development of Intelligence Tests

The measurement of intelligence began with the publication in 1905 of a series of tests to measure mental development of children by Alfred Binet and his assistant Theodore Simon. Binet created his tests at the request of the French Minister of Public Instruction in order to identify mentally retarded children in the French schools. It was Binet who introduced the concept of mental age by assigning an age level from 3 to 13 to each of his 59 tests in the 1908 revision. Binet's early work on intelligence was quickly picked up and developed in the United States. In 1916 Louis M. Terman published the Stanford revision of the Binet Scale, which included a manual describing a standardized procedure for the administration and scoring of the tests. In this revision of the Binet Scale, Terman applied the concept of "intelligence quotient," or I.Q., based on the ratio of mental age to chronological age. Terman's version of the Binet Scale was revised in 1937, 1960, and in 1972.

Prior to Binet, other researchers worked on the measurement of individual differences, but their approach was different and not as successful as Binet's. Binet's tests were largely of the complex mental processes including reasoning, judgment, and thinking. Previous work concentrated on sensorimotor measures. In the late nineteenth century, Sir Francis Galton developed extensive measures of physical and sensorimotor characteristics of human beings. At the turn of the century, James McKeen Catell, influenced by Galton's work, established psychological laboratories at the University of Pennsylvania and Columbia University. He introduced the term "mental tests" but his measures, like Galton's, were sensorimotor, including tasks that measured sensory threshold, speed of reaction, and keenness of vision and hearing. Ultimately this method of measuring intelligence proved a failure when Wissler in 1901 found that there was no relationship between Catell's measures and course grades of students at Columbia University.

It was World War I that gave a boost to the intelligence testing movement. The existing methods for classifying people in terms of ability were inadequate for the task of assessing large groups of men coming into the military service. The Binet test was an individually administered test that required about one hour of testing time and a trained examiner; it was too cumbersome for large-scale testing.

Arthur Otis came up with a new idea in testing that solved the problem. He developed a *group intelligence test* that was self-administering. His work became the basis for the Army Alpha and Beta Tests. The Alpha required sixth-grade reading ability and the Beta no reading. These tests later evolved into the Army General Classification Test, which is still in use. Otis's success spurred the development of other group tests—intelligence, aptitude, interest, and personality. The quickness and ease of their administration made them very suitable for the assessment needs of government, industry, and schools.

In 1939 David Wechsler introduced the Wechsler-Bellevue test for adolescents and adults. This test was divided into two parts, one verbal and the other nonverbal, making it possible to obtain both separate intelligence scores for each part and a total score. Wechsler emphasized the interest value of the items on the test for adults and the diagnostic value of analyzing the pattern of scores on the 11 subtests that comprised his test. The Wechsler-Bellevue was revised and introduced as the Wechsler Adult Intelligence Scale (WAIS) in 1955. The latter is for age 16 and above. Wechsler also devised the Wechsler Intelligence Scale for Children (WISC-R) for ages 6 to 16 and the Wechsler Preschool and Primary Scale of Intelligence (WPPSI) for ages 4 to 6, both patterned after the Wechsler-Bellevue Test. The Wechsler tests have gained great popularity in recent years because of the inclusion of *nonverbal* tests at the higher age levels, which have proven useful for testing people with various language handicaps.

I.Q. Concept

The I.Q. method of computing intelligence, which was introduced in the 1937 revision of the Binet, has become almost synonymous with intelligence. Literally, I.Q. means intelligence quotient. As a quotient, I.Q. is computed in the following manner:

$$\frac{\text{Mental Age}}{\text{Chronological Age}} \times 100 = \text{I.Q.}$$

Today, intelligence measurements are, in general, no longer computed in this manner. In the Wechsler-Bellevue Scale, the concept of I.Q. is expressed as a deviation score. *Deviation scores* are computed in relation to the mean or average score of an age group. A person is expected to maintain his relative position throughout his lifetime. (Our discussion of the standard deviation in Chapter 19 will make this concept of deviation score clearer.) The intelligence quotient concept made assumptions that the deviation score method avoids. The intelligence quotient assumes that mental and chronological age develop in parallel fashion, at the same rate. This is clearly not the case for the gifted and the retarded. With the retarded, for example, mental age progresses slowly and levels off early; under the old quotient concept this results in a decline in I.Q. scores since chronological age continues its upward movement while mental age increases more slowly. For many other individuals as well, mental age does not develop evenly, producing fluctuations of I.Q. scores from age to age. Because of these technical problems the major intelligence tests today employ the deviation score method of measuring intelligence. The term "I.Q." is still retained, however, for traditional and historical reasons.

Classification of Intelligence

The span of intelligence from severely retarded to genius is divided according to ranges of I.Q. scores. Below are the classifications based on the Wechsler tests, followed by the designations of the American Psychiatric Association's diagnostic manual. The APA manual, which is also the classification system of the World Health Organization, only classifies subnormal intelligence.

Wechsler Classification

130 and above	Very superior
120 to 129	Superior
110 to 119	Bright normal
90 to 109	Average
80 to 89	Dull normal
70 to 79	Borderline
69 and below	Mental defective

American Psychiatric Association Classification

68 to 83	Borderline mental retardation
52 to 67	Mild mental retardation
36 to 51	Moderate mental retardation
20 to 35	Severe mental retardation
Under 20	Profound mental retardation

Intelligence Test Items

What areas of functioning are tapped in assessing intelligence? The best way to answer this question is to examine the items contained in one of the major intelligence tests. Below we have listed the different subtests of the Wechsler Adult Intelligence Scale (WAIS). The WAIS reflects a good sampling of the types of items typically found on intelligence tests. Also, the items on the adult scale are more difficult versions of similar items contained in the Wechsler Intelligence Scale for Children (WISC). Items on each subtest are arranged in increasing order of difficulty. The examiner discontinues a subtest when the examinee fails a specified number of items on that test.

Verbal Tests

1. *Information.* Assesses fund of common information. At the beginning are simple questions like "What are the colors of the American flag?" and "How many months are there in a year?" Later on, a more difficult question is "Who wrote Faust?"

2. *Comprehension.* Assesses understanding of common situations. Typical items are "Why should people pay taxes?" and "Why does the state require people to get a license in order to get married?"

3. *Arithmetic.* As the name implies arithmetic computation and reasoning are assessed. Example: "How many oranges can you buy for 36 cents if one orange costs six cents?"

4. *Similarities.* Assesses abstract verbal concept formation. Example: "In what way are a poem and a statue alike?"

5. *Digit Span.* Assesses recent memory (short-term recall) by requiring the examinee to repeat increasingly longer series of numbers. First there is a digits forward series and then a digits backwards series.

6. *Vocabulary.* Assesses knowledge of word meaning. Example: "What does ominous mean?"

Performance (Nonverbal) Tests

1. *Digit Symbol.* Assesses ability to follow directions and ability to perform rote perceptual motor tasks. The examinee is presented with combinations of numbers and symbols. Then, with the model as a reference, he is shown numbers that have blank spaces under them and is given 90 seconds to fill in the symbols that go with the numbers.

2. *Picture Completion.* Assesses awareness of the environment and familiarity with common objects. Tasks require identifying missing parts from pictures of common objects.

3. *Block Design.* Assesses nonverbal concept formation and perceptual-motor coordination. Examinee must arrange colored blocks to form designs identical with the models that are presented.

4. *Picture Arrangement.* Assesses logical thinking and the ability to make inferences. Series of pictures comprising a story are presented to the examinee in a mixed-up order. The task is to put them in the correct order.

5. *Object Assembly.* Assesses ability to perceive part-whole relationships and to integrate parts into meaningful wholes. Task consists of puzzle parts that must be put together.

Subtest and Total Score. In recognizing that the total intelligence score is derived from the sum of separate subtests, we can see how two individuals with the same overall score can have different strengths and weaknesses. One person may be strong on the performance items and weak on the verbal items while another person may have just the opposite pattern. Yet both may achieve a total I.Q. score of, let us say, 100. Many others can also achieve a score of 100 and have totally different subtest patterns. Intelligence looked at this way is not a single unified factor but is made up of numerous abilities and skills. While it is true that most people function in a fairly uniform fashion across subtests, there are discrepancies. We are all familiar with the "intelligent" person who is a brilliant scholar but quite limited in practical matters or psychomotor skills. Similarly, there are those who are outstanding in practical intelligence but weak in verbal-abstract functioning. The overall intelligence score doesn't tell us the components of the person's intelligence; for that we have to look at performance on specific tasks.

CREATIVITY AND INTELLIGENCE

Criticism has been leveled against intelligence tests for not including measures of creativity. Many investigators have argued that creativity is a characteristic independent from the usual conceptualization of intelligence (Getzels and Jackson, 1962; Guilford, 1967; Torrance, 1964). Intelligence tests tend to focus on commonplace or convergent ways of problem-solving and thinking, whereas creativity entails unique, unusual, varied, or divergent approaches to problem-solving and thinking. Torrance (1964), in his test battery of creativity, measures such factors as "fluency, flexibility, originality, and elaboration."

While it is generally true that highly creative individuals also tend to obtain high scores on intelligence tests, there are many discrepancies. Getzels and Jackson (1962) and McKinnon (1962) cite cases of highly creative subjects who were not in the highest I.Q. group. Many institutions and business organizations are beginning to recognize creativity as an important separate entity and are selecting personnel who may not have the best formal credentials but show the ability to function creatively. Graduate and professional schools are also taking a close look at the creative potential of applicants.

Can creativity be taught? This is a very important question for nursing because the nurse is constantly confronted with complex decision-making situations that require creative inventiveness. Hallman (1963) believes that everyone has creative potential that will be expressed if nurtured properly. Torrance (1961) has decried the ways in which schools, especially in the early years, inhibit and penalize creativity. Even professional training often emphasizes narrow, rigid role models and is hostile toward the divergent thinker. Techniques that encourage creativity must reward originality, risk-taking, curiosity, independent thinking, and mental playfulness.

The measurement of creativity has been a thorny problem. Many of the tests developed look like the verbal items on standard intelligence tests. Even nonverbal items require a test-taking attitude that can inhibit the creative process. Torrance (1964) has been concerned with identifying the creatively gifted among the disadvantaged, who usually do not do well on tests, thereby masking their creativity. Torrance, therefore, lists observational features of behavior that can indicate creativity. This list is of particular interest to nurses since the nurse's primary mode of evaluation is observation of behavior.

1. Intense absorption in listening, observing, or doing.
2. Intense animation and physical involvement.
3. Use of analogies in speech.
4. Bodily involvement of an intense nature in writing, reading, drawing, etc.
5. Tendency to challenge ideas of authorities.
6. Habit of checking many sources.
7. Taking a close look at things.
8. Eagerness to tell others about discoveries.
9. Continuing in a creative activity after the scheduled time for quitting.
10. Showing relationships among apparently unrelated ideas.
11. Following through on ideas set in motion.
12. Various manifestations of curiosity, wanting to know, digging deeper.

13. Spontaneous use of discovery or experimental approach.
14. Excitement in voice about discoveries.
15. Habit of guessing and testing outcomes.
16. Honesty and intense search for the truth.
17. Independent action.
18. Boldness of ideas.
19. Low distractability.
20. Manipulation of ideas and objects to discover new combinations.
21. Tendency to lose awareness of time.
22. Penetrating observations and questions.
23. Self-initiated learning.
24. Tendency to seek alternatives and explore new possibilities.
25. Willingness to consider or toy with a strange idea. (p. 175)

INTELLIGENCE, HEREDITY, AND ENVIRONMENT

Since intelligence is a highly valued trait in our society, many people are concerned with their potential for developing it further. Is intelligence biologically determined or can it be nurtured by one's experiences and environment? This is a very difficult question to answer. Part of the problem resides in the fact that immediately upon conception a person's biological makeup becomes intertwined with his environment, making it difficult to separate the two completely. However, intelligence studies of families, and of siblings and twins reared apart in different environments, lead experts to believe that there is a biological base for intelligence. Nevertheless, there is also convincing evidence that the environment in which a person is raised can have a significant effect on his intelligence beyond biological factors. There are a number of famous cases that illustrate this point. The case of Isobel, reported by Davis (1947), is one dramatic instance. Isobel was found hidden away in an attic, raised under conditions of extreme sensory deprivation and isolation by her deaf-mute mother. When discovered at age 6, she had an I.Q. of 30, which is in the severely retarded range. She was moved to a more stimulating, normal environment, and by age 8 her I.Q. was average. Studies of institutionalized children who were separated from their parents at an early age show a decline in I.Q., again illustrating the impact of the environment.

In our society there are many disadvantaged people. Their environments are characterized by poverty, social disorganization, unemployment, poor schooling, and lack of opportunity. The disadvantaged generally score somewhat lower on tests of intelligence and ability than the advantaged groups. We trace the poor performance of the disadvantaged to the negative features of their environment, which prevent them from fulfilling their true potential.

Related to the question of heredity versus environment is the concept of *average expectable environment*. All tests of intelligence and ability assume that the average range of experience afforded by most environments is sufficient for the person's potential to unfold to its maximum. Many children, however, do not have the average range of experience. From this point of view test scores may be unfair to many groups when these scores are taken to indicate ultimate potential for development. We must keep in mind the experience factor and evaluate a person's scores accordingly.

CONTROVERSIAL ISSUES

In addition to the divided opinion over hereditary and environmental influences on intelligence there are other areas of controversy. One concern is that assessment of intelligence can be used to deny people opportunities. For example, if the medical staff concluded that a patient did not have high enough intelligence to comprehend the complexities of a rehabilitation program, then the patient could be denied an important opportunity. But, you might wonder, what if the staff were correct in their assessment? The problem is that assessment never gives a complete picture of a person. We cannot predict what personality strengths and powerful motivations a person might muster to rise to an occasion. If we use assessments to help people overcome their weaknesses and then give them opportunities to demonstrate their abilities in real situations, assessment will have a positive, growth-facilitating function that few would resist.

Many people feel that tests and assessments, particularly of intelligence and personality, intrude on rights of privacy. In an age of wiretapping, eavesdropping, and computerized information processing this concern may not be unreasonable. Here too, if we are to fulfill a growth facilitating role we must demonstrate that our assessments are used to help clients and not to hurt or exclude them. A related concern is that assessment data will not be handled confidentially. Nobody wants personal data recorded in easily available files that may find their way to unknown persons and places. For the nurse the issue of confidentiality applies to all areas of functioning. Intelligence assessment requires even more sensitive consideration of confidentiality if we are to gain the trust and openness of our clients, which are essential in human relations work.

DEVELOPMENT OF INTELLIGENCE

In Chapter 11 we have presented a detailed account of Piaget's conception of intellectual development. Piaget's stages describe the evolution of intellectual processes from infancy through adolescence. In this section, therefore, we will confine our discussion to the data on the growth and stability of intellectual processes in adulthood and old age.

At one time it was believed that intelligence stopped increasing in late adolescence. That is not to say that a person could no longer acquire more information, skills, or training, but that the level or "power" of his intelligence ceased to grow any further. The early Binet scale set 16 years of age as the maximum chronological age for computing the intelligence quotient. Other test constructors quibbled over this and variously set 15 through 20 as the limit of intellectual growth. But many testing specialists were uneasy about these assumptions since evidence continuously arose suggesting that intellectual development continues into adulthood. Growth patterns of intelligence show, however, that intelligence increases rapidly in infancy and the preschool years, progresses more slowly during the elementary school years, and then grows very gradually after the onset of adolescence.

The behaviorist John Watson, who believed in the "limitless plasticity" of the human being, attributed the leveling off of intelligence in adulthood to lack of motivation. When people reach a level of comfort, Watson believed, they stop developing because they cease to expose themselves to growth or stimulating situations. It may be no coincidence that intellectual development slows down for most people after the school years. Similarly, it is interesting to note that studies showing increases in intelligence in adulthood find such increases most prevalent among the educated. Educated people apparently continue to pursue interests that are growth-facilitating (e.g., reading and exposure to cultural experiences).

I.Q. scores in general show considerable stability over time. A recent study by Honzik and MacFarlane (1973) followed 50 men and 60 women from 21 months of age to age 40. Their findings confirm other studies that show that I.Q. scores after age 6 compare closely with those obtained in adulthood. Again, those who gained the most tended to have the highest education. Women showed a greater increase in verbal I.Q. than men although their initial scores were lower. Scores increased in nonverbal as well as verbal tests for both men and women. Only one psychomotor speed test showed a decline between 18 and 40 years of age.

Among physically healthy people there is evidence of stability and increases in intelligence, even well into old age. For the healthy aged, the popular notion of memory loss in old age has no evidence in research. Lissy Jarvik et al. (1973) report cases from research at the New York State Psychiatric Institute showing increases in cognitive functions into the ninth decade of life: "At age 82 the lady scored higher than she did at age 62 on vocabulary, similarities and digits backward and she equalled her earlier performance on digits forward. Only on the speed of motor tasks were there prominent decrements." After evaluating the new evidence on intellectual functioning in adulthood and old age, Jarvik et al. direct our attention to the factors associated with the maintenance of intellectual functioning in later years of life, an area in need of further explanations and research. In a study by Owens (1953) 127 men were administered intelligence tests at thirty-year intervals. The scores were significantly higher on the second administration, with the greatest increases in tests of reasoning and abstraction. Eichorn (1973), reporting on the Berkeley Growth Study, confirms the increases in intelligence in adulthood. She states: "that increments in mental ability occur during adulthood no longer seems debatable. The questions become: in what, for what, and whom?" These data on intellectual stability and growth in adulthood and old age should be useful and encouraging to those nurses working with the aged.

INTELLIGENCE AND ILLNESS

People who ordinarily are bright, alert, and competent may appear otherwise when ill. Psychological reactions to illness can depress intellectual functioning and give patients a dull appearance. Anxiety, depression, apathy, and obsessional concerns interfere with thinking, memory, and psychomotor functioning. It is not uncommon for people in a heightened emotional state to have little awareness of their immediate surroundings, difficulty in coping with stress, and difficulty in attending to personal and practical matters. The dependency fostered by illness can also contribute to a helpless, infantile, unintelligent appearance. Medications are another possible cause of reduced intellectual functioning. Some medications produce anxiety, confusion, depression, poor motor coordination, and other symptoms that interfere with effective functioning (Chapter 18 treats the topic of medication and behavior in greater detail).

Most of these depressing effects on intelligence are transient; they vanish when the person regains his psychological stability or when the medication is withdrawn. Nevertheless, we are reminded of the need to be cautious in evaluating a person's intelligence or ability when he or she is observed in a state of illness or emotional upset.

SUMMARY

Intelligence exerts an influence on development throughout the life cycle. Many directions that a person's life takes are related to his intelligence. Definitions of intelligence vary. Formal definitions derive from the contents of the various tests of intelligence. Some tests like the Binet emphasize verbal and abstract reasoning; others like the Wechsler tests include perceptual-motor and personality characteristics. Intelligence is no longer computed as a quotient but as a deviation score. The latter gives the relative intelligence of an individual compared with his chronological age group peers. The designation I.Q. (meaning intelligence quotient) continues to be used for historical tradition. Intelligence is classified according to ranges of scores from the severely retarded level to the very superior level. The two most widely used classification systems are those of David Wechsler and the American Psychiatric Association. Creative ability is frequently separate from intelligence. There are many behavioral characteristics that reveal creative potential.

Heredity is an important factor in intelligence, but a person's experience also plays a major role. An advantaged environment can enhance intellectual development and a disadvantaged environment can depress it. Because of the experience factor measures of intelligence should not be taken as a reflection of a person's ultimate potential. Intelligence has been shown to develop and increase at all stages of the life cycle through old age. This is especially true for the educated who continue to expose themselves to growth experiences.

Some of the controversies that surround the use of intelligence evaluations relate to the fear that some will be denied opportunities based on test scores, that the individual's right to privacy will be invaded, and that confidentiality will be violated. When health professionals show that evaluations are used to help people these fears can be allayed.

Some patients appear less intelligent than they are because of emotional states associated with illness or the effects of medications.

SUGGESTED READINGS

Anastasi, A. *Psychological testing.* New York: Macmillan, 1968.
Flynn, J. T., and Garber, H. *Assessing behavior.* Reading, Mass.: Addison-Wesley, 1967.

Jarvik, L. F., Eisdorfer, C., and Blum, J. E. *Intellectual functioning in adults.* New York: Springer, 1973.

Wechsler, D. *The measure and appraisal of adult intelligence.* Baltimore: Williams and Wilkins, 1958.

Part  *IV*

Maladaptive Development and Behavior

THE HUMAN PERSONALITY *develops from a complex interaction of the individual's constitutional endowment, sociocultural environment, special life experiences, and relations with friends, teachers, and relatives. All these elements shape the development of the child's personality and continue to shape and change the adult's personality. In an evolutionary sense it is to man's advantage that he is so plastic and modifiable that his inherited qualities determine only a relatively small part of his ultimate personality characteristics.*

While developmental flexibility provides the potential for continued adaptation, this great modifiability also has unhappy consequences. Being open to many influences, the developing personality faces the possibility of taking many "wrong turns." For example, most families supply a sense of love and security—but if they don't, an individual may go through life unable to love or relate effectively to others. Other maladaptations arise from the culture in which an individual is raised, as in the case of a society that regards sexual pleasure for women as sinful, thereby inducing in women feelings of conflict and pain with regard to sexual impulses. In some instances a person's "wrong turn" can be traced to an accidental occurrence (e.g., an illness or traumatic event) that has little to do with his original personality but nevertheless has long-range effects on the course his development takes.

It is not only the environment that can go wrong. The child's constitution is equally critical. Here we are less concerned with con-

317

stitutional factors as such than with the ways in which they predispose the individual to certain experiences and perceptions that have developmental consequences. Consider the case of a newborn child who has 3-month colic. The colicky baby cries day and night. Nothing soothes or quiets him for more than brief periods. The parents try alternately to rock, hold, and ignore the baby, but nothing succeeds. His apparently immature digestive system causes cramps that will subside only with time. During this early period frustrations and patterns of interaction are already developing in the child. Because his pain persists, he may perceive the environment as nonsupportive. The parents may, in their exhaustion, be unable to sustain the caring behaviors they are capable of showing with a less demanding child. Subsequently, a less affectionate interaction may mark the family's relationship with the child, and this in turn can shape his future development; conversely, the family may take an inappropriately protective attitude toward the child, with different but also important consequences. Neither the child nor his parents can be blamed. Rather a combination of the child's constitutional make-up and the limitations of his parents' tolerance of frustration merge to produce an unfavorable environment for personality growth.

Regardless of the route taken, when development proceeds in a manner that leaves the child or adult with personality characteristics that markedly limit his functioning, we label that development maladaptive. As we shall see, limitations can be traced to various sources (e.g., organic or functional) and can be expressed through a number of psychological processes. But the actual limitation usually disrupts one or more of four basic areas: school, job, social relations, and sexual functioning.

When we speak of limitations in functioning, we don't mean transient disturbances such as doing poorly on a particular exam because of anxiety. But if a person were so anxious that he could not learn in a school setting, the limitation would be considered marked, and maladaptive development would be present. It is important to realize that some "symptoms" are normal. It is normal to be anxious in new or in very crucial life situations. Anxiety before a big exam is normal. It is also normal to have some emotional upheavals at critical points in life. We expect most people to be discouraged at times and occasionally to feel sufficiently depressed that their work and human relations are impeded. In fact, not to feel depressed after certain events, such as the loss of a parent or friend, would be abnormal.

Various surveys indicate that approximately 80% of the population experience some symptoms of psychological distress with nervousness or depression most common. At the same time, 20% of the population have sufficiently maladaptive development to experience considerable limitations in their functioning. (D. C. Leighton and A. H. Leighton, 1967). These 20% can be said to be suffering from emotional disturbances or mental illness.

We must, of course, emphasize once again the relative nature of the term normal. You will recall our discussion of normality in Chapter 13. The extent to which symptoms or behavior are disabling depends on the social context in which the person must live and work. From this standpoint there are no exact measures, and professional judgments are therefore necessary.

In Chapter 16 we explore the various types of maladaptive development, looking first at the nature of the system for classifying mental disorders. We will consider the organic disorders and the functional disorders, including the functional psychoses and the less serious disturbances, the neuroses and personality disorders. There is a brief discussion of sexual deviations and addictions. The chapter concludes with a survey of childhood mental disorders. Chapter 17 examines the various therapeutic approaches to the treatment of maladaptive development. We have included Chapter 18 on the effects of medications on mental states and behavior because patients often manifest pathological behaviors that stem from medication rather than from deeply rooted personality disturbances.

Chapter *16*

Psychopathology

THE STUDY OF diseases of the mind is still in its infancy. Although we know a great deal, there is much more that we don't know. For this reason you will hear many different opinions and arguments about who is and is not emotionally disturbed. For the most part such arguments have to do with problems of definition. In Chapter 13 we discussed the complications of arriving at a universally acceptable definition of psychological normality (or abnormality). We also pointed out that in most instances the nurse need not be too concerned with labels, because her focus is on understanding the patient in order to help him mobilize resources toward the goal of recovery and health. Nevertheless, to be able to communicate with others about mental disorders, working definitions and a system of classification are essential.

321

DEFINING MENTAL DISORDER

For practical purposes we reduce the complex and varied processes of psychological functioning to three areas, which we then assess to determine the type and extent of the psychopathology or psychological illness. All three areas are usually implicated in psychopathological states, but one will stand out to characterize a given disorder. These three areas are thinking, behavior (including relationships with others), and affect (feeling).

Working Definitions

When you are asking yourself whether a patient is emotionally disturbed, it is helpful to note first what characterizes his thinking. Do his thoughts flow logically from the information he has available to him? Then look at his general behavior. How does he relate to other people? Finally, consider how he feels. Is he fearful or unusually aggressive or withdrawn? Is he overwhelmed by anxiety or other disturbing emotions?

> Mr. R. was a middle-aged businessman and the father of three teen-age girls. One day while driving home he noticed a blue car behind him. The next day he *thought* he saw the same blue car parked near his business establishment. He was *certain* he was being followed. He called the police, and when they could not substantiate his suspicions he declared that *they were also involved* in the conspiracy. What conspiracy he was not sure, but the TV networks were involved since he *clearly had seen* a hidden message from the conspirators on a TV show the night before.

In this actual and not unusual sequence of events a man observes that a car, similar to one behind him the day before, shows up near his store. It may or may not be the same car, but that is not important. What is important is the man's unrealistic thought process, which leads him to conclude that he is being followed.

Confronted for the first time with a patient displaying this type of thought process, we are tempted to accept his interpretation. The intensity of the patient's belief and his fear can be very convincing. We feel he must be right. But when we have time to think through the sequence of his thoughts we begin to realize that the objective facts of his experience do not justify the conclusions that he draws. His thought process distorts what he sees, and his fears shape neutral events into a *delusion of persecution*. Events that may lead another individual to comment casually "I thought I saw that car yesterday" lead him to conclude that there is unquestionably a conspiracy afoot to control him. We are led to the conclusion that the man is suffering from a mental disorder.

International Classification System

Once we have agreed to define mental disturbance in terms of thinking, behavior, and affect, we need a system for classifying the different disorders of these functions. Classification enables us to communicate in an abbreviated fashion the nature of a patient's difficulties. The World Health Organization sponsored the effort to arrive at an internationally agreed-upon classification of mental illness that culminated in the acceptance, in 1968, of the presently used system. This system is the official basis for diagnostic classification throughout the United States and is the required form for statistical reporting. In spite of this official acceptance, the classification of mental illness reflects the still primitive state of psychiatric knowledge; we do not yet know enough to provide a logically consistent system of categories of illness. The use of other terms for the same illness or condition is not infrequent, and we will mention some of the more common synonyms as we discuss the major diseases.

There are two dimensions that form the scaffold upon which the current system of classification rests. These are *severity of dysfunction* and *etiology*. It should be clear that a system relying on severity of dysfunction as a basis for categorization will result in many instances of disagreement. Illnesses are fluid and can, therefore, seem severe at one point and mild at another point, resulting in different category placements for the same illness.

Severity. In the case of the businessman with the delusion of persecution, the pathology interfered in a very gross way with the ability to function effectively. The man was dominated by irrational fears, and could not concentrate on or attend to the management of his affairs. His suspiciousness was so marked that he allowed only a few people to speak with him or have access to him. If such a condition became extreme, the man might barricade himself in his room, isolating himself even from his family. At such a point the family would become alarmed and seek psychiatric help. In more acute conditions hospital treatment may be necessary, especially if the patient becomes dangerous to himself and others. In this case the patient's severe dysfunction would be diagnosed as psychotic. If, on the other hand, his suspiciousness and fearfulness occurred without the presence of delusional thinking and he was not significantly impaired in his daily functioning, he would be considered a paranoid personality disorder (nonpsychotic).

In the case of a person experiencing a mild to moderate depression in which there is no apparent precipitating reality factor (such as the loss of someone or something important—a parent, a job, etc.) we say he is suffering from a *depressive neurosis.* But if the individual becomes increasingly depressed or is from the outset severely depressed, we say he is suffering from a *depressive psychosis.* We will discuss further what goes into assessment of the degree of severity, but at this point it is helpful to keep in mind two levels of severity of malfunction and their subcategories:

1. *Mild to moderate dysfunction:* Neuroses, personality disorders, children's behavior disorders, physical (organic) conditions of the brain that affect functioning to a moderate degree (e.g., the mild forgetfulness and occasional confusion associated with arteriosclerosis of the brain).

2. *Severe dysfunction:* The psychoses, including manic-depressive illness, schizophrenia, delirium tremens, and severe confusional states.

Etiology. The second dimension on which classification is based is etiology—that is, the origin of the disorder or illness. Here again there is a two-way division, with many gray areas: (1) *organic disorders,* in which there is something physically wrong with the brain, and (2) *functional or nonorganic disorders*—those disturbances for which there is no known physical impairment.

Summary

The study of mental illness is still in its infancy. The difficulties of diagnostic classification reflect this primitive state of psychiatric knowledge. Mental illnesses are classified on a two-axial system. The two axes are severity of illness and etiology. The severity dimension extends from mild disturbances to psychoses. Psychosis is present when a person can no longer function independently under ordinary life circumstances.

The major divisions of types of disorders are organic and functional. The organic disturbances have detectable physical impairment of brain tissue. The functional disturbances are not due to physical impairment but to environmental and developmental influences.

ORGANIC DISORDERS

In all organic disorders there is a known physically induced impairment of brain tissue function. This impairment may be transient, as in drunkenness, or it may be permanent, as when a blood vessel ruptures and brain tissue is destroyed. Cases of brain damage that are reversible, as in certain chemically induced disturbances such as *delirium tremens,* are called "acute" brain disorders. When brain damage is permanent, it is called a *chronic organic brain syndrome* ("syndrome" here means "complex of symptoms").

Although brain damage can be very localized—as when a bullet destroys just a small part of the frontal lobe—most diseases of the brain cause diffuse brain damage. Probably the most common source of brain damage is the narrowing and closing of many of the small arterioles of the brain, which occurs as part of the general process of arteriosclerosis (hardening of the arteries). Arteriosclerosis involving the extremities does not, however, necessarily imply arterioscleritic brain damage. Similarly diffuse is brain damage resulting from infections (encephalitis or meningitis) or toxic materials (alcohol, LSD, lead poisoning). Tumors and cysts do not necessarily cause diffuse damage, though the pressure from an expanding tumor in the confined space of the skull does cause increased intracranial pressure and a diffuse damage to the brain may result.

Symptoms of Diffuse Brain Damage

Diffuse damage to the brain, whether it is temporary or permanent, severe or moderate, has certain characteristic symptoms. A useful aid in understanding these characteristics is to think in terms of someone intoxicated with alcohol. The intoxicated individual is suffering from an *acute (temporary) organic brain syndrome.* How would we describe his functioning? First of all, he has *difficulty in reasoning.* His thinking is obviously muddled, and he has trouble understanding what is said to him. His difficulties in reasoning may be subtle or gross depending on the degree of brain tissue impairment (proportionate to the amount of alcohol in his blood stream) and the degree to which he is susceptible to the effects of alcohol. Just as in other types of brain damage, the extent of the dysfunction will vary quite markedly among individuals, although all individuals will show some impairment. That reasoning is impaired is readily demonstrated. Give even a mildly intoxicated individual a mathematical problem that he is normally able to solve, and you will quickly see how impaired his reasoning has become.

Another important area affected is *memory*. As you know, the individual who is markedly intoxicated will often forget not only what he said and did while intoxicated but where he was and for how long. Again the degree of memory loss depends on the extent of intoxication and individual susceptibility.

Another symptom related to memory loss is *impairment in orientation*. Orientation has a very specific meaning in mental status exams and you will see it routinely referred to in psychiatric examinations; it means the ability to recognize and identify people, to know where you are, and to be able to keep track of time. For instance, an intoxicated man brought to the emergency room of a general hospital at 1 A.M. for suturing of a scalp wound might say: "I've got to get out of here. I'm late for work. You can keep my money. Just get me a cab and I won't bother you no more. I'm sorry I broke that bottle of whiskey. It was just an accident. . . ." And he may then struggle to leave and fight your efforts to cleanse his wound. What has happened is that he is disoriented. He has been told that he is in a hospital but does not understand, even though the physical setting is unmistakable; he also does not recognize the hospital staff as such; and, finally, he thinks it is time for work even though it is the middle of the night. We would say he is disoriented in the three spheres of *person, place,* and *time.*

Another symptom of diffuse impairment of brain tissue is *impaired judgment.* The intoxicated individual thinks his coordination is adequate to drive a car, when in fact it is totally inadequate. It is not just bravado that makes him overestimate his capacity. The complex abilities required for judgment of what is appropriate behavior are often severely diminished. For this reason families are often embarrassed by the behavior of adult members who display impaired judgment subsequent to an organic brain disorder. An otherwise distinguished man may decide to urinate in the street; he feels the pressure to evacuate his bladder but fails to realize the inappropriateness of the place he chooses to do it.

The last major symptom common to the organic disorders is *lability of affect. Lability* refers to frequent and abrupt ups and downs, while *affect* means feeling state. The individual with diffuse impairment will seem quite cheerful at one moment and then, following a minor disagreement, will burst into tears or become excessively hostile. The hostility or tears, however, quickly fade. Family and friends are left baffled by the sudden shifts unless and until they understand that it is a characteristic of the brain disorder their relative or friend is experiencing. Even then it is difficult for a friend to maintain composure in the face of the lability of affect. Fortunately, the mood swings are most often not severe.

Organic Psychoses

Psychoses are those disturbances in which a

> *patient's mental functioning is sufficiently impaired to interfere grossly with his capacity to meet the ordinary demands of life.* The impairment may result from a serious distortion in his capacity to recognize reality. Hallucinations and delusions, for example, may distort his perception. Alterations of mood may be so profound that the patient's capacity to respond appropriately is grossly impaired. Deficits in perception, language and memory may be so severe that the patient's capacity for mental grasp of the situation is effectively lost. *(Diagnostic and Statistical Manual of Mental Disorders,* 1968, p. 23; emphasis added)

To be called psychotic, then, an individual must be unable to function in the ordinary demands of life. If someone is so depressed that he is unable to go to work or take adequate care of himself, he is psychotic. Similarly someone whose memory is so impaired that he is unable to remember how to get home when he is just a few steps out the door is considered psychotic. It is important to realize that the term refers to severe impairment of functioning and not to bizarre behavior. Thus most people who are psychotic do not look "crazy." Although bizarre appearance and behavior are statements about a person's ability to cope, these statements need to be assessed in a larger context before one can determine whether a particular individual is psychotic.

The *organic psychoses* are those disorders in which physical impairment of brain tissue function has reached the point where the individual is no longer able to function in ordinary life circumstances.

> Mrs. M. was a 55-year-old mother of four children, now married. Mrs. M. had lived with her oldest daughter and son-in-law since her husband died two years ago. Until a month prior to hospitalization, she had worked as a secretary; she took a leave of absence when she found herself forgetting what she had to do next. Her children brought her for a diagnostic evaluation after she repeatedly wandered out of the house in her nightgown in the middle of the night. They were afraid she would be hurt since she wandered in a confused state into the street. On admission, Mrs. M. was a slender, timid, markedly anxious woman who did not understand the family's explanations for the trip to the hospital, was not sure of the season of the year or the month, and was quite suspicious. She thought her labor union was behind the hospitalization because they wanted to stop her disability payments. Physical examination revealed markedly elevated blood pressure and evidence of generalized arterio-sclerosis (retinal and EEG changes). There was also a history of early

senility in the family. After careful work-up revealed no other source of brain dysfunction, she was sent home to the watchful eye of her family, with medication to combat her suspiciousness. However, these changes were permanent and progressive and the family could anticipate that in a few years she would need to be watched 24 hours a day.

The organic psychoses are as numerous as the conditions that can affect the brain. We will discuss only the ones most commonly encountered.

Alcoholic Psychoses. Alcoholic psychoses are conditions caused by alcohol poisoning. Simple drunkenness is not considered a psychosis but a nonpsychotic organic brain disorder. (This is one of the many inconsistencies of terminology, since the malfunctioning of the drunken individual, even though temporary, can be of psychotic severity). The most frequently occurring of the alcoholic psychoses is *delirium tremens*. In this condition, which follows withdrawal from chronic alcoholism, the patient has tremors of the extremities and frightening visual hallucinations, usually of animals. In his intense fear a patient may be driven to escape, even if it means jumping from a window. The agitation of delirium tremens can lead to exhaustion and death, so that sedation and close observation are required. Nursing care is crucial in the treatment. Fortunately the condition is limited in duration and, when adequately treated, recovery is usually complete.

Infectious Psychoses. Infections of the brain are now relatively infrequent. However, any infection that causes an encephalitis (inflammation of the brain) may have as an outcome an organic brain syndrome of psychotic or nonpsychotic severity. At one time the most common cause of psychosis and chronic hospitalization was syphilitic infection of the brain. Now, however, thanks to modern medication, it is unusual to see a case of psychosis due to syphilis even in a large institution. Illnesses that earlier were also major sources of encephalitis—middle-ear infections, tuberculosis—are today infrequent. Viral encephalitis still takes its toll and is responsible for some cases of psychotic organic brain syndrome, but again the incidence is small.

Psychosis Due to Other Degenerative Conditions. The conditions other than infection that cause degeneration or destruction of brain tissue are quite numerous. All of these conditions may cause only mild impairment and therefore result in minimal disability, or they may produce extensive destruction of brain tissue with impairment severe enough to interfere grossly with an individual's capacity to care for himself. Among the conditions that may result in a psychotic disorder are cerebral arteriosclerosis, brain tumors, brain trauma, and senile and presenile dementia. (Senility is a hereditary degeneration of brain tissue of unknown cause.)

An important group of psychotic disorders are associated with disorders of hormonal regulation and metabolism: psychoses that may accompany severe thyroid disease (both hyper- and hypo-thyroidism), those associated with the excessive cortisone production of Cushing's syndrome, and the psychoses that may be present in severe vitamin deficiency diseases such as pellagra.

Drug-Related Psychoses. It is important to be aware of the potential psychotic reactions that can result from medications. Steroids (cortisone, prednisone, etc.) in high doses, as they are used in the treatment of many conditions (ulcerative colitis, arthritis, organ transplants), quite frequently trigger confusion, delusions, and paranoid behavior, which subside when the medication is reduced or discontinued. The unwary practitioner may find herself with a patient in panic after a kidney transplant because of the psychotogenic properties of the cortisone being used as an immuno-suppressant. In such cases, the fearfulness can be better controlled if the patient is made aware that what he or she is experiencing is an expected reaction. Sometimes tranquilizers also help. Careful monitoring of such patients is essential. Special nursing is often required, because self-destructive behavior can readily occur in the delusional panic that may overtake the patient. In Chapter 18 there is a more detailed discussion of the effects of medication on mental states and behavior.

Physical Conditions. Physical conditions can also produce psychotic episodes or reactions. The elderly arteriosclerotic patient who has experienced transient or sustained hypoxia (lack of oxygen) as the result of circulatory collapse during an operation or secondary to a myocardial infarct can easily become transiently delusional. The staff needs to recognize and treat such psychiatric emergencies in the intensive care unit or recovery room, wherever and whenever they develop.

Nonpsychotic Organic Brain Disorders

All the conditions that can cause psychosis may in less severe form cause a nonpsychotic disorder. The dividing line is whether the individual can adequately function in his ordinary life pursuits. This distinction is often a difficult one to make; sometimes the labeling is not overly important. On the other hand the labels can be a quick way of communicating to professionals the assessed needs of a patient. When a patient is diagnosed as psychotic, the clinician is saying that the patient lacks adequate judgment and the ability to reason and to take care of himself; therefore, those around him will have to provide a great deal of supervision and help.

Dr. H., a physician in his late thirties, had been becoming gradually more irritable and irrational over a period of eight years previous to his first hospitalization. Wealthy, happily married, with two children, he began to change in subtle ways: he lost his temper somewhat more easily, he became increasingly extravagant in his use of money. He began to quarrel with his wife over issues previously taken for granted—how they spent their summers, what activities each engaged in, and so on. On the urging of colleagues he entered psychotherapy with a highly respected psychiatrist. His symptoms worsened and after two years of treatment he was referred for an extensive neurological work-up. By now the irritability was marked; he also showed abrupt mood swings and could be quickly precipitated into a rage or bout of crying by relatively minor incidents. He often forgot patients' appointments and at times even their names, and his practice was dwindling.

The neurological work-up revealed that he had Huntington's Chorea —a progressive, hereditary disease with diffuse degeneration of brain tissue (the brain at necropsy looks like Swiss cheese). Although he knew the diagnosis was correct, he could not accept it, knowing the progressive, incapacitating, and eventually fatal outcome, and he attempted to continue to do things (such as fly his private plane) of which he was no longer capable. He was hospitalized at a point where he was unwilling to accept the supervision that his poor judgment required. For eight years this physician had been symptomatic. However, only in the year before hospitalization were his memory, reasoning, and judgment so impaired that he could not work at all and required extensive care and supervision.

Therefore, for approximately seven years, Dr. H. would be said to be suffering from a nonpsychotic organic brain disorder; after that time he would be considered psychotic.

Most nonpsychotic organic disorders, unlike Huntington's Chorea, are not progressive. For instance brain injury sustained in a car accident is usually a nonprogressive and nonpsychotic type of dysfunction. The symptoms in such a case might be a mild intellectual impairment with excessive moodiness and irritability.

Similarly, children who eat lead-based paint commonly develop a nonpsychotic organic brain disorder. Their symptoms frequently include hyperactivity, impulsivity, and short attention span. As can be seen, the nonpsychotic organic disorders encompass a wide spectrum of symptoms and etiologies.

Summary

Organic disorders are due to physical impairment of brain tissue function. Reversible brain impairment is called acute organic brain syndrome. Permanent brain dysfunction is called chronic organic brain syndrome. Brain damage may be localized or diffuse. Most often it is diffuse. There are five major symptoms of diffuse brain damage: (1) impairment of reasoning, (2) impairment of memory, (3) impairment of orientation, (4) impairment of judgement, (5) lability of affect.

Organic psychoses occur when brain tissue dysfunction makes it no longer possible for the individual to function in ordinary life circumstances. Delirium tremens resulting from alcohol withdrawal is a frequently seen acute organic psychosis. Chronic organic brain syndrome of psychotic proportion may result from infections, arteriosclerosis, brain tumors, certain metabolic diseases, brain tissue degeneration, and trauma. The same causes of organic psychoses may yield a nonpsychotic organic brain syndrome when the brain damage is less severe.

Suggested Readings

Brain, L., and Walton, J. W. *Brain's diseases of the nervous system.* London: Oxford University Press. 1969.

DSM II, *Diagnostic and statistical manual of mental disorders.* Washington, D.C.: American Psychiatric Association, 1968.

Freedman, A. M., and Kaplin H. I. *Comprehensive testbook of psychiatry.* Baltimore: Williams and Wilkins, 1967.

FUNCTIONAL DISORDERS

Functional disorders arise from the individual's experiences and emotional interaction with the environment. Neuroses are one type of functional disorder. A fear of heights, for example, arises from some experience in the course of the individual's development that resulted in a marked need to avoid high places. For such an individual heights may activate an earlier trauma or may symbolically represent an earlier fear. It is obvious that such a fear is not the result of physical impairment of the brain. It is nonorganic or functional in origin.

In physical illness a symptom may point to a single disease process; severe left chest pain radiating down the left arm, for instance, is a cardinal symptom of myocardial ischemia. Of course, more commonly certain symptoms may have a variety of causes. The tense, inactive, painful abdomen of peritonitis can result from perforation of a gastric ulcer, pancreatitis, appendicitis, etc. The symptoms of functional mental disorders are more likely to have many possible different causes, as in the case of the painful abdomen; therefore they are classified according to symptoms. The child who is inhibited, lacking in self-confidence, or extremely fearful may have an intrusive, overprotective mother—or he may have a father who is abusive or extremely punitive. Symptoms are the final common pathway of functional disturbances; two individuals with the same symptoms may have developed the symptoms for different reasons.

Functional Psychoses

There are two major groups of functional disorders of psychotic severity: the *schizophrenias* and the *affective illnesses*. As you know, a mental illness is a psychosis if it is severe enough to prevent the individual from coping with ordinary life needs. A common criterion for determining psychosis is *reality-testing*. This criterion states that an individual is psychotic if he is unable to distinguish between fantasy and reality. Perhaps most, but *not all*, psychotic patients give evidence of serious problems in reality testing. An example will clarify this issue.

> Mrs. R. came from a wealthy family and gave no evidence of serious disturbance until the age of 23. She lived some distance from her family, and they first began to be concerned when she stopped making use of her generous allowance. Shortly thereafter she disappeared from her apartment. It was three months before they found her in a state hospital, where she had been committed after being arrested for attempting to cash a forged check. The name she signed was that of a movie actress whose identity she had assumed. She denied being anyone but the actress and when her family came to take her to a private facility, she maintained that they were the ones who were mistaken in identifying her as their daughter. Mrs. R., who was pretty but not beautiful, had quite transparently begun to believe her fantasy of being an actress. Her belief made it impossible for her to manage in ordinary life circumstances.

In contrast to Mrs. R., a patient who had adequate reality-testing but still would be considered psychotic, is Mr. T.

Mr. T. had been a successful businessman until the age of 62. At that time his wife suddenly died, and although other members of the family were supportive, he reacted to her death not only with intense sorrow but with a depression maintained well beyond the usual and normal three months of deep mourning. He seemed at a loss as to how to start the day. He was preoccupied by irrelevant details and found himself without ability to concentrate on his work. His business had to be sold after a year of increasing incapacity on Mr. T.'s part. He was plagued by insomnia and spent the entire day sitting in an apathetic manner in his favorite chair staring out the window. He would not even eat unless someone practically forced him to take something. However, when he could be prodded into conversation, it was clear that none of his capacity to test reality or to remember was impaired. He was simply too depressed to make use of his intellect.

These two brief descriptions are examples of the two major functional psychotic disorders. Mrs. R. is suffering from a schizophrenic disorder, and Mr. T. is suffering from an affective illness.

Affective Psychoses

An affective psychotic illness is just what the name implies—an illness characterized by marked and incapacitating changes in affect or mood. Extreme elation or extreme depression may occur. However, the most frequent type of mood disturbance by far is depression.

Depression. Psychotic depression may occur at any time in life but is most common for women in their 50s and men in their 60s. Psychotic depression is marked by a sense of hopelessness and helplessness. It is often precipitated by an external event such as loss of a loved one, children leaving home, or retirement. Such depressions are called *exogenous,* that is, they are generated from the outside world. A depression occurring without an identifiable event of some importance preceding it is called an *endogenous depression* (one that comes from within).

One of the most frequent symptoms, and the one that rightfully causes the most concern, is the desire of the depressed individual to kill himself. Even when the depression is not of psychotic proportions most afflicted individuals have the thought that they want to die. In fact few if any human beings go through life without having suicidal thoughts in a time of sadness or despair. These thoughts are especially common in adolescence and in old age. But for the psychotically depressed individual, the suicidal thought may well become an act, and careful clinical monitoring of the patient's mental state is required.

Fortunately, the distress of psychotic depression is one of the more treatable of the serious mental illnesses. Several means are available: medication, electroshock therapy, environmental management, and psychotherapy. Most severely disturbed patients respond to one or a combination of these modes of treatment, and complete cures are frequent even when the depression has endured one or more years. Often the depressed person had led an active and productive life prior to the depression, and once treatment is successful, a return to this earlier, adaptive life style is possible.

Several features of the depressive illnesses are hard on families, friends, and those who seek to diminish the suffering. First, attempts to cheer up the depressed person are almost always met with apathy. Most severely depressed patients simply cannot respond to such efforts, and this frustrates those who wish to be of help. Second, reassuring depressed individuals that their worries or fears are unrealistic does no good. Their agitation and worry may be grossly unrealistic (e.g., one woman insisted that she had an incurable disease even after it was "proven" to her that she did not), but evidence to the contrary will not allay the obvious fear they experience. In such instances, a single statement of what the reality is makes most therapeutic sense; repeated reassurances serve no purpose but only frustrate the helpers. It is nonetheless hard to resist reassuring even when experience tells us that it is of no avail and may only increase the patient's distress. The obvious pain of the depressed patient's demeanor and behavior are pulls that tend to overwhelm what our clinical knowledge tells us is best.

Mania. Extreme elation characterizes the patient with a manic illness. They are frequently smiling, making jokes, and are truly "high"—but not on drugs. Characteristically, a person who is psychotically manic is episodically so. He will have periods in which his mood is normal or depressed. When manic, the patient describes himself as feeling "wonderful, beautiful, free," etc., and at first he does indeed appear happy. But it is only a short while before the observer detects the underlying anger, anxiety, and marked irritability that is only lightly covered over by the jokes and excessive laughter. Insomnia, incessant activity, and poor judgment e.g., giving expensive gifts to strangers whom he meets and immediately adopts as "best friends" are frequent. Recent advances in the use of medication (lithium) have for the first time made a prolonged recovery possible for patients suffering from manic-type psychosis.

Schizophrenia

The schizophrenic disturbances are all severely disabling. The illness is characterized by profound interpersonal isolation, hallucinations, delusions, fears of persecution, disorientation, difficulty expressing feelings, and states of prolonged panic. There are several types of schizophrenia, classified on the basis of the predominant symptoms. A patient with a paranoid type of schizophrenia, for example, will have as a main manifestation of his illness unfounded fears that he is being persecuted. He may build up in his mind a complex theory of who is persecuting him and why. Such a false belief is termed a *delusion of persecution.* A paranoid patient might also believe that he is someone of extraordinary importance, e.g., a prophet or possessor of secrets of inestimable value. Such a delusion is called a *delusion of grandeur.* These delusions need to be distinguished from beliefs that are part of a culture and not idiosyncratic to an individual. For instance the belief of a tribal "medicine man" that he has special and important powers is not delusional but part of a cultural belief. On the other hand, the belief of an American that he is Napoleon would be delusional.

The term *schizophrenia* was coined by a Swiss psychiatrist, Eugene Bleuler, whose classic treatise on the subject appeared in 1911. Translated literally, schizophrenia means "split-mindedness." The splitting of the mind Bleuler referred to was not the split or double personality, as is popularly believed. Rather he meant the splitting of the personality into unintegrated functions, so that the intellectual functions are not integrated with the motivational and affective aspects of the personality.

Interpersonal Isolation. Characteristically the schizophrenic patient is withdrawn, in the sense that he has profound fears of relating to others. This springs from a basic failure in his development—the failure to develop trust in his capacity to be loved. This lack of confidence in his "lovability" leads to an avoidance of contact with others, because he is certain that they will reject him. Consequently attempts by helpers to reach him, unless very cautiously carried out, are apt to create a panic of anxiety. The fear of intimacy with another human being is overwhelming. Again, it is important to remember that we are describing characteristics that are psychotic in severity: they grossly interfere with the schizophrenic's ability to function under ordinary life circumstances. In a less severe form, these symptoms are seen in personality disorders (to be discussed later), in which they limit an individual's adaptive capacity but to a less extreme degree.

Thought Disorder. The characteristic that defines schizophrenia (that is, without which the condition is not labeled schizophrenia) is thought disorder. The thought disorder that characterizes schizophrenia has a variety of expressions, but basically it renders the individual incapable of logical thought. The main aspect of the deficit in logic is the so-called looseness of associations. By this term is meant the inability to maintain continuity of associations. Now at times we all experience some difficulty in maintaining continuity of associations, especially when anxious or fatigued. But for the schizophrenic this difficulty is dominant. For example, a patient asked by a psychiatrist about his relationship with his father replied:

> My father, he was a carpenter, he built houses. Houses are expensive these days and expensive things like cars are hard to come by. What kind of car do you drive?

Here the initial response was to give his father's occupation. Then, instead of either following the initial question or developing the picture of his father, the patient drifted off to talk about houses and cars and ended by asking the interviewer about what kind of car he drove. The link between thoughts is extremely loose, in the sense that a thematic focus is not maintained, and the statements are related only by attributes of secondary importance.

Hallucinations. An associated disturbance and one of the most frightening is hallucination. Hallucination is the seeing or hearing of things that do not exist. Hallucinations also occur in various toxic states such as delirium tremens and LSD intoxication. In one relatively common schizophrenic hallucination, the patient hears voices cursing at him and calling him names. Auditory hallucinations may also take the form of commands to carry out some act. It needs to be emphasized, however, that the schizophrenic patient is rarely harmful to others. Most often he is an isolated, confused, pathetically frightened individual.

Etiology. How does an individual develop such a disabling illness?

We do not know entirely, but there are certain family characteristics that account in part for the disturbance. One characteristic of such families is that there is a continuous interruption of thematic focus, that is, someone is always interrupting someone else before he can finish a thought (Wynne et al, 1958). Another is that a clear expression of feelings, especially negative or angry feelings, is not permitted. Still another is a very early failure to provide the child with a sense of basic trust in the human environment. Nonetheless, the studies of the etiology of schizophrenia have thus far failed to define fully all the factors that are causal for the disturbance. There is probably, in addition to family factors, a hereditary predisposition or vulnerability to psychosis. A number of studies have shown that identical twins (twins from one ovum), even when raised separately, are more likely to develop schizophrenia if one has the illness than are fraternal twins (twins from two ova).

Treatment. At present the most effective means for helping the schizophrenic patient is to arrange his environment (job, family) to make use of and support his strengths, and to use tranquilizers to diminish the omnipresent and limiting anxiety. A large number—approximately one-third—of patients with a first schizophrenic psychotic episode will return to normal functioning with little or no long-term treatment. The remaining two-thirds will need help from time to time or on a regular basis for the rest of their lives. This chronicity is the reason that schizophrenia accounts for more occupied hospital beds than any other mental illness.

Summary

There are two major types of functional psychotic disorders: affective psychoses and the schizophrenias. The affective psychoses are characterized by severe changes in mood. The most common affective disturbance is depression. Severe depression is marked by feelings of despair, helplessness, and hopelessness, by frequent somatic complaints, insomnia, and apathy. Mania is, in appearance, the opposite of depression. It is characterized by intense elation, overactivity, inappropriate laughter and joking, and often poor social judgment.

The schizophrenic patient constitutes the largest group of hospitalized patients. The disturbance is usually chronic and often requires life-long treatment. The main symptoms are: (1) interpersonal isolation, (2) thought disorder, and (3) difficulties in expressing feelings. The etiology of schizophrenia is not fully understood, but family interaction plays a major role. Twin studies also indicate that heredity is probably an important factor in susceptibility to the illness.

Suggested Readings

Beers, C. *A mind that found itself*. New York: Doubleday, Doran, 1939.

Beck, A. T. *The diagnosis and management of depression*. Philadelphia: University of Pennsylvania Press, 1973.

Faberow, N. L., and Shneidman, E. S., eds. *The cry for help*. New York: McGraw-Hill, 1965.

Green, H. *I never promised you a rose garden*. New York: Holt, Rinehart and Winston, 1964.

Kasanin, J. B., ed. *Language and thought in schizophrenia*. New York: Norton, 1964.

Lidz, T. *The origins and treatment of schizophrenic disorders*. New York: Basic Books, 1973.

NEUROSES AND PERSONALITY DISORDERS

The neuroses and personality disorders are less severe functional disturbances than are the psychotic disorders. In the neuroses and personality disorders the individual can reason adequately and differentiate between fantasy and reality. Despite a tendency to be over- or underemotional in behavior, the neurotic is not completely overwhelmed by emotions. Although conflicts may prevent such an individual from functioning at his full potential, he is still able to get along and meet at least the minimal requirements of life. In some instances people with neuroses and personality disorders can achieve at a high level in "conflict-free" areas of their lives. Sometimes their behavior is a successful compensation for their difficulties.

Neuroses

The neuroses are the most readily understood of the emotional disturbances because their major characteristic—anxiety—has been experienced by everyone. Taking an important test, going for a job interview, entering a new social situation—these are all occasions that elicit that vague sense of fear, often described as centering in the upper abdominal region, which we call anxiety. We all know the perspiring and increased heart rate and muscular tension that accompany anxiety. When is anxiety symptomatic of a psychoneurosis and when is it considered a normal response? Anxiety is an expression of a neurosis when its presence and/or intensity are not logically explainable by the stress of the situation. Thus the anxiety associated with an important test is a normal response. An intense fear of cats is not, on the other hand, explainable by the danger posed by a cat, and such a fear would be considered a phobic neurosis.

While anxiety is the chief characteristic of the neuroses, it is not always directly expressed but may be controlled by various psychological mechanisms—at a considerable price to the individual, however. Such is the case in the hysterical neuroses in which a symptom such as blindness may occur as a means of resolving the *internalized conflict* that has given rise to the anxiety. The internalized conflict, a conflict between opposing needs or between desires and the taboos of conscience, is the source of the irrational anxiety of the neurotic. There are five major types of neuroses: anxiety neurosis, hysterical neurosis, phobic neurosis, obsessive-compulsive neurosis, and depressive neurosis.

Anxiety Neurosis. A person suffering from an anxiety neurosis experiences the distress of anxiety in a diffuse, pervasive manner. Typically he will describe a sense of discomfort that is with him almost all the time and on occasion becomes a sense of panic. The individual is usually well aware that his fear has no objective basis, yet subjectively it is very real.

Mrs. T. consulted her physician with the complaint of feeling "nervous" for the past several months. She described it as a tense shaky feeling that was with her most of the time and seemed focused in her upper abdomen. She thought that "she was losing her mind" or perhaps had some serious illness. Examination disclosed that there was nothing physically wrong, and that although she was distinctly uncomfortable she did continue to take care of her home and family in her usual effective way. After rather prolonged psychotherapeutic treatment it became evident that a major source of the anxiety had to do with an internal conflict which she was initially only vaguely aware of. The conflict was between her wish to view her marriage as ideal and the anger, frustration, and unhappiness she was actually experiencing in her relationship with a husband whose only true investment was in his business. Her unwillingness to admit to herself that she could harbor such negative feelings towards her idealized husband led to an internal conflict which was subjectively experienced as anxiety. It also prevented the possibility of her and her husband working towards a better relationship since she was not able to communicate to him the intensity of her anger and unhappiness.

Hysterical Neurosis. A person suffering from an hysterical neurosis may not directly experience the degree of anxiety that Mrs. T. felt. The anxiety in the hysterical neurosis is to a great extent set aside by a resolution in which there is a *conversion* of the psychological conflict into a physical disability or complaint. While it is always important to be certain that the complaint is not due to physical causes, it is equally important not to attribute a physical basis to an emotionally derived complaint. If one fails to appreciate the psychological basis of a conversion or hysterical symptom, one will treat it somatically, and the treatment will of course fail.

> Mrs. O. was 18, very attractive, but fearful to an extreme of breaking away from her husband, a violent and abusive man. She had a 1-year-old son. In a fit of anger one night her husband held a gun against her head and threatened to kill her. She passed out; when she awoke she was paralyzed from the waist down. She was taken to the hospital, where a tentative diagnosis of stroke was made, but careful tests failed to reveal evidence of intracranial hemorrhage. She made a slow recovery of some function of her lower extremities but marked weakness remained. The diagnosis was then changed to multiple sclerosis. After eight years (a period in which there had been no progression in symptoms) she was seen by a psychiatrist because of problems her son was presenting in school. Under hypnosis it was revealed that she did have full use of her lower extremities, though there was some muscular atrophy due to disuse. The paralysis was an expression of her desperate fear of her husband and, at the same time, her feeling that she was forced to remain in the marriage. The paralysis, a conversion symptom, relieved her of her conflict. She was unable to run away, but her husband did leave her since he was not willing to take care of an invalid.

Phobic Neurosis. A phobic neurosis involves a fear of some specific situation or thing. Some examples are fear of heights, fear of crowds, and fear of trains. The fear represents an anxiety that has become symbolized by or associated with something that in itself is not a source of danger. For instance, a woman may have an intense fear of animals, such that she feels a sense of panic when one is nearby. Yet this same woman may be personally able to approach other truly dangerous situations with relative calm. The animal is not a real danger but symbolizes and therefore summons forth associated sources of high anxiety.

Obsessive-Compulsive Neurosis. The obsessive-compulsive neurosis involves two related behaviors, both of which are repetitive in nature. The obsessive aspects of the neurosis consist of the repeated occurrence of a thought, word, or series of thoughts. We have all experienced the annoying recurrence of thoughts. A common obsessive experience is of a melody or song that we keep humming "in spite of ourselves." The individual afflicted with an obsessive neurosis experiences a great deal of anxiety and discomfort because of constantly repetitious thoughts. For instance, a young woman was obsessed with the idea that her baby would suffocate in her crib. This is a common enough worry, but for her it was an almost incessant thought that went far beyond the usual concern.

Compulsions, the second aspect of this neurosis, are acts or activities an individual feels forced to do over and over again. The obsessive thought and the compulsive act are often coupled. A rather common obsessive-compulsive neurosis is the handwashing compulsion. A man has the repeated thought that his hands are dirty or contaminated. So he washes them, but the thought is still there. So he washes them again. He will spend several hours each day washing his hands. And still he is filled with a sense of anxiety that they are dirty and germ-laden. He recognizes that he is driven to wash his hands by an unrealistic fear, but he is unable to silence the thoughts or stop the washing. His hands are dried out and painful and still he washes. The obsession and its compulsion symbolize psychological conflict that the individual is not able to resolve. The man's handwashing may be a symbolic attempt to cleanse himself of some act or thought for which he feels deep guilt. The thought or wish to strike or do harm to a parent may induce in this man the symbolic attempt to wash away his guilt. A famous literary example of such a compulsion—which, however, took on psychotic proportions—is Lady Macbeth, in Shakespeare's play, who tries in vain to wash the blood of the murdered king from her hand.

Depressive Neurosis.   A depressive neurosis is characterized by a prolonged depression that is either unrelated to a real situation or out of proportion to it.

> Mr. R. was 22 when he received his engineering degree. He appeared to have a very bright future with many job opportunities. He felt, however, inexplicably depressed. After a searching consideration of his feelings and life events it became apparent that his success represented a graduation into the responsibility of competing in the adult world. Competing meant being aggressive, and although he was in reality a markedly aggressive individual, these feelings had been suppressed in keeping with his strict upbringing. Now when aggression was to be called on, he could not adaptively give in to it and became "unaccountably" depressed.

In this case Mr. R. is torn by a conflict between the opposing forces of aggression and passivity. This inhibits his functioning, leading to the pervasive depressive affect.

Personality Disorders

The personality disorders sometimes called character disorders are very much related to the neurotic disorders. Often the line separating them is thin or even blurred. In order to make some of the distinctions clear it is necessary to overstate the differences.

The anxiety and the distress over specific symptoms that characterize the neuroses are often either absent or not dominant in the personality disorders. In the personality disorders anxiety is largely bound up in the pervasive patterns of interaction that limit and constrict the person's functioning. For example, we spoke of the obsessive-compulsive neurosis, in which a thought intrudes over and over again and/or an act is repeatedly carried out. There is also what is called the *obsessive-compulsive personality disorder*. The individual with this personality disorder is not obsessed by an idea so much as his whole life style is dominated by an excessive need for orderliness and conformity. He is seen by associates as rigid and overly inhibited, and subjectively he finds himself overly concerned with details and unable to relax. We speak of such obsessive characteristics as emotional disturbances in that they limit quite markedly the range of behavior and interaction available to the individual. There are of course situations in which obsessive concern with detail and perfectionism is adaptive and rewarded. Every professional must to an extent adopt obsessive mechanisms if he is to carry out his duties adequately. Obsessive concern for detail is essential in an operating room and in administering medication. A slight error can be fatal. Being obsessive when this is necessary is a sign of health, but being obsessive at all times is a sign of disturbance. The nurse who never loses count of her instruments and sponges in the operating room is successfully perfectionistic where it is a necessity. If she seeks the same perfection in choosing a mate, she may never find one who is suitable.

The person suffering from a personality disorder is often very much identified with his narrow or distorted pattern of behavior. Thus the person with the obsessive-compulsive personality disorder may "like" being compulsive. His behavior is what is called *ego-syntonic*, meaning consonant with his self-image. It is this identification with the disorder that shields him from the anxiety and symptomatology experienced by the neurotic obsessive-compulsive. The neurotic is more conflicted and bothered by his own behavior.

Other personality disorders include the schizoid personality (overly shy, withdrawn, but not out of contact), the hysterical personality (overly dramatic, frequently seductive, highly emo-

tional), and the passive aggressive personality (much of his behavior has an aggressive expression but is carried out in a passive
manner—late for appointments, "forgets" to do things for someone
he's angry at, meets anger with silence).

Sexual Deviations

What is or is not deviant sexual behavior is hotly debated and
disputed. The term *deviant* is itself a poor term, but we are stuck
with it for the moment, since it is the term currently employed in the
International Classification of Diseases (same as the *Diagnostic and
Statistical Manual* of the American Psychological Association,
1968).

Sexual practices are greatly influenced by social attitudes, and
consequently purely scientific evaluations of behavior are difficult
to arrive at. Homosexuality is a case in point. It is widely held that
homosexuality represents an identity problem based on a "wrong
turn" in development. But is the identification problem of the homosexual more limiting or damaging to overall functioning than other
identification problems or "wrong turns"? We really can't say for
sure because society has placed a stigma on the homosexual. The
stigma creates new problems, which in turn give rise to conflicts and
anxiety perhaps greater than the homosexuality itself. The homosexual, male or female, must conceal his or her sexual orientation for
fear of ridicule and rejection; he or she may lose a job or be denied
the choice of place to live if it becomes known. The recent changes in
attitude toward homosexuality indicate how uncertain and how
socially influenced we are concerning designations of deviancy. In
1973 the American Psychiatric Association removed homosexuality
from its list of mental disorders.

As the scientific study of human sexuality progresses, we come to
realize more and more that many behaviors previously considered
deviant are practiced by most people with no apparent damage to
themselves. The research of Kinsey et al. (1948, 1953) and Masters
and Johnson (1966) has brought the study of sexuality out of the
dark ages and into the modern world of open inquiry. These
researchers have found that masturbation, fetishism, variations in
position during sexual intercourse, role-playing, and oral sexual
behavior are common aspects of the sexual experience in our society.
The prevailing view today is that what is mutually agreed upon by a
couple, mutually satisfying, and without painful or destructive
consequences should not be considered disturbed or abnormal. The
designation of "disturbed" becomes more appropriate when compo-

nents of the sexual experience are ends in themselves, the exclusive mode of sexual pleasure, or when the individual is unable to experience pleasure in sexual intercourse.

Exhibitionism. Genital exposure is almost exclusively a male disturbance. Typically the man exhibits himself to women or children, in a public place such as a park, a street, or a train. The compulsion is often intense, and he may expose himself several times in a day. Surprisingly, exhibitionists are frequently married men who are unable to explain their behavior. They are also characteristically timid individuals who do not represent any physical danger to others.

Voyeurism. In voyeurism, the individual obtains his or her primary or only sexual gratification by looking at genitals or by watching others engaged in sexual activities. Looking is of course an important aspect of normal sexual relations, but for the voyeur it represents the major source of gratification.

Fetishism. Fetishism, like exhibitionism, is mainly a male disturbance. The fetishist obtains his primary or only sexual pleasure from some sexual object rather than from a partner. Common festishes are a woman's shoe, undergarments, and hair.

Sadism and Masochism. The sadist derives sexual pleasure from inflicting pain, either physical or psychological (e.g., by humiliating the partner). The masochist obtains sexual gratification by being physically or psychologically abused. Often it appears that both aspects are present in the same individual, and the disturbance is consequently called sadomasochism.

Homosexuality. Homosexuality is generally defined as the preference for sexual relations with one's own sex when there are partners available of the opposite sex. This definition excludes the behavior of those adults, such as prisoners, who engage in sexual relations with their own sex during periods when they have no access to the opposite sex. Also generally excluded from what is considered to be true homosexuality is the transient homosexual experimentation of young adolescents.

It is difficult to know how many individuals are homosexual, given the social stigma attached to homosexuality. The fact that an indeterminate number of individuals engage in both homosexual and heterosexual activities further complicates the matter. According to Kinsey (1948) 4% of white adult males remain exclusively homosexual after adolescence while 37% have at some time in their life overt homosexual experiences. For women Kinsey (1953) reported that less than 1% remained exclusively homosexual and 13% had overt homosexual contacts.

The origins of homosexuality are still incompletely understood. There are probably numerous paths to the development of a homosexual pattern, just as there are for other developmental outcomes. One of the possible origins is the situation in which a boy fears his father or a girl fears her mother to an extreme degree and therefore cannot identify with the parent of the same sex. Or a child may find the parent of the opposite sex so abhorrent that future relations with the opposite sex become too frightening.

wrong

It has also been proposed that hormonal or constitutional factors may play a role. Aside from the gross mislabeling of gender that occurs in rare instances because of anatomical defects at birth, however, there has been little solid evidence that constitution influences sexual object choice.

It is important again to note that homosexuality, although it may represent a problem for an individual or for society, is no longer considered a mental disorder. In the light of this altered view there are efforts to gain equal rights for homosexuals.

Addiction

Addiction is physiological dependence on a chemical agent. "Physiological dependence" means that a person suffers physical symptoms when the chemical substance is withdrawn. The symptoms are invariably distressing, for example the painful abdominal cramps experienced in opium withdrawal. Withdrawal may even have a fatal outcome, as withdrawal from alcohol sometimes does. There are as many addictions as there are addicting agents. Among the agents most commonly employed today are: alcohol, opium derivatives, barbiturates, and amphetamines. Other substances, such as the hallucinogen LSD, are not addicting but can have damaging effects.

Alcohol Addiction.   Addiction to alcohol is by far the commonest of the addictions. There are an estimated five million alcoholics in the United States. The effect of the addiction on the individuals and their families is enormous. The chronic alcoholic is frequently unable to hold a job, and as the need for alcohol is dominant, his behavior toward friends and relatives tends to become increasingly erratic and irresponsible.

Why do people become alcoholics? As in all the functional

disorders, there is no clear and simple answer. Alcohol depresses the higher cortical functions and thereby acts as a disinhibiter and tranquilizer. The anxiety-reducing effect is rapid and may be the main effect sought by the alcoholic. But many people suffer from severe anxiety and only certain individuals become addicted to alcohol. One factor is probably cultural. The Moslems, Jews, and Chinese, for instance, rarely become alcoholics, whereas alcoholism is relatively frequent among other groups. Alcoholism is also more common among men than among women.

Withdrawal from alcohol is usually accomplished through the use of barbiturates, given at first in a quantity equal to the extent of the addiction and then gradually reduced. The procedure prevents the potentially fatal withdrawal symptoms of delirium tremens from developing. Because alcohol also suppresses the appetite, alcoholics are subject to vitamin deficiencies and other forms of malnutrition. Cirrhosis of the liver, also potentially fatal, is a common sequel to chronic alcoholism.

Drug Addiction.   Drug-taking to some extent has become part of the youth culture. But it is not exclusively a youth activity, as evidenced by the widespread use by adults of tranquilizers, antidepressants, and other mood-altering substances. Drugs are initially taken for many reasons: fitting in with the gang, escape from a boring job or life situation, release from transient tensions (e.g. exams, a "tough" week on the job, etc.), and relief from vague anxieties and persistent psychological conflicts. For many, smoking pot or "popping" pills remains at the level of experimentation or an infrequent basis similar to social drinking; others maintain an habitual use of tranquilizers, sleeping pills, and other drugs but never go to the harder drugs such as heroin and cocaine.

Addiction cannot be assigned only to those substances that are physiologically addictive. Psychological addiction can be as great and as compelling as physiological addiction. For example, the person who runs out of sleeping pills may experience extreme reactions of panic and anxiety because of psychological dependence.

Addiction to the opium family of compounds—heroin, morphine, demerol—has reached epidemic proportions in recent years though there are signs that the epidemic is subsiding and that heroin addiction especially is losing favor. The morphine compounds produce a state of euphoria in susceptible individuals—hence their widespread abuse. Not everyone is susceptible; most individuals not in pain find that an injection of morphine produces an unpleasant giddiness and nausea. If one is in pain, the morphine relieves the pain as well as the apprehension that often accompanies it, but there is little in the way of a "high" unless one is susceptible. What determines who will react to the morphine compounds with euphoria is not known. However, repeated and prolonged use seems to make a euphoric response and addiction more likely, as is demonstrated in patients who initially receive morphine for pain relief. If the use is prolonged beyond the therapeutic requirements, the patients frequently become addicted.

While the heroin epidemic in the United States has been largely (though not exclusively) limited to the lower socioeconomic strata, the abuse of morphine and demerol is a major problem throughout the world at all socioeconomic levels. The availability of morphine to health professionals has resulted in physicians and nurses having the highest incidence of addiction to these drugs of any professional group.

There is no one personality type that can be identified with drug addiction. But it is recognized that addicts are emotionally immature people who cannot deal with the ordinary conflicts and frustrations of life and seek quick escape from stress.

Summary

The neuroses have anxiety as their primary symptom. The major types of neuroses are: (1) anxiety neurosis, (2) hysterical neurosis, (3) phobic neurosis, (4) obsessive compulsive neurosis, and (5) depressive neurosis. Anxiety neuroses have *diffuse* anxiety as the major symptom. Hysterical neuroses usually deal with the anxiety by a symbolic physical expression of the psychological conflict. The phobic neurosis focuses on some thing or situation that arouses inordinate fear. The obsessive compulsive neurosis calls forth repetitive thoughts and acts. Depressive neurosis shows an irrational depression.

The personality disorders are pervasive patterns or life styles with pronounced maladaptive features. Examples are obsessive-compulsive personality disorder, schizoid personality disorder, and the passive-aggressive personality disorder.

Sexual deviations take many forms. They are considered disturbances when primary sexual gratification is derived from other than heterosexual relations. Examples are fetishism, exhibitionism, voyeurism, and sadomasochism. Homosexuality, however, is no longer considered a mental disorder by the American Psychiatric Association.

Alcoholism and drug addiction are related illnesses. They

represent a state of physiological and psychological dependence on alcohol, barbiturates, morphine, amphetamine, or similar compounds. Addictions are very debilitating and costly both to the individual and society.

Suggested Readings

Cameron, N. *Personality development and psychopathology: a dynamic approach.* Boston: Houghton Mifflin, 1963.

Cleckley, H. *The mask of sanity.* 4th ed. St. Louis: C. V. Mosby, 1968.

Fenichel, O. *The psychoanalytic theory of neurosis.* New York: Norton, 1945.

The Ford Foundation. *Dealing with drug abuse.* New York: Praeger, 1972.

Goode, E. *Drugs in American society.* New York: Knopf, 1972.

Horney, K. *The neurotic personality of our time.* New York: Norton, 1937.

Kolb, L. C. *Modern clinical psychiatry.* 8th ed. Philadelphia: W. B. Saunders, 1973.

CHILDHOOD DISORDERS

Emotional disturbance at any age is a serious problem, but its impact is especially great in childhood. The reasons are readily apparent. Disturbance in childhood interferes with critical aspects of development in such a way that future personality growth is severely distorted. Consider, for instance, the damaging effects of a phobia. Phobias are common in children as well as in adults. If an adult develops a job phobia in which his fears of going to work keep him unemployed for two years, he will, to be sure, experience some difficulty in regaining his former level of competence once the phobia is overcome; his skills, however, will not have greatly diminished. On the other hand, a child with a school phobia who because of his fears remains home for two years will experience marked lags in social skills, even assuming that home tutoring has helped him to maintain his cognitive growth. It will be hard for the child to recoup his loss since the social skills he failed to acquire will now be more difficult to learn. Other children and adults have little patience for the disturbed child's lags.

Nonetheless, children are endowed with an amazing capacity "to make the best of it." Conditions that severely stress an adult, such as the tensions of wartime, are much more readily adapted to by children. As long as the basic necessities of food, shelter, and family stability are present, children do quite well.

As with adult disorders, the World Health Organization's categories of children's maladaptive development are based not on cause but on major presenting symptoms. We will discuss three primary divisions or categories of childhood psychopathology in this section: mental retardation, childhood schizophrenia, and behavior disorders. (Additional categories, such as childhood neuroses, do not differ sufficiently from adult disorders to warrant description in this overview.) It should be emphasized that these categories are only one of many attempts at classification. A well-thought-out alternative system of classification is that formulated by the Group for Advancement of Psychiatry and detailed in their monograph "Psychopathological Disorders in Childhood" (1966).

Mental Retardation

Mental retardation is below-normal intellectual functioning. The problem of what is normal intelligence and how it is measured is a difficult one that has already been discussed at length in Chapter 15. For practical purposes the clinician needs to indicate the level of functioning that the child or adult is capable of in order to maximize the individual's life satisfaction by tailoring expectations to capability. You will recall that the categories of intellectual functioning defined by the American Psychiatric Association (APA) and the World Health Organization (WHO) are, borderline mental retardation (68–85 I.Q.); mild mental retardation (52–67 I.Q.); moderate mental retardation (36–51 I.Q.); severe mental retardation (20–35 I.Q.); and profound mental retardation (under 20 I.Q.).

What do these levels mean as far as the child is concerned? To take one instance, it means that a child who is mildly mentally retarded will be able to reach approximately the fifth or sixth grade level of academic achievement, provided he has special educational and family assistance. It also means he has the ability to learn job skills that may provide a fair degree of self-support as well as social satisfaction and an independent existence. The moderately retarded child, however, cannot be expected to progress beyond second grade in academic skills. Social judgment and memory are similarly limited so that he will continue to require a good deal of supervision throughout his life. Through occupational training, semiskilled or unskilled work under supervision may provide some self-support.

We perhaps need to remind ourselves at this point that a child of 7 (second grade age) would have a wide range of potential gratifications and skills even if he did not progress beyond that level of development. Such is the situation of the 30-year-old who is moderately retarded. And just like the 7-year-old, he can also provide those around him with a great deal of gratification. Nonetheless, a young child's mind in an adult body presents serious social problems for the retarded person and his family. How well the child is able to acquire social skills (personal hygiene, control of sexual and aggressive impulses, etc.) is the crucial issue for the family's and the child's adjustment and fulfillment. Actually, the social skills are more important than level of vocational skill, although the two kinds of skills are interdependent.

Etiology. Numerous events may affect the developing brain and result in subnormal intelligence. Prenatal genetic abnormalities, as in the case of mongolism (related to the presence of an extra chromosome), can cause mental retardation. Congenital illnesses such as rubella and syphilis may also play a role. The fetus or infant can also be affected by nutritional deficiencies (e.g., vitamin B) and ingested poisons (e.g., lead). Acquired illness sometimes leads to retardation; for example, encephalitis often results in extensive brain damage. Then there are environmental deprivations of sensory, affectional, and social stimulation, which can produce functional retardation. In spite of the long list of detectable causes, perhaps as many as 75% of retarded children fall into the "unknown cause" category.

Research is constantly adding to our knowledge about mental retardation. Discoveries have even led to preventive therapeutic measures in cases where genetic or metabolic defects usually produce mental retardation. Phenylketonuria (PKU) is one such instance. PKU is a form of mental retardation caused by the lack of an enzyme for the conversion of phenylalanine. Infants are now tested soon after birth for abnormal amounts of phenylpyruvic acid in their urine. When detected, the condition is successfully treated with a special phenylalanine-free diet. In other cases nutritional treatment, immunization procedures, and new laws (e.g., outlawing lead in paints used for cribs and children's toys) are additional preventive measures. For the future, there is the prospect of correcting defects by actually inducing genetic changes in the fetus (called the science of *euphenics*).

Education. It is essential to keep in mind that retarded children *do learn* and *do develop intellectually*. The rate at which they learn is slowed and the ultimate level of reasoning they attain is limited. Also, there will be individual differences as to the areas of cognitive and intellectual functioning affected and the extent of damage to the brain. But to achieve their highest level of functioning the retarded must receive special learning and training experiences with a great deal of structure, support, and patience from the family and teachers.

Childhood Schizophrenia

Schizophrenic symptoms before puberty are fortunately infrequent. When they do occur, the prognosis is generally poor because the disturbance drastically interferes with developmental processes. The most devastating disturbances occur in the preschool years: childhood autism and symbiotic psychosis of childhood.

The autistic child is almost completely withdrawn into a world of his own and actively avoids contact with others. Such basic responses as making eye contact with other people are actively avoided. The *autistic child* will look everywhere but into the eyes of the person trying to get to know him. Frequently speech is absent, or it may be what is termed "noncommunicative." That is, the child speaks but does not address anyone but himself.

> Jeffrey's mother already felt he was different in the first few months of life. He was a "good baby," making few demands (he only cried when very hungry), but he did not smile and was not nearly as responsive as her first child. She herself had been quite depressed during the last months of her pregnancy because of marked marital conflict. She felt tired and at first welcomed the low level of demands placed on her by the new baby. But by the time he was 2 she knew something was wrong. He made no effort to be with his brother and did not seem to care if anyone were around or not. He was constantly in a world by himself. At times it even appeared that he could not hear because he would not respond to his name, but examination revealed that his hearing was normal. By the age of 3 he would sit for hours looking at a record spinning if he were permitted to do so. No speech developed. At the age of 8 he was placed in a custodial institution because his increasing physical strength made for serious management problems.

The *symbiotically psychotic* child is in some ways the opposite of the isolated, autistic child. The symbiotic child is so intensely attached to his mother that he cannot let go. He must be with her constantly and fails to develop the autonomy normal for a 3-year-old child. One such child at the age of 5 spoke almost entirely in the language of TV commercials. His communications, however, were only understandable to his mother who could interpret them quite accurately to others. Of course this form of communication limited his major interactions to his mother.

Schizophrenia in middle childhood comes closer to resembling the adult illness, although thought disorders are uncommon before puberty. It still remains a matter of controversy whether childhood psychosis is really a younger form of adult schizophrenia. The childhood and adult schizophrenias are probably similar only in some respects and do not truly represent a single disease. They are similar, however, in that both childhood and adult schizophrenia are severely disabling illnesses that affect both cognitive and emotional aspects of the individual's functioning.

Behavior Disorders

These disorders are the most frequently diagnosed psychiatric disturbances in child guidance clinics. They are considered less firmly established (and therefore more subject to change) as patterns of maladaptation than the neuroses, personality disorders, or psychoses. The behavior disorders are classified by the type of behavior that is distressing. Again we are classifying patients by major symptoms rather than on the more desirable basis of etiology, but that is the "state of the art." The term *reaction* that follows the symptom, as in "hyperkinetic reaction," implies that the symptoms are responses or reactions to unfavorable life situations.

Hyperkinetic Reaction. "Hyperkinetic" refers to more than normal movement. The hyperkinetic child is in almost continual movement. He gets up and sits down repeatedly, moves incessantly about the room, has difficulty keeping at a task, and is easily distracted from what he is doing. These symptoms make it especially difficult for the child to perform in school, even though his intelligence is not affected. If a child cannot sit still, it is hard for him to learn. This disorder is much more frequent in boys than girls. At times the hyperactivity is in response to anxiety generated by problems in the home, but often it appears to be due primarily to neurological immaturity since with age the hyperactivity tends to diminish. Medications are often beneficial and necessary since the child who is not able to keep up in school is handicapped both by his failure to learn and the inevitable development of low self-esteem.

Withdrawing Reaction. The child with this disorder is very shy and overly sensitive to what others say, and he avoids interpersonal relationships. The low self-image this child has developed springs from serious deficiencies in the parent-child relationship.

Overanxious Reaction. Excessive fearfulness characterizes this disorder. The child responds to new situations with inordinate anxiety and in daily life is inhibited in spontaneous expression and performance. The anxiety usually reflects fears of rejection for imagined inadequacies. Examination of the family relationships usually reveals the source of these fears.

Runaway Reaction.   These children repeatedly flee from home for one or more days at a time. The running away is a cry for help and assurance of being loved and wanted. The assurance is difficult to provide since the child is convinced of the rejection even when circumstances improve. Psychotherapy helps but only gradually does the child overcome his sense of not being cared for.

Unsocialized Aggressive Reaction.   This disorder is the single most common disturbance in child guidance clinics. It includes those children who are persistently fighting, destructive, and inappropriately hostile and disobedient. The reasons for the deviant aggressive behavior vary greatly, but regardless of etiology the consequences are usually serious. The aggressive behavior alienates the child from peers, frequently causes interruption in his schooling, and not infrequently develops into serious adult disturbances with chronic psychiatric disability.

Group Delinquent Reaction.   This disorder refers to the child who is antisocial in his behavior as a consequence of his participation in a deviant peer group. The children are often highly conforming but the conforming is to the group's antisocial norms, which are likely to include stealing, truancy, and drug use.

Summary

The three major categories of childhood disturbances that we have considered are mental retardation, childhood schizophrenia, and behavior disorders of childhood. Mental retardation is a condition of below-normal intellectual functioning. Although in the majority of cases the cause of the retardation is unknown, it is presumed to be due to physical maldevelopment of the brain. The retarded child is capable of learning and needs specialized educational opportunities to achieve optimal functioning.

Childhood schizophrenia is a very severe disorder. The younger the child when he first manifests psychotic behavior, the poorer the prognosis. Autistic children are isolated and almost completely in a world of their own. Symbiotic children relate only to their mothers and panic at any brief separation.

The most common childhood disturbances are the behavior disorders. These disorders are divided according to the major behavioral symptom the child displays: hyperactivity, anxiety, withdrawal, running away, aggression, or delinquency.

Suggested Readings

Gardener, R. A. *MBD: the family book about minimal brain dysfunction.* New York: Jason Aronson, 1973.

Goldfarb, W. *Childhood schizophrenia.* Cambridge: Harvard University Press, 1961.

Group for the Advancement of Psychiatry. *Psychopathological disorders in childhood: theoretical considerations and a proposed classification,* New York: Group for the Advancement of Psychiatry, 1966.

Redl, F. *The aggressive child.* New York: Free Press, 1957.

Love, H. D. *The mentally retarded child and his family.* Springfield, Ill.: Charles C. Thomas, 1973.

Thomas, A., Chess, S., and Birch, H. G. *Temperament and behavior disorders in children.* New York: New York University Press, 1969.

Wolman, B. B., ed. *Manual of child psychopathology.* New York: McGraw-Hill, 1973.

Chapter *17*

The Therapies

THE IMPETUS FOR the development of personality theories derives from two main sources: the need to understand how individuals become what they are, and the need to help persons who have psychological problems. In response to the second need, a wide range of treatments for alleviating psychological distress has been developed. Some of these techniques spring directly from the theories we have discussed. Others have evolved on an empirical basis, that is, rather than stemming from theory they have been the result of trial and error or fortuitous clinical observation. An example of the latter is the revolutionary impact of the observation that a medication (chlorpromazine) used as a postoperative anti-emetic was an effective tranquilizer. Chlorpromazine has been the chief means of advancing the treatment of schizophrenia since Pinel unshackled the mentally ill.

There are two categories of therapies: the *organic therapies* and the *psychotherapies*. The organic therapies are treatment modalities employing physical agents that act on the brain (often in an unknown manner) to alleviate the distress. The major organic therapies are phramacotherapy, electroconvulsive therapy, insulin coma therapy, and psychosurgery. Today, pharmacotherapeutic agents such as the minor tranquilizers are prescribed routinely by physicians, even in cases of mild anxiety. Most psychiatrists are opposed to the use of electroconvulsive therapy, insulin coma therapy, and psychosurgery except as last resorts. The psychotherapies—treatment modalities that employ psychological means to alleviate emotional disturbance—are even more varied than the organic therapies and more difficult to classify. One way to group the psychotherapies is by the context of treatment. Thus there are individual, group, family, and milieu psychotherapies. Treatments can also be classified by their aim, yielding the distinction between depth and supportive therapy. Another means of classifications is by the theoretical or treatment approach employed by the therapist: psychoanalysis, primal therapy, behavior therapy, and so on. Thus two individuals entering into two different group therapy situations may be experiencing very different types of treatment.

ORGANIC THERAPIES

Pharmacotherapy. There are currently three major functional categories of medications: tranquilizers, antidepressants, and antimanic agents. The tranquilizers are the largest group of medications employed for the relief of psychological stress. They range from very mild tranquilizers such as meprobamate, used for the relief of minor anxiety, to the major tranquilizers such as chlorpromazine, employed where anxiety is chronic and intense as in psychotic states. The antidepressants (e.g., imipramine, amitryptyline) are used for the relief of depression. There is only one antimanic agent, lithium, in general use for the treatment of mania.

Electroconvulsive Therapy (ECT). ECT is employed today primarily with the severely (psychotically) depressed individual. In such cases, it remains the most effective means of alleviating the symptoms, although the physician will usually try first to achieve results by using antidepressant medications. The mechanism of ECT remains a mystery. The method consists of sending an electric current of carefully controlled amount and duration into the brain by means of electrodes placed against the head. The current induces a convulsion,—thus the name, electroconvulsive therapy. Just prior to the administration of the electric current, the patient is rendered unconscious by intravenous medication so that he experiences no pain during the procedure.

Insulin Coma Therapy.   Although infrequently used today in the era of tranquilizers, severely disturbed patients are still occasionally treated by insulin coma therapy. The therapy consists of inducing a comatose state by injecting insulin in carefully monitored amounts. The procedure is costly because highly trained personnel must continually be present during the several hours the patient may be maintained in the coma.

Psychosurgery.   In the chronically and severely disturbed patient, neurosurgery has been used with some success. Cutting certain connections to the frontal lobe of the brain—prefrontal lobotomy—decreases in some patients the marked agitation and discomfort that may be constantly present, and may make their lives less tortured than before. However, it also decreases their ability to judge the social needs of a situation and therefore makes continued supervision necessary.

PSYCHOTHERAPIES

As professionals who are serving more and more as therapists, nurses need to be familiar with the various psychotherapies in use today. Nurses are frequently called upon to make referrals or recommendations about psychotherapy or counseling. In such instances, consultation with other professionals is desirable, but it is helpful for the nurse to have her own reservoir of accurate information about psychotherapy. After outlining the general characteristics of the psychotherapies, we will present descriptions of specific psychotherapeutic techniques. The techniques already treated in Part II (e.g., psychoanalysis and behaviorism) will only be reviewed briefly here.

Psychotherapy is a generic term that applies to all the psychological treatments of behavior and mental problems. Because psychotherapy includes so many diverse methods and theories, it is not easy to come up with a single meaningful definition. However, we can characterize the overall aim of the different psychotherapies: *all psychotherapies strive to change aspects of the person through verbal, affective, or interactional means.* There is some dispute, as we have already seen in Part II on theories of development, as to whether the desired change pertains to overt behavior or to internalized structures such as cognitions, beliefs, feelings, or other personality variables. Also in dispute is whether the aim is to change parts of behavior or the person as a whole. Nevertheless, some form of change, regardless of how the psychology of the person is conceptualized by a given theory, is the common definitional property of all psychotherapies. Aside from a commitment to the possibility for growth and change, there are other features common to the various psychotherapies. Since practitioners of all the psychotherapies report success, the therapeutic effects may be accounted for by any number of these shared characteristics: acceptance of the patient, concern for the individual, availability of the therapist, regularity of treatment sessions, and confidentiality of the therapeutic relationship.

General Types of Psychotherapy

Individual Psychotherapy. As the term suggests, this type of therapy is directed toward one person. Most often it will involve a one-to-one relationship between therapist and patient. The fact that a therapy is individual does not tell you which school of psychotherapy it is based on. Individual psychotherapy is performed by many different schools including those of psychoanalysis, Gestalt therapy, behavior therapy, Adlerian therapy, primal therapy, and others.

Group Therapy. The essence of group therapy is that an expert leads a group of people who wish to achieve some beneficial changes for themselves. Types of groups are as numerous as their goals. For instance, a didactic group may seek to effect better child-rearing patterns in a group of parents primarily by teaching and discussion. A religious group may seek to help some of its members abstain from alcohol. A psychoanalytic group may seek insight into members' anxieties or problems as a means of effecting changes in their lives. A group dynamics group may seek to help the individual members become aware of how they interact with others, and use the group as a means to change patterns of interaction. For any of these groups to reach its goal it is essential that the leader be truly expert in the method by which the group goals are attained.

Family Therapy. In family therapy, the goal is to help individuals through changes in the family process. Especially in the case of children and adolescents, it is difficult if not impossible to achieve

significant changes in the individual if the disturbed family relationships that created the psychopathology persist. Through family
therapy sessions the family's faulty interactions can be observed and
alternate modes of interacting can be tried out.

One of the difficulties of family therapy is in getting all members
to participate. Often the "identified patient" is a child who is brought
to the therapist by a parent. When the therapist attempts to bring the
parent and other siblings as well as the child into the therapeutic
process, there may be strong resistance. Some parents just want the
therapist to "fix up" the child and are unwilling or unable to see the
disturbed family process or their own contribution to the child's
difficulties. Great skill on the part of the therapist is necessary to
overcome the many resistances and abrasive interactions that this
form of therapy arouses.

As in other forms of therapy, family therapy techniques vary in
method and aims according to the treatment orientation of the
therapist. Consequently the therapist's role may range from very
passive to actively directing and drawing the family members out.
The goal can be immediate relief from a single pressing problem or
an extensive revision of the family process.

Milieu Therapy. This approach to therapy employs the social
system of the hospital ward to strengthen coping mechanisms and
correct impaired functioning. Milieu therapy is based on the concept
that many symptoms of the psychologically disturbed individual are
a consequence of faulty social learning, and that the learning of new
modes of social interaction will make possible more effective
functioning and a reduction in anxiety. To facilitate new social
learning, the milieu (i.e., the environment of the psychiatric unit) is
structured to encourage the expression of latent capacities and the
restitution of areas of previously adequate functioning. To achieve
these goals, several practices are commonly employed. Daily
"community" meetings are held on the ward to promote clarity of
communication between staff and patients. Patients participate in
the administration of the ward, often by means of a formal patient
government. And group therapy sessions emphasize the impact of
each person's behavior on others in the social system of the ward.
Milieu therapy is also practiced on an outpatient basis in day
hospitals and clinics; patients spend the day in the therapeutic milieu
but return home for evenings and weekends.

Depth versus Supportive Therapy. In some instances the goal of
therapy or counseling is not to solve the deep, long-standing

problems of the patient but to help him restore or maintain his usual level of adjustment or to strengthen existing positive features of personality. In giving support to a patient, the therapist provides sympathetic understanding, listening, reassurance, encouragement, and empathy. Depth therapy might also include supportive measures but it strives additionally to break through the patient's defenses to achieve insight or behavioral change, i.e., there is an effort to alter the usual neurotic pattern of the patient. Supportive therapy is appropriate for short-term contacts (such as in brief hospitalization), acute stress, and crisis situations. Patients in acute states of emotional reaction are unable to profit from depth therapy until some equilibrium has been restored. Also, in cases of extreme psychopathology (e.g., psychosis), depth therapy may be too threatening to the patient's poor adjustment mechanisms. The specific techniques of supportive and depth treatment will vary depending on the theoretical framework within which they are practiced.

Specific Psychotherapies

Psychoanalysis. The treatment called psychoanalysis is a highly specialized method related to the theories of Sigmund Freud. Freud wrote a number of technique papers describing the requirements of psychoanalytic treatment. These prescriptions include five to six visits per week, free association, relative passivity of the therapist, dream interpretations, tracing present behavior back to past traumas, and analysis of the relationship between the patient and therapist (transference) to clarify earlier conflicts in development. According to psychoanalysts, behavior change takes place when the patient has insight into the unconscious origins of his conflicts. Insight then frees the patient to use his drives and impulses positively. Insight is gained primarily through the analysis of the transference neurosis, in which the patient transfers on to the analyst all of the neurotic conflicts deriving from childhood experiences. In working through the transference neurosis in the analytic situation the patient is able to reintegrate his personality.

Very few analysts today follow the strict dicta of Freud. The pace of modern life makes classical psychoanalysis impractical in most instances. Few patients can afford five or six sessions per week, and the demands of modern life require more immediate release from inhibiting symptoms than would be the case in the usual course of classical psychoanalysis. Most psychoanalysts, therefore, do what is called psychoanalytically oriented psychotherapy. The basic technique of uncovering unconscious conficts is retained, but the therapist is more directive and active in helping the patient with immediate and practical problems as well. In Chapter 9 we have described some of the applications of psychoanalytic concepts to nursing situations.

Behavior Therapy. In behavior therapy (also called behavior modification) the focus is on directly changing those behaviors that the patient reports to be problematic. Behavior therapists believe that maladaptive behavior is maintained by environmental conditions that reinforce them, and they reject notions of internal conflict or unconscious processes as the root causes of maladaptive behavior. The task of therapy is to change behavior using a variety of techniques of which reinforcement and conditioning are the most prominent. In Chapter 10 some specialized techniques of behavior therapy were described in detail. Behavior therapy has been shown to be successful in the treatment of many symptomatic problems including fears, phobias, impotence, and frigidity.

Rational Emotive Therapy (RET). This technique was introduced by Albert Ellis, who is not a behavior therapist but who nevertheless uses techniques that are closely related to behavior therapy. In Rational Emotive Therapy the aim is to clarify for the person his implicit attitudes, cognitions, and guiding assumptions, which presumably cause him pain and conflict. For example, to the Rational Emotive Therapist, a person's sensitivity to rejection may be based on an implicit assumption that he needs to be liked by everyone or that he is a worthless person if he is not liked by everyone. In clarifying the implicit assumptions, the RET therapist then helps the patient to construct more rational beliefs and notions about himself which eliminate the need to feel guilty, anxious, or frightened in life situations. Since RET works directly on changing aspects of behavior, although behavior in this instance is defined as cognitions, there is a link with behavior modification approaches. Many behavior modification specialists are currently using RET in conjunction with their own techniques.

Gestalt Therapy. Gestalt therapy is primarily associated with the work of Frederick Perls. The term *gestalt* derives from gestalt psychology, which emphasizes the wholeness and unified nature of experiences. Gestalt psychology is opposed to analyzing experiences into fragmented parts; meaning is derived from wholeness ("the whole is greater than the sum of the parts"). In gestalt therapy the focus is on awareness of the total "nowness" of the person's existence: past does not exist anymore and the future is not yet, so that it is the here-and-now experiences that must be scrutinized and clarified. Even dreams and childhood events and memories are looked at in their present manifestations and impact. The therapist in gestalt therapy serves as a projective screen upon which the patient can discover and then re-own the covered-up and lost parts of himself. Perls states that "awareness per se—by and of itself—can be curative." In becoming oneself rather than the sum of expectations of parents or others, the patient is able to utilize his potential for self-actualization. Gestalt therapy is practiced in both individual and group settings.

Encounter and Sensitivity Therapy. The aim of encounter and sensitivity therapy is to get people in closer touch with their own feelings and to help them gain greater awareness of others. The methods are generally practiced in a group setting. The group is a loose, nonstructured format that allows the participants to be themselves and to let their real selves emerge. While not directing the group toward any particular topic, the group leader will encourage the expression and experience of feelings. A variety of exercises may be used to heighten awareness. These exercises may include touching other people, embracing, expressing feelings (both positive and negative) honestly to others in the group, and revealing fears and anxieties. In encounter sessions with married couples, the husband and wife may confront and explore each other's deepest feelings for the first time. Sensitivity and encounter techniques have also been employed in industry and other settings to improve human relations by helping people deal with hidden feelings that hamper productive work and meaningful interaction. Encounter and sensitivity sessions are usually lengthy so that the participants have enough time to get to know each other and "let go." Sessions can run for a few hours or a few days.

Primal Therapy. Primal therapy, a recent innovation of Arthur Janov, proposes that all neurotic behaviors are symbolic reactions to the accumulated repressed pains of childhood experiences. To uproot neurosis Janov believes that the defenses must be "blasted open" so that the patient can reconnect with his cut-off feelings and thereby become a "real" and "whole" person again. Through specialized techniques the primal therapist regresses the patient back to childhood for a total psycho-physical reliving of feelings of abandonment, loneliness, fear, rejection, and other affective states. Since many psychological pains occur before the child acquires language skills, primals (the reliving of states of deep feeling) often involve crying, screaming, moaning, as well as other reactions associated with infancy. According to Janov, as the "pool of pain" is drained through primals, the patient can begin to reconstruct his life in a healthy direction. In Janov's method, the patient spends an initial three-week period isolated from family, friends, and work (usually in a hotel). During this period there are daily individual sessions that extend for a number of hours, depending on the patient's need. After the "three-week intensive" the patient returns to normal activities and continues the therapy in a group that meets one to five times per week. Other therapists using the primal methods do not insist on the three-week period of isolation and prefer to integrate treatment with ongoing life activities.

Transactional Analysis. The thrust of transactional analysis is for the therapist to point out continuously the Child and Parent aspect of the patient's interpersonal transactions. (See the discussion of transactional theory in Chapter 12.) Understanding carry-over transactions to the present, which embody the Child and Parent, is not enough. The therapist must constantly work with the Adult part of the patient to encourage him to engage in new transactions that can promote an "OK feeling." The more the patient sees the success of his OK transactions, the stronger the Adult becomes while the Parent and Child selves recede. Transactional analysis is practiced in both individual and group settings.

The Child and Adult aspects of the person can be seen in the transactional games that people play. In all of these games there is a characteristic dishonesty and destructiveness. Harris (1969, p. 120) gives a good example of the transactional game "Why Don't You, Yes, But." In this game the player opens with a complaint such as, "I am so plain and dull that I never have any dates." The friend counters with, "Why don't you go to a good beauty salon and get a different hairdo?" The player responds with, "Yes, but that costs too much money." The interaction goes on with each repeated constructive suggestion made by the friend countered with "Yes, but." In this instance the player maintains the "Not OK" image that is deeply ingrained in her. The game has the secondary advantage of getting her the attention and concern of a friend while the "Not OK" image is sustained.

"Want Out" is a game of particular interest to health professionals since it is frequently played in hospital settings. In this game the Parent and Adult do what is necessary to get out, but at the critical moment the Child will sabotage gains, making release impossible. "How Do You Get Out of Here" is another game related to "Want Out." Here the patient learns all the rules for getting out and complies with them to the fullest. It is frequently played by hospitalized psychiatric patients who, in many instances, are seriously ill and should not be released. "I'm Only Trying To Help You" is a game commonly practiced by health professionals. The underlying destructiveness of the game is in the aim of personal martyrdom at the expense of the patient, who is cast as ungrateful and disappointing.

In "Now I've Got You, You Son of a Bitch," the player takes every opportunity to seize upon faults or mistakes of another person. In health-care situations the game can be played by either client or professional. Sometimes the player sets up the situation in order to take the gleeful position, "Now I've Got You, You Son of a Bitch."

SUMMARY

There are two categories of therapies, the organic therapies and the psychotherapies. The organic therapies use physical agents while the psychotherapies use verbal, affective/and/or social interaction. The organic therapies include pharmacotherapy, electroconvulsive therapy, insulin therapy, and psychosurgery. The general types of psychotherapy are individual, group, family, and milieu. In terms of its goal, therapy can be supportive (helping to restore stability and strengthening existing structures), or depth (changing basic personality structures). For short-term contacts, severe stress reactions and extreme psychopathology supportive therapy is usually employed. Seven specific psychotherapies were described to illustrate the variety of approaches: psychoanalysis, behavior therapy, rational emotive therapy, gestalt therapy, sensitivity and encounter therapy, primal therapy, and transactional analysis.

SUGGESTED READINGS

Harris, T. A. *I'm OK—you're OK*. New York: Harper & Row, 1969.

Hayworth, M. R. *Child psychotherapy*. New York: Basic Books, 1964.

Janov, A. *The primal scream*. New York: Dell, 1970.

Menninger, K. *Theory of psychoanalytic technique*. New York: Harper & Row, 1964.

Perls, F. S. *Gestalt therapy verbatim*. New York: Bantam, 1971.

Small, L. *The briefer psychotherapies*. New York: Brunner/Mazel, 1971.

Wolberg, L. R. *Technique of psychotherapy (2 vols.).* New York: Grune and Stratton, 1967.

Wolpe, J. *The practice of behavior therapy.* New York: Pergamon Press, 1973.

Chapter  18

The Effect of Medications
on Mental States and Behavior

MEDICATIONS RARELY have one single effect on patients. Among the multiple effects usually only one, or at most two, are useful ones that are designated the therapeutic or main effects. Other effects, those which do not have therapeutic value, are by definition side effects. We do not focus on side effects unless they are damaging, painful, or life-threatening. The suppression of white cell production caused by the use of chloramphenicol is an example of a dangerous and sometimes lethal side effect. Among the most serious and common side effects of medications are psychological changes, which can influence the patient's willingness and ability to participate in rehabilitation. Here is one example.

Mrs. R. had a successful kidney transplant operation, with complete restoration of normal kidney function. She was maintained on the usual fairly high dose of prednisone (a cortisone derivative) to suppress the body's immune response and thereby prevent rejection of the transplanted kidney. After two days of necessarily high doses of prednisone, the patient became increasingly irritable and uncooperative. She felt the doctors were intentionally hurting her and that no one understood her. She panicked when she saw a cat at the foot of her bed. (She had enough ability to test reality to know that she was then hallucinating). Restraints were required to prevent her removing the IV and the urethral catheter. As the dosage of prednisone was decreased, there was a marked lessening of her delusional thinking and agitation, but she remained suspicious and just marginally cooperative. Even though the kidney functioned well, Mrs. R. never recovered the sense of competence and ability to cope that had characterized her behavior before she needed to take the high doses of prednisone. Her failure to cooperate proved fatal some six months later when, after refusing to return for follow-up examinations, she developed pneumonitis and died.

Cortisone and its derivatives are among the "wonder drugs" that make modern medicine what it is. Although cortisone is considered indispensable in the treatment of many serious illnesses, it usually has psychological effects that influence the patient's ability to get well. Small doses often produce an initial unrealistic euphoria and hypomanic behavior. High doses, even in stable individuals, can result in severe disturbances in patients' thinking and emotional states. Delusions of persecution and hallucinations are relatively common. These side-effects must be treated early or effective patient care may become almost impossible.

Perhaps nowhere else is the nurse's role as diagnostician more acutely in demand than in detecting the psychological side effects of medications. This task requires astute and continuous observation of the subtle personality and mood changes that may be related to the introduction of a medication, a change of dosage, or the rhythmic changes associated with the time of receiving a medication and its peak absorption. Sometimes, when we listen carefully, we will hear patients describe the onset of symptoms that occurred concomitantly with the administration of a particular drug. Usually, however, patients' complaints are not clearly time-related. It is only when we think of the medication as a possible source of complaints that we can help the patient delimit the time of onset of their uneasiness, sense of apprehension, confusion, or irritability. Most useful is the nurse's observation that such personality changes have taken place within the course of treatment. We are all, unfortunately, too quick to ascribe behavioral changes to the presumed personal deficiencies of the patient, rather than exercise diagnostic acumen and search for other possible sources of the patient's distress.

Mechanism of Action. How medications induce psychological changes is not fully known, but for some medications theories of action have been put forth. For example, phenothiazines supposedly produce their tranquilizing effect by depressing the responsiveness of the reticular activating system, a network of nerves in the brain stem thought to be responsible for the level of wakefulness of the higher levels of the brain. It should be noted, however, that almost all the psychological effects of medications, whether therapeutic or side effects, are empirical findings. That is to say, the effects are known but the mechanism on which their action is based remains unclear.

Individual Differences. The psychological effects of medications vary greatly with the constitutional and emotional makeup of the patient. These differences in response to drugs are so marked that it is usually not possible to predict which side effect will appear with a given dosage in any one patient. This can be seen in the case of morphine, which produces a mild euphoria and dulling of pain sensation in most patients, while others react with nausea, vomiting, and no euphoria. The bases for such differences are not known and can only be ascertained by trial and error. Individual differences complicate the nurse's job of relating medications to affect and behavioral changes in patients.

Differences in drug response that are due to age are somewhat more predictable. Many medications produce a reaction in children opposite to that experienced by most adults. For example, amphetamines stimulate most adults and result in an increase in activity level, while children are usually made calmer. In fact, amphetamines are even used to treat hyperactivity in some children. Similarly, barbiturates tend to excite children and are therefore usually avoided except when absolutely necessary (as in the treatment of epilepsy), while they are among the most common sedatives used for adults. Many medications also cause different psychological states among the elderly. Sedatives and tranquilizers, especially, frequently induce a state of confusion and agitated excitement in the elderly, thus producing an effect opposite to the desired one. Then there is the suggestible patient or placebo responder who develops symptoms he anticipates will occur. For such patients, countersuggestion is often helpful, e.g., the suggestion that the symptoms will last only a short time.

Indirect Effects. Sometimes a psychological change occurring in connection with the administration of a medication is not due to the medication per se but rather to the patient's reaction to certain physical changes induced by the particular drug. A medication that slows down the reactions and pace of a person accustomed to a high level of activity can produce depression and anxiety; in such a case it is not the medication that causes the emotional response but the patient's inability to alter his style of living. The same reaction can occur in the slower-moving reflective person whose activity level is increased by a medication. Such patients may react with distress because of their inherent need to "pull back" and contain themselves. Any medication that interferes with sexual responsiveness can also result in indirect psychological effects because of the fear of impotence or frigidity. Counseling patients to expect certain changes can go a long way in reducing the impact of these indirect psychological effects.

Drug Interaction. Some medications that do not yield noticeable psychological side effects when taken alone do have marked effects when given in combination with other drugs. When we consider the variety of medications given to patients and the variations in dosage, we must realize the large number of possible combinations. It is no wonder that drug interactions are relatively incompletely accounted for. Most warnings about combination effects relate to the simultaneous administration of two medications. Yet many patients receive more than two medications simultaneously. While some specific drug interactions are known, there are many individual differences of response. One common interaction is that of the sedatives and the tranquilizers with alcohol. These drugs potentiate each other, sometimes leading to confusion, stupor, coma, and even death. Since there are so many unknowns in this area, it is important for the nurse to be alert to the possibility of interaction effects and to keep abreast of the new findings continuously emerging.

TABLE OF PSYCHOLOGICAL SIDE EFFECTS

In Table 18.1, on pages 370-381, some of the most commonly prescribed medications are listed, with indications of the possible psychological side effects. No such table can include all of the medications that might be encountered, but those most commonly used are listed. Awareness of the effects of medications representative of certain groups will alert the nurse to the types of personality changes that are most likely to occur.

SUGGESTED READINGS

Falconer, M. W., Norman, M. R., Patterson, H. A., and Gustafson, E. A. *The drug, the nurse, the patient.* Philadelphia: W. B. Saunders, 1966.

Garb, S., Grim, B. J., and Thomas, G. *Pharmacology and patient care.* 3rd ed. New York: Springer, 1970.

Walker, S. *Psychiatric signs and symptoms due to medical problems.* Springfield, Ill., Charles C Thomas, 1967.

Table 18.1 **Psychological Side Effects of Medication**

Official Name	Trade Names	Therapeutic Uses
Amitriptyline	Elavil, Etrafon, Triavil	Treatment of depression
Amphetamines	Benzedrine	Powerful central nervous system stimulant, used to stimulate respiration, increase peristalsis, decrease appetite (in treatment of obesity), and alleviate mild depression. It is also used to reduce hyperactivity in children
Amyl nitrate	amyl nitrate Aspirols, Vaporole	Vasodilatation, especially in coronary artery disease
Aspirin		Pain relief, fever reduction; treatment of rheumatic fever and rheumatoid arthritis
Barbiturates		Sedation and sleep induction; suppression of convulsions in treatment of epilepsy
barbital	Veronal	
phenobarbital	Luminal	
amobarbital	Amytal	
pentobarbital	Nembutal	
secobarbital	Seconal	

Psychological Side Effects

Jitteriness and appetite loss; as depression lifts, excitement and hypomania may occur; at high doses, temporary confusion and disturbed concentration may be evidenced; rarely, hallucinations and psychosis may occur

Restlessness, insomnia, and irritability are very common; at high doses and after prolonged use, psychotic states are not infrequent with the patient experiencing feelings of persecution, delusion, and, occasionally, hallucinations. In children, similar symptoms may occur but they are much less frequent. In adults, drug dependence is a common danger because of the drug's euphoric effects

Mental confusion

Sense of apathy

Confusion, failure of recent memory, depression and feelings of depression; especially in the elderly, excitement and agitation are fairly frequent (effects opposite to the therapeutic goal of sedation are found even with increased doses). Barbiturates are addictive and their abrupt withdrawal in addicted individuals may lead to delirium tremens with its accompanying confusion and hallucinations

Table 18.1—continued

Official Name	Trade Names	Therapeutic Uses
Bromides	Neurosine, Bromo-Seltzer	Sedation; and, now rarely, treatment of convulsions (epilepsy)
Caffeine	Present in Cafergot, APC, Empirin Compound, Excedrin, etc.	Cerebral stimulant used in treatment of narcotic poisoning, sedative overdose, and radiation sickness
Chloral hydrate	Noctec, Kessordrate	Sedation
Chlordiazepoxide	Librium, Librax, Menrium	Reduction of anxiety, muscle relaxation, and sedation
Chlorpheniramine	Allerest, Teldrin, Chlor-Trimeton	Antihistamine for allergic conditions
Chlorphenteramine	Pre-Sate	Appetite suppression in treatment of obesity
Cocaine and related compounds		Topical, local, and/or regional anesthesia
Dibucaine	Nupercaine	
Lidocaine	Xylocaine	
Procaine	Novocain	
Tetracaine	Pontocaine	

Psychological Side Effects

Irritability, confusion, depression, and sexual impotence; the disturbance may reach psychotic proportions with delusions and hallucinations occurring

Nervousness, restlessness, and insomnia almost always occur

Confusion and, in the elderly, agitation and excitement; in high doses delirium and paranoid delusions may occur

Drowsiness, confusion, and excitation

Drowsiness and, rarely, confusion

Nervousness, irritability, and insomnia

Drowsiness, nervousness, excitement, and a feeling of apprehension (all except the drowsiness are attributable to the epinephrine usually added to the medication)

Table 18.1—continued

Official Name	Trade Names	Therapeutic Uses
Cortisone and derivatives	Cortone, Cortogen	Suppresses the immune reaction of the body and inhibits the inflammatory process. As such it is used for treatment of numerous severe allergic conditions and autoimmune diseases, rheumatoid arthritis, lupus erythematosis, and bronchial asthma; it is also used following organ transplant operations
Hydrocortisone	Cortef, Cortril, Hydrocortone	
Prednisone	Deltra, Deltasone, Meticorten	
Prednisolone	Delta-Cortef, Hydeltra, Meticortelone	
Dexamethasone	Decadron, Deronil, Gammacorten	
Cycloserine	Seromycin	Treatment of tuberculosis
Diazepam	Valium	Relief of anxiety; muscle relaxant
Diphenhydramine	Benadryl	Antihistamine used for treating allergies and as a mild sedative
Diphenylhydantoin	Dilantin	Treatment of epilepsy
Ephedrine	Amesec, Bronkotabs, Tedral, Isuprel	Treatment of hypotension, bronchial asthma, and other allergies
Epinephrine	Asmolin	Treatment of allergic conditions such as bronchial asthma, urticaria, and angioneurotic edema

Psychological Side Effects

An initial euphoria with nervousness and irritability is common; depression (which may be profound), feelings of persecution, and vivid hallucinations are fairly frequent at prolonged high doses

Confusion

Decreased mental alertness; confusion and depression.Paradoxical reactions have occurred with symptoms of excitement, anxiety, insomnia, hallucinations, and rage. Psychological and physical dependence may occur with barbiturate-type withdrawal symptoms, i.e., convulsions and delirium

Drowsiness, confusion, nervousness, restlessness, and insomnia

Insomnia, irritability, and nervousness

Irritability, anxiety, and insomnia

Tremors, sense of anxiety, and apprehension (may be intense); restlessness, insomnia, and feeling of weakness

Table 18.1—continued

Official Name	Trade Names	Therapeutic Uses
Imipramine	Tofranil	Antidepressant; treatment of refractory enuresis in children
Indomethacin	Indocin	Treatment of rheumatic fever and arthritis
Insulin	Iletin	Treatment of diabetes mellitus
Isocarboxazid	Marplan	Antidepressant
Isoproterenol	Isuprel Norisodrine	Treatment of bronchial asthma
Levodopa		Treatment of Parkinson's disease
Meperidine group	Demerol, Mepergan	Pain relief
Methadone	Dolophine	Pain relief; replacement for heroin in the treatment of addiction
Methamphetamine	Amphedroxyn, Desoxyn, Methedrine	Appetite suppression in the treatment of obesity; relief of mild depression
Methyldopa	Aldomet	Reduction of blood pressure in hypertension

Nervousness, restlessness, and agitation; occasionally a confusional state with hallucinations and disorientation, particularly in older age groups and at higher dosage

Feelings of detachment and unreality may develop

Symptoms secondary to hypoglycemia: fatigue, tremulousness, anxiety. If hypoglycemia is severe, delirium will develop before the eventual stupor and unconsciousness of insulin shock

Insomnia, restless agitation, mania, confusion, memory impairment, and transient impotence may occur

Nervousness, tremor, restlessness, and insomnia

Addiction and physiological dependence

Mild euphoria; addiction

Restlessness, insomnia, and irritability are common; with high doses delusions and occasionally hallucinations occur. Highly addictive

Initially, sedation; anxiety, apprehension, and depression may occur

Table 18.1—continued

Official Name	Trade Names	Therapeutic Uses
Methylphenidate	Ritalin	Treatment of hyperactivity in *children;* appetite suppression in treatment of obesity; cerebral stimulation
Nitrous oxide		General anesthesia
Norepinephrine		Treatment of acute hypotension
Phenelzine	Nardil	Antidepressant
Opiates		Relief of acute, severe pain; suppression of cough reflex in various compounds including proprietary cough medicines; also used for inducing sleep and reduction of peristalsis (in diarrhea)
Morphine		
Codeine		
Dihydromorphine	Dilaudid	
Paregoric		
Phenmetrazine	Preludin	Appetite reduction in treatment of obesity; euphoriant
Phenacemide	Phenurone	Anticonvulsant for treatment of epilepsy
Phenothiazines		Reduction of severe anxiety, agitation, and aggressiveness in serious psychological disturbances; also used as antiemetic, cough suppressant, and potentiator of anesthetics
Promazine	Sparine	
Chlorpromazine	Thorazine	
Fluphenazine	Permitil, Prolixin	
Perphenazine	Trilafon	
Pnochlorperazine	Compazine	
Trifluoperazine	Stelazine	
Thioridazine	Mellaril	

Psychological Side Effects

May induce drowsiness; more commonly results in restlessness, nervousness, palpitations, and insomnia; may result in delusions and, rarely, hallucinations

Mental confusion and hallucinations may occur

Tremors and a nervous apprehension frequently occur

Drowsiness in some; a more common side-effect is euphoria, which may increase to agitation and mania; impotence may also occur

Initial effect is euphoria and a sense of physical ease; in overdose stupor will occur; highly addictive

Insomnia, overactivity, restlessness, and in high doses hallucinations and delusions

Marked personality changes, including depression and suicidal and aggressive behavior of psychotic proportions, may occur

Drowsiness, confusion, and transient diminished sexual potency. In some patients phenothiazines may paradoxically cause agitation and worsening of psychotic symptoms

Table 18.1—continued

Official Name	Trade Names	Therapeutic Uses
Progesterone	C-Quens, Enovid, Ortho-Novum, Cyclogesterin	Contraception, treatment of endometritis, hypermenorrhea, and amenorrhea
Quinine	Quinamm	Treatment of malaria
Reserpine	Raudixin, Serpasil	Reduction of high blood pressure; relief of anxiety
Streptomycin	Wycillin	Antibiotic
Sulfonamides	Gantrisin, Azulfidine	Antiinfective agent
Sulfones		Treatment of leprosy
Thiopental	Pentothal	General anesthesia
Thyroid	Android, Thyrar, Proloid	Treatment of thyroid deficiency

Psychological Side Effects

Headache, nervousness, dizziness, and, occasionally, depression

Sense of fullness in the head

Relatively frequent depression, which may be severe

Depression, especially during prolonged administration as in tuberculosis

Depression

Mental confusion

Confusion and agitation

Excessive nervousness, agitation, and feelings of persecution

Chapter *19*

Epilogue:
Research Methods and Statistics

THE FINAL CHAPTER of this book treats research methods and statistics as they apply to health care. A note of explanation is necessary, since it is unusual to find these topics in a human development text. There are two reasons behind our decision to include the chapter. First, in surveying nursing programs throughout the United States, we found that research and statistics are increasingly included in human development courses. This is not surprising, since it would be difficult for nursing students to consult the human development literature intelligently without some background in research methodology. But most important in our decision was the feeling, as we came to the end of our book, that something was missing. We realized that an excursion through the still young science of human psychology raises more questions than it answers. When we are left with many "whys" and "hows," only research can provide more complete answers. So as we reach the end of our task we need a new beginning. Research and statistics will help you pick up where the book leaves off.

More and more, nursing is evolving into an empirical science that seeks evidence through research. Research is the investigatory arm of science; it establishes fact. In science we ask questions, then design research procedures for finding out the answers. The process of establishing facts is a slow and painstaking one, because answers and facts are rarely absolutely substantiated. Rather, the accumulation of research evidence gives us increasing confidence that our "facts" are *probably* correct. The research orientation of the scientist is one of inquisitiveness, self-criticism, and the quest for evidence. Proof must always be the final determinant of scientific knowledge. At the same time, intuition plays an important role in research. The creative insight of the scientist is often the starting point of new discoveries. The formulation of meaningful questions to be researched can only be raised by astute and sensitive observers.

In this chapter, we will review the major concepts necessary for understanding research methods in health care. The grasp of these concepts will enable the reader to comprehend better the nursing and health care literature. To further our task we will briefly describe a hypothetical research study, which we will refer to in discussing the basics of research and statistics. Read the study bearing in mind that the unfamiliar terms will be clarified in the ensuing discussion. Try not to be put off by the technical terms. They are only convenient words that you can easily learn and will need in your advanced studies. While further study will be necessary to master the technical end of research, the more essential creative spark is within the grasp of every student, novice as well as advanced.

HYPOTHETICAL RESEARCH STUDY

In this study the researchers were interested in investigating the effect of hospital admission procedures on surgery patients. For the *experimental group* a human relations approach was used while the *control group* received a standard admission procedure used at the hospital where the study was conducted.

Hypotheses.   The hypotheses of the study stated that the human relations approach to admission of surgery patients when compared with the standard approach would result in:

1. significantly less anxiety for the human relations group during the preoperative period.

2. significantly less anxiety for the human relations group during the postoperative period.

3. significantly better adjustment to hospital routine and procedures for the human relations group.

4. significantly more positive attitudes toward hospital personnel for the human relations group.

Definitions

Human relations approach. This approach consists of the following:

1. Nurse and surgeon meet the patient at admission and greet her warmly, introducing themselves.

2. Identifying data is taken by the nurse after the patient is settled in the ward or room.

3. The nurse and physician explain their roles to the patient.

4. Three to four hours after admission the nurse explains the nature of the operation, the anticipated discomfort, and the expected postoperative course of recovery.

Standard admission procedure. The patient initially reports to an admissions desk where she is required to give identifying data and fill out forms. She is escorted to a room and given a hospital gown. Her belongings are put away and the nurse comes in to take her vital signs. Next comes a technician to take some blood, and an intern follows to give a physical. No explanation of the procedure is made and only brief answers are given when questions are asked. The surgeon does not see the patient until six hours after admission.

Subjects. All the patients in the study were females between the ages of 35 and 40 who were admitted for hysterectomy. There were 15 patients in each of the two groups.

Tests. The tests measured anxiety, adjustment to hospital routine and procedures, and attitudes toward hospital personnel. Measures were based on ratings of the patients' behaviors and verbal communication. For each of the three variables being measured the possible ratings ranged from 0 to 100, with 0 representing a low score and 100 a high score. Thus a patient with a rating of 10 on anxiety would show relatively low anxiety while a patient with a rating of 80 would show relatively high anxiety. Similarly for the measures of adjustment to hospital routine and attitude toward hospital personnel. We assume, for the sake of enhancing the discussion, that the investigators had valid and reliable measures.

Procedures.   Patients between the ages of 35 and 40 entering the hospital for hysterectomy were randomly assigned to the human relations group (experimental group) or the standard procedure group (control group). Scores for the two groups were compared on the four measures (variables). The preoperative measure of anxiety was obtained 1 hour before surgery; other psychological measures were obtained 48 hours after surgery.

Results.   The results of the study are summarised in Table 19.1. The results show that all four hypotheses are supported, indicating that the human relations approach to admission of surgical patients has positive effects on anxiety level, adjustment to the hospital, and attitudes toward hospital personnel.

Table 19.1   **Mean and Standard Deviation Scores on Anxiety, Adjustment, and Attitude Toward Hospital Personnel**

	Preoperative Anxiety		Postoperative Anxiety		Adjustment		Attitude Toward Personnel	
	Mean	*SD*	*Mean*	*SD*	*Mean*	*SD*	*Mean*	*SD*
Human relations group (experimental)	40*	10	30*	15	75**	14	82**	15
Standard procedures group (control)	60	8	68	16	25	10	43	13

* Difference significant at .05 level (p<.05).
** Difference significant at .01 level (p<.01).

DISCUSSION OF THE STUDY

Now that we have outlined the essentials of the study, we can backtrack and trace the principles involved. You should be aware that an actual research study would be reported in much greater detail. We have simplified the reporting for the sake of clarity and to focus on some major points.

Experimental versus Descriptive Research

The study just described is experimental research. What makes it experimental is the systematic manipulation of a variable that can yield a cause-and-effect conclusion. The experimental group (human relations) is given one treatment, and the control group (standard) is given another treatment. In some experimental designs the control group is given no treatment. The experimental design enables you to attribute differences in results between groups to the experimental condition, thereby establishing a causal relationship.

In descriptive research a group or phenomenon is described, but there are no direct implications of cause and effect, although causality may be suggested. For example, a descriptive research project might detail the various characteristics of patients who have a particular blood disease. The systematic description of these patients might lead to important insights. Perhaps the disease would turn up significantly more frequently in a particular age group or among patients of a particular ethnic background. Such findings could ultimately lead to causal explanations about the disease.

Both descriptive and experimental research are important, and both have contributed to scientific discovery. Which method a researcher chooses will depend on the nature of the research question. The hypothesis of our study proposes that the human relations approach is more effective than the standard approach to hospital admission of surgical patients in the four specific ways that were noted; stated as such, the hypothesis lends itself to an experimental study.

The Hypothesis. Stating a hypothesis is an essential part of experimental research. The hypothesis is the experimenter's assertion of what he thinks the "facts" are. It is a proposal of fact. The task of the experiment is to support or refute the hypothesis (or hypotheses).

Rationale. The researcher should give plausible reasons for studying the problem under investigation and the basis for the hypothesis. We want to know why the problem is important and how the research will add to our knowledge. Similarly, we want to know the basis for the assertion of the hypothesis. A rationale gives a study breadth by relating it to general principles. The importance of our hypothetical study could easily be indicated. The relationship of hospital procedures to the psychological needs and behavior of patients is of great importance for the effectiveness of health-care delivery and for the role of health professionals. The rationale for

Epilogue

the hypothesis in this study could be derived from many theories of personality that tie gratification of psychological needs (as implied in the human relations approach to psychological adjustment. In stating a rationale in this fashion, the study becomes a test not only of the specific hypothesis but also of the theoretical concept that provides the rationale.

Need for Systematic Research

To some readers the outcome of the hypothetical study may seem obvious. It would certainly appear more desirable to use a human relations approach than an impersonal one. However, the cost in staff time required by the human relations approach would be difficult to justify to most hospital administrators without evidence of its positive effectiveness in patient care. From the pure research point of view, the study is necessary to pinpoint the specific areas that the human relations method affects. It may affect some areas of behavior and not others. For knowledgeable nursing care we need to know exactly what impact our procedures have.

Why can't the nurse merely try out the human relations technique with a number of patients in an informal manner to determine whether it is better than the standard method? In other words, is a systematic study necessary? Many practitioners actually do function by informal trial. The difficulty in formulating conclusions based on informal trial is that it is impossible to establish objective fact. The impression, based on a few cases, that the human relations approach is superior may simply reflect the nurse's desire to have that method work. Without objective measures we cannot verify these impressions. However, trying out hunches is excellent for determining the advisability of proceeding with a more elaborate systematic study. But drawing conclusions from isolated informal trials violates two important aspects of research that we will now discuss—controls and sampling.

Controls

It is essential in research to insure that only the condition under study varies while everything else is held constant. In this way we can determine what effects, if any, result from the experimental condition. In the study outlined above the variable (i.e., the factor that varies in research) under study is the method of admission, and in particular the human relations approach versus the standard approach. Presumably any differences occurring between the two groups at the end of the experiment can be attributed to the differences between the experimental and control conditions with regard to method of admission. If other factors are also permitted to vary, it becomes impossible to pinpoint the cause of differences. Thus the need for controlling variables. For example, in our study the groups were limited to women between the ages of 35 and 40. This insures that the two groups have patients similar in age. If the two groups differed in age, the outcome of the research might be due to this difference. If one group had a preponderance of patients over age 50 and the other consisted of women in their 30s, the reactions of the two groups might be due to their age rather than the particular method of admission that was used. The explanation might be that the anxiety of the younger women over a hysterectomy is greater because they are still in the reproductive years. This is just speculation but we wouldn't be able to draw any firm conclusion about the effect of admission procedures (which was the main purpose of the study). It would be possible to study the effect of age on admission method by including groups of women of different ages and then comparing their responses to the methods of admission. This of course would require a larger number of patients than was included in the research as outlined and would change the purpose of the study. In any case, the factor of age must be controlled by the researcher and not left to chance.

Another variable in our study that would have to be controlled is social class. This was not mentioned in the study and would be a weakness if it were not included. As we learned in Chapter 13, social class is frequently associated with particular attitudes toward health care. If the human relations group consisted largely of low socioeconomic women and the standard procedure group of middle-class patients, class status might be the most important determinant of the outcome. No differences between the two groups might possibly reflect a greater anxiety on the part of low socioeconomic women faced with hospital procedures, a situation that would mask the effectiveness of the human relations approach. Again we could not be certain and the main purpose of the research would not be accomplished.

We could go on with examples of other variables, but in each case the rule would be the same: control any factor that can reasonably be thought to have significant impact on the condition under study. Variables that are frequently controlled in behavioral research are: age, educational level, socioeconomic level, intelligence, sex, and religion.

Controls do not mean that a study must be limited to a narrow range of a variable such as age or social class. A wide range can be included if there are enough of each type to make an analysis of each subgroup possible. In our study we could have included many groups of patients, such as ages 29-34, 35-39, 40-44, 45-49, and 50-60. For each age group we could also have included both middle and low socioeconomic class patients. Such a study would be well controlled—but it would require a large number of patients, a large research staff, and considerable research time. Also, the array of patients required would probably not be available in any one institution. In any given study, practical considerations as well as the nature of the research problem will determine which variables to control and how complex to make the study. Sometimes a simple design can accomplish as much as a more complex one, saving unnecessary expenditure of resources.

Sampling

A *sample* is a group selected from a population. Members of populations and samples have similar characteristics but the population is larger. Sampling and controlling variables are very much related, since once we have defined a sample, the controls are implied. For our study, the 30 female patients between the ages of 35 and 40 referred for hysterectomies comprised the sample. The population would be the larger group of all women of that age group referred for hysterectomies. (An even larger population would consist of all surgery patients.) Sampling is an important part of research and statistics, because it provides a practical method for drawing conclusions or making inferences about larger populations. It would be quite prohibitive, if not impossible, to do our study with the entire population of hysterectomy patients. We might question the sample choice of women between the ages of 35 and 40, since most hysterectomy patients are older than that age group. However, the choice may be less crucial in this case because the focus of the study is on hospital admission procedures rather than hysterectomy. But we can see how sample choice can weaken, strengthen, or bias a study.

Most people are familiar with sampling in connection with market and opinion research. TV ratings, for example, are based on samples of TV viewers. Political forecasts are made by questioning samples of voters and making inferences about the entire population of voters.

After the population is defined, the next task is to use a method for selecting the sample that is *unbiased*. In the opinion poll example, selecting viewers only from large cities would be biased, because those viewers would not necessarily reflect the TV viewing habits of smaller communities. Random sampling is a method that avoids bias. In a random sample each member of the population from which the sample is taken has an equal chance of being selected. Pulling names out of a hat is a random method. From a list of all TV viewers we might select every twentieth name, another random method. Proportionate or stratified sampling is still another technique. In this method a percentage of the sample might be selected for each area of the country proportionate to the population of that area. Within each area a random method of selection would be used.

In our study on admission of surgery patients the population is quite limited. Most likely the study would be conducted at a hospital where there would be a limited number of hysterectomy admissions of the specified age group. Ideally, it would be better to have a larger population of patients from which to select. But this is one of the limitations of real-life behavioral studies.

Assignments to experimental and control groups must also be done in an unbiased fashion. This can be accomplished by using any one of a number of arbitrary methods of assignments. For example, in our study every other patient between the ages of 35 and 40 entering the hospital for a hysterectomy could be assigned to the experimental group, with the remainder assigned to the control group. This would avoid any conscious or unconscious bias of, say, placing the more seriously ill or high-risk patients in the control group and thereby "fixing" the results.

Reliability and Validity

Reliability and validity are characteristics of tests or measures. A study can be no better than the reliability and validity of its measures. In our hypothetical study four measures were obtained: preoperative anxiety, postoperative anxiety, adjustment to hospital routine, and attitudes toward hospital personnel. To simplify the presentation, we assumed that the tests used to obtain the measures were reliable and valid. Actually reliability and validity can never be assumed and the researcher must indicate evidence of both.

Reliability. Reliability refers to the accuracy of a test or measure —specifically, to its ability to obtain the same data when repeated. Repeatability is a basic question of all measurement. Tests, in a sense, are like tape measures. If we measure the length of an object such as a table with a tape measure and get a reading of 36 inches on one occasion, $37\frac{1}{2}$ inches on another, and 39 inches on still another occasion, we would conclude that the tape measure was unreliable, and suspect it of stretching. In any case, we would not want to use that tape measure for any serious purpose. The same goes for measurements of human behavior characteristics. We want to be assured that the tests we use yield approximately the same scores when given to the same individuals repeatedly. Since people are not inert objects as tables are, we expect somewhat less accuracy in psychological measurement than in physical science measurement. Nevertheless, a test must be reliable to deserve our confidence. The reliability of tests will be indicated in test manuals or research reports.

There are three common methods for determining reliability. The *test-retest* method involves the administration of a test to the same group on two different occasions. If the test is reliable the scores on the two administrations should be fairly similar for each individual. The *split-half* method takes one administration of a test and divides it into two equal parts (using odd and even items or some other random method of dividing in half). Then the two halves are treated as if they were two administrations of the test. If the test is reliable then each individual should get similar scores on each half. The *alternate-form* method is similar to the test-retest method, the only difference being that the second administration is not of exactly the same test but of an alternate form of the test with equivalent items. In all of these methods the purpose is to determine that successive administrations yield comparable scores, thereby reflecting accurate measurement.

Validity.   Does the test measure what it purports to measure? This is the question of validity. "So you say it is a test of anxiety—prove it." There are a number of methods for establishing the validity of a test. One way is to compare the scores on a new unproven test with the scores on a test that is already accepted and established. When scores on the two tests compare favorably, we say that the new test is valid. Sometimes validity is ascertained through predictions of other performances. For example, if the unproven test measures anxiety, then we might expect those with high scores on that test to do poorly on some task or life activity that requires intense concentration. Low anxiety scorers, on the other hand, should do well on those tasks. Again, the test manual or research report will indicate the degree of validity of a test.

Defining Terms

Whenever terms are used that can have various meanings, the researcher must define those terms for the purpose of the study. Such is the case with the terms "human relations approach" and "standard approach," which can mean different things to different people. Therefore, definitions were provided spelling out what the terms meant in our research study. One preferred type of definition is called *operational*. In an operational definition the total acts or operations that define the term are given. Operational definitions remove confusion over definition by eliminating the need for interpretation. In the case of our study, operational definitions were given for the two methods of admission—that is, the procedures defining each method of admission were detailed.

Limitations of Research

The question raised at the beginning of the hypothetical research study pertains to the effect of different admissions techniques on the reactions of surgical patients. The actual study deals only with hysterectomy patients of a particular age group. Can the results of such a study be applied to surgery patients in general or even to all age groups of hysterectomy patients? There are always great risks in generalizing beyond the population actually studied. We could not, with any degree of confidence, be assured that other types of surgical patients would react in the same way as did the hysterectomy patients. The same uncertainty applies to different age groups. The results of a particular study may very well increase our confidence about the general effect of a procedure, but further research on other patients would be required to give substance to this confidence. Here we can see the slow, step-by-step building of knowledge of scientific research. One study is one of the building blocks but cannot answer all questions.

INTERPRETING RESEARCH RESULTS

It is important to be familiar with the meaning of statistical terms and symbols because they inevitably appear in research reports in the professional literature. Statistics are measures based on populations and samples. Two types of statistics can typically be found in research: descriptive and inferential. Descriptive statistics provide measures that depict the characteristics of a sample or population. Inferential statistics use measures to make inferences about the larger population and to test for the significance of results.

Descriptive Statistics

Under descriptive statistics we will discuss *mean, mode, median,* and *standard deviation.* All of the descriptive statistics are valuable for giving a shorthand characterization of a group or distribution of scores. For example, when you want to know about the scores of a class on a test, it is common to say, "What was the mean or average score?" The mean gives a quick sense of what the scores were like. Of course you could ask to see all of the scores, but that can be cumbersome, especially when large numbers of scores are involved.

Mean.   The mean (or average score) is computed by adding all the scores and then dividing by the total number of scores.

$$\overline{X} = \frac{\Sigma X}{N}$$

$\overline{X}$ = mean
Σ = sum of
X = individual scores
N = number of scores

The mean is not a perfect indicator of the way in which scores of a group are distributed, and sometimes it can be misleading. Many different combinations of scores can yield the same mean. A class would have a mean score of 50 on an exam if half the class received 0 and half 100. On the other hand, if everyone in the class scored around 50, the mean score would still be 50. Thus, to get a more accurate picture of a distribution, additional descriptive statistics are required.

Mode.   The mode is the most common or frequent score. It can indicate where a preponderance of the scores lie.

Median.   The median is the middle score, i.e. the score above which and below which 50% of the scores fall. A median of 50 on a test would mean that half the class scored less than 50 and half the class more than 50. Unlike the mean, which can be pulled up by a few very high scores and pulled down by a number of very low scores, the median is not affected by the actual magnitude of scores. The mean and the median give a better picture of a distribution of scores when taken together. When there is an odd number of scores, the median will be the middle score. For an even number of scores the median is the midpoint between the two middle scores.

Standard Deviation.   The standard deviation expresses the variation of scores from the mean. In this way it gives a clear picture of the distribution or spread of a group of scores. A small standard deviation would indicate that most scores are bunched around the mean, while a large one would indicate a wide spread of scores. The standard deviation is one of the most important descriptive statistics and it is essential for many statistical tests. The Greek symbol σ (called sigma) is frequently used to represent the standard deviation (it may also be written as SD). The nature and use of the standard deviation will become clearer as we discuss the normal curve.

Normal curve. The normal curve, sometimes referred to as the bell-shaped curve, is a particular distribution of scores that is the cornerstone of most statistics (Figure 19.1). The shape of the curve is symmetrical with low scores and high scores similarly distributed; most of the scores are around the mean or center of the distribution, with fewer scores at the upper and lower extremes. The normal curve is used as the model for the distribution of scores on many behavioral traits. For example, if an intelligence test were administered to a large, randomly selected group of people, the distribution of scores would very likely resemble the normal curve. Most of the scores would be around the mean (100), with decreasing numbers of scores at the genius and defective levels.

The standard deviation is used to indicate units along the normal curve. Since we know the proportion of scores between the mean and different standard deviation units, the standard deviation becomes a highly informative statistic in relation to the normal curve. Figure 19.1 shows the normal curve and the percentage of scores between the standard deviation units; 68% of all scores fall between +1 and −1 standard deviation units, 95% of the scores between +2 and −2 standard deviation units, and 99% of the scores between +3 and −3 standard deviation units.

Figure 19.1 **The Normal Curve**

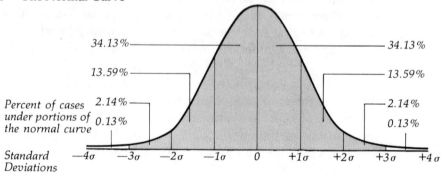

Let's take an example to see how the normal curve can be used. If an individual's score on a test or rating were 1 standard deviation above the mean, we would know immediately that his score was better than 84% of the scores (50% of the scores below the mean plus 34% from the mean to +1 standard deviation equals 84%). If the score were 2 standard deviations above the mean it would exceed 97% of the scores. Any score can be converted into a standard deviation score (standard score) by subtracting the mean from the score and then dividing by the standard deviation. In most studies the standard deviation will be given.

$$\text{Standard score} = \frac{\text{Score} - \text{Mean}}{\text{Standard deviation}}$$

Let us look at the data from our own study to see the application of the normal curve. Turn to Table 19.1 on p. 385. The table shows that the mean score on preoperative anxiety for the human relations group is 40 and the standard deviation 10. This means that 10 is equal to one standard deviation unit for that group. As Figure 19.2 shows, 68% of all the preoperative anxiety ratings for the human relations group are between 30 and 50 (between 1 standard deviation unit above and 1 standard deviation unit below the mean). A score of 50 would be equivalent to one standard deviation unit above the mean (50-40)/10. Any score of that group could similarly be converted into a standard score by subtracting the mean from it and dividing by 10. Presenting a score in standard units has the advantage of conveying the meaning of the score in relation to the other scores.

Figure 19.2 **Normal Curve Distribution of Scores on Preoperative Anxiety**

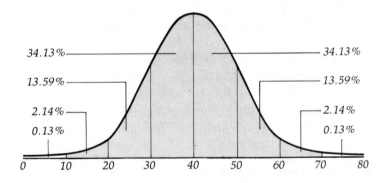

SIGNIFICANCE OF FINDINGS

Looking at the mean scores in our study reported in Table 19.1, we note that the scores for the two groups differ on all the measures. The human relations group has lower mean scores on preoperative and postoperative anxiety, and higher scores on adjustment and positive attitudes. These differences are in the direction predicted by the hypotheses and would, therefore, seem to support the hypotheses. But are these differences significant differences? The question of significance of differences is the most crucial one for testing hypotheses and evaluating the outcome of research. In order to understand the meaning of significance in statistical research, it is necessary to grasp the concepts of variability, probability, and tests of significance.

Variability

It is fairly safe to say that no two events occur exactly the same way. Take a common activity such as bowling. You may get one score on one occasion and a different score the next. If we observed you bowling a half-dozen times, you would probably get different scores each time. Most of the scores may be close or within a narrow range, but some may differ greatly. Such variability does not usually surprise us, unless the differences are very great. In other words, we expect human behavior and performance to vary. We do not, therefore, consider minor variability to be significant. But at what point does variability cease to be regarded as insignificant or normal variability? The same question arises when we compare the scores of an experimental and control group. Can the differences obtained be attributed to normal variability, since we would not expect two groups to obtain the exact same scores? Put in terms of our own study, is the difference of 40 and 60 on preoperative anxiety due to normal variability, or is it the effect of our experimental condition (method of admission)? Just looking at the size of the difference cannot tell you whether or not it is significant. We do not have the space here to go into the full explanation of why this is so, but the rule of not drawing conclusions about significance from the size of differences should always be followed. There is a great temptation to conclude that relatively large differences are significant, but this should be avoided. *Tests of significance are necessary to settle the question of significance of difference.*

Probability and Tests of Significance

Any event can occur by chance or accident. Natural variability, as in the bowling example, is an aspect of chance occurrence. In contrast to chance events are those that are caused by an agent that can be identified or assumed. Any event, no matter how improbable, has a possibility of occuring by chance. The probability of winning a lottery may be one in a million, yet someone does win—by chance.

In flipping a coin, the chance of getting a head on any given flip is 50/50. But if you actually flip a coin 10 times you might get 6 heads and 4 tails, or 7 and 3, or 8 and 2, or sometimes even 10 and 0. None of these occurrences is particularly startling; each combination has a certain probability of occurring. Even the 10 heads and 0 tails could be expected a certain number of times if we did many series of 10 flips (the probability of 10 heads and 0 tails is 1 in 1024). But 100 heads and no tails would arouse suspicion, although even that combination has a probability of occurring by chance (more than 1 in a billion). Here we are likely to smell something fishy—a weighted coin, or a two-headed coin, or some other trick. In other words, when the probability for the occurrence of an event is very small we are inclined to reject chance as the explanation, and we look for a causal explanation ("what did it?").

All scientific "facts" are based on the notion of probability. The task in establishing fact is the designation of the probability level beyond which we reject chance as the explanation. There is something of a contradiction in recognizing the chance possibility of any event but rejecting chance in a particular case because it is too chancy. The *null hypothesis* states that the difference between groups is due to chance variability. For establishing significance the aim is to reject the null hypothesis. In research the method for designating the probability level beyond which chance is rejected and a cause assumed is called setting significance levels. These significance levels are arbitrary and vary depending on the nature of the subject under study. In the physical sciences, where measurement is highly accurate and experimental controls very good, more demanding levels of significance are set than in the behavioral sciences.

In the behavioral sciences a 5% level of significance is usually accepted. This means that if the difference between two measures could occur by chance five or less times out of a hundred, then the difference is not chance but significant. It is written as follows:

$$p < .05 \qquad\qquad p = \text{probability}$$
$$< = \text{less than}$$
$$.05 = 5\% \text{ or 5 times in 100}$$

Turning to the results of our own study (Table 19.1), the asterisks (*) indicate the level of the significance of difference between the means. The difference between the means of 40 and 60 on preoperative anxiety is significant ($p < .05$). The difference between the means of 30 and 68 on postoperative anxiety is also significant at the .05 level. The differences between the means on adjustment and attitudes toward personnel are even more significant, with probabilities of $p < .01$, meaning that these differences could occur by chance less than one time in a hundred. If any of the differences between the means had been insignificant, they would have been reported as p> .05 (the sign > means greater than), meaning that the differences could occur often enough by chance that they could be attributed to natural variation. The statistical test used most often for testing the significance of differences between means is the t test. You will frequently see references to this test in research studies. However, regardless of which statistical test is used, it is most important to read the report on the level of significance of a study's findings.

Correlation

Correlation is another statistical technique you will frequently come across in behavioral research. Correlation expresses *the degree of relationship between variables*. Another hypothetical example will help to illustrate the kind of information provided by the correlation. Suppose we were studying the relationship between age and anxiety of women admitted for hysterectomy. The sample for this study consists of 50 women between the ages of 26 and 60. The hypothesis is that as age increases anxiety over the operation decreases.

The results of the above study would be reported in terms of correlation, i.e., the degree of relationship between the two variables of age and anxiety. Stated more technically, the hypothesis would assert a negative correlation between age and anxiety. In a negative correlation a high score on one variable goes with a low score on the other variable. Since higher age is expected in this study to be associated with lower anxiety, the expected correlation would be negative. A positive correlation means that a high score on one variable goes with a high score on the other variable, and low scores on one go with low scores on the other. Correlations are almost never perfect but indicate tendencies in either the positive or negative direction. When we say, for example, that two tests have a high positive correlation we mean that there is a tendency for students who achieve high scores on one of the tests to achieve high scores on the other test as well, and for low-scoring students on one test to be low-scoring students on the other test.

The degree of correlation is reported as a correlation coefficient. Correlation coefficients are values that can range from −1 to +1. A zero correlation would mean no consistent relationship (i.e., a random relationship between the two variables). The greatest possible negative relationship is represented by −1 and the greatest possible positive relationship by +1. The symbol r represents the

Epilogue   398

most commonly used correlation coefficient. Here is the meaning of some correlation coefficients that might be reported in a study.

r = +.8 (relatively high positive correlation)
r = −.8 (relatively high negative correlation)
r = +.3 (relatively low positive correlation)
r = −.3 (relatively low negative correlation)

After a correlation coefficient is obtained, its degree of significance must be determined. You will recall that we faced the same problem in evaluating differences between means. The question for correlation is, how high must the correlation be for it to reflect a significant degree of relationship? Is the obtained correlation one of chance occurrence based on natural variability? As in the case with the size of differences between means, the amount of a reported correlation cannot tell you the degree of significance. In some instances a correlation of .8 will be insignificant and a correlation of .3 significant. For determining significance a test of significance must be applied that is reported as a probability. Again, the 5% level of significance is commonly used for behavioral research. Is the probability of a reported correlation occurring by chance 5 or less times in 100 ($p<.05$)? The results section of a study will provide this information. If a correlation is significant, it will be reported as $p < .05$, and if it is insignificant it will be reported as $p > .05$. (The figure, of course, depends on the level of significance established by the researcher.)

EVALUATING RESEARCH

In reading a research report, you will have to ask yourself, "How much confidence should I place in this study?" Even without a highly sophisticated knowledge of statistics it is possible to answer this question and make a reasonable evaluation. Many of the points necessary for the evaluation of research have already been made in the course of our discussion, but we will now review them.

1. *Rationale.* Did the researcher state a meaningful purpose for the study and hypothesis? Were there indications of how the study would add to our knowledge?

2. *Hypothesis.* Was the hypothesis (or hypotheses) clearly formulated and stated?

3. *Controls.* Were there adequate controls so that clear conclusions could be reached?

4. *Sample.* Was the sample representative of a population that

is relevant to the problem under study? Was the sample selected in an unbiased manner?

5. *Tests.*　Were the tests (or measures) used in the study reliable and valid?

6. *Significance.*　Did the results show statistical significance?

7. *Conclusions.*　Were the conclusions reached justified in terms of the scope and method of the study? Were the conclusions too broad or overgeneralized?

BEGINNING A RESEARCH PROJECT
Getting an Idea

How do ideas for research originate? Ideas have many sources. A question may arise in the course of your work or study that intrigues you, resulting in further investigation and ultimately in the formulation of a research project. Reading other research studies and journal articles is also an important source of research ideas. We said earlier that no single research study ever answers all questions; sometimes it may end up raising more questions than it answers, and thus suggest further research. Talks with colleagues and teachers about experiences, doubts, and questions can also generate ideas. Informal discussions are often fruitful; the "coffee klatch" has probably led to as many research ideas as "hard thinking." At times a research idea will seem to just pop into your mind. These seemingly "out-of-nowhere" ideas are usually based on a receptiveness to ideas and a long period of incubation. The inquisitive, scientifically oriented, open-minded nurse will have no difficulty finding research ideas.

Researching the Literature

Once you have an idea and have formulated a research question, the next step is to find out what others have said and done about the topic. Learning about the related work of others can help you sharpen your question and develop it in a fruitful direction. At first the task of locating the related literature may seem overwhelming, but if you approach the job calmly and systematically, it can be done quickly and painlessly. You can become quite expert in reviewing many years of research on a topic in the course of a few hours of library work.

Indexes and abstracts are the best sources for locating related articles and research. Professional journals are also excellent resources. Here is a list of the most important behavioral references for the nurse-researcher:

International Nursing Index. Published quarterly by the American Journal of Nursing in cooperation with the National Library of Medicine. Contains a comprehensive index to the worldwide nursing literature. Lists articles on nursing and related subjects in over 240 nursing and other professional journals, magazines, and books and in over 2,200 medical publications. The emphasis is on U.S. publications. References are indexed under topical headings. Excellent for researching all areas of nursing and health care.

Index Medicus. Published monthly by the National Institutes of Health. It is a bibliographic reference for approximately 2,200 worldwide biomedical publications.

Psychological Abstracts. Published quarterly by the American Psychological Association. Includes abstracts of most worldwide psychological journals and books. Emphasis is on U.S. publications. Abstracts consist of brief summaries, which can be used to judge quickly the relevance of articles and books. References are listed topically and by authors. Excellent for all psychological and behavioral research.

American Journal of Nursing. Official monthly publication of the American Nurses' Association. Includes clinical, theoretical, and other articles relating to all facets of nursing and allied fields. Emphasis is on promoting an understanding of current developments in nursing.

AORN Journal. Official monthly organ of the Association of Operating Room Nurses. Provides operating room personnel and related services with original, practical information in their fields.

Canadian Nurse. Published monthly in English and French by the Canadian Nurses' Association. Contains articles of general interest to those in the nursing profession.

International Nursing Review. Official organ of the International Council for Nurses; published four times a year. Contains news and articles on all phases of nursing in many countries.

Journal of Continuing Education in Nursing. Bimonthly journal; contains articles and news directed to nurses interested in continuing and/or inservice education.

Journal of Nursing Administration. Bimonthly publication;

contains articles of particular interest to nurses in administrative positions.

Journal of Psychiatric Nursing. Bimonthly journal; articles focus on psychological problems and nursing of the mentally ill.

Nursing Clinics of North America. Quarterly specializing in recent clinical nursing developments. Gives broad appraisal of both new and existing concepts of clinical nursing and descriptions of new techniques in health care.

Nursing Forum. Quarterly that concentrates on original and stimulating ideas, concepts, and thoughts in nursing.

Nursing Mirror and Midwives Journal. Weekly British publication; contains news and articles of interest to nursing and related professions.

Nursing Outlook. Monthly publication; official organ of the National League for Nursing. Contains articles of interest to nurses and allied professionals as well as lay persons interested in nursing education, nursing service administration, and community health nursing.

Nursing Research. Published bimonthly by the American Journal of Nursing Company; carries reports, articles, abstracts, and other material related to scientific studies in nursing.

Nursing Times. Weekly British publication. Contains brief articles and news items of general interest to nurses and allied professionals.

Occupational Health Nursing. Monthly publication; official organ of the American Association of Industrial Nurses. Carries news and articles intended to keep industrial nurses in touch with current practices in their specialized field.

Perspectives in Psychiatric Care. Quarterly; contains in-depth articles and clinical material of special interest to nurses working with psychiatric patients and related problems.

RN Magazine. Independent monthly journal; carries broad range of articles on clinical and nonclinical subjects of interest to nurses and allied professionals.

Supervisor Nurse. Bimonthly; specializes in articles of particular interest to nurses in supervisory positions.

Working with References

It is useful to approach reference works (indexes, abstracts, journals, and books) with a list of headings and topics (cross-references) under which your subject may be found. In our study of admission procedures the cross-references would include: admission procedures, hysterectomy, surgery, ward behavior, and any others that would help locate important material (can you think of other cross-references?). Before using an index or other references, check the topical headings that are used in their listings. Begin with the most recent year of the reference material, and work backwards through successive years. You must use your own judgment in deciding how far back to go. For new areas of research it may be necessary to review only a few years. For other topics that have a long history, it would be wise to go back much further. When reading a relevant article or book, be sure to study its bibliography, which will appear at the end of the work, for additional leads. Very often the bibliographies will give you confirmation of the important literature in the area and indicate how far back to research. When you have completed your review of the indexes, abstracts, and the material they have led you to, it is a good idea to thumb through the indexes of the most current issues of journals. The "currents" have probably not yet been covered by the indexes and abstracts.

List all the references that you locate on separate cards. These cards can later be arranged alphabetically for your own bibliography. Attention to the routine mechanics of organizing your research can save a tremendous amount of time and work in the long run.

SUMMARY

Research is the scientific method for establishing facts. Statistics are used in most forms of research. Knowledge of research and statistics is important not only for the prospective researcher but for anyone who needs to consult research literature and reports.

To illustrate the basic concepts of research and statistics, we presented a hypothetical study dealing with admission procedures for surgery patients. A "human relations" approach was compared with a "traditional" approach. In analyzing the study, we discussed the difference between experimental and descriptive research, the need for systematic research, the nature of hypotheses, the importance of sampling, controls, validity and reliability of measures, and the limitations of research. Basic statistical concepts were introduced because they are necessary for evaluating the significance of results. Significance of findings was explained in terms of probability and tests of significance. Tests of significance are essential for differentiating between "normal" or chance variability and events that are caused by experimental conditions. Some suggestions were made concerning how to go about getting a research idea and initiating a study. Coming up with a research idea is a creative process that is within the reach of all students.

SUGGESTED READINGS

Elzey, F. F. *A programmed introduction to statistics.* Belmont, California: Brooks/Cole, 1971.

Fox, D. J. *Fundamentals of research in nursing.* New York: Appleton-Century-Crofts, 1970.

Notter, L. E. *Essentials of nursing research.* New York: Springer, 1974.

Siegel, S. *Nonparametric statistics.* New York: McGraw-Hill, 1956.

Weinberger, G. H., and Schumaker, J. A. *Statistics: an intuitive approach.* Belmont, California: Brooks/Cole, 1969.

Sidman, M. *Tactics of scientific research.* New York: Basic Books, 1960.

Bibliography

Ackerman, N. W. *The psychodynamics of family life.* New York: Basic Books, 1958.

Adorno, T. W., Frenkel-Brunswik, E., Levinson, D. J., and Sanford, R. N. *The authoritarian personality.* New York: Harper, 1950.

Aisenberg, R. What happens to old psychologists? a preliminary report. In *New thoughts on old age,* ed. R. Kastenbaum. New York: Springer, 1964.

Alexander, F., and French, T. M. *Studies in psychosomatic medicine.* New York: Ronald, 1948.

American Association on Mental Deficiency. *A manual on terminology and classification.* Baltimore: Garamond & Pridemark Press, 1973.

Anastasi, A. *Psychological testing.* New York: Macmillan, 1968.

Anderson, G., and Tighe, B. Gypsy culture and health care. *American Journal of Nursing,* 1973, 73 (2), 282-85.

Anguilera, D. C. Sociocultural factors: barriers to therapeutic intervention. *Journal of Psychiatric Nursing,* 1970, 8, 14-18.

Ansbacher, H. L., and Ansbacher, R. R. *The individual psychology of Alfred Adler.* New York, Basic Books, 1956.

Anthony, E. J., and Benedek, T., eds. *Parenthood: its psychology and psychopathology.* New York, Little, Brown, 1970.

Aries, P. *Centuries of childhood.* New York, Knopf, 1962.

Axline, V. M. *Dibs: in search of self: personality development in play therapy.* Boston, Houghton Mifflin, 1965.

Baer, E., Davitz, L., Davitz, J., and Lieb, R. Inferences of physical pain and psychological distress. *Nursing Research,* 1970, 19, 388-92.

Bair, S. L. *Wives' legal rights.* New York: Dell, 1965.

Bandura, A. *Principles of behavior modification.* New York: Holt, Rinehart and Winston, 1969.

Basu, A. Socio-cultural influences on patients' reaction to pain. *Nursing Journal of India,* 1966, 57, 231-32.

Beach, R. A., ed. *Sex and behavior.* New York: Wiley, 1965.

Beck, A. T. *The diagnosis and management of depression.* Philadelphia: U. of Pennsylvania Press, 1973.

Beauvoir, S. de. *The second sex.* New York, Bantam, 1961.

———. *The coming of age.* New York: Putnam, 1972.

Becker, W. C. Consequences of different kinds of parental discipline. In *Child development research,* ed. M. L. Hoffman and L. W. Hoffman. New York: Russell Sage, 1964, 169-208.

Beecher, H. K., and Boston, M. D. The powerful placebo. *Journal of the American Medical Association,* 1955, 159, 1602-6.

————. Relationship of significance of wound to pain experienced. *Journal of the American Medical Association*, 1956, 161, 1609-13.

Beers, C. *A mind that found itself.* New York: Doubleday, Doran, 1939.

Bell, N. W., and Vogel, E. F. *A modern introduction to the family.* Rev. ed. New York: Free Press, 1968.

Bell, R. R. *Studies in Marriage and the family.* 2nd ed. New York: Crowell, 1973.

Bell, R., and Costello, N. Three tests for sex differences in newborn. *Biologia Neonatorum*, 1964, 7, 335-475.

Bell, R., and Darling, J. The prone head reaction in the human newborn: relationship with sex and tactile sensitivity. *Child Development*, 1965, 36, 943-49.

Benedict, R. *Patterns of culture.* New York, Penguin, 1934.

Bergman, T., and Freud, A. *Children in the hospital.* New York: International Universities Press, 1965.

Berne, E. *Games people play.* New York: Grove Press, 1964.

Berni, R., and Fordyce, W. *Behavior modification and the nursing process.* Saint Louis: Mosby, 1973.

Birch, H. C., ed. *Brain damage in children.* Baltimore: Williams & Wilkins, 1964.

Birren, J. E. When the aged, dying patient needs a listener. *RN*, 1966, 29, 72-77.

Blank, R. H. Mourning. In *Death and bereavement*, ed. A. H. Kutscher. Springfield, Ill.: Thomas, 1969.

Blaylock, J. The psychological and cultural influences on the reaction to pain. *Nursing Forum*, 1968, 7, 262-74.

Bleuler, E. *Dementia praecox or the groups of schizophrenias* (1911). New York, International Universities Press, 1950.

Blos, P. *On adolescence: a psychoanalytic interpretation.* New York: Free Press, 1962.

Blumberg, J., and Drummond, E. E. *Nursing care of the long-term patient.* New York: Springer, 1971.

Boring, E. G. Intelligence as the tests test it. *New Republic*, 1923, 34, 35-36.

Bott, E. *Family and social network.* London: Tavistock, 1957.

Botwinick, J. *Aging and behavior.* New York: Springer, 1973.

Bowlby, J. *Maternal care and mental health.* 2nd. ed. Geneva: World Health Organization, 1952.

————. *Attachment and loss.* Vol. 1. *Attachment.* New York: Basic Books, 1969.

————. *Attachment and loss.* Vol. 2. *Separation.* New York: Basic Books, 1973.

————, Ainsworth, M., Boston, M., and Rosenbluth, D. The effects of mother–child separation: a follow-up study. *British Journal of Medical Psychology*, 1956, 29, 211-47.

Brady, J. V. Ulcers in "executive" monkeys. *Scientific American*, October, 1958, 250-53.

Brain, L., and Walton, J. W. *Brain's diseases of the nervous system.* London: Oxford U. Press, 1969.

Breuer, J., and Freud, S. Studies on hysteria. In *Standard edition of the complete psychological works of Sigmund Freud,* vol. 2. London: Hogarth Press, 1955.

Brinton, D. M. Health center milieu: interaction of nurses and low-income families. *Nursing Research,* 1972, 21, 46-52.

Brody, B. A., and Capaldi, N. *Science, men, methods, goals.* New York: W. A. Benjamin, 1968.

Brody, S. *Patterns of mothering.* New York, International Universities Press, 1956.

Bruce, R. Don't let the patient be nursed to death. *Nursing Mirror,* 1967, 125, 124-25.

Bullough, B. *Poverty, ethnic identity, and health care.* New York: Appleton-Century-Crofts, 1972.

Burgess, E. W., and Locke, H. J. *The family: from institution to companionship.* New York: American Book, 1945.

———, and Thomas, M. M. *The family: from traditional to companionship.* 4th ed. New York: Van Nostrand, 1971.

Busse, E. W., and Pfeiffer, E., eds. *Behavior and adaptation in late life.* Boston: Little, Brown: 1969.

Butler, R. N. The life review: an interpretation of reminiscence in the aged. *Psychiatry,* 1963, 26, 65-76.

———. The life review: an interpretation of reminiscence in the aged. In *New thoughts on old age,* ed. R. Kastenbaum. New York: Springer, 1964.

———, and Lewis, M. I. *Aging and mental health.* St. Louis: Mosby, 1973.

Byers, M. L. The hospitalized adolescent. *Nursing Outlook,* 1967, 15, 32-34.

Caldwell, B. M. The effects of infant care. In *Child development research,* ed. M. L. Hoffman and L. W. Hoffman. New York: Russell Sage, 1964, 9-87.

Cameron, W. *Personality development and psychopathology: a dynamic approach.* Boston: Houghton Mifflin, 1963.

Campbell, D., and Thompson, W. R. Developmental psychology. In *Annual review of psychology,* ed. P. R. Farnsworth. Palo Alto, Calif.: Annual Reviews, Inc., 1968.

Canter, A., Imboden, J. B., and Cluff, L. E. The frequency of physical illness as a function of prior psychological vulnerability and contemporary stress. *Psychosomatic Medicine,* 1966, 28, 344-50.

Carlsson, G. Swedish character in the twentieth century. *The Annals of the American Academy of Political and Social Science,* 1967, 370, 93-98.

Chesler, P. *Women and madness.* New York: Avon, 1973.

Chess, S. *An introduction to child psychiatry.* New York: Grune & Stratton, 1959.

Child, I., Potter, E. H., and Lavine, E. M. Children's textbooks and personality development. *Psychological Monographs,* 1946, 60, 1-54.

Church, J. *Understanding your child from birth to three.* New York: Random House, 1973.

Clark, K. *Dark ghetto.* New York, Harper & Row, 1965.

Cleckley, H. *The mask of sanity.* 4th ed. St. Louis: Mosby, 1968.

Coles, R., and Kagen, J., eds. *Twelve to sixteen: early adolescence.* New York: Norton, 1972.

Cox, R. D. *Youth into maturity.* New York: Mental Health Materials Center, 1970.

Crate, M. Nursing functions in adaptation to chronic illness. *American Journal of Nursing,* 1965, 65, 73-76.

Cumming, E. M. New thoughts on the theory of disengagement. In *New thoughts on old age,* ed. R. Kastenbaum. New York: Springer, 1964.

Davenport, W. Sexual patterns and their regulation in a society of the southwest Pacific. In *Sex and behavior,* ed. F. A. Beach. New York: Wiley, 1965.

David, M. and Appell, G. A study of nursing care and nurse-infant inter-action. In *Determinants of infant behavior,* ed. B. M. Fros. New York: Wiley, 1961.

Davies, J. T. *The scientific approach.* New York: Academic Press, 1965.

Davis, K. Final note on a case of extreme isolation. *American Journal of Sociology,* 1947, 57, 432-57.

Davitz, L. J. *Interpersonal processes in nursing.* New York: Springer, 1970.

Diagnostic and statistical manual, II. Washington, D.C.: American Psychiatric Association, 1968.

Dorroh, T. L. *Between patient and health worker.* New York: McGraw-Hill, 1974.

Drakontides, A. B. Drugs to treat pain. *American Journal of Nursing,* 1974, 73, 508-13.

Duvall, E. M. *Family development.* 4th ed. New York: Lippincott, 1971.

Eichorn, D. H. The institute of human development studies, Berkeley and Oakland. In *Intellectual functioning in adults,* ed. L. F. Jarvik, C. Eisdorfer, and J. E. Blum. New York: Springer, 1973.

Elkind, D. *Children and adolescents.* New York, Oxford U. Press, 1974.

Elliott, K., ed. *The family and its future.* London: J. and A. Churchill, 1970.

Elzey, F. F. *A programmed introduction to statistics.* Belmont, Calif.: Brooks/Cole, 1971.

Erikson, E. H. *Childhood and society.* 2nd ed. New York: Norton, 1963.

————. *Identity and the life cycle.* New York: International Universities Press, 1969.

Faberow, N. L., and Shneidman, E. S., eds. *The cry for help.* New York: McGraw-Hill, 1965.

Falconer, M. W., Ralston, N. M., Patterson, H. R., and Gustafson, E. A. *The drug, the nurse, the patient.* Philadelphia: Saunders, 1966.

Fancher, R. E. *Psychoanalytic psychology: the development of Freud's thought.* New York: Norton, 1973.

Farnsworth, P. R., ed. *Annual review of psychology.* Palo Alto, Calif.: Annual Reviews, 1968.

Fast, J. *Body language.* New York: Evans, 1970.

Felner, R. D., and Stolberg, A. The effects of the crisis predisposing events of parental separation and divorce or death on the referral patterns of children. Paper presented at the Eastern Psychological Association Convention, April, 1974.

Fenichel, O. *The psychoanalytic theory of neurosis.* New York: Norton, 1945.

Flavell, J. H. *The developmental psychology of Jean Piaget.* Princeton, N. J.: Van Nostrand, 1963.

Fletcher, J. Ethics and euthanasia. *Americal Journal of Nursing,* 1973, 73, 670-74.

Flynn, J. T., and Garber, H. *Assessing behavior.* Reading, Mass.: Addison-Wesley, 1967.

Fond, K. I. Dealing with death and dying through family-centered care. *Nursing Clinics of North America,* 1972, 7, 53-64.

Ford, C. S., and Beach, F. A. *Patterns of sexual behavior.* New York: Harper, 1951.

Ford Foundation, The. *Dealing with drug abuse.* New York: Praeger, 1972.

Fox, D. J. *Fundamentals of research in nursing.* New York: Appleton-Century-Crofts, 1970.

Fraiberg, S. H. *The magic years.* New York: Scribner's, 1959.

Freedman, A. M., and Kaplan, H. I., eds. *Comprehensive Textbook of Psychiatry.* Baltimore: Williams & Wilkins, 1967.

Freud, A. *The ego and the mechanisms of defense.* New York: International Universities Press, 1960.

——. *Normality and pathology in childhood: assessments of development.* New York: International Universities Press, 1960.

——, and Burlingham, D. T. *Infants without families.* New York, International Universities Press, 1944.

Freud, S. *Collected papers.* 5 vols. New York: Basic Books, 1959.

——. *Beyond the pleasure principle.* New York: Bantam, 1959.

——. Mourning and melancholia. In *Collected papers.* London: Hogarth Press and Institute of Psychoanalysis, 1925.

——. *Civilization and its discontents.* London: Hogarth Press, 1930.

——. *A general introduction to psychoanalysis.* Garden City, N. Y.: Garden City Publishing, 1943.

——. *Psychopathology and everyday life.* New York: Mentor, 1951.

Friedan, B. *The feminine mystique. New York: Dell,* 1970.

Friedenberg, E. Z. *The vanishing adolescent.* New York: Dell, 1962.

Fromm, E. *Escape from freedom.* New York: Farrar and Rinehart, 1941.

Fuszard, M. B. Acceptance of authoritarianism in the nurse by the hospitalized teenager. *Nursing Research,* 1969, 18, 426-32.

Garb, S., Grim, B. J., and Thomas, G. *Pharmacology and patient care.* 3rd ed. New York: Springer, 1970.

Gardner, R. A. *MBD: the family book about minimal brain dysfunction.* New York: Jason Aronson, 1973.

Gaumer, W. R. Electrical stimulation in chronic pain. *American Journal of Nursing,* 1974, 73, 504-5.

Gesell, A. *The first five years of life: a guide to the study of the preschool child*. New York: Harper, 1940.

Gesell, A., and Amatruda, C. S. *Developmental diagnosis*. New York: Harper & Row, 1949.

Gesell, A., Ilg, F. L., and Ames, L. B. *Youth: from ten to sixteen*. New York: Harper, 1956.

Getzels, J. W., and Jackson, P. W. *Creativity and intelligence*. New York: Wiley, 1962.

Ginsburg, H., and Opper, S. *Piaget's theory of intellectual development*. Englewood Cliffs, N. J.: Prentice-Hall, 1969.

Golden, J., Mendel, N., Glueck, B. C. Jr., and Feder, Z. A summary description of fifty "normal" white males. *American Journal of Psychiatry*, 1962, 119, 48-55.

Golfarb, A. I. Geriatric psychiatry. In *Comprehensive textbook of psychiatry*, ed. A. M. Freedman and H. I. Kaplan. Baltimore: Williams & Wilkins, 1967.

Goldfarb, W. Effects of psychological deprivation in infancy and subsequent stimulation. *American Journal of Psychiatry*, 1945, 102, 18-33.

Goldfarb, W. *Childhood schizophrenia*. Cambridge, Mass.: Harvard U. Press, 1961.

Goldfogel, L. Working with the parent of a dying child. *American Journal of Nursing*, 1970, 70, 1675-76.

Goldstein, H. S. Internal controls in aggressive children from father-present and father-absent families. *Journal of Consulting and Clinical Psychology*, 1972, 39, 512.

Goloskov, J., and LeRoy, P. Use of the dorsal column-stimulator. *American Journal of Nursing*, 1974, 73, 506-7.

Gog, R. W. Reproductive behavior in mammals. In *Human reproduction and sexual behavior*, ed. C. W. Loyd. Phila.: Lea & Febiger Co., 1964.

Goode, E. *Drugs in American society*. New York: Knopf, 1972.

Gornick, V. Why women fear success. In *The first Ms. reader*, ed. F. Klagsbrun. New York: Warner, 1973.

Gould, R. L. The phases of adult life. *American Journal of Psychiatry*, 1972, 129, 521-32.

Green, A. Nursing the young adolescent in hospital. *Nursing Times*, 1968, 64, 1242-43.

Green, H. *I never promised you a rose garden*. New York: Holt, Rinehart & Winston, 1964.

Green, M. Care of the dying child. *Pediatrics*, 1967, 40, 492-97.

Group for the Advancement of Psychiatry. *Psychopathological disorders in childhood: theoretical considerations and a proposed classification*. New York: Group for the Advancement of Psychiatry, 1966.

Guilford, J. P. Creativity: yesterday, today, and tomorrow. *Journal Creative Behavior*, 1967, 1, 3-14.

Haley, J. *Strategies of psychotherapy*. New York: Grune & Stratton, 1963.

Hall, C. S., and Lindzey, G. *Theories of personality*. New York: Wiley, 1970.

Hallman, R. J. The commonness of creativity. *Educational Theory*, 1963, 13, 132-36.

Hamburg, D. A. and Lunde, D. T. Sex hormones in the development of sex differences in human behavior. In *The development of sex differences*, ed. E. E. Maccoby. Stanford, Calif.: Stanford University Press, 1966, 1-24.

Hammar, S. L., and Eddy, J. A. *Nursing care of the adolescent.* New York: Springer, 1966.

Haring, D. G. Japanese character in the twentieth century. *The Annals of the American Academy of Political and Social Science*, 1967, 370, 133-42.

Harlow, H. The affectional responses in the infant monkey. *Science*, 1959, 130, 421-32.

Harris, D. B., Gough, H. G., and Martin, W. E. Children's ethnic attitudes: relationship to parental beliefs. *Child Development*, 1950, 21, 169-82.

Harris, T. A. *I'm O.K.—you're O.K.* New York: Harper & Row, 1967.

Harrison, S. I., Davenport, C. W., and McDermott, J. F. Children's reactions to bereavement: adult confusions and misperceptions. *Archives of General Psychiatry*, 1967, 17, 593-97.

Hartley, R. *Understanding children's play.* New York: Columbia U. Press, 1952.

Haworth, M. R. *Child psychotherapy.* New York: Basic Books, 1964.

Hendin, H. *Suicide and Scandinavia.* New York: Grune & Stratton, 1964.

Hilgard, E. R. *Theories of learning.* New York: Appleton-Century-Crofts, 1956.

Hill, J. Parental determinants of sex-typed behavior. Unpublished doctoral dissertation, Harvard U., 1964.

Himes, N. E. *Medical history of contraception.* New York: Gamut, 1963 (1936 ed. republished).

Hoffman, M. L., and Hoffman, L. W. *Child development research.* Vol. 1. New York: Russell Sage, 1964.

Holland, J. T. *The psychology of vocational choice.* Waltham, Mass.: Blaisdell, 1966.

Hollingshead, A. B., and Redlich, F. C. *Social class and mental illness.* New York: Wiley, 1958.

Honzik, M. P., and Macfarlane, J. W. Personality development and intellectual functioning from 21 months to 40 years. In *Intellectual functioning in adults*, ed. L. F. Jarvik, C. Eisdorfer, and J. E. Blum. New York: Springer, 1973.

Horney, K. The flight from womanhood. *International Journal of Psychoanalysis*, 1926, 7, 324-39.

———. *The neurotic personality of our time.* New York: Norton, 1937.

———. *New ways in psychoanalysis.* New York: Norton, 1939.

———. *Neurosis and human growth.* New York: Norton, 1950.

———. *Feminine psychology.* New York: Norton, 1967.

Hunter, R. C. A. On the experience of nearly dying. *American Journal of Psychiatry*, 1967, 124, 122-26.

Illingsworth, R. S. *The normal child.* 5th ed. Baltimore: Williams & Wilkins, 1972.

Ingram, I. M. The obsessional personality and obsessional illness. *American Journal of Psychiatry,* 1961, 117, 1016.

Jackson, D. D. Family rules. *Archives of General Psychiatry,* 1965, 12, 1535-41.

Jackson, E. N. Attitudes toward death in our culture. In *Death and bereavement,* ed. A. H. Kutscher. Springfield, Ill.: Thomas, 1969.

Janov, A. *The primal scream.* New York: Dell, 1970.

Jarvik, L. F. Discussion: patterns of intellectual functioning in the later years. In *Intellectual functioning in adults,* ed. L. F. Jarvik, C. Eisdorfer, and J. E. Blum. New York: Springer, 1973.

Jarvik, L. F., and Falek, A. Intellectual stability and survival in the aged. *Journal of Gerontology,* 1963, 18, 173-76.

Jarvik, L. F., Eisdorfer, C., and Blum, J. E. *Intellectual functioning in adults.* New York: Springer, 1973.

Jersilid, A. T. *Psychology of adolescence.* 2nd ed. New York: Macmillan, 1963.

Johnson, V. E., and Masters, W. H. Sexual incompatibility: diagnosis and treatment. In *Human reproduction and sexual behavior,* ed. C. W. Lloyd. Philadelphia: Lea & Febiger, 1964.

Kalish, R. A. Social distance and the dying. *Community Mental Health Journal,* 1966, 2, 152-55.

Kalish, R. Experiences of persons reprieved from death. In *Death and bereavement,* ed. A. H. Kutscher. Springfield, Ill.: Thomas, 1969.

Kanner, S. *Child psychiatry.* 4th. ed. Springfield, Ill.: Thomas, 1972.

Kaplan, H. S. *The new sex therapy.* New York: Brunner/Mazel, 1974.

Kasanin, J. B., ed. *Language and thought in schizophrenia.* New York: Norton, 1964.

Kastenbaum, R. Longevity and life patterns. In *New thoughts on old age,* ed. R. Kastenbaum. New York: Springer, 1964a.

———. The reluctant therapist. In *New thoughts on old age,* ed. R. Kastenbaum. New York: Springer, 1946b.

———. The mental life of dying geriatric patients. *Gerontologist,* 1967, 7, 97-100.

———, and Aisenberg, R. *The psychology of death.* New York: Springer, 1972.

Killeffer, D. H. *How did you think of that? An introduction to the scientific method.* New York: Doubleday, 1969.

Kimmel, D. C. *Adulthood and aging: an interdisciplinary, developmental view.* New York: Wiley, 1974.

Kinsey, A., Pomeroy, W. B., Martin, C., and Gebhard, P. *Sexual behavior in the human male.* Philadephia, Pa.: Saunders, 1948.

Kinsey, A. C., Pomeroy, W. B., Martin, C., and Gebhard, P. *Sexual behavior in the human female.* Philadelphia, Pa.: Saunders, 1953.

Klagsbrun, S. Cancer, nurses and emotions. *RN,* 1970, 33, 46-51.

Klein, D. F., and Blank, R. H. Psychopharmacological treatment of bereavement. In *Death and bereavement,* ed. A. H. Kutscher. Springfield, Ill.: Thomas, 1969.

Knight, J. A., and Herter, F. Anticipatory grief. In *Death and bereavement*, ed. A. H. Kutscher. Springfield, Ill.: Thomas, 1969.

Kolb, L. C. *Modern Clinical Psychiatry*. 8th ed. Philadelphia: Saunders, 1973.

Koprowicz, D. C. Drug interactions with coumarin derivatives. *American Journal of Nursing*, 1973, 73, 1042-44.

Korner, A. Sex differences in newborns with special reference to differences in the organization of oral behavior. *Journal of Child Psychology and Psychiatry*, 1973, 14, 19-29.

Kübler-Ross, E. *On death and dying*. New York: Macmillan, 1969.

————. What is it like to be dying. *American Journal of Nursing*, 1971, 71, 54-61.

Kutscher, A. H., ed. *Death and bereavement*. Springfield, Ill.: Thomas, 1969.

Lasko, J. K. Parent behavior toward first and second children. *Genetic Psychology Monographs*, 1954, 49, 97-137.

Lazarus, A. A. *Behavior therapy and beyond*. New York: McGraw-Hill, 1971.

Lebow, M. D. *Behavior modification: a significant method in nursing practice*. Englewood Cliffs, N. J.: Prentice-Hall, 1973.

Lebra, W. P., ed. *Transcultural research in mental health*. Hawaii: East-West Center (University of Hawaii), 1972.

Leighton, D. C., and Leighton, A. H. Mental health and social factors. In *Comprehensive textbook of psychiatry*, ed. A. M. Freedman and H. I. Kaplan. Baltimore: Williams & Wilkins, 1967.

Leininger, M. The culture concept and its relevance to nursing. *The Journal of Nursing Education*, 1967, 6, 27-37.

————. *Nursing and anthropology: two worlds to blend: culture factors in nursing care*. New York: Wiley, 1970.

Leopold, A. Psychological problems in hemodialysis. *RN*, 1968, 31, 42-45.

Lesser, G. S. The relationship between overt and fantasy aggression as a function of rational response to aggression. *Journal of Abnormal & Social Psychology*, 1957, 55, 218-21.

Lester, J. E. The psychic principle in nursing infants. *American Journal of Nursing*, 1915, 16, 109-11.

Levin, S. Depression in the aged: the importance of external factors. In *New thoughts on old age*, ed. R. Kastenbaum. New York: Springer, 1964.

Levy, N. B. *Living or dying: adaptation to hemodialysis*. Springfield, Ill.: Thomas, 1974.

Lewis, M. *Clinical aspects of child development*. Philadelphia: Lea & Febiger, 1971.

Lewis, O. *Five families*. New York: Basic Books, 1959.

————. The culture of poverty. *Scientific American*, 1966, 215, 19-25.

Lidz, T. *The person. His development throughout the life cycle*. New York: Basic Books, 1968.

————. *The origins and treatment of schizophrenic disorders*. New York: Basic Books, 1973.

Liley, H. M., and Day, B. *Modern motherhood*. New York: Random House, 1967.

Lindemann, E. Symptomatology and management of acute grief. *American Journal of Psychiatry*, 1944, 101, 141-48.

Lindsley, O. Geriatric behavioral prosthetics. In *New thoughts on old age*, ed. R. Kastenbaum. New York: Springer, 1964.

Lipkin, G. B., and Cohen, R. G. *Effective approaches to patients' behavior*. New York: Springer, 1973.

Lipset, S. M., and Lowenthal, L. *Culture and social character*. New York: Free Press, 1961.

Lishman, W. A. The psychology of pain. *Nursing Times*, 1970, 66, 1577-78.

Lloyd, C. W., ed. *Human reproduction and sexual behavior*. Philadelphia: Lea & Febiger, 1964.

Looft, W. R. Sex differences in expression of vocational aspirations by elementary school children. *Developmental Psychology*, 1971, 5, 366.

Love, H. D. *The mentally retarded child and his family*. Springfield, Ill.: Thomas, 1973.

Love, L. R., Kaswan, J., and Bugeutal, D. E. Differential effectiveness of three clinical interventions for different socioeconomic groupings. *Journal of Consulting and Clinical Psychology*, 1972, 39, 347-60.

Loxley, A. K. The emotional toll of crippling deformity. *Americal Journal of Nursing*, 1972, 72, 1839-40.

Maccoby, E. E., ed. *The development of sex differences*. Stanford, Calif.: Stanford U. Press, 1966.

Maccoby, M. On Mexican national character. *The Annals of the American Academy of Political and Social Science*, 1967, 370, 63-73.

Macgregor, F. C. *Social science in nursing*. New York: Russell Sage, 1960.

————. Uncooperative patients: some cultural interpretations. *American Journal of Nursing*, 1967, 67, 88-91.

Maddi, S. R., and Costa, P. T. *Humanism in personology*. New York: Aldine/Atherton, 1972.

Malinowski, B. *Sex, culture, and myth*. New York: Harcourt, Brace & World, 1962.

Maslow, A. H. *Toward a psychology of being*. New York: Van Nostrand, 1968.

Masters, W., and Johnson, V. *Human sexual response*. Boston, Mass.: Little, Brown, 1966.

Mastrovito, R. C. Psychogenic pain. *American Journal of Nursing*, 1974, 73, 514-19.

Matarazzo, J. D. *Wechsler's measurement and appraisal of adult intelligence*. Baltimore: Williams & Wilkins, 1972.

McBride, A. B. *The growth and development of mothers*. New York, Harper & Row, 1973.

McCaffery, Margo. *Nursing management of the patient with pain*. Philadelphia: Lippincott, 1972.

McDaniel, J. W. *Physical disability and human behavior.* New York: Pergamon, 1969.

McKinnon, D. W. The nature and nurture of creative talent. *American Psychologist,* 1962, 16, 484-95.

Mead, M. *From the South Seas.* New York: Morrow, 1939.

————, and Newton, N. C. Cultural patterning of perinatal behavior. In *Childbearing—Its social and psychological aspects,* ed. S. Richardson and A. F. Guttmacher. Baltimore: Williams & Wilkins, 1967.

Mechanic, D. Some factors in identifying and defining mental illness. *Mental Hygiene,* 1962, 66-75.

Medinnus, R., and Johnson, R. C. *Child psychology.* New York: Wiley, 1965.

Melzack, R. The perception of pain. *Scientific American,* 1961, 204, 41-49.

————. *The puzzle of pain.* New York: Basic Books, 1974.

————, and Wall, P. D. Pain mechanism: a new theory. *Science,* 1965, 150, 971-79.

Mendelson, J., Kubzansky, P. Liederman, P., Wexler, D., and Solomon, P. Physiological and psychological aspects of sensory deprivation: a case analysis. In *Sensory deprivation,* ed. P. Solomon. Cambridge, Mass.: Harvard U. Press, 1961.

Menninger, K. *Theory of psychoanalytic technique.* New York: Harper & Row, 1964.

Milio, N. Values, social class, and community health services. *Nursing Research,* 1967, 16, 23-31.

Miller, D. *Adolescence: psychology, psychopathology, and psychotherapy* New York: Jason Aronson, 1974.

Mitchell, B. Working with abusive parents. *American Journal of Nursing.* 1973, 73, 480-82.

Money, J. Psychosexual differentiation. In *Sex research, new developments,* ed. J. Money. New York: Holt, Rinehart, and Winston, 1963.

Moore, K. L. *Before we are born: basic embryology and birth deficits.* Philadelphia: Saunders, 1974.

Morram, G. D. Patients' evaluation of their care. *Nursing Outlook,* 1973, 21, 322-24.

Mullahy, P. *Oedipus—myth and complex.* New York: Hermitage House, 1948.

Munroe, R. L. *Schools of psychoanalytic thought.* New York: Dryden, 1955.

Murphy, G. E., et al. Life stress in a normal population: a study of 101 women hospitalized for normal delivery. *Journal of Nervous and Mental Disability,* 1962, 134, 150.

Muus, R. E. *Theories of adolescence.* 2nd ed. New York: Random House, 1968.

————, ed. *Adolescent behavior and society.* New York: Random House, 1971.

Narain, D. Indian national character in the twentieth century. *The Annals* of the *American Academy of Political & Social Science*, 1967, 370, 124-32.

National Center for Health Statistics. 100 years of marriage and divorce statistics, 1867-1967. In *Vital and health statistics*. PHS Pub. No. 1000, Series 21, No. 21, Public Health Service. Washington, D.C.: U.S. Government Printing Office, Sept., 1971.

————. Divorces: Analysis of changes. United States 1969. In *Vital and health statistics*. PHS Pub. No. 1000, Series 21, No. 22. Washington, D.C.: U.S. Government Printing Office, April, 1973.

————. Remarriages, United States. In *Vital and health statistics*. PHS Pub. No. 1000, Series 21, No. 25. Washington, D.C.: U.S. Government Printing Office, Dec., 1973.

National Institute of Mental Health. *The mental health of urban America*. Washington, D.C.: U.S. Government Printing Office, 1969.

Natterson, J. M., and Knudson, A. G. Observations concerning fear of death in fatally ill children and their mothers. *Psychosomatic Medicine*, 1960, 22, 456-66.

Neale, R. E. *The art of dying*. New York: Harper & Row, 1973.

Neugarten, B. L., ed. *Middle age and aging: A reader in social psychology*. Chicago: U. of Chicago Press, 1968.

Orlansky, H. Infant care and personality. *Psychological Bulletin*, 1949, 46 1-48.

Owens, W. A., Jr. Age and mental abilities: a longitudinal study. *Genetic Psychology Monograph*, 1953, 48, 3-54.

Parsons, T., and Bales, R. F. *Family socialization and interaction process*. New York: Free Press, 1955.

Pavenstedt, E. A comparison of the child-rearing environment of upper-lower and very low-lower class families. *American Journal Orthopsychiatry*, 1965, 35, 89-98.

Pearlman, J., Stotsky, B. A., and Dominick, J. R. Attitudes toward death among nursing home personnel. *Journal of Genetic Psychology*, 1969, 114, 63-75.

Perls, F. S. *Gestalt therapy verbatim*. New York: Bantam, 1971.

Petrie, A. *Individuality in pain and suffering*. Chicago: The U. of Chicago Press, 1967.

Petrillo, M., and Sanger, S. *Emotional care of hospitalized children*. Philadelphia: Lippincott, 1972.

Pfeiffer, E. and Davis, G. C. The use of leisure time in middle life. *Gerontologist*, 1971, 11, 187-95.

Piaget, J. *The construction of reality in the child*. New York: Basic Books, 1954.

————. *Six psychological studies*. New York: Random House, 1967.

Plank, E. N., Coughey, P., and Lipson, M. J. A general hospital child-care program to counteract hospitalism. *American Journal of Orthopsychiatry*, 1959, 29, 94-101.

Provence, S. A., and Lipton, R. C. *Infants in Institutions: a comparison of their development with family-reared infants during the first year of life*. New York: International Universities Press, 1962.

Bibliography   416

Prugh, D. G., Staub, M. A., Sands, H. H., Kirschbaum, R. M., and
Lenihan, E. A. A study of the emotional reactions of children and
their families to illness and hospitalization. *American Journal
Orthopsychiatry*, 1953, 23, 70–106.

Puck, T. T., and Robinson, A. Some perspectives in human cytogenetics.
In *The biological basis of pediatric practice*, ed. R. E. Cooke. New
York: McGraw-Hill, 1960.

Quint, J. C. *The nurse and the dying patient*. New York: Macmillan, 1967.

Rapaport, D., and Gill, M. M. The points of view and assumptions of meta-
psychology. *International Journal of Psychoanalysis*, 1959, 60, 153–62.

Redl, F. *The aggressive child*. New York: Free Press, 1957.

————, and Wineman, D. *Controls from within*. New York: Free Press,
1952.

Richardson, S. A., and Guttmacher, A. F., eds. *Childbearing—its social
and psychological aspects*. Baltimore: Williams & Wilkins, 1967.

Riesman, D. Some questions about the study of American national
character in the twentieth century. *The Annals of the American
Academy of Political & Social Science*, 1967, 370, 36–47.

Roberts, J. A. F. *An introduction to medical genetics*. 6th ed. London:
Oxford U. Press, 1973.

Robertson, J. Some responses of young children to loss of maternal care.
Nursing Times, 1953, 49, 382–86.

————. *Young children in hospitals*. New York: Basic Books, 1958.

Robbins, L. C. The accuracy of parental recall of aspects of child development and of child rearing practices. *Journal of Abnormal & Social
Psychology*, 1963, 66, 261–70.

Rodman, H., ed. *Marriage, family, and society*. New York: Random
House, 1967.

Rokeach, M. *The open and closed mind*. New York: Basic Books, 1960.

Rose, C. L. Social correlates of longevity. In *New thoughts on old age*,
ed. R. Kastenbaum. New York: Springer, 1964.

Rosenberg, B. G., and Sutton-Smith, B. Sibling association, family size,
and cognitive abilities. *Journal of Genetic Psychology*, 1966, 109,
271–79.

Rothenberg, M. Reactions of those who treat children with cancer.
Pediatrics, 1967, 40, (3), Part II, 507–10.

Rubenstein, B., and Levitt, M., eds. *Youth and social change*. Detroit:
Wayne State U. Press, 1972.

Runyan, J. W. Jr., Phillips, W. E., Herring, O., and Campbell, L. A
program for the care of patients with chronic diseases. *Journal
of the American Medical Association*, 1970, 211, 476–79.

Saario, T. N. Sex role stereotyping in the public schools. *Harvard
Educational Review*, 1973, 43, 386–416.

Savino, A., and Sanders, R. W. Working with abusive parents: group
therapy and home visits. *American Journal of Nursing*, 1973, 73,
482–84.

Schaefer, H. R., and Callender, W. M. Psychological effects of hospitalization in infancy. *Pediatrics*, 1959, 24, 528–39.

Schaefer, H. H., and Martin, P. L. Behavioral therapy for "apathy" of hospitalized schizophrenics. *Psychological Reports*, 1966, 19, 1147-58.

Schmale, A. H., Jr., and Engel, G. L. The giving up-given up complex illustrated on film. *Archives of General Psychiatry*, 1967, 17, 135-45.

Schmale, A. H., and Iker, H. P. The effect of hopelessness and the development of cancer. *Psychosomatic Medicine*, 1966, 28, 714-21.

Schmieding, N. J. Relationship of nursing to the process of chronicity. *Nursing Outlook*, 1970, 18, 58-62.

Schultz, N. V. How children perceive pain. *Nursing Outlook*, 1971, 19, 670-73.

Sears, R., Maccoby, E., and Levin, H. *Patterns of child rearing.* Evanston, Ill.: Row, Peterson, 1957.

Segall, M. E. Blood pressure and cultural change. *Nursing Science*, 1965, 3, 373-82.

Sewell, H. W. Infant training and the personality of the child. *American Journal of Sociology*, 1952, 58, 150-59.

Sheehy, G. Catch-30 and other predictable crises of growing up adult. *New York Magazine*, February 18, 1974, 30-44.

Sidman, Murray. *Tactics of scientific research.* New York: Basic Books, 1960.

Siegele, D. S. The gate control theory. *American Journal of Nursing*, 1974, 73, 498-502.

Skeels, H. M. Adult status of children with contrasting life experiences. *Monographs of the Society for Research in Child Development*, 1966, 32 (105, whole #3).

Skinner, B. F. *Walden II.* New York: Macmillan, 1948.

———. *Beyond freedom and dignity.* New York: Knopf, 1971.

———. *About behaviorism.* New York: Knopf, 1974.

Small, L. *The briefer psychotherapies.* New York: Brunner/Mazel, 1971.

Smart, M. S., and Smart, R. C. *Preschool children.* New York: Macmillan, 1973.

Solomon, I. L., and Starr, B. D. *The school apperception method (SAM).* New York: Springer, 1968.

Solomon, P., Kubzansky, P., Leiderman, P. H., Mendelson, J. H., Trumbell, R., and Wexler, D. *Sensory deprivation.* Cambridge, Mass.: Harvard U. Press, 1961.

Solomon, P., and Patch, V. D. *Handbook of psychiatry.* Los Altos, Calif.: Lange Medical, 1971.

Sorensen, R. C. *Adolescent sexuality in contemporary America.* New York: World, 1973.

Speers, R. W., and Lansing, C. *Group therapy in childhood psychosis.* Chapel Hill, N.C.: U. of North Carolina Press, 1965.

Spinetta, J. J., and Rigler, D. The child-abusing parent: a psychological review. *Psychological Bulletin*, 1972, 77, 296-304.

Spitz, R. A. Hospitalism: an inquiry into the genesis of psychiatric conditions in early childhood. *The Psychoanalytic Study of the Child*, 1945, 1, 53-74.

————. Hospitalism: A follow-up report on investigation described in Vol. 1, 1945. *The Psychoanalytic Study of the Child*, 1946, 2, 113-17.

Spock, B. *Baby and child care.* New York: Hawthorn, 1968.

Stanton, A. H., and Schwartz, M. S. *The mental hospital.* New York: Basic Books, 1954.

Starr, B. D. Disciplinary attitudes of both parents and authoritarianism in their children. Unpublished doctoral dissertation, Yeshiva University, 1965.

Steele, B. F., and Pollock, C. B. A psychiatric study of parents who abuse infants and small children. In *The battered child*, ed. R. E. Helfer and C. H. Kempe. Chicago: U. of Chicago Press, 1968.

Stein, R. F. Sociological foresight and hindsight in nursing. *International Journal of Nursing Studies*, 1967, 4, 311-17.

Stone, T. J., and Church, J. *Childhood & adolescence.* 3rd ed. New York: Random House, 1973.

Sullivan, H. S. *The interpersonal theory of psychiatry.* New York: Norton, 1953.

————. *The psychiatric interview.* New York: Norton, 1954.

Sunley, R. Early nineteenth-century American literature on child rearing. In *Childhood in contemporary cultures*, ed. M. Mead and M. Wolfenstein. Chicago: The U. of Chicago Press, 1955.

Symonds, P. M. *The psychology of parent-child relationships.* New York: Appleton-Century-Crofts, 1939.

Szasz, T. S. The myth of mental illness. *American Psychologist*, 1960, 15, 115-18.

Tanner, J. M. *Growth at adolescence.* Oxford: Blackwell, 1962.

Taylor, C. D. The hospital patient's social dilemma. *American Journal of Nursing*, 1965, 65, 96-99.

Taylor, G. P., Jr., and Persons, R. W. Behavior modification techniques in a physical medicine and rehabilitation center. *Journal of Psychology*, 1970, 74, 117-24.

Terman, L. M. *Stanford-Binet intelligence scale (Form L-M).* Boston: Houghton Mifflin, 1973.

Thomas, A., Birch, H. G., Chess, S., Hertzig, M. E., and Kron, S. *Behavioral individuality in early childhood.* New York: New York U. Press, 1965.

Thomas, A., Chess, S., and Birch, H. G. *Temperament and behavior disorders in children.* New York: New York U. Press, 1968.

Tijo, J. H., and Levan, A. The chromosome number of man. *Heriditas*, 1956, 42, 1.

Toman, W. *Family constellation.* New York: Springer, 1969.

Torrance, E. P. Curriculum frontiers for the elementary gifted pupil: flying monkeys and silent lions. *Exceptional Children*, 1961, 28, 119-27.

————. Identifying the creatively gifted among economically and culturally disadvantaged children. *The Gifted Child Quarterly*, 1964, 8, 171-76.

Travelbee, J. *Interpersonal aspects of nursing*. Philadelphia: F. H. Davis, 1971.

Ujhely, G. *Determinants of the nurse-patient relationship*. New York: Springer, 1968.

Ursprung, H. Developmental genetics. In *The biologic basis of pediatric practice* (Vol. II.), ed. R. E. Cooke. New York: McGraw-Hill, 1968.

U.S. Bureau of the Census. Marriage, divorce and remarriage, by year of birth: June, 1971. *Current population reports*, Series P-20, No. 239. Washington, D.C.: U.S. Government Printing Office, Sept., 1972.

————. Marital status and living arrangements: March, 1973. *Current population reports*, Series P-20, No. 255. Washington, D.C.: U.S. Government Printing Office, Sept., 1973.

Vedder, C. B. *Problems of the middle aged*. Springfield, Ill.: Thomas, 1965.

Virtanen, R. French national character in the twentieth century. *The Annals of the American Academy of Political and Social Science*, 1967, 370, 82-92.

Walker, S. III. *Psychiatric signs and symptoms due to medical problems*. Springfield, Ill.: Thomas, 1967.

Wallace, A. F. C. *Culture and personality*. New York: Random House, 1970.

Watson, J. D. *The double helix. A personal account of the structure of DNA*. New York: Atheneum, 1968.

Watson, J. B. *Psychological care of infant and child*. New York: Norton, 1928.

————. *The ways of behaviorism*. New York: Harper, 1928.

Watson, L. S., Jr. *Child behavior modification*. New York: Pergamon, 1973.

Wechsler, D. *Wechsler intelligence scale for children*. New York: The Psychological Corporation, 1949, 1974 (revised).

————. *Wechsler adult intelligence scale*. New York: The Psychological Corporation, 1955.

————. *The measurement and appraisal of adult intelligence*. Baltimore: Williams & Wilkins, 1958.

————. *Wechsler pre-school test of intelligence*. New York: The Psychological Corporation, 1963.

Weinberger, G. H., and Schumaker, J. *Statistics: an intuitive approach*. Belmont, Calif.: Brooks/Cole, 1969.

Weinstein, S., Vetter, R., and Sersen, E. *Physiological and experiential concomitants of the phantom*. New York: Albert Einstein College of Medicine, 1964 (VRA research report No. 4217).

Werts, C. E. Social class and initial carer choice of college freshmen. *Social Education*, 1966, 39, 74-85.

Wheelis, A. B. Flight from insight. In *Psychoanalytic psychiatry and psychology*, ed. R. P. Knight and C. R. Friedman. New York: International Universities Press, 1954.

Winch, R. F. *The modern family.* New York: Holt, Rinehart and Winston, 1963.

Wolberg, L. R. *Technique of psychotherapy.* 2 vols. New York: Grune & Stratton, 1967.

Wolf, K. *Geriatric psychiatry.* Springfield, Ill.: Thomas, 1963.

Wolff, P. The natural history of crying and other vocalizations in early infancy. In *Determinants of infant behavior,* ed. B. M. Foss. London: Metheun, 1969, 113–38.

Wolfenstein, M. Fun morality: an analysis of recent American child-training literature. In *Childhood in contemporary cultures,* ed. M. Mead and M. Wolfenstein. Chicago: The U. of Chicago Press, 1955.

Wolman, B. B., ed. *Manual of child psychopathology.* New York: McGraw-Hill, 1973.

Wolpe, J. *The practice of behavior therapy.* New York: Pergamon, 1973.

Wright, B. A. *Physical disability, a psychological approach.* New York: Harper & Row, 1960.

Wright, E. The period of mourning in chronic illness. In *Medical and psychological teamwork in the care of the chronically ill,* ed. M. Harrower. Springfield, Ill.: Thomas, 1955.

Wright, L., Nunner, A., Eichel, B., and Scott, R. Behavioral tactics for reinstating natural breathing in infants with tracheostomy. *Pediatric Research,* 1969, 3, 275–78.

Wu, R. *Behavior and illness.* Englewood Cliffs, N. J., 1972.

Wynne, L. C., Ryckoff, I. M., Day, J., and Hirsch, S. I. Pseudo-mutuality in the family relations of schizophrenics. *Psychiatry,* 1958, 21, 205–20.

Yalom. I. D. *The theory and practice of group psychotherapy.* New York: Basic Books, 1970.

————, Green, R., and Fish, N. Prenatal exposure to female hormones. *Archives of General Psychiatry,* 1973, 28, 554–61.

Yarrow, L. J. Separation from parents during early childhood. In *Child development research,* ed. M. L. Hoffman and L. W. Hoffman. New York: Russell Sage, 1964.

Yarrow, M. R., Campbell, J. D., and Burton, R. *Child rearing.* San Francisco: Jossey-Bass, 1968.

Zahourek, R., and Jensen, J. S. Grieving and the loss of the newborn. *American Journal of Nursing,* 1973, 73 (#5), 836–39.

Zbsrowski, M. Cultural components in responses to pain. *Journal of Social Issues,* 1952, 7, 16–30.

Zelditch, M. Role differentiation in the nuclear family: a comparative study. In *Family, socialization and interaction process,* by T. Parsons and R. F. Bales, New York: Free Press, 1955.

Zeligs, R. *Children's experience with death.* Springfield, Ill.: Thomas, 1974.

Index

Anal stage of psychosexual development, 192, 197
Analysis, transactional, 244-45
Anaxagoras, 175
Androgens, 43, 46, 54
Anger:
  and death, 149, 158, 165
  and mania, 334
  psysiological effects of, 2
Animism in the preoperational stage,
230
Antidepressants, 156, 356
Antimanic agents, 356
Anxiety:
  and the aged, 143
  basic, and development, 247-48
  and death, 149, 158
  and defense mechanisms, 185-86,
    196-98
  effect of mother-child interaction on,
    253
  and grief, 156, 159-60
  and hospital procedures, 283
  in the infant, 243
  and intelligence, 313
  from lack of stimulation, 284
  and mastectomy, 296-97
  neurosis, 339, 347
  and pain, 277
  physiological effects of, 2, 100-102,
    139
  during pregnancy, 110-11
  psychological effects of, 250, 263,
    334, 338-39, 342, 346, 352
  and relaxation thereapy, 212
  resulting from medication, 368
Anxiety, separation:
  in childhood, 43
  and hospitalization, 285-86, 288-89,
    291-92, 300
Apathy:
  and behavior modification, 216
  in old age, 140
Aphasia, 298
Appell, G., 286
Arapesh Tribe, culture of, 258-59
Aristotle, 277
Army Alpha Test, 305
Army Beta Test, 305
Army General Classification Test, 305
Arteriosclerosis:
  and diffuse brain damage, 325, 331
  genetic factors in, 22
  in old age, 130-31, 138-39
Artificialism in the preoperational
stage, 230, 235
Artistic experience in old age, 134
Aspirin, 370-71

Assertiveness training, 213
Assimilation:
  functional, of infant, 225
  generalized, of infant, 225
  recognitory, of infant, 225
  of stimulation, 220, 237
Atherosclerosis, 130-31
Attention and the ego, 185
Authoritarianism in child-rearing,
  119-20
Authority concept of normality, 264
Autism, childhood, 32-33, 351
Autonomy of the child, 240
Average concept of normality, 261-62

Baer, E., 11
Bales, R. F., 115
Bandura, A., 207, 213
Barbiturates, 368, 370-71
Bargaining stage, in the process of
  dying, 149, 165
Basu, A., 270
Beauvoir, Simone de, 117
Becker, W. C., 120-21
Beecher, H. K., 279, 280
Behavior:
  and biological needs, 251
  complexity of, 6
  and conditioning, 210-14
  disorders, in children, 349, 352-54
  infantile, 3, 7, 12
  interpretation of, 171
  multidetermined nature of, 7, 14
  multilevel nature of, 7, 14
  operant, 209
  overdetermination of, 7
  respondent, 209
  sex difference in, 45
  sociocultural influences on, 7, 257-71
  therapy, 361, 364
Behaviorism, 167, 201-16
  and observable behavior, 205
  and old age, 135
Behavior modification, 201-4
  techniques of, 211-13, 216
  and ward management, 214-15
Bell, R., 45
Berkeley Growth Study, 313
Berne, Eric, 244
Binet, Alfred, 304
Binet, Alfred, Laboratory, 218
Binet Scale, 312
Birren, J. E., 128
Birth, see Childbirth
Blank, R. H., 155
Blastocyst, 25
Blastula, 25
Blaylock, J., 270-71, 279

Index

Neonate:
   care of, 113
   characteristics of, 18, 26-27, 28, 29, 43, 44, 45-46, 49, 203, 219
   and death, 162-63
Nervous system, development of, during infancy, 28
Neurological apparatus, development of, 26
Neurosis, 324, 338-48
   and isolation, 250
Neurotic needs and anxiety, 247
Newborn, *see* Neonate
New Guinea, tribes, 271
New York State Psychiatric Institute, 313
Nitrous oxide, 378-79
Nonverbal measures of intelligence, 303
Nonverbal tests, 305
Norepinephrine, 378-79
Normal curve, distribution of scores on, 394-95
Normality:
   concepts of, 260-66
   definitions of, 261-62, 263-64
Nuclear family, *see* family, nuclear
Null hypothesis and levels of significance, 397-98
Nurse-patient relationship:
   importance of, in treatment process, 3
   patient-oriented, 12-13
Nursery school, role in childhood development of, 38
Nursing:
   applicability of psychological theories to, 2-4, 13, 170, 175, 177, 196-99, 234-36, 237
   and behavior modification, 213, 216
   care in delirium tremens, 328
   care of children, 234-36, 286, 289
   care of the dying, 151-52, 159-60, 161-62
   and creativity, 309
   and the definition of pathology, 265-66
   and denial of illness, 280, 300
   and the effects of culture, 257, 274
   and humanist social theories, 252
   and intelligence assessment, 311
   and pain, 277-80, 299-300
   and psychotherapy, 357
   and research, 383
   and restricted sensory stimulation (isolation), 284
   and self-image, 282, 300
   and side effects of medications, 367

Nursing homes, and the aged, 133, 142-43
Nurturing role, 115-16, 124
Nutritional deficiency, and mental retardation, 350

Object constancy, 221, 226-27
Object relationship with mother, 286-87
Observation as source of information, 10-13
Obsessive-compulsive neurosis, 340-41, 342, 347
Occupation, choice of, 74-79, 87
   in adolescence, 64-65, 68
   in early adulthood, 73-74, 87
   effect of sex role training on, 47
   and identity, 241
   See also Employment
Occupational status and longevity, 137
Oedipal stage and anxiety during hospitalization, 289
Oedipus complex, 178, 193-94, 240
Old age, *see* Aging
Old Man's Prayer, An, 164
Opiates, 378-79
Opium compounds and addiction, 346
Oral stage of psychosexual development, 191-92, 197
Ordering in the concrete operational stage, 231-32
Ordinal position, effect of, on personality, 121-22
Organic psychoses, 327-29
Organic therapies, 356-57, 364
Organization of mental functioning, 219, 237
Organogenesis, 25
Orgasm, female, 101
Orientation, impairment in, and diffuse brain damage, 326
Orlansky, H., 119
Otis, Arthur, 305
Overanxious reaction, 352-53
Overcontrol, 71
Owens, W. A., 313

Pain:
   and cultural orientation, 270-71
   perception, 279-80
   psychological factors in, 277-80
   reaction to, 277-80, 299
Paranoia, 324
Parent, identification with, 74-75
Parental control, emancipation from, in adolescence, 65-66
Parenting in monkeys, 115, 124

Parents:
and chronic illness, 293-95, 300
and dying child, 158-59, 160
and hospitalized child, 289
influence of, 40, 47, 76, 245
interaction of, with child and social class, 271-72
relationship of, with child and withdrawing reaction, 352
role of, 114-15, 117-18
Parsons, T., 115
Passive-aggressive personality disorder, 343, 347
Pavenstedt, Eleanor, 271-72
Pavlov, Ivan, 201, 202-4, 216, 278
Pearlman, J., 150-51
Peer group, role of, in development, 40-42, 50, 55-56, 68
See also Groups
Perls, Frederick, 361-62
Permissive child-rearing, 100-101
Penis envy in phallic stage, 193
Pennsylvania, University of, 304
Persecution, delusion of, 322-23
Personality:
characteristics, and intelligence, 303
characteristics, of maturity, 70-72, 87
differences, 4-5
disorders, 342
dynamics, 4-5
effect on, of child-rearing practices, 119, 124
effect on, of national character, 266-68
effect on, of ordinal position in family, 121-22, 125
evolution of, 249-50
structures of, 200
traits and career choice, 75-76, 87
Personification and the infant, 243
Persons, R. W., 214-15
Petrie, A., 278
Phallic stage of psychosexual development, 192-93, 197
Phantom pains, 278
Pharmacotherapy, 356, 364
Phenacemide, 378-79
Phenelzine, 378-79
Phenmetrazine, 378-79
Phenothiazines, 367, 378-79
Phenotype, 18, 22
Phenylketonuria, 350
Phobia, 288, 348
Phobic neurosis, 339, 340, 347
Physical development in infancy, 27-28, 36-37
Physiological changes:
in adolescence, 67-68

in old age, 127-28, 145
Piaget, Jean, 16, 34, 158, 167, 206, 218-37, 312
Picasso, Pablo, 133
Pill, the, 104
Pinel, Philippe, 355
Placebo:
effect, 279-80
responder, 368
Planning, ability for, 72, 87
Play:
associative and parallel, 38
separation of sexes in, 41, 45
Pleasure principle, 180
Poisoning and mental retardation, 350
Pollock, C. B., 123
Population control, 102-3
Poverty:
and child rearing, 272
and health care, 273
See also Culture
Preconscious, the, 190
Pregnancy, 109-12, 124
Prejudice:
toward the aged, 135-36, 143
and authoritarianism, 119-20
Premature infant, characterstics of, 25
Prenatal care and social class, 272
Prenatal development, 23-24, 46
Preoperational stage of development, 224, 227-31, 237
and hospitalization, 288
Preschool child, development of, 33-38, 50
See also Childhood, Development
Primal therapy, 362-63, 364
Primitive society:
nurturing and child care in, 116
and sexual gratification, 180
Privacy:
and the hospitalized adolescent, 290-91
and intelligence tests, 311
Privileges in marriage contract, 109
Probability, 396-98
Problems, psychological, resulting from disability, 300
Progesterone, 46, 110, 380-81
Projection of impulses, 188
Projective stimulus demonstrates differences in perception, 5
Protein synthesis, 19
Provence, S. A., 31
Prugh, D. G., 286, 288-89
Pseudohermaphroditism of infant, 44-45
Psychoanalysis, 167, 179, 199, 360, 364
Psychological crises and disability, 300

Sadism, 250, 344, 347
Sampling in research, 389-90, 399-400, 403
Sanders, R. W., 123
Savino, A., 123
Schemas of behavior, 219-20, 221, 224, 236, 237
Schizoid personality disorder, 342, 347
Schizophrenia, 324, 332, 335-36, 337, 349, 351-52, 353
Schmale, A. H., Jr., 2
School:
  curricula and sexuality, 58
  nursery, role of in childhood development, 37-38
  readiness for, 38-39
  role of, in development, 39-40, 50, 56, 66-67, 68
  sex role stereotyping in, 48
Schultz, N. V., 270
Schweitzer, Albert, 133
Seawell, H. W., 119
Secondary schemas, coordination of, 226
Security operations of the self system, 243
Self, 175
Self-actualization, 72, 252
Self-assessment:
  in middle age, 85-86
  in old age, 134
  risk of distortions in, 9
Self-Awareness Exercise:
  The Aging Process, 145
  Disability, 299
  The Marriage Contract, 108-9
  The Obituary, 165
Self-concept, in adolescence, 64
Self-image:
  development of, in adolescence, 63-64, 68
  role of, in illness, 281-82, 300
Self-report, 8-9
Self system, 243
Senility, 234
Sensitivity therapy, 362, 364
Sensorimotor stage of development, 224-27, 237
Sensory deprivation, effects of, 284
Sensory development in infancy, 29
Sensory stimuli, coordination of, 220-21
Separation anxiety:
  and death, 158
  in illness, 284-92, 300
Seriation in the concrete operational stage, 231-32

Sex:
  role stereotyping, 47-48, 115
  role typing, 41, 47-49, 50, 76-77
Sexual deviation, 343-45, 347
Sexual dysfunction, 100
Sexual identity and mastectomy, 296-97
Sexuality:
  in adolescence, 58, 59, 60, 61, 68, 290-91
  in childhood, 43-49, 50, 57
  in old age, 135-36, 146
Sexual relationships:
  and chronic illness, 294-95
  in marriage, 99-100, 124
  and pregnancy, 111
Shaping of desired behavior, 211-12, 216
Sheehy, G., 81
Sibling rivalry, 240
Side effects, psychological, of medications, 370-81
Siegele, D. S., 278
Significance, tests of, 396-98, 400, 403
Simon, Theodore, 304
Sixties, characteristics of, 86-87, 88
Skeels, H. M., 31
Skeletal structure, development of, 27
Skinner, B. F., 208-11, 216
Smoking and aversive conditioning, 212
Social behavior:
  in the formal operational stage, 234
  in the concrete operational stage, 232
Social class:
  and child-rearing environment, 271-72
  and health care, 272-73, 275
Social conditioning:
  and development of a sense of industry, 241
  effect of on heterosexual socialization, 58
  of emotional expression, 71
  of intimacy, 242
  of role and identity, 241
  of sexual practices, 343
  of sexual typing, 47-49, 50
  of values, 105
Social development, 30-33, 34-38, 41, 55-61
Social environment:
  and conflict, 247
  effect of, on development, 240, 252
  and personality, 249
Social factors affecting old age, 131-33, 145-46
Social interaction and behavior modification, 214